A Family of Faith

A Family of Faith

An Introduction to Evangelical Christianity

Timothy R. Phillips and Dennis L. Okholm

Baker Academic

A Division of Baker Book House Co
Grand Rapids, Michigan 49516

© 1996, 2001 by Timothy R. Phillips and Dennis L. Okholm

Published by Baker Academic
a division of Baker Book House Company
P.O. Box 6287, Grand Rapids, MI 49516-6287

Printed in the United States of America

Library of Congress Cataloging-in-Publication Data

Phillips, Timothy R. (Timothy Ross), 1950–2000
    A family of faith : an introduction to evangelical Christianity / Timothy R. Phillips & Dennis L. Okholm.—2nd ed.
      p. cm.
    Rev. ed. of: Welcome to the family.
    Includes bibliographical references (p.) and index.
    ISBN 0-8010-2265-7 (paper)
    1. Evangelistic work—History. 2. Evangelistic work—United States—History. I. Okholm, Dennis L. II. Phillips, Timothy R. (Timothy Ross), 1950–2000 Welcome to the family. III. Title.
    BR1640.P48 2001
    280'.4—dc21
                                       00-049804

For information about academic books, resources for Christian leaders, and all new releases available from Baker Book House, visit our web site:
http://www.bakerbooks.com

To
W. Ross and Huntley,
Amilee and Barbara,
Sandy and Trevecca,
who have shaped us in ways
they do not even know
to live faithfully as Christians

and in memory of
Timothy R. Phillips
1950–2000
"whose rest is won" and with whom
the church family on earth remains in
"mystic sweet communion"

101108

Contents

Acknowledgments 9

Part 1 Basic Concepts
1. All in the Family 13
2. Browsing the Worldview Catalog 22

Part 2 Our Christian Identity
3. Revelation: The Source of Our Christian Identity 47
4. Setting the Stage: The Creation of the World
   and Human Beings 67
5. After the Fall: Sin and Its Consequences 79
6. Hallelujah, What a Savior: God's Salvific Work
   in Jesus Christ 91
7. Already but Not Yet: The Church and the Kingdom 108
8. Back to the Future 124

Part 3 Living Faithfully Now
9. How the Family Got Its Start: The Early Church 137
10. A Mixed Marriage: The Medieval Church 150
11. From Protest to Revolution: The Protestant
    Reformation 166
12. Anabaptists: The Church Living in Antithesis
    to the World 182
13. Martin Luther: The Conversionist Church 196
14. John Calvin: The Transformationist Church 209
15. Slouching toward Secularism: Modernity and
    Accommodation 222

16. We Are Family: American Evangelicalism
    and Its Roots   240
17. Recommendations for the Family in a Culture
    against Christ   262

    Epilogue: The Legacy   273
    Appendices   275
    Notes   305
    Glossary   320
    Index   325

Acknowledgments

$\mathcal{I}$n one sense this book began when our names were placed on the cradle roll at our churches. We have been reared by families and churches in evangelical Christianity as it has been believed and practiced by Pentecostals, Baptists, and Presbyterians.

In a profound sense this book began to take shape when we were both students at Wheaton College, being introduced to issues with which we still wrestle, in classes like "Christ and Culture" and "Introduction to Philosophy" and with professors like Robert Webber and Arthur Holmes.

In graduate studies and in our teaching careers, we have been further shaped by those who mentored us by their lives and by their books—people like Donald Bloesch, Shirley Guthrie, George Marsden, Robert Roberts, and William Wells. There are a host of others, and if one recognizes the ideas or tone of voice of those we have mentioned and others we have not, it is because we are indeed children who have been nurtured by these parents and siblings.

Our colleagues at Wheaton College have contributed to this book by their encouragement in a common endeavor and their honest engagement of us in ceaselessly grappling with the issue of faithfully living out the faith we profess. Specifically, we thank Scott Clark and Jim Lewis for taking the time to read portions of the manuscript and offer helpful suggestions that have improved the final product.

Perhaps we owe the most to our students in a freshman course titled "Theology of Culture." They have used various redactions of this book in manuscript form for several years. They have been invited to interact with it and critique it. We have learned from them, and that is reflected in much of what we have written. We hope that this introduction to evangelical

9

Christianity will continue to serve future generations of students who must carry on the family name.

Thanks must also go to several individuals who have made significant contributions to this volume. Peter Anders made helpful suggestions and worked on the index for the first edition. Emmylou Fast and Rachel Johnson made the second edition more coherent, accessible, and accurate with notations that marked nearly every page. We are very grateful for the editorial work of Bob Hosack (first edition) and Amy Nemecek (second edition). We suspect a book editor's job description includes "ability to handle stress and anxiety, and patience with authors." Bob and Amy displayed Christian virtues and editorial skills that have made this book better than it was when the manuscript was first submitted.

Finally, one of the authors must acknowledge an incalculable debt to the other. As the dedication implies, Tim Phillips died a few months after the revisions were completed for this second edition. With stubborn passion for Christ, Tim fought cancer and the Adversary until the end, meeting with students, teaching classes, and working on theological projects. As his son Aaron once said in describing his father's work, "My dad studies God." Tim's studies made some significant contributions to the church and for the kingdom, primarily because Tim was in love with the Object of his study. He will be greatly missed by two families—the one to which he was related by births, adoption, and marriage, and the one into which he was baptized.

Part 1

Basic Concepts

one

All in the Family

Seven-year-old Tommy Zoblinski was struggling just to get a spoonful of wiggly Jell-O up and into his mouth. Right at that moment, a spoonful of green beans was abruptly launched across the room. This missile found its target, right smack dab in Tommy's face. He was stunned. His concentration dissipated, and the Jell-O plopped into his lap. The dining table erupted with laughter. Tommy knew that a first strike would have resulted in punishment fitting the crime. But since his father had initiated this, traditional expectations were off. So he retaliated, launching the Jell-O at his attacker. Warfare erupted from all sides. Suddenly Mrs. Zoblinski appeared at the dining room door, hands on her hips. "Act like Zoblinskis!" she shouted. As quickly as the fracas had begun, the food fight ceased.

At one time or another, most of us have been reprimanded by our parents to act in a manner characteristic of our family name. Our surnames are like a public "badge" by which we represent our family to the rest of the world.

Tommy has learned his family's expectations and standards through his parents' modeling and the oral traditions of his ancestors which circulate among family members. The child knows something about the family's reputation, which he is now commanded to uphold, because over a period of years and particularly on special occasions he has met various members of the Zoblinski family—grandparents, aunts and uncles, nieces and nephews, and cousins. Like it or not, he is becoming aware that the Zoblinski heritage includes a Zoblinski way of thinking, acting, and viewing the world.

If we had substituted the name "Christian" for "Zoblinski" in the preceding paragraph, what we have described would be true for a whole host of people who are related as brother and sister (1 John 3:1–3; 4:20–21), grandparent and parent and child (Ps. 78:1–8), and commonly adopted children of a heavenly Father (Rom. 8:15–17; Gal. 4:6–7)—all of whom are invited by Jesus Christ to address God as "Daddy" (Matt. 6:9). To keep this heritage alive, they are encouraged to meet together regularly (Heb. 10:25)—especially to hear the stories of their ancestors and their heritage (see Ps. 78)—so that they will know how to think and act and view the world as people who go by the family name of "Christian." In fact, from the time kids in this family are in the church nursery, they are meeting other members of the family (both dead and alive) and hearing their stories, particularly on special occasions like Christmas, Easter, and Pentecost, as well as at baptisms and the Lord's Supper.

During their entire lives, the people in this family have to be reminded to "act like a Christian!" But what that means is not always easy to define, let alone to do. One reason—but certainly not the only one—is that the world is so much more complicated than it used to be. While the early Christians and their Jewish ancestors were quite familiar with war, they knew nothing of nuclear arms that could annihilate the world. While our ancestors knew of communicable diseases such as leprosy, they knew nothing of the horrifying epidemic of AIDS, complicated by the fact that it is more prevalent among people who practice certain kinds of lifestyles that are wrong in the eyes of the Christian family. This list goes on, with some issues having only the slightest resemblance to anything in the family's past, while others are simply modern variations of ancient themes: poverty and hunger, racism and apartheid, feminism, government corruption, legalized and assisted euthanasia, pornography, civil disobedience in a democracy, abortion, hand-gun control, pollution, urban homelessness, and the New Age movement. And perhaps the gravest challenge the Christian family faces today, though not without its precedent for our ancestors, is the insistence on moral and religious diversity, such that even a Christian's critical evaluation of the diverse options appears arrogant and intolerant.

So, the key question here is this: "What does it mean to think, act, and view the world like a Christian in today's culture?"

The Evangelical Christian Family

Before we even begin to answer this question, we have to understand more clearly what it is we are asking.

Every family's heritage includes various branches. Some of the branches have common links with their close neighbors, while others got separated long ago and are now far removed from each other. They still belong to the same family tree—they share some of the same heritage and one can detect some commonalities, but there are some peculiarities that set them off from other branches in the family tree. For instance, our Zoblinskis might think of themselves as more authentically "Zoblinski" over against some distant cousins who have a sordid reputation. And sometimes when Junior balks at the reprimand to act like a Zoblinski, he is reminded that he might end up like the "other side of the family"!

Unfortunately, the Christian family shares much in common with the Zoblinskis in this regard. It would be dishonest not to admit this historical fact. In fact, certain branches of the Christian family often cannot even eat together at the table of their common brother Jesus. It is sad, but nonetheless true.

In fact, the separation of the branches on the Christian family tree are sometimes so wide that we must admit that the various branches actually do see things differently and do act differently in today's world. And, like our Zoblinski family, we probably would not remain on our particular branch if we did not think that it is somehow just a little more authentic—a little more like the original trunk—than most of the other branches.

Accordingly, this book is written from the perspective of those who sit on the "evangelical" branch of the Christian family tree and who do so quite self-consciously.

Evangelical Christians share much in common with other branches of the family. But what is it about this branch that makes it distinctively "evangelical"? It certainly is not a denominational tie (like Baptist, Lutheran, or Presbyterian). Instead, it is a distinctive perspective on the Christian faith that is held by many people from different denominations. Keeping in mind that there are many "twigs" on the evangelical branch, there are certain key elements and a history that tie us together. The history will be explained later, helping us to understand better why the following list might be said to be the distinctive elements of evangelical Christianity.

1. *Evangelicals insist that Jesus Christ is the incarnate God and thus the definitive self-revelation of God.* Jesus Christ is fully God and fully human. As such, Jesus Christ is God personally present and active in the flesh. He is the fulfillment of the promise of God and the one in whom the faith of all of God's people has been placed since the beginning of human existence (whether with full understanding or not). Simply put, Jesus Christ is the only way to a salvific relationship with God. This belief separates evangelicals theologically from any group which maintains that salvation can be found outside of Jesus and his work.

And this impacts their view of Jesus' person as well. The liberal branch conceives of Jesus as the highest development of humanity. Evangelicals, however, confess that Jesus is not merely different from us in degree (the most perfect human), but also different from us in kind (the unique God-human).

2. *Evangelicals affirm the authority of the Bible as the truthful, absolutely reliable, divinely inspired, and uniquely normative guide for Christian belief and practice.* Scripture is the Word of God which reveals Christ through the work of the Holy Spirit, who inspired the original writers of Scripture and who now illumines the readers. This unique status makes the Bible normative above any church's traditions or officials. By contrast, liberals deny the unique status of the Bible, seeing it as just one religious writing among many or as a classic text that derives its authority from those who resonate with what it says.

3. *Evangelicals believe that our salvation was established only through Jesus Christ's life, atoning death, and resurrection, and that Christ's work must be personally appropriated by faith alone.* In other words, Jesus Christ alone has established our salvation; he does not simply reflect God's universal saving work. Unlike many liberals, evangelicals deny that Jesus of Nazareth is one among many ways to God. Furthermore, evangelicals insist that salvation involves a personal relationship to Jesus Christ. That is, evangelicals insist that the saving work of Christ must be personally appropriated through faith and necessarily involves the conversion and commitment of the individual.

4. *Evangelicals commit themselves to a life of active piety under the lordship of Christ.* For the evangelical, Christian faith is not simply a set of beliefs about God, but a life lived out in response to the initiating grace of God. Obedience is required of the one who professes faith in Christ, and one's spiritual condition is demonstrated by one's fruit. Disciplines are necessary for the holy life and Christian growth, including Bible study, prayer, and fellowship with other Christians.

5. *Evangelicals engage themselves in evangelism, aimed at the conversion of individuals and of the church.* Because of their belief that Jesus Christ is the sole means of salvation and because of their emphasis on discipleship, evangelicals place a great deal of stress on carrying out the "Great Commission" (Matt. 28:18–20). They view themselves as those sent by Jesus to be his witnesses and ambassadors (Luke 24:48; Acts 1:8; 2 Cor. 5:18–20)—the instruments of his work throughout the whole world. This is reflected in the history of revivalism, and it sets evangelicals apart from those who view evangelism primarily or solely in terms of social work.

Differences among Us

It may sound like evangelicals are all the same. In one sense they are. They are people who are personally committed to Jesus as their Lord. Jesus should determine their orientation toward life. In fact, the term "Christian" reflects this. *Christ-ianoi*, first used in Antioch (Acts 11:26), was a common way of identifying the followers or servants of the one named "Christ."

In their tenacious loyalty as disciples of Jesus, one might be surprised to find such diversity in the evangelical family. For instance, we grew up in churches where drinking and smoking were not acceptable habits for Christians. We were shocked when our post-high-school world expanded and we came into contact with people who considered themselves committed evangelicals, yet who drank beer and placed ashtrays on their tables.

Diversity in lifestyle issues goes far beyond alcohol and tobacco. For example, one evangelical argues that Christians should live as a community, where the property is owned by the church and where the income distributed by the church provides for only basic sustenance. He claims that the operative principle is derived from the early church in Acts: "each in proportion to their abilities and each in proportion to their needs" (Acts 2:44–45; 4:32).[1] Still another evangelical delights in his luxury car and "mini-castle" in an exclusive neighborhood, all acquired through his diligent labor, savings, and investments. This lifestyle, he argues, accords with God's providential ordering of creation and commands in Scripture.[2] Both maintain they are obedient to Jesus Christ as Lord, yet their lifestyles differ radically.

Evangelicals also dispute political and ethical issues. Some are Democrats; some are Republicans; still others are independents. While some have been pacifist draft resisters, others proudly shout, "America, love it or leave it." Some live a simple lifestyle to feed the hungry and practice civil disobedience against cuts in welfare; others protest the welfare state and quote the Bible to insist on a "no work, no eat" policy. On one hand are those who believe abortion is permissible in certain cases, on the other are those who believe that it never can be allowed. Yet such differences are not new to evangelicalism. Throughout its history there have been divisions over basic ethical issues. The Southern Baptists, for example, though they have since repented of their stance, during the mid-nineteenth century split from the national denomination, maintaining the ethical rightness of owning slaves. Contemporary tempestuous issues such as AIDS, feminism, homosexuals in the military, and inequities between the rich and the poor have only stoked more religio-political fires!

Being Faithful to Jesus Christ Now

So evangelicals, it seems, disagree about quite a few things—behavioral standards, lifestyles, and even political and moral issues. Certainly some of this diversity can be traced back to our family and cultural heritage. These actions and attitudes reflect the basic orientation and values absorbed from our family. But whether these behaviors were Christian was never questioned. Frequently we just accept the "Zoblinski way," instead of exploring whether a specific lifestyle or a political option is Christian.

Is that an adequate response? We don't think so. How can one claim to be a Christian—literally, a disciple of Jesus Christ—and never explore the most basic question: Am I being obedient to Christ in every area of life? Consider his influence in the areas of politics, lifestyle, family life, and work. Instead of being Christ's agent, perhaps you actually hinder his work.

The importance and urgency of this question escalates once we realize that all of us apprehend Scripture and even Jesus Christ through the lens of a specific culture. Within that cultural lens are specific prejudgments and assumptions which are so basic that they function as our *control beliefs*.[3] By *control beliefs* we are referring to the most basic values and assumptions that define and even regulate a culture's interpretation of reality. These control beliefs shape, in either a positive or negative manner, a Christian's commitment to Christ.

One of the most startling illustrations of the power of a culture's control beliefs occurred this century in the Western world. At the beginning of this century, ethnic nationalism dominated German culture. Even its leading intellectuals defended the superiority of German blood, culture, and militarism. At the start of World War I its leading academics, including some evangelicals, vigorously sanctioned Germany's militarism as intrinsic to German culture: "Without German militarism, German culture would have long since perished from the earth."[4]

Two decades later when Hitler arrived on the scene promoting German militarism, these control beliefs still molded the understanding and commitment of many Christians. The result was the "German Christian" Movement, which sanctioned Hitler's reign, even its racist anti-Semitism.[5] As its Guiding Principles (1932) declared:

> We see in race, folk, and nation, orders of existence granted and entrusted to us by God. God's law for us is that we look to the preservation of these orders. Consequently miscegenation (racially mixed marriages) is to be opposed. For a long time German Foreign missions . . . has been calling to the German people: "Keep your race pure," and tells us that a faith in Christ does not destroy one's race but deepens and sanctifies it.

In the mission to the Jews we perceive a grave danger to our nationality. It is an entrance gate for alien blood into our body politic. . . . As long as the Jews possess the right to citizenship and there is thereby the danger of racial camouflage and bastardization, we repudiate a mission to the Jews in Germany.

We want an evangelical (Protestant) Church that is rooted in our nationhood. We repudiate the spirit of a christian world-citizenship.[6]

While this episode may seem incomprehensible to us today, this movement cannot be dismissed as a fringe group. Notable conservative Christian scholars defended its basic theses.

The very existence of the German Christian Movement illustrates the domineering and distortive power of certain control beliefs. Here the control belief of German nationalism constricted and concealed who Jesus is and to what he calls us. The "German Christians" may have professed to confess Jesus as Lord. But wasn't their real God and Lord found elsewhere, in Germanism? Wasn't Jesus accepted only to the degree that he could be twisted to support their more basic truth, that of German nationalism? This process of assimilating Christ to a culture's control belief co-opted Christ!

This result uncovers the most important requirement for "being faithful to Jesus Christ now." *To acknowledge Jesus as "the Truth," in "whom are hidden all the treasures of wisdom and knowledge" (Col. 2:3), means that he alone should be our foundational control belief, judging every other aspect of reality. Either Christ confronts us with his exclusive claim as Lord and judge over all, or he does not confront us as Lord at all. There can be only one Lord!*

Like the Germans, we also absorb basic beliefs from our cultural environment. Why should we assume that our Western American culture is any more obedient to God than German culture, or even the Jewish world into which Jesus was born? Scripture does not describe Jesus' Jewish culture as producing obedient believers. As John bluntly puts it, "he came to that which was his own, but his own did not receive him" (John 1:11). We cannot assume immunity from distorting control beliefs.

As a result, the most crucial question facing the Christian today—indeed, the question that confronts every generation of believers—is: What does it mean to think, act, and view the world like a Christian in today's culture?

Our Task

While this question has been asked and answered before—*many* times before—each generation in the family must ask whether it is *truly* being faithful to Jesus *now*. We are not the heirs of some dead tradition, but, as John Leith has put it, we are people who are "traditioning" the faith.[7] Being

faithful to Jesus Christ entails taking the "faith which was once for all delivered to the saints" (Jude 3, RSV) and asking how to live it faithfully now.
What does the Word of God demand from us regarding nuclear arms, AIDS,
urban homelessness, or environmental pollution? In a sense, we are being
asked to apply our past—our rich family heritage—to our present. We are
attempting to be *faithful* to the Word of God we were reared on *by* bringing it to bear on today's issues in a *relevant* way.

To do this—to answer our key question—we are going to have to know
at least two things. First, we need to know more about the family we are in.
What is our family heritage? Or, put another way, what is the Christian
worldview? Second, we need to learn from different branches of the family,
including the evangelical, just how the church has brought that worldview
to bear on the culture in which the church has existed. Here we will find several options throughout the church's history, and it will be these options that
will help us to answer the question for our present circumstances.

So, we will proceed to find out what a Christian *worldview* is and how it
differs from other worldviews, but to do that, we first need to say something about the concept of a worldview itself.

For Further Reflection

1. As we have done in this chapter with the Zoblinskis, can you draw
   some parallels between your upbringing in your family and your
   upbringing in the church? If you were not "reared" in the church,
   would your Christian upbringing be something like that of an
   orphan?
2. Can you think of a "control belief" drawn from your national identity that might interfere with your faithful allegiance to Christ, similar to the example of Nazi Germany in this chapter?
3. Evaluate this statement: There is no sociopolitical issue in the twentieth century that is not addressed in the Bible.

For Further Reading

Bloesch, Donald G. Foreword to *The Future of Evangelical Christianity: A Call for Unity amid Diversity*, by Mark Noll. Colorado Springs:
Helmers and Howard, 1988.

McGrath, Alister E. *Understanding Doctrine: What It Is—and Why It Matters*. Grand Rapids: Zondervan, 1990.

———. *Evangelicals and the Future of Christianity*. Downers Grove, Ill.: InterVarsity, 1995.

Wells, David R., and John D. Woodbridge, eds. *The Evangelicals: Who They Are and What They Believe*. Nashville: Abingdon, 1975.

Wells, William W. *Welcome to the Family*. Downers Grove, Ill.: InterVarsity, 1979.

two

Browsing the
Worldview Catalog

We have talked about thinking, acting, and viewing the world like a Christian. This is the language of "world-views." A worldview is a way of seeing or picturing the world and everything in it. It's a conceptual framework. It determines how we interpret our experience and it guides our actions—whether we are conscious of it or not.

One of the most elementary (and literal) ways of illustrating what a worldview is may be seen by looking at a popular map of the world purchased in, say, Chicago. The map has the American continents in the center, with the Asian continent split so that the western and eastern halves of Russia appear on different sides of the map. In fact, the United States is right in the middle! It probably comes as no surprise that the map is printed in the U.S. This is a case in which the world is seen literally through North American eyes.

Maps are an easy way to illustrate the concept of a worldview and particularly the fact that a worldview is often held unconsciously. What would happen if we turned the world map upside down? Would it seem odd to us if Russia were in the middle of the map, with half of the United States on each end? These kinds of experiences jolt our consciousness into becoming aware of aspects of our worldview that may have gone undetected before.

The reason that such assumptions can go undetected is that at the bottom of our worldviews are those "control beliefs" that guide our thinking.[1] The term "belief" here does not denote a tentative opinion but one's most basic convictions regarding the world and morality. These beliefs anchor our world by defining the most basic "facts" about reality.

These include beliefs about the relationship between God and the world which determine how we interpret what is happening around us, how we respond to events, and so forth. In fact, our way of seeing the world brings with it a set of emotional responses, value judgments, character traits, and behaviors. That is to say, worldviews involve the *whole* person, not just the mind.

For example, one person's worldview might include a valuation of the game of golf such that on a gorgeous spring day her heart might race when she drives by a beautifully manicured course; on the other hand, another's worldview may be such that in driving by the same course, he would consider golf a silly way to ruin a nice walk on the grass.

Let's consider another illustration that makes the point more profoundly. Consider how a person's worldview affects the way he or she *sees* a person rummaging around in a trash can. If our worldview has been shaped by beliefs such as "a person gets what's coming to him" and "people are homeless and out of work because of something *they* did to deserve it," then we might see a morally defective, lazy, dishonest, inherently inferior, or intellectually deficient individual and respond to that person accordingly. But if our view of that person is guided more fundamentally by beliefs such as "God makes *all* people in his image" and "Jesus Christ died and rose again for all people," then we might *see* a person whom God created, for whom Christ died, and who is caught up in the same causal nexus of sin in the world that we find ourselves struggling with in other contexts. And when we see a person *this* way, our emotional responses toward that person and judgments about his or her value, as well as our behavioral responses, are profoundly affected.

How Worldviews Are Acquired

How does one get a worldview? Answering this question might help us to see why most people in the United States would not give a second thought to the ethnocentric world map, while a Russian visitor would find the map amusing at best. More to the point, answering this question goes a long way to explain why people have different reactions to seeing an ill-clad person rifling through the garbage.

"Christian ethics . . . is not first of all concerned with 'Thou shalt' or 'Thou shalt not.' Its first task is to help us rightly envision the world. . . . We can only act within the world we can envision, and we can envision the world rightly only as we are trained to see. We do not come to see merely by looking, but must develop disciplined skills through initiation into the community that attempts to live faithful to the story of God. Furthermore, we cannot see the world rightly unless we are changed, for as sinners we do not desire to see truthfully. Therefore, Christian ethics must assert that by learning to be faithful disciples, we are able to see the world as it is, namely God's creation." (Stanley Hauerwas, *The Peaceable Kingdom,* 29–30)

The short answer is that we are shaped into a certain way of looking at the world. We are born into a culture where certain beliefs are a given, and we absorb these behaviors and attitudes just by living in a particular community. Children are great imitators. They learn early to mimic what they see in their parents and significant others. Children who are read to regularly will pretend to read on their own long before they actually have such skills. The "learned behavior" is a powerful influencer. For the same reason, television and music are significant influences in our contemporary society.

Indeed, a worldview is formed in us by what we read, watch, listen to, and have modeled for us. We acquire it through the peers with whom we associate, our parents, and our church. It is developed by the activities we engage in and the experiences we have. And most importantly, it is shaped by what we love—by the focus of our soul's eye.

We know a doctoral student who made a living by working evenings in a department store as a detective, on the lookout for shoplifters. For him this was simply an interesting job to make money. But for most of the people with whom he worked it was a career or a step toward related work. Their experiences as white middle-class women and men working in a mall that was a ten-minute bus ride from the core of Trenton, New Jersey—which was largely African-American and poor—shaped the way they viewed the department store customers, reinforced not only by their upbringing, but by such things as their reading of a local paper that majored more on sensationalism and, most importantly, by the love of their work (success in which involved arresting a quota of shoplifters for the month). The resultant worldview that was operative on the job meant that the crew spent most of their time watching urban African-Americans, rather than white-haired women in their fifties (like the guilty one they accidentally "nabbed") and young local college professors (like the one they caught stealing a sweater). If there was any doubt about the guiding philosophy at work, it was dispelled by his closest coworker, who was incited by one of the stories he read in the newspaper one day and proceeded to lecture our friend about the way in which "the blacks had driven all the whites out of Trenton." Because of his worldview it did not occur to him that the whites might have abandoned the city in the sixties because they did not want to live near blacks.

The bottom line is that the way a person views the world and thus acts in it is shaped by his or her deepest and most cherished beliefs, hopes, and loves. And those are often acquired through associations and experiences in our lives. So, if we trust, hope in, and love the God who revealed himself in Jesus Christ with all of our heart, soul, mind, and strength—in other words, with the total person that a worldview involves—we will be shaped into a Christian way of looking at life and the world.

But this does not happen naturally or accidentally. Perhaps an illustration will help. One of us has worn eyeglasses since he was four years old. A severe astigmatism was discovered early on. While a lens prescription went a long way to correct it, the doctor insisted that the vision would improve later in life if exercises which focused the eyes together were worked on at an early age. These exercises involved slowly moving a large colored pinhead in front of the eyes, training them to focus on this single object.

In the same way, we must consciously train our spiritual eyes to focus on God and his kingdom if we are to avoid the kind of "double vision" that results from a world-

Abraham Kuyper (1837–1920)

What if you went to a university in which the entire curriculum was based on the philosophy that Christianity calls us to a total life perspective and way of living—to a *weltanschauung* or worldview? That is precisely what Abraham Kuyper set out to do when he founded the Free University of Amsterdam.

Kuyper accomplished more in his life than most of us would in three lifetimes. A Dutch Calvinist who experienced an evangelical conversion, Kuyper believed that Calvinism made demands on the entire person who lives in culture—whether it be in the realm of politics, art, science, or education. His involvements bore this out. Besides founding the Free University and serving as the prime minister of Holland, Kuyper wrote many books and articles on theology, philosophy, politics, art, and social issues.

In these writings he developed the idea that faith is a structural part of universal human nature—an aspect of "common grace." We all have a "faith-structure" that operates in all of our knowing. For instance, our conviction that what we perceive are really objects that exist "out there" and not just in our minds, is a presupposition that precedes the evidence of our senses. Faith is the root of all rationality (even in the sciences). Granted, sin has "fatal effects" in our lives, including our thinking. Yet the Christian and the non-Christian can still agree on sensory data and measurements of phenomena. There is a decisive difference between the regenerate and the unregenerate, but it is not a complete difference. Even the non-Christian, then, can operate within an autonomous sphere of human endeavor and have much in common with the Christian.

view which tries to focus on two loves at the same time. If we want to love God with our whole person, then we must consciously exercise our spiritual lives through regular Scripture reading, meditation, prayer, church attendance, giving things away, serving others, not striking back when hit, and so forth. In these very intentional ways we are training ourselves to become like Christ and to see the world, emotionally respond to it, and act in it in a way characteristic of Christ. We are "putting on" the characteristics of Christ (see Eph. 4:20–23; Col. 3:9–17) so that by "dressing up" like Christ (in our attitudes and behaviors) we might eventually be like Christ, thinking and acting in a way that is literally second nature to us.

Somehow we have adopted the notion that on the physical level development requires training and exercise, while on the spiritual level souls come prepackaged as mature or move passively along the assembly line until they come out at the other end "mature and complete, lacking in nothing" (James 1:4, NRSV). We know that we cannot look like the people on the cover of *Weightlifting* magazine only by thinking or reading about it. Similarly, we know that simply reading about Michael Jordan's career and merely puttering around in the driveway will not develop our basketball skills very far. But what we do not always recognize, even though it is repeated over and over in Scripture (e.g., Eph. 5:1–2; Phil. 2:1–5; 3:12–16; Heb. 12:1–2, 12–14), is that if we want to have the thoughts, values, and emotions of Christ and act in the world like him, then we have got to be involved in a very intentional training program. Our souls must be conditioned through exercise in a way that is analogous to the shaping of our bodies or our ball-playing abilities.

For a believer developing a Christian worldview, this training initially takes place by repenting (turning one's spiritual eyes away from one's former picture of the world to see life from Christ's point of view) and then, through God's transforming grace, by being formed more completely into the kind of person who sees and acts the way Christ does (a process that theologians call sanctification). And, as we said, the latter comes through spiritual disciplines like reading Scripture and praying, all in the context of believers with whom we regularly associate. We should add that this regular association is indispensable, not because we are legalistically bound to attend the church of our choice for an hour when Sunday morning rolls around, but because the people with whom we associate are in the same training program—they belong to the same health club! And if we are to be successful in our training, then we need each other's encouragement, insights, support, reprimands, and guidance. In fact, as Robert Roberts has said, the test of a church's faithfulness to its mission is the way its members are being shaped into Christlikeness.[2]

As one's worldview is shaped, we find that our thinking is guided by certain biblical and Christian concepts—certain control beliefs that turn out to be the essentials of Christianity. We will need to define the essential Christian concepts or "nonnegotiables" of the Christian worldview. That will be the business of the second part of this book. Before we turn to that, more needs to be said about worldviews, especially those that rival Christianity. That will lead us to a discussion about preliminary criteria that might help us to make informed decisions about which worldview we want to hold and develop.

Rival Worldviews

People's views are often at odds with each other. Democrats do not see eye to eye with Republicans. Muslims have different ideas from Christians. Even within Christianity there are opposing groups: Protestants, Roman Catholics, and Eastern Orthodox. Underlying these differences are worldviews that lay the foundation for our sense of meaning and purpose. In fact, worldviews can be outlined in terms of their response to four basic questions which undergird all religious thinking and activity:

(1) What is real? What is the nature of ultimate reality? Is this sensible universe all that there is? Is this physical universe an illusion? Who or what is God?

(2) Who am I? What does it mean to be human? What is the purpose of human existence? What are we doing here? What is the stuff of which we are made?

(3) What is wrong? What is the origin of suffering and evil? Why do we die? What keeps humans from utopia?

(4) What is the solution? How does one remedy this problem? How does one attain "salvation"?[3]

Fundamentally different answers to these questions exist, resulting in rival worldviews.

These rival worldviews can be placed along a continuum from monistic at one extreme to dualistic at the other. In monistic worldviews only one kind or level of reality exists. Dualistic worldviews, on the other hand, maintain that more than one kind of reality exists and that these realities limit each other. As we examine each major option, you should appreciate its distinctive vision of life: its conceptions of ultimate reality, human beings, and evil and suffering, and its remedy for finding peace or attaining utopia.

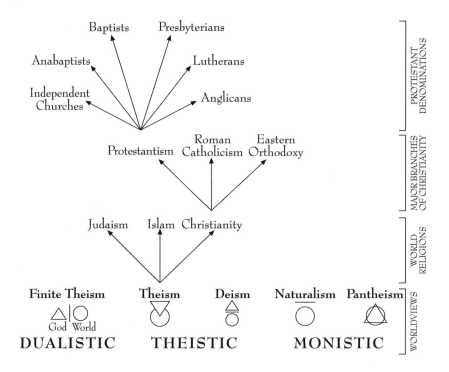

Monistic Worldviews

In monistic worldviews there is only one kind or level of reality. Naturalism and pantheism are two major representatives of these monistic worldviews.

Naturalism

Naturalism holds that there is only one level of reality: matter. Nature is all that exists. "What you see is what you get." (Of course, some things can't be seen with the naked eye—like quarks and distant stars, but in one form or another they can be detected or measured by physical instruments.) In this worldview, God and the supernatural are out of the picture entirely. Naturalism is atheistic and is often what many people popularly refer to when they use the term "secular humanism." The world is simply a bundle of physical occurrences with random side effects. There are no miracles, because there is nothing coming in from outside the bundle. As Carl Sagan succinctly puts it, "The Cosmos is all that is or ever was or ever will be."[4] The cosmos is a self-contained system; nature does not need explanations beyond itself to account for the reality of natural objects. Whatever exists is in principle explicable by means of science.

Sagan's worldview is typical of naturalism. But he is certainly not the first to espouse such a worldview. This view has been around for millennia, represented by ancient Greek philosophers like Democritus. Perhaps its most famous modern proponents are Thomas Hobbes, Ludwig Feuerbach, Karl Marx, Sigmund Freud, Bertrand Russell, and B. F. Skinner.

In this worldview human beings are simply the result of natural processes and the product of this system. They are physical animals with no real spiritual component that lives on. The idea of a soul is derided as just "a ghost in the machine." Since nothing other than nature exists, personal identity ceases at death. "All claims to unique human immortality [are an] expression of wish fulfillment, a vain reading into nature of human hope and fancy."[5]

Still, humans are sophisticated beings who can think in complex ways such that they can become victims of their memories, particularly if they try to deal with bad memories in unhealthy ways. But this thinking is all done by a brain that is as much a part of the physical body as is the foot. The problem with human animals is that they have a hard time accepting the scientific fact that they are nothing but physical entities in a symbiotic relationship with the environment, affecting and being affected by everything else in the universe that is also physical. If we could be mature and "rational" about all of this we would get along much better as individuals and as a race. The solution is quite simply to become more scientific in our thinking about *everything*.

One of the distinctives of humans is that they naturally pursue certain goals. Actually this identifies the challenge and impasse confronting the future of humankind. For individuals and groups possess radically different and conflicting values. In our society, some individuals define the highest good as promiscuous sex, an affluent lifestyle, or the advancement of their own career or company at all costs. Conflicts invariably arise. How can disputes regarding values be adjudicated?

Since naturalism has eliminated a supernatural ground for resolving moral disputes, it insists that humans must define what is right and wrong. The "Humanist Manifesto II" (1973), for instance, maintains that "moral values derive their source from human experience. Ethics is *autonomous* and *situational*, needing no theological or ideological sanction. Ethics stems from human need and interest. To deny this distorts the whole basis of life" (italics added). As an example, within the sphere of sexuality the naturalist denies that sex is a relationship ordained by God for a specific purpose: furthering the personal relationship—an unconditional transparency, trust, and mutual submission—established by the marriage covenant. According to the naturalist, sex is simply a human convention which can be revised by humans. Since humanity is the highest end, sexuality must be defined relative to human needs and desires. In other words, sexual ethics must be shaped by "human need and interest," not by a "theological sanction." And so the "Humanist Manifesto II" sanctions premarital and extramarital sex.

But why doesn't the Manifesto make rape legitimate? Doesn't this view of ethics, where the human being is seen as the creator of all moral values, eventuate in anarchy? Not according to the naturalist. For the answer is to become more rational and scientific in our thinking. One scientific fact is that individuals can have no real sense of security and happiness unless everyone plays fair in society. A community in which everyone expects to be shot in the back by his neighbors simply will not survive. Moreover, because we are social beings, acting in the interests of others is necessary for enriching our own existence. According to the naturalist, morality arises when humans recognize the scientific fact that in order for individuals to realize the good life and satisfy their own dreams, everything must be done to further the welfare of all humankind. Therefore, humans should attempt to work for the greatest possible human good.

Naturalism does have an ethic, and it is consistent with a very moral life. Indeed, the secular humanist's mission is to advance humanity's future. As the Manifesto bluntly asserts:

> We can discover no divine purpose or providence for the human species. While there is much that we do not know, humans are responsible for what we are or will become. No deity will save us; we must save ourselves. . . . Human life has meaning because we create and develop our futures.[6]

As the product of nature, history has no inherent goal. So the naturalist argues that humanity should work for a better world, which can be achieved by the appropriate use of science.

We will return to some of the challenges that Freud's brand of naturalism presents to the Christian worldview when we deal with the modern period in the third part of this book.

Pantheism

Pantheism shares with naturalism the label "monism," though it is a different species of monism. In contrast to naturalism, it admits the existence of some nonmaterial reality, which some might or might not call "God." Actually, we must be careful at this point, because there are many varieties of pantheism, the most recent and popular of which have been "New Age" varieties—usually Western popularizations of Eastern religious ideas.

Originating from the Greek words *pan* (all) and *theos* (God), the term pantheism refers to the view that "God and the world are one; everything is God and God is everything." That is to say, the distinction between God and the world is blurred. In fact, there are no ultimate boundaries between

God, human, cauliflower, and rock, regardless of what reason and sense perception tell us about reality. All is one in the end.

But all is also God. Everything partakes of God or is part of God. (The latter is usually called panentheism.) One of us first encountered this on a popular level through a visiting saleswoman. As she was making small talk and warming us up for her sales pitch, the conversation turned to the pleasant weather we were having. She noted enthusiastically that the sunshine had encouraged her to roll down her car window and "let God in." For her, even the air was animated with the existence of God. God was not so much a person, but an "it"—an impersonal energy or force or presence that was everything.

Pantheism can take a variety of forms. For instance, many Eastern versions conceive the material world as an illusion. On the other hand, the diverse religious groups associated with the New Age espouse a pantheistic vision of reality which generally affirms the reality of the material world.

While the New Age is an association of loosely linked groups, one essential theme is the unity of all being. All that exists—whether it be a pencil, a porcupine, or a person—is interrelated and part of one continuous reality, namely, God. God unifies the plurality of things in this visible world. Because God unifies and incorporates everything that exists, this Absolute cannot be conceptualized. Concepts require making distinctions, and God transcends all distinctions. Similarly, for the New Agers, God cannot be a person. People are able to know who they are and differentiate themselves from things around them. This inclusive whole, which is called God or the One, cannot. Typically these religious groups relate God and this visible world through a cosmic theory of evolution and involution, in which the whole cosmos—all its various and polar aspects (male-female, light-darkness, and so on)—emanate from the divine source and then return to the All. "The material world is not permanent and will eventually be subsumed into the One; nonetheless, as the world unfolds, every atom of it, animal, vegetable, and mineral, is filled with the divine life."[7]

Humans are distinctive and unique because they can have a greater awareness of this oneness with God than any other creature. More than any doctrine or specific belief system, the New Age movement is built around this mystical transforming experience of unity with the God found within oneself. One New Age participant described his experience in this way:

> It was at Esalen, my first trip there several years ago. I had just had a Rolfing session, and I walked outdoors.
> Suddenly I was overwhelmed by the beauty of everything I saw. This vivid, transcendent experience tore apart my limited outlook. I had never realized the emotional heights possible. In this half-hour solitary experience I felt

unity with all, universal love, connectedness. This smashing time destroyed my old reality permanently.[8]

As this account indicates, the crucial feature of this higher consciousness is an awareness of the universal energy which unifies things that ordinarily appear separate. This experience of the connectedness of everything is different from ordinary cognitive thought, where an individual as a person is separate and different from other people. In this higher consciousness, one steps outside of the system of ordinary consciousness, and things which had been thought of as separate and distinct are now seen as interdependent and interconnected. This higher consciousness does not reject the lower way of thinking, but views it as limited and partial.

Because so many humans lack this higher consciousness, New Agers argue, senseless suffering persists. They acknowledge that much evil is simply a matter of misinterpretation; what seems evil to us may actually have a beneficial function in the overall cosmic plan. And to the degree that everything that exists is a part of God, nothing is contrary to God's will. Yet many New Agers still persist in speaking of evil and even insist that ignorant and selfish humans are responsible for much senseless evil. Yet humans are not evil, simply misguided. In the Western civilizations, for instance, humankind persists in dualizing reality: God against the world, humans against nature, self against community, good against evil. They have failed to see the connections of all things within each other. Not only does this ignorance and egocentricity hinder the evolutionary process of reunion with the All, but the result is senseless suffering evidenced by war, political oppression, the ecological crisis, and all other ills that haunt us.

According to the New Agers, humans possess the most highly developed consciousness in the cosmos and thus are the most responsible for reshaping the future. Humans must save the cosmos! Propagating the experience of higher consciousness can bring about a new allegiance to the planet and the human race which supersedes the old loyalties of race, nation, or religion. While certain techniques may aid the process, this experience of higher consciousness is always accessible to the individual.

But hope for the future does not just rest upon the dissemination of this experience. Humankind is part of this divine cosmic process; thus this process is advancing through us. The All transforms itself through us. Therefore we have the power to advance this process. The New Age proponent Barbara Marx Hubbard explains:

The concept of life as an evolutionary process has subtly taken hold of me. I don't live in a static eternity but in an evolving universe. I'm going somewhere. Being of the race of human, not animal, for the first time in history there's an opportunity to choose, at least a little. . . . Now, we, humanity are in the process of forming ourselves into a synthesis, a planetary organism, one being—humankind.[9]

In sum, the New Agers are very optimistic regarding the future: "We are in an evolutionary process upward to a culture where our allegiance is to the one world, cooperation, and the survival of planet Earth!" Once humans get in touch with this continuum and realize that we are all a part of it—that we are all one and that all is God—then our world community will get better. We will live in harmony with each other. We simply need a communal spiritual "tune-up." Then, out of the ashes of the old Western worldview, they see a New Age dawning.

Dualistic Worldviews

The incessant suffering in life suggested to many groups that two antithetical principles exist, one the source of all good and the other the source of all evil. Dualism comes in many brands. It is found in some Eastern religions (and therefore in some New Age philosophies) and in some ancient and modern aberrations of theism. Two well-known ancient brands of dualism are Zoroastrianism and Manichaeism.

Dualism teaches that there are two fundamental eternal principles of reality that are *equal and independent.* They are eternally opposed to each other on the battleground of history and therefore mutually limiting. There was not originally one good world that went wrong and introduced a principle of evil into an otherwise good creation, as Christianity teaches. But there has always been an evil force as well as a good force—or at least two opposing realities.

Actually, we have to shy away from calling one evil and one good, because if dualism is going to be defensible at all it really cannot label the two opposing principles in that manner, as C. S. Lewis argued.[10] Either the labels are arbitrary or there is a third reality that is a higher standard or reference point for both. That is to say, if we all agree on which of the two is the evil one, then we must be making this judgment on the basis of some transcendent principle of reality—the real God—to which the good principle is in right relationship and the bad principle is in wrong relation. Thus, the two opposing forces are no longer independent powers; their being and their value are dependent on God.

In the contemporary world, there are few "pure" illustrations of dualism. However, its influence pervades the contemporary scene in theories where no being has sufficient power to guarantee his or her hope and vision for the future. As a result, history is simply the struggle and dissension of all that exists. God cannot guarantee his own future; God can only limit and obstruct others. Contemporary American process philosophy, for instance, maintains that God cannot exist without a world and that his power is limited and confined by the creation's actions.

Harold Kushner expounds a popular version of this limited metaphysical dualism in his popular book, *When Bad Things Happen to Good People*. The death of his first son, due to progeria (rapid aging), forced this Jewish rabbi to deal with the problem of senseless and even "innocent" suffering in God's creation. While Kushner's answer picks up some classic lines from theistic religious writers, the whole focus is altered because he denies that God is omnipotent. A view more akin to dualism than theism results. As Kushner bluntly confesses, "I worship a God who hates suffering but cannot eliminate it."[11] Other than originally equipping us with a conscience, God has no power over us.

> Why then do bad things happen to good people? One reason is that our being human leaves us free to hurt each other, and God can't stop us. . . .[12]

God is outraged and grieves with us in our innocent suffering. Our sorrowful existence can be lessened, Kushner proposes, if unjust suffering turns us from our self-centered ways so that we work for justice and demonstrate to others compassion in their times of grief. But there is no escape from the history of suffering, neither for us nor for God.

Theistic Worldviews

In contrast to monistic worldviews, theism insists that at least two different kinds of reality exist: God the creator and his creation. Over against dualistic worldviews, theism insists that God is the omnipotent creator, and nothing will obstruct his final goal for creation. However, there are many brands of theism, and they should not be confused with Christian theism.

Deism

Deism insists that God created the universe and humans with a moral conscience, but that he is no longer active in history. God is letting history run on its own, maintaining a hands-off approach until the end when human vice will be judged and human virtue will be rewarded. Miracles are not necessary in this scheme. God is viewed as a sort of "celestial watchmaker" who wound things up in the beginning so that the machine keeps working on its own. Meanwhile, human beings are responsible to live moral lives that are based on sound rational principles.

This view arose in seventeenth-century France and made its way to England by the next century. It was imported into the United States by people like Benjamin Franklin and Thomas Jefferson. Franklin's autobiography is tediously typical of the prudential lifestyle of a deist: "Keep your nose clean and God will bless you; get in trouble and God will get you." And Jefferson's "Gospels," in which he snipped out all of the miracles in the life of Jesus but recommended the high moral precepts to his son, illustrates the rationalism of deism's approach to religion. It is simply not true that the "founding fathers" of the United States were all Christians, though the myth that anyone in the U.S. who says the word "God" in a civil context is talking about the God who revealed himself in Jesus of Nazareth continues to live on in the minds of well-meaning Christians. In today's pluralistic society, when someone says "in God we trust" it would be prudent to inquire what he or she means by "God."

Christian Theism

In the modern world there are three major theistic religions: Judaism, Christianity, and Islam. In general, all three agree that God is the only ultimate reality who existed before anything else existed. Therefore, God is not the world. God is the creator of the world and is intentionally, personally, intimately, and continuously involved with the world he brought into being. God is not a force or energy which can easily be confused with some cosmic processes. So, God both *transcends* the world and is *immanent* within it. He is other than but present to the world at the same time.

As the archetypal person, God created humans as persons who are to be subservient to himself. Humans are moral agents who are responsible for their acts in this life; they will answer for them in the life to come.

Other than this meager description, there are vast differences between the "peoples of the book," as Muslims refer to these religions. The more precise definitions of God, the human task, sin, salvation, and redemption differ. In Christianity, it is the advent of God in Jesus Christ that is ultimately responsible for defining these terms.

According to the Christian worldview, the human problem is sin. Humankind has rebelled against God's fellowship and love. As a result, Satan has become the temporary ruler of creation, "the god of this age" (2 Cor. 4:4), and humankind is enslaved to this sinful condition. There is no power in humankind or creation which can free us from evil's grasp. We are "dead in [our] transgressions and sins" (Eph. 2:1). Only God can defeat the Evil One and redeem us from our condition. Despite humankind's rebellion and bondage in sin, God acted in history to call a people to himself. Through this historical revelation God identified who he is in contrast to this fallen cosmos, demonstrated his graciousness to the sinner, and promised Israel that he would reestablish his kingdom over creation. Jesus Christ fulfilled this promise. In this One alone, God assumed human flesh, took on our guilt, defeated Satan, created a new humanity, and brought about the reconciliation of creation. In Jesus Christ alone, God has descended to our condition, meeting us where we are and offering us a personal relationship with him whereby we may grow into his image. In Jesus Christ, God is reclaiming creation for himself. The Bible promises that one day all creation will again submit to him as Lord (cf. Eph. 1:20–21; Phil. 2:9–11).

It should be obvious from just this brief definition that Christian theism cannot live in peaceful intellectual coexistence with naturalism, pantheism, dualism, or deism. This is the worldview that we will explore in part 2, and at that point we will have other opportunities to note some further distinctions between Christian theism's answers to the questions we listed above and the answers given by its rival worldviews.

Pluralism in a Postmodern Culture: Are There Really Any Differences after All?

For nearly 200 years the U.S. was defined by Judeo-Christian values. But increasingly this moral and worldview consensus has broken apart. There is no escape from the rival religious and moral claims surrounding us. Today we live in an age of "pluralism," a challenge to evangelical Christians who make exclusive claims such as "Jesus Christ is the Lord of the universe." This exclusivism does not set well with a culture that prides itself on letting each person have his or her own opinion when it comes to matters of religion, expression, or moral behavior. Such claims are increasingly viewed as intolerant and arrogant by a culture that prizes pluralism, demanding that we accept different ethical and religious beliefs as equally valid. The implicit claim is that there are no real differences between moral and religious systems; these are just culturally-derived matters of taste. In the academic arena some theologians at Christian seminaries have bluntly rejected Christianity's exclusive truth claims: "The idea that Christianity [has] a monopoly on religious truth is an outrageous and absurd religious chauvinism."[13]

The most prominent spokesperson for this view, John Hick, defends religious pluralism in *An Interpretation of Religion: Human Responses to the Transcendent*. His thesis is that "we always perceive the transcendent through the lens of a particular religious culture with its distinctive set of concepts, myths, historical exemplars and devotional or meditative techniques."[14] Hick is not merely *describing* the diversity of religious beliefs; if that is all there is to his statement then it would be undeniable, for the twentieth-century world is filled with diverse cultural and religious beliefs about God and the world. But Hick is insisting that the existence of religious pluralism is itself a religious *truth*: the major world religions end up referring to the same ineffable transcendent Reality. That is to say, Hick goes beyond a descriptive pluralism to insist upon a *normative* pluralism. For Hick, all religions are "true" to one degree or another (depending on their ethical orientation). What appear to us as differences between religions arise only because of our varying cultural and historical contexts. If they result in a life of love and concern for others, the claims of the Buddhist, the Muslim, the Christian, and even the atheist must be accepted as equally true and salvific.

This sits well with many people in our culture—from academicians to talk show hosts. The point of many discussions in the university and on *The Oprah Winfrey Show* is not to arrive at the truth of the matter, if the "matter" has to do with religious beliefs and moral values; the point is simply to keep the discussion going and respect the divergent points of view, because, as one talk show guest said about pornography, "The great thing about our society is that you can have your opinion, and I can have mine."

How did we get to this point? Lesslie Newbigin helps us to understand this in *Foolishness to the Greeks*. Contemporary Western culture has divided the world into two realms. One realm is the *public* world of scientific fact that explains *how* something occurred by examining its causal relationships. Statements which can be verified through the scientific method (such as "atoms exist" and "atoms can be split to produce energy") are assumed to be true, and people would be fools to deny them. The other realm is the *private* world of religious beliefs and moral values, which deal with *why* questions: Why is there a creation? What is the purpose of human existence? As a society we have found no way to reach agreement on what human life ought to be. So statements like "Homosexual behavior is morally wrong" and "It is only through Jesus of Nazareth that a person can be saved" are relegated to the realm of private opinion. Our religious beliefs and moral values have been "democratized." That makes for good ratings on talk shows, but it should not be acceptable to Christians who confess their credo on Sunday.

It should not even be acceptable to any thinking person who is *forced* to admit that there *are* some things that are absolutely wrong and some things that are absolutely right in the realm of morality. For instance, killing six million Jews just because you have anti-Semitic sentiments is not a matter to be left up to personal taste or opinion. Presumably, any honest person in our pluralistic society would not say, "What Hitler did was okay for him, but it would not be okay for me."

But what about religious beliefs? Isn't our culture right to assume that if pantheism works for one person and Christian theism for another then that's okay—that what is true is "what works for you"? There is something to be said for this kind of pragmatic test. But when a Christian makes a reli-

gious claim such as, "Jesus of Nazareth is the *only* way to God," he or she
is stating a truth about reality itself which, if true, excludes all rival claims
of the naturalist, pantheist, dualist, and deist—let alone of non-Christian
theists. Either this claim is true and all other similar claims are false, or it
is false and some other (or no other) claim is true.

In addition, the way in which the pantheist or the naturalist construes
this world—even events and data within the scientific realm—is not the
same as the Christian. The Christian's perception is indelibly shaped by his
or her control belief regarding God's purposeful creation. Worldviews are
not confined to just the private sphere, as the pluralist assumes. Rather,
each shapes the totality of reality. And there is no universally common
standpoint; there is no view from nowhere. Each worldview represents a
uniquely particular and different apprehension.

"Postmodernism" is the term that is often used today to label the situation in which we find ourselves. In philosophical circles the word refers
especially to the thought of some continental (i.e., European) philosophers
since the 1970s (e.g., Lyotard, Foucault, and Derrida). In the U.S., names
like Richard Rorty and Stanley Fish are sometimes associated with postmodernism. But the first time one of us recalls seeing the term in popular
print was in an advertisement to describe the movie *Pulp Fiction*.

In this popular sense postmodernism refers to the pluralism we have
been discussing. It rejects the Enlightenment modernism (see chapter 15)
that truth is "out there," waiting to be discovered by rational humans who
all think according to the same rational principles in a predictable machine-
like world. Hence the "post" in postmodernism: all knowledge is bound up
with one's culture and way of thinking. How one looks at reality depends
on one's ethnicity, gender, nurturing community, and so forth. Meaning
and truth are, in part, social constructions created by groups that share a
common tradition and perspective.

Modern technology has certainly enabled this new perspective. Instant
Web access and rapid transportation put us in touch with new ways of living and thinking with which we might never have come into contact a century ago. This is further exacerbated by the proliferation of choices, from
cable TV to grocery store inventories. As one social analyst put it:

> Too many of the things we do in our lives, large and small, have come to
> resemble channel surfing, marked by a numbing and seemingly endless pro-
> gression from one option to the next, all without the benefit of a chart, logis-
> tical or moral, because there are simply too many choices and no one to help
> sort them out. We have nothing to insulate ourselves against the perpetual
> temptation to try one more choice, rather than to live with what is on the
> screen in front of us.[15]

What specifically, then, are the crucial features of postmodernism in our everyday channel-surfing lives?

1. *Postmodernism rejects any "master narrative."* Since postmodernists reject a universal acultural point of view, they insist there are no master narratives (or metanarratives) that define reality or history for all people at all times. Instead, we are to celebrate centerlessness, diversity, choice. To claim that there is a master narrative is seen as oppressive.

2. *Postmodernism locates authority in the socially-constructed self.* The authority of the autonomous self takes the place of the master narrative. The self is the source of truth and reality. Nothing else should interfere. As Roger Lundin points out, we live in "an age that believes that freedom will make you true."[16]

   If each self is autonomous to construct its own reality and truth, then we must respect others who define themselves. In postmodernism there is an acute awareness of the "other." Again, this is a consequence of the fact that there is no metanarrative, no universal way of interpreting things. Each December equal respect must be paid to Hanukkah, Christmas, and Kwanza. And so we live by the dictum of "political correctness" and use "PC language," all buttressed by the supreme virtues of niceness and civility. All selves have an equal voice and, more importantly, all are considered equally valid.

3. *Postmodernism reminds us of the power of language.* Some collections of like-minded selves manage to gain a privileged status, silencing or marginalizing the views of others and insisting that their interpretation of reality and truth is the only true one. Even concepts such as "rational" and "justice" are up for grabs. Those who pretentiously define the terms for everyone else are the "victors." Postmodernism claims that the entire cultural and social history of the "victims" is ignored, denied, or brought into line with the dominant narrative of the victor. The victim is, therefore, implicitly labeled by the victor a deviant or simply wrong. So, knowledge of reality is not the discovery of what is waiting to be grasped in the same way by everyone. In the most radical sense of postmodernism, reality has to do with who has the power. For example, do we call what gestates in the womb of a pregnant woman a "fetus" or a "baby"? Is the termination of the pregnancy an "abortion" or "murder"?

   We create reality with words that we use for pragmatic purposes. Language and symbols do not necessarily represent truth. Language is used to tell stories that rearrange information to describe whatever reality a person or group is constructing. Richard Rorty once put it this way: "Anything can be made to look good or bad by being redescribed." The lines between fantasy and fact begin to be erased.

Pretty soon everything becomes a continuous interpretation of (and debate about) words. Words refer to words. Even the word "is" might be up for grabs!

4. *Postmodernism emphasizes the construction of reality.* Now it should be obvious that what is perhaps most characteristic of postmodernism is its emphasis on the social construction of reality—something like the virtual reality in the movie *Star Trek: Generations* in which a spaceship hurling through the galaxy becomes a tall ship sailing through the high seas. Typically, if one can reconstruct reality, then there is no moral responsibility in the end. Captain Kirk can simply go back in time and replay an event in which he acted less than virtuously until he gets it the way he wants it. In the movie *Matrix* we witness both the computerized construction of reality by machines and the attempt to sabotage such a construction by a small minority of quasi-religious human remnants.

5. *Postmodernism gives priority to images.* In the construction of reality images are important, whether one is courting sympathy in a murder trial, invading an enemy who is portrayed as another "Hitler," slipping in sound bites and irrepressible images in a political campaign, or capturing a family vacation on videotape. In fact, in one sense the event being videotaped becomes less important than getting it just right so it will play well in the family room a year later.

6. *Postmodernism celebrates the importance of management and therapy.* In the postmodern culture the manager and the therapist are the important occupations. The pragmatic postmodernist seeks to manage her experience and environment in the interests of a "manipulable sense of well being."[17] The primary concern is self-improvement and comfort with one's self over against the ethical ultimates and obligations imposed by "universal truth."

Evangelical Christians should not jump to the conclusion that everything about postmodernism is bad or wrong. In fact, a careful reader of this book's final chapter will conclude otherwise. But if the modernist's claims to have a universally acceptable and defensible common knowledge turn out to be illusory, and if subscription to a universal rational point of view, a universal morality, and a universal religious truth has expired, then how can we tell whether or not the Christian's claim is true? Can we prove that it is true? Some Christians suggest that we can prove the truth of Christianity beyond a shadow of a doubt, in part by showing the falsity of other worldviews. But Scripture does not promise this. In fact, some are blinded by their sin and cannot even understand biblical truths (John 1:5; 1 Cor. 2:14). Furthermore, the attempt to prove Christianity true with absolute certainty by means of an appeal to rational grounds—which always reflects a particular conception of reality—is inher-

One Christian's view about worldviews—". . . the most persuasive case for Christianity lies in the overall coherence and human relevance of its worldview." (Arthur Holmes, *Contours of a Worldview*, viii)

Another Christian's view about worldviews—". . . coming into contact with Jesus inspires worship, gives us access to the very mind of God, and provides enough confidence to endure martyrdom, while worldview philosophy brings one out of dogmatism but has tendencies toward skepticism. . . . The best case for Christianity, then, is not the coherence and comprehensiveness of its worldviews." (Gregory Clark, "The Nature of Conversion: How the Rhetoric of Worldview Philosophy Can Betray Evangelicals" in Phillips and Okholm, *The Nature of Confession*, 217)

ently contradictory. For this very attempt implies that something more basic than Scripture is our norm for truth. But the most basic "fact" for the evangelical is that the Word of God, namely, Jesus Christ, is the norm for truth. Everything else must be accountable to him!

Simply put, the truthfulness of Christianity is not dependent on being justified as true to adherents of rival worldviews! In the same way, a hung jury does not imply that a murderer did not commit that crime. Our standards for truth must be determined by God, not sinful humans.

But this does not mean that we are left with Hick's normative pluralism and that adopting Christian theism is just a matter of personal taste. If we cannot prove with absolute certainty that Christian theism is true over against rival worldviews, we can at least show that it is plausible to hold as a worldview—that the natural and social sciences, for instance, do not disprove the truth of Christianity but can, as a matter of fact, demonstrate just how plausible it is to believe what Christians believe. And demonstrating the plausibility of Christianity is as far as Scripture commands us to go: "Always be prepared to give an answer . . . for the hope that you have" (1 Peter 3:15).

Indispensable to this calling are the various "tests" for worldviews. For instance, a worldview should be consistent. Recall C. S. Lewis's argument that the dualist's distinction between a good and an evil principle is inconsistent in that worldview. Another test is "empirical fit." That is, does the worldview "fit" all of our experience? If naturalism does not ring true to the human craving for immortality, what does that say about the adequacy or the "live-with-ability" of naturalism? Coherence is a third test. The pantheist's claim that all is God might be difficult to coherently affirm in light of some of the horrendous evil humans have perpetrated against each other.

Of course, the Christian is not immune from these tests, and it could be argued that the Christian's claim that God the Son died on the cross is inconsistent or that Christ's imperative to turn the other cheek when struck does not ring true for our human experience. The problem of evil is a perennial one for the coherence of Christian theism. In fact, such objections have been and are continually made against the truth of Christianity. Such debates will go on as long as we remain on this side of heaven.

Our task is to be faithful to the Gospel—to the fundamental, nonnegotiable beliefs of the Christian faith. Spelling out what those are and how we got them is the task that is next on our agenda. But it will not be enough to know what to say; we must also know how to speak the claims of the Christian worldview to our own culture, and that means that we must be faithful and relevant. As Karl Barth put it, a good theologian (and a good Christian) must have a Bible in one hand and a newspaper in the other. How to apply the Good News to today's news is rarely a simple task, and an exploration of how the church has done it in the past will occupy our attention in the third part of this book.

For Further Reflection

1. Compare what was said about the way we picture the world (such as looking at a map of the world) with the way that Paul says people view the cross (see 1 Cor. 1:18–2:6) or with the way that Jesus says people view the necessities of life (Matt. 6:24–34). Do Paul and Jesus imply that emotional, valuational, or behavioral responses are part of these views?

2. Given what was said about how our worldview affects the way that we see and respond to a person rummaging through a trash can, consider the story of Jesus, Simon the Pharisee, and the prostitute in Luke 7:36–50. Could the same point be illustrated here? What is significant about Jesus' question in verse 44?

3. If a worldview is a way of seeing the world, based in part on what one loves, then how will a person's worldview be affected if he or she tries to love both God and mammon? (cf. Matt. 6:24) Is it possible for a person's worldview to have "double vision"? If so, what is the impact of that if a worldview involves the whole person?

4. Watch the video Worldview Boutique, produced by the media department of InterVarsity Christian Fellowship. Relate it to what was said about pluralism and proving the truth of the Christian worldview in this chapter. (The video is available from 2100 Productions, P.O. Box 7895, Madison, WI 53707-7895; 1-800-828-2100.)

For Further Reading

Allen, Diogenes. *Christian Belief in a Post-Modern World*. Louisville: Westminster John Knox, 1989.

Grenz, Stanley. *A Primer on Postmodernism*. Grand Rapids: Eerdmans, 1996.

Holmes, Arthur. *Contours of a World View*. Grand Rapids: Eerdmans, 1983.

Lewis, C. S. *Mere Christianity*. New York: Macmillan, 1952.

Newbigin, Lesslie. *Foolishness to the Greeks*. Grand Rapids: Eerdmans, 1986.

Roberts, Robert C. *Spirituality and Human Emotions*. Grand Rapids: Eerdmans, 1982.

Sire, James. *The Universe Next Door*. Downers Grove, Ill.: InterVarsity, 1988.

———. *Discipleship of the Mind*. Downers Grove, Ill.: InterVarsity, 1990.

Walsh, Brian J., and J. Richard Middleton. *The Transforming Vision*. Downers Grove, Ill.: InterVarsity, 1984.

Willard, Dallas. *The Spirit of the Disciplines*. New York: Harper and Row, 1988.

Wolterstorff, Nicholas. *Reason within the Bounds of Religion*. Grand Rapids: Eerdmans, 1976.

Part 2

Our Christian Identity

three

Revelation: The Source of Our Christian Identity

he Zoblinski heritage has shaped Tommy's specific outlook on the world. Nevertheless, simply because he is a member of the human race, Tommy Zoblinski's worldview will share much with the Luppolds, the Walters, the Santiagos, and most other families. Our outlook on the world is derived from ingredients that form our daily lives—from the media that pervades our lives to the people we rub shoulders with everyday. The worldview a person acquires must be relevant to all aspects of life and should have beneficial consequences for society. In fact, one general purpose of education is to acquire more experiences and other ways of seeing the world, for these new encounters enrich and broaden an individual's outlook.

For example, Jeremy, an African-American, sits next to Tommy Zoblinski at school. On their very first day in the second grade, Tommy and Jeremy discover a common love of trains. Tommy has an HO train layout that his father played with as a little boy, which Jeremy would love to see. But Tommy's repeated requests for his mother to invite Jeremy over to play have been futile. Despite his mother's curious behavior, Tommy and Jeremy delight in imagining train trips at recess and have become best friends.

Tommy's college-aged sister, Stella, has just returned home after a semester of social work in Nigeria. Working in the rural areas, she has gained a deep appreciation for the sense of community and family in Yoruba culture. American individualism now appears selfish and even materialistic. Even the Yoruba religious traditions, especially their deep emotional ties with nature and their relevancy to everyday life, are becoming more attractive than her family's Christianity.

In other words, through education and significant life experiences, Tommy and Stella have gained appropriate new ways of seeing the world that transcend their Zoblinski perspective. Perhaps the multiplicity of outlooks on the world is bewildering at first. But the educational enterprise helps the student to recognize enduring categories, and eventually to evaluate them on the basis of internal consistency and their ability to comprehend all of life. Through this process, the student becomes the master of his or her own outlook on the world, instead of being submissive to the prejudices and unreflective habits of the past. Of course, every student realizes that education is an endless process, and an appreciation of probability is a hallmark of the educated person.

This raises the decisive question of authority, crucial for every worldview. What is your norm for deciding truth concerning God, humankind, even the cosmos? Who is your ultimate authority? In the end, who determines what is true in your worldview?

Broadly speaking there are two options to this question. Some people attempt to ground truth claims in the human subject, whether it be feeling, conscience, or human reason. Here authority revolves around the human subject. Certainly for Stella Zoblinski the ultimate norm is the current shape of reason and its probable stabs at assessing consistency and comprehensiveness. And as Stella illustrates, the problem with this option is that it domesticates Christianity to what she thinks is true.

In the opposing option, the authority is outside the subject. For instance, evangelicals have traditionally claimed that to have a Christian worldview, the God who has made himself known in Jesus Christ must be the center and even the norm by which we evaluate every other element. This means that a Christian worldview must be grounded first and foremost in God's revelation of himself, that is, the Old and New Testaments.[1] And revelation here does not refer to the subject's probable assessment that this is a divine revelation. Rather Scripture confronts one as having God's authority; it establishes itself as the norm over the believer's life. And the believer submits to God's Word of judgment and grace (Ps. 139:23–24). In this chapter we will examine the Christian's authority—God's revelation in Jesus Christ through Holy Scripture.

Revelation

The word revelation literally means *the unveiling of a hidden mystery.* In this instance, we are speaking of the unveiling of an otherwise hidden and incomprehensible God. This revelation is not something God has to do. It is a gift! God is under no obligation to us, other than that which he has imposed upon himself. And certainly we have not deserved to know anything about the Creator, given the way we have disobeyed him, treated his creation, and preferred to construct our own ideas of "god." Nevertheless, God is gracious; He *wants* to be in a relationship with us.

Maybe you have tried to get to know someone of the opposite sex. But every time you initiate a conversation and ask questions about his or her family, interests, and hopes, the person "clams up." Talking to a roommate or friend, you might complain, "I just can't get close to him/her." Thank God (literally) that God did not "clam up." By being attentive to the ways in which God has revealed himself and shared with us his interests, hopes, likes and dislikes, we can get close to him.

General Revelation

Scripture distinguishes between God's general and special revelation. *General revelation* refers to God's self-revelation through creation. God—the origin, ground, and goal of human existence—leaves traces of himself in the universe. First, the fabric of our human existence—the *microcosm*—witnesses to us something of the existence and purposes of God. Here one can point to our sense of morality, our conscience, and our abilities to reason and be creative. Paul refers to this in his speech on Mars Hill in Acts 17:22–31 and in Romans 1:18–20 and 2:15, when he notes that the "requirements of [God's] law are written on [our] hearts." Humans know their obligation to the Creator as their moral judge. Second, nature—the *macrocosm*—is also a testimony to God's existence. It is the stage for God's glory; or as the psalmist puts it, "The heavens are telling the glory of God; and the firmament proclaims his handiwork" (Ps. 19:1, NRSV). Third, human history suggests God's providence as we trace backward through our own autobiographies, witness sociopolitical events, or examine the development of other religions.

But these sources seem particularly ineffective in guiding humanity to God. How often do the magnificent California redwood forests or the stark beauty of an Arizona landscape evoke recognition of God's existence or even praise to God? Isn't the creation, not the Creator, more often worshiped?

The unregenerate "has, in a spiritual sense, eyes and sees not. . . . He has no true knowledge of the things of God. . . . But as soon as he is born of God, there is a total change. . . . The 'eyes of his understanding are opened' . . . 'he sees the light of the glory of God,' His glorious love, 'in the face of Jesus Christ.'" (John Wesley, *Wesley's Standard Sermons*, 2:233)

Why don't all humans recognize this general knowledge of God? In this post-Edenic world, the problem is twofold. First, there is a radical difference between the infinite God and finite humans. While we can know something about God, much more is beyond our grasp. Due to our *finitude*, general revelation appears ambiguous and is readily interpreted in conflicting ways. Take nature's awesome spectacles—piercing arctic winters, Florida's terrifying hurricanes, animals ripping into the entrails of other animals (including human animals!). Is it any wonder humans project an impotent, fearful, or even hateful God? Without God's supernatural demonstration of his gracious love and sovereignty in the midst of history, how can we consider ourselves as any more than forsaken specks in a foreboding cosmos intent on returning us to dust? Or, in the words of the Kansas anthem: "All we are is dust in the wind."

In addition, this general knowledge about God *is* twisted. Paul notes in Romans 1:18–2:1 that the sinner is fearful of God the Judge, since there is nothing in general revelation suggesting God's mercy for sinners. To pacify their terrified consciences, sinners distort general revelation and contrive an idea of God under their control and whim. Our ideas about God end up being the idolatrous fabrications of our own minds, even if they started out with good ingredients (such as the beauty and orderliness of nature). So due to sin general revelation is not enough. And Paul concludes that after the Fall, general revelation only renders us inexcusable before God (Rom. 2:1).

Special Revelation

Recognizing the human predicament, God mercifully chose to reveal himself in a special way and to deal decisively with sin. Special revelation concerns God's supernatural entrance into our space-time reality to redeem the human race from sin and reclaim creation for himself. God originally promised salvation when Adam and Eve fell, by prophesying to Satan, "I will put enmity between you and the woman, and between your offspring and hers; he will crush your head, and you will strike his heel" (Gen. 3:15).

	Origin in Creation	Subjective Access to this Reality	Purpose of this Revelation
General Revelation	Part of the natural order of creation	Through natural means, i.e., conscience and reason	Show inexcusability
Special Revelation	Supernatural or miraculous act	Through supernatural means, i.e., illumination of the Holy Spirit	Establish salvation and develop the believer

Comparison between General and Special Revelation

Scripture is the history of God acting to enrich his people's understanding of that promise and then fulfilling it in Jesus' life, death, and resurrection.

Through these miraculous acts and words in history God discloses truths that are not written on the face of nature (Heb. 1:1–2). Such acts—the Abrahamic theophanies, the burning bush which spoke to Moses, God's freeing the Israelites from slavery in Egypt, the word of God spoken by the prophets—correct our distorted knowledge of God by revealing his holy standards as well as his merciful intentions toward the sinner. Today, through the special revelation in Jesus Christ we learn that God has provided the way for bringing us into relationship with himself and longs to be every sinner's friend. That is why believers can "approach God with freedom and confidence" (Eph. 3:12) without fearing a wrathful judge.

In addition, fallen humans are so bent and twisted that they do "not accept the things that are from the Spirit of God"; they appear as "foolishness," for sinners "cannot understand them" (1 Cor. 2:14). Someone more powerful than we humans must correct this twisted spiritual eyesight. Consequently, access to special revelation occurs only through the Holy Spirit's work which illumines or opens our eyes and ears.

Finally, special revelation places us in a personal confrontation with God where we are forced to obey or reject God. The story of Moses at the burning bush (Ex. 3) forms the paradigm. When he received God's special revelation—the voice speaking through the burning bush—Moses knew that he stood in the presence of God. He immediately fell to the ground and prostrated himself. Moses recognized God's authority and his own sinfulness; that is why he was afraid. God met Moses there. Yet God offered his mercy and even enlisted Moses in his work in this world. (Note the similarity with Saul's encounter with God in Acts 9.) And Paul argues in 2 Corinthians 4:4–6 that the same thing occurs today: God in Jesus Christ encounters us in Scripture!

Special revelation is somewhat like getting to know another person. Strictly speaking, knowledge of another person is beyond the reach of our best efforts. The external actions of the other person at best provide an ambiguous and uncertain basis for discerning the other's intentions. Certainly we can impute motives to another, but that is precisely the problem. For we are all aware of the ways in which incomplete knowledge of someone's actions quickly leads to deception, as well as the ease with which we project motives on others to fit our own fantasies. Our knowledge of others depends primarily on their decision to reveal or unveil who they are and thereby confront and correct our projections regarding their intentions. And only if they choose to reveal their intentions—who they are—are we able to understand them.

For example, a shy and undiscerning college freshman might mistake the innocent smile of a certain woman whose path he happened to cross on campus as a sign of some interest on her part. Not knowing her real intentions for smiling, he imputes self-interested motives to her actions. That is, until he calls and asks for a date. Then her negative answer would shatter his fantasies. Only then would he have certainty regarding her intentions! But not *until* then.

God's work in special revelation is somewhat similar. For through special revelation God acts to disclose something that was not available in any other way. Simply put, special revelation is not a human discovery of God, but God's activity (Heb. 1:1–2). In the event of special revelation (recall Moses and Saul) God shatters our illusions regarding who he is as well as who we are in relation to him, and God offers us a loving personal fellowship. Here knowledge of God does not result from my approximations of the cosmos, but God's personal confrontation.

This model of personal knowledge also helps us to understand better the problem of general revelation. After the Fall, general revelation is distorted by our idolatrous illusions. That is why the Protestant Reformers argued that special revelation must correct our distorted vision. John Calvin provides a compelling image at this point. He referred to the Bible as the "spectacles" through which we can correctly read nature and history.

> Just as old or bleary-eyed men and those with weak vision, if you thrust before them a most beautiful volume, even if they recognize it to be some sort of writing, yet can scarcely construe two words, but with the aid of spectacles will begin to read distinctly; so Scripture, gathering up the otherwise confused knowledge of God in our minds, having dispersed our dullness, clearly shows us the true God.[2]

Special revelation sheds light on what would otherwise be seen dimly or distorted due to the darkness of our sin.

Scripture as Special Revelation

All Christians recognize that God has in some way spoken in Jesus Christ and that this history has claims on our attention. But Christians differ on where and how to listen to God. Evangelicals believe that God speaks today through his written Word, the Bible. They insist that the Bible must stand as the sole norm for all of life (*sola Scriptura*).[3] Evangelicals affirm the right of the Bible to stand in judgment over the church, human reason, and conscience. Scripture alone demands our obedience; it alone stands as the rightful authority in all matters of faith and practice. The Bible is the source of special revelation and the norm for constructing a Christian worldview. Four theological terms—Christocentricity, illumination, inspiration, and self-authenticating authority—provide further insight into the evangelical doctrine of Scripture.

Christocentricity

Jesus Christ is the nucleus of God's salvific acts in history. According to his eternal plan, God the Word promised salvation and then assumed our flesh and established our salvation (see Eph. 1:3–14). Similarly, Jesus Christ constitutes the central theme of Scripture. The very phrase, *the Word of God,* indicates this. Above all, this refers to God's definitive disclosure of himself in Jesus Christ, *the* Word of God (John 1:1–18). Second, this phrase refers to the whole Bible. Not only is Scripture God's revelation to us, but its purpose is "to show forth Christ." For this was how Jesus used Scrip-

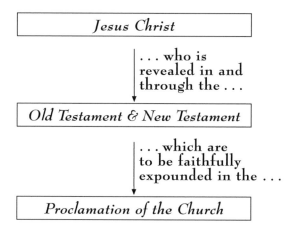

The "3-fold Form" of the Word of God

ture: Jesus "beginning with Moses and all the Prophets . . . explained to them [the disciples] what was said in all the Scriptures concerning himself" (Luke 24:27). In addition, this phrase, *the Word of God,* sometimes refers to God's revelation of himself through the church's proclamation, particularly as it faithfully attends to Scripture.[4] This is what Paul thankfully reminds the Thessalonian church about their response to the apostles' preaching: "when you received the word of God that you heard from us, you accepted it not as a human word but as what it really is, God's word" (1 Thes. 2:13, NRSV).

The threefold form of the Word of God is arranged in a hierarchy. Each level serves the next higher level, so that ultimately all refer to Jesus Christ, the definitive Word of God. Simply put, Jesus Christ and his work is the interpretive key to Scripture.

Scripture's Illumination and Inspiration

As special revelation, access to Scripture's content and its origin is not simply a natural phenomenon. That is to say, Scripture's reality as the Word of God includes both the Spirit's *illumination* of the contemporary reader, as well as the Spirit's *inspiration* in originating this text.

Illumination empowers contemporary readers to understand and obey God's Word (1 Cor. 2:14). As an individual reads the Word, relying upon the Holy Spirit for illumination, the Word will convert and sanctify that individual. As Paul notes in 2 Timothy 3:16, because the same Holy Spirit who inspired the writers of the Bible now illumines its readers, the Bible will effectively teach, rebuke, correct, and train believers in righteousness.

The term inspiration typically refers to someone motivating us: "Your hard work inspires me!" In theology, however, *inspiration* has a very different meaning. The Greek word underlying the English term "inspiration" is *theopneustos,* a compound of God (*theos*) and breath (*pneusto*) (2 Tim. 3:16). It means that the Scriptures are the product of God's own breath, recalling God's supernatural power by which he creates the world and performs his mighty acts (Ps. 33:6). When Paul describes Scripture as inspired, he is asserting that these writings transcend the human author's own abilities.

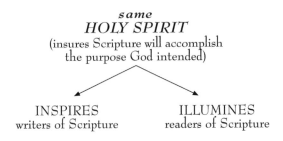

same
HOLY SPIRIT
(insures Scripture will accomplish
the purpose God intended)

INSPIRES   ILLUMINES
writers of Scripture   readers of Scripture

Inspiration is God's supernatural work so that what God wanted, the biblical authors wrote.

Moreover, 2 Timothy 3:16 indicates that *all* Scripture is inspired, not just some parts. So evangelicals confess plenary and verbal inspiration—the whole (plenary) is inspired, even the very words (verbal). By contrast, some theologians claim that God inspired only the images or thoughts of Scripture and that the words were chosen outside the inspiration process by the authors. But this quickly results in evading the Bible's authority by identifying some dimension of Scripture as just humanity's best insights, not what God wanted to say. Plenary and verbal inspiration confirms the normative authority of the Word of God over all life.

On the other hand, verbal and plenary inspiration must not be confused with dictation. There simply is no evidence that the biblical writers were God's passive robots or even that God consciously spoke to them everything they wrote. Luke 1:1–4 tells us that he carefully investigated his sources. In addition, the biblical books vary in style and substance, reflecting each writer's own personality as well as his cultural, historical, and stylistic peculiarities.[5] The affirmation of verbal and plenary inspiration is not an attempt to explain *how* inspiration occurred or its mechanics, but the *extent of inspiration.* Since this was a supernatural and thus miraculous process, it would be foolish to specify how God inspired the biblical writers. For miracles cannot be explained by ordinary causes!

God though was at work in this process so that these writings are truly the inspired Word of God. Here divine revelation is incarnate in human words, not unlike the mystery of the divine and human natures of the incarnate Christ. And consequently we have the confidence that Scripture is true and trustworthy, the supreme and final authority for our life.[6]

Scripture's Self-Authenticating Authority

How do we know that the Bible is the Word of God? The Protestant Reformers—Martin Luther, John Calvin, and Ulrich Zwingli—contended that Scripture is self-authenticating: it proves its authority to every believer. They were not referring to the Bible's statement that it is God's inspired Word; almost every religious book makes similar claims. Nor did the Reformers appeal simply to archaeological and historical evidences to confirm that these recorded events occurred. While such evidences for the reliability of Scripture are useful and even necessary, by themselves they do not establish that Scripture is God's Word. Nor were the Reformers appealing to a new revelation by God in which he happens to whisper in one's ear that Scripture is inspired. For then, the real norm would be this new revelation and not Jesus Christ.

"For as God alone can properly bear witness to his own words, so these words will not obtain full credit in the hearts of men, until they are sealed by the inward testimony of the Spirit. The same Spirit, therefore, who spoke by the mouth of the prophets, must penetrate our hearts, in order to convince us that they faithfully delivered the message with which they were divinely entrusted." (Calvin, *Institutes* 1.7.4)

Rather, Scripture's self-authenticating authority refers to the conjunction of the inspired Holy Scripture and the Spirit's supernatural illumination. Here Scripture confronts one as having God's own authority. God's Word shatters the subject's own ideas and establishes itself as the authority over the believer. Only then is Scripture's authority as God's own Word self-evident to the believer. As John Calvin describes this reality, "If we turn pure eyes and upright senses toward it [Scripture], the majesty of God will immediately come to view, subdue our bold rejection, and compel us to obey."[7] "Indeed, Scripture exhibits fully as clear evidence of its own truth as white and black things do of their color, or sweet and bitter things do of their taste."[8]

Moreover, this authority is "superior to human judgment; [we] feel perfectly assured . . . we have a thorough conviction that we hold to an unassailable truth; . . . because we feel a divine energy living and breathing in it [Scripture]—an energy by which we are drawn and animated to obey it, willingly indeed, and knowingly, but more vividly and effectually than could be done by human will and knowledge."[9]

This sense of Scripture's divine authority rests upon its central message: God's grace to us in Jesus Christ. Scripture is the clothing in which Jesus comes to us. And when Jesus Christ confronts us in Scripture, it includes judgment and grace: God is showing us who we really are as sinners and thus judging us, but he is also bestowing his grace upon us, putting us right with him and changing us. As Paul explains, we perceive "the glory of God in the face of Christ" (2 Cor. 4:6), God's own salvific presence. Scripture's power to convert and sanctify is its self-authenticating authority.

Canon

We have referred to the Old Testament and the New Testament as if these terms represented two clearly defined groups of books. In general they do. But even today questions regarding the precise limits of the Old Testament disturb the church. And new Christians are sometimes quite surprised to learn of books not included in the New Testament which were read as Scripture by some early Christians, such as the *Didache*.[10] This naturally provokes questions. How did we get the precise shape of Scripture? Why do some denominations include more books in their Bibles than others? Each of these questions concerns itself with one basic problem—that of establishing the *canon* of the Bible.

The term *canon* is derived from the Hebrew *qaneh*, which referred to a "reed" or "rod"—a straight stick—that was used to measure length and straightness. Hence, the reed that measures is a rule. The early church used the term canon to identify those books considered authoritative. The canon of Scripture, then, is the rule by which we measure the "straightness" of our beliefs and actions.[11]

The Old Testament Canon

The only Bible the early church had was the Old Testament. These were books considered to have prophetic authorship, since a prophet was one whose life was devoted to revealing the message and purposes of God for his people (see 1 Peter 1:10–11). They also had to be in conformity with the Torah (the five books of Moses at the beginning of the Old Testament, called the Law or Pentateuch).

But the Old Testament existed in two forms. From 250–100 B.C. some Alexandrian Jews translated the Hebrew Old Testament into Greek for Jews of the Diaspora who no longer spoke Hebrew. This Greek translation, also called the Septuagint, contained additional books that explained the situation of Jews in Palestine during the intertestamental period. These books, called the *Apocrypha*, did not appear in the Hebrew Bible. Since most of the known world spoke Greek, the Septuagint circulated widely. As a result, these apocryphal books have become the cause of much controversy.

A working Hebrew Old Testament canon was probably in place by 300 B.C., and this was recognized by a council of rabbis in Jamnia (in Palestine) around A.D. 90. It consisted of thirty-nine books which correspond to ours today. But only Jews living in Palestine—such as Jesus and his apostles—recognized the Hebrew Old Testament as canonical. Outside that area the Septuagint was preferred. Since the New Testament authors wrote in Greek, they often used this latter version when quoting from the Old Testament. However, they rarely alluded to apocryphal books and never attributed canonical status to them.

The post-apostolic church also used the Septuagint, including its extra writings. By the fifth century, much of the church treated these books as canonical, though some (such as Jerome) revered them highly as instructive spiritual literature while not granting them canonical status. The Protestant Reformers raised the question concerning the Apocrypha's authority again and decided to return to the Hebrew canon, following the practice of Jesus and the apostles. In response, the Roman Catholic Church at the Council of Trent reaffirmed its traditional acceptance of the larger Greek canon. Protestant and Catholic Bibles still reflect that difference today. Note, however, that the only issue in dispute is whether the Apocrypha is canonical.

The New Testament Canon

The earliest Christians depended on the Old Testament, oral traditions about Jesus' teaching and work, and direct revelations from God through Christian prophets. When Jesus described the Old Testament as the Word of God (John 10:35), he not only sanctioned the idea of a canon but prepared the way for a collection of new scriptural writings. For if the Old Testament simply foretold of Jesus' coming, a similar set of writings became necessary for preserving his teachings and the story of his ministry. And Jesus' final command to his apostles—the Great Commission (Matt. 28:18–20)—to "go and make disciples of all the nations" (v. 19) initiated these writings.[12]

As the New Testament books were written, they were read in the churches and even exchanged. As the circulating materials increased, similar materials were collected and bound together. The earliest collection consisted of ten of Paul's letters, and then the four Gospels were united into one collection.

But a wide range of literature was read and valued by the church. While some was apostolic and referred to in the same breath with the Old Testament books (2 Peter 3:16), other writings were questionable, if not outright heretical.[13] By A.D. 140, the church began recognizing that some literature was God's inspired Word. This is evident from the activities of Marcion, a Christian living in Rome about that time. Marcion believed that the Jewish God of the Old Testament could not be identical with the God of love revealed in Jesus Christ. So he established his own canon free from any Jewish influences. He selected Luke as his sole Gospel and accepted only some of the Pauline writings. The very fact that Marcion considered it necessary to establish his own canon and reject certain works shows that the wider church had accepted some books as Scripture in his day.

While the church had begun to define the canon, this process occupied the church's attention for about the next two hundred years. Not one of the New Testament books was accepted due to pressure from the church hierarchy. The councils that discussed the canon were at the very end of the fourth century, 393 and 397. By that time, the New Testament canon—the same twenty-seven books that we recognize today—had already become the Scripture of the church. By the same token, the church indicated that the rest of the literature circulating among the churches was not inspired, even though some writings might be beneficial. And finally, the church reaffirmed the divine authority of the Old Testament. (To use the New Testament to the exclusion of the Old is called "Marcionism.") So

Christians are guided by both the Old and New Testaments, though they interpret the Old in light of the New—the life and teachings of Christ.

One decisive criterion for New Testament books was apostolic sanction. The apostle was not just a spectator or reporter of Christ, but an active participant with and witness to Christ in a unique and unrepeatable way. Each author of a book in the New Testament canon was either an apostle (like John), one intimately connected with an apostle (like Mark), or an apostle "untimely born" (like Paul). But in the end the decisive question was: Does it speak with God's authority? The church did not give the Bible its authority. On the contrary, the church recognized and listened to the voice of her Lord speaking in and through certain pieces of literature. These she recognized as God's Word or Scripture and so acknowledged them as canonical.

Through these conflicting historical pressures a book emerged which Christians apprehend as the Word of God. The resulting canon of Scripture is the unique and absolute norm for the believer's faith and practice. It is that by which all else is judged. And it must function that way for us as we develop a Christian worldview.

The Faith Which We Believe

The initial human response to divine revelation is called faith. There are two aspects to faith.

First, we sometimes speak of the act of faith, using the *verbs* "to believe, to trust, or to give assent." The church has referred to this in Latin as *fides qua*—the faith *by which* we believe. This is the subjective side of faith. It is a trust and confidence in God to be true to his revealed Word, grounded in God's actions in the past. It is what most people mean when they ask whether or not a person "has faith."

This aspect of faith is important because without it our Christian doctrines will become mere academic exercises. It is this *personal appropriation* of the elements of a Christian worldview that makes it come alive and makes a difference in the world.

But merely believing is not sufficient, no matter how intensely you do it. You may have heard people speak of members of certain religious groups in very respectful tones because these religious folks *really* believe what they preach. The problem is that all the believing in the world does not make something believed in true or right. In fact, sometimes an intense faith in the wrong thing can be disastrous, even among those who profess to be Christians. As a result, the most crucial question facing the Christian today—indeed, the question that confronts every generation of believers—

is: Do we really acknowledge Jesus as Lord over all life? Are we truly being faithful to Jesus now?

The Christian church refers to right belief or *orthodoxy* (from two Greek words meaning "straight/correct" and "opinion"). The word is similar to *orthopedics,* a branch of medicine devoted to preventing and correcting skeletal deformities; orthopedics can help people walk well. In the same way, orthodoxy is concerned to prevent or correct theological deformities. By keeping her beliefs "straight," a Christian can live well. *Heresy* (from a Greek word meaning "I choose") appeals to our sinful tendencies (such as self-centeredness) and cripples our ability to live the full life that God intended.

This is why it is equally important to stress the second aspect of faith—namely, the *content* of faith. This is what earlier theologians referred to as *fides quae*—the faith *which* we believe. This is faith in the noun sense—the object of our intense belief. This is the objective side of faith—knowledge. In the Christian worldview it is as important to be correct about the object in which you put your trust as it is to have that trust in the first place. And when these beliefs are put into verbal or written form we refer to them as *doctrines* or *dogma*. They get expressed in creeds (such as the Apostles' Creed and the Nicene Creed, often used as summaries of orthodoxy against heresies), confessions (such as those used by your local church as a guide and contemporary expression of the faith for a particular people at a particular time), theology books, and even hymns (see the trinitarian "Holy, Holy, Holy," or the great song about the church, "The Church's One Foundation").

There is nothing mysterious about the notion of doctrine. The word simply means "things that are taught." As such, doctrines are summaries of biblical teaching on particular topics, such as the person of Christ or the nature of the church. And these summaries continue to be investigated and mulled over by each generation of believers. As Alister McGrath describes it, this involves taking the various threads of Scripture and weaving them into whole cloth.[14] This is the task of theology.

The Task of Every Believer: Theology

Unfortunately when the term *theology* is mentioned, we are usually met with glazed eyes. Whether in the college or local church setting, we know what students are thinking: theology is simply a human enterprise; it is found in dusty, boring books; it has no relevance for our lives.

On the contrary, we think theology is the most practical and essential activity for the Christian. Let us explain. Etymologically, "theology" is derived from two Greek words, *theos* meaning God, and *logos* referring to an explanation or an account. Theology is one's "understanding about

God." Everyone has some thesis regarding God, even if it is just that God does not exist. So everyone has a theology, whether acknowledged or not. The central question is: Is your theology true? As evangelicals, we believe the Bible is our norm and final authority for determining whether our understanding of God is true or not. This is the norm for determining whether we obediently acknowledge Jesus as Lord over all.

But precisely at this point even stronger objections to theology arise. If the Bible is our final authority, why bother with theology? Why not just stick to the Bible? Some Christians even assert, "No creed but the Bible." This statement, of course, misrepresents the aim of an evangelical theology. An evangelical theology does not displace Scripture with a creed. Scripture alone is our norm. But still, if we have Scripture, the inspired and normative understanding of God, why do we need theology, our own erring and human understanding of God?

Let us return to the situation of a believer in Germany during Hitler's rise to power in the 1930s. The theologically conservative Lutherans who supported the "German Christian" movement were explicitly committed to Scripture's authority. Their biblical arguments were plentiful. First, they argued that God is the Creator of all. As Paul concludes, nothing therefore can be viewed as inherently unclean (1 Cor. 10:26), certainly not one's racial and national identity! Paul had defended his missionary strategy with the line, "to the Jews I became like a Jew, to win the Jews" (1 Cor. 9:20). Similarly, shouldn't Christians endorse German nationalism and adapt the Gospel to it in order to win the Germans to Christ? Paraphrasing Paul, their strategy was "to the nationalist German, we have become nationalist Germans, to win them."[15] Second, Paul makes clear that the state reflects God's will and thus support for the state is a necessary part of obedience to God (Rom. 13). Consequently, they claimed that "as Christians we honor with thanks toward God every order, therefore also every authority, even if deformed, as a tool of divine preservation." Simply put, Christians are required to obey Hitler. Third, they maintained that their anti-Jewish policy was biblical, paralleling Jesus' own woes against "world Jewry" (Matt. 23:15; John 8:40–44).[16]

Believers uneasy with these racial purity statements were probably sidetracked by historical exigencies. For in the late 1920s and early 1930s Germany was grappling with the moral and social breakdown of its culture. The crisis of modernity—which North America is facing now—posed the question: How could social and political unity be maintained when relativism, permissiveness, and pluralism precluded a common vision? How can social chaos and disintegration be averted without a core of common values? At this particular moment, the only viable political options appeared to be Fascism and atheistic Marxism. For in the early twentieth century, Hitler represented one of the few political forces against atheistic Marxism; and fascism appealed to the militarism of the German people. In view of these biblical and cultural arguments, the majority of Christians, both the laity and the clergy, viewed Hitler as representing God's will for the German nation.

Why did Christians so badly misinterpret Scripture? Why did so many Christians fail to confront Hitler? The answers are complex, but the discipline of theology helps provide some explanations. They, in turn, demonstrate why theology is so essential for the Christian.

Theology Is Necessary for Correctly Interpreting Scripture

Why was Scripture so poorly understood and misinterpreted? Some German Christians failed to recognize that any biblical claim and assertion must be theologically evaluated.

Scripture is God's Word. But to understand Scripture, we must interpret it. This activity of interpreting Scripture is theological. Either implicitly or explicitly, we are making claims about God. For instance, the German Christians concluded from Paul's declaration, "to the Jews I became a Jew," that Scripture sanctioned Germanic identity and nationalism. Interpretation cannot be escaped by just repeating Scripture. For the selection of this specific verse in contrast to another set of passages demonstrates that one believes this verse is central to Scripture's conception of race. That is a theological interpretation!

Of course, all these theological interpretations are human and in principle fallible. For that reason, the essential question that must always be asked is: Is this theological interpretation and claim true? But this question is seldom pursued. Far too often a collection of Bible verses seems to diminish and even deaden a Christian's critical and discriminating powers.

Scripture has always been interpreted from conflicting standpoints. Divergent readings of Scripture, some of which are just as mind-boggling as the German Christians', are common today and always will be. This does not imply that every reading is correct; only certain interpretations account for all the biblical teaching most adequately and accords with God's intent. But the validity of this interpretation must be argued and defended. It is not a given. A successful defense usually requires a comprehensive knowledge of Scripture, and especially of the essential biblical terms and categories which were developed in the Old Testament and fulfilled in Jesus Christ. This framework is actually a form of theology, frequently called biblical theology.

Theology Is Necessary for Understanding and Evaluating the Contemporary World

Why did so many Christians dismiss the gravity of Fascism's challenge? The evil of Fascism was not directly confronted because many Christians

Byang Kato (1936–1975)

The son of a priest among the Jaba people in Nigeria, as a teenager Byang Kato turned away from his people's traditions and accepted Jesus Christ as his Savior. After completing his doctorate overseas, Kato returned and became a leading evangelical African theologian. Until his tragic death, Kato courageously countered the threat from liberal African church leaders who maintained that the salvation offered in Jesus Christ is expressed in the African traditional religions. Through his own Jaba tradition, Kato illustrated that while this general revelation reflects humanity's yearning for the Creator, after the Fall it is inevitably distorted and idolatrous. The Jaba acknowledged the existence of God, but offered him no worship. Salvation was conceived totally in terms of appeasing the evil spirits and regulating the social life and order in the village; it offered only oblique and contradictory hints regarding the life after death. According to Kato, the Jaba religion reflects the "cry of the human heart, but the solution lies elsewhere"—namely, in this Word that became flesh as a particular person in Bethlehem. Liberal syncretistic Christianity only "depersonalizes" Christ. If Jesus is truly Lord, then this Word must "judge the African culture"; one must "never allow the culture to take precedent over Christianity."

had not sufficiently reflected on Scripture in order to apply it to their contemporary world.

Frequently, Christians are tempted to just repeat biblical categories. For instance, in the church where one of us grew up, a revivalist once warned that we should not attempt to think too seriously about what the Bible says. Human reasoning inevitably leads to doubts about the faith; rather, one should simply accept what the Bible says and not ask questions.

But is that stance appropriate? Scripture was written over 2,000 years ago. How can a mere repetition of biblical categories elaborate the significance of Jesus' person and work for our contemporary world? How can the church help resolve contemporary challenges and problems, except by developing and elaborating the key themes of Scripture so that they apply to the present? How else can the church speak with biblical authority to the social problems of AIDS, the widening division between the first and third worlds, the intellectual challenges of the New Age, pluralism, and so on? Being faithful to Jesus Christ entails not only understanding his Word, but applying it to our world so that we are his disciples *now*.

The danger—and too often the reality—is that believers will accommodate themselves to the ideals, desires, and practices of their world unless a comprehensive understanding of God's revelation dealing with contemporary issues is developed. That is why the believer must develop an understanding of God's revelation which deals with *every* dimension of life. Then one can perceive the Christian implications for behavior, lifestyles, political and moral issues, and even for academic disciplines such as economics, biology, and psychology. This further development of theology, usually called systematic theology, strives to understand all reality in an organized and integrated way from the perspective of revelation. Then one can confess Jesus Christ as Lord over every area of life. Isn't this what our Lord meant when he commanded us to love him with all our mind? (Mark 12:33; Luke 10:27)

Theology Is Necessary for Our Identity

Finally, the heresy of "German Christianity" arose because many Christians had forgotten their identity as disciples of Jesus Christ and as the body of Christ, the historic Christian church. German nationalism shaped their identity more than Jesus Christ.

When we receive Christ as our Savior, we become part of a new community, the body of Christ. This new family into which we are welcomed, the church, helps shape and form our identity as disciples of Jesus Christ. We grow, becoming more like Christ, Paul argues, within the church (Col. 2:19). Indeed, church leaders—apostles, prophets, evangelists, pastors, teachers—are given in order "that the body of Christ may be built up" so that we all "become mature, attaining to the whole measure of the fullness of Christ" (Eph. 4:11–13). Much in the same way that our biological family has shaped and nurtured us, the church through its modeling, nurturing, and chastising activities builds our identity.

However, Paul does not confine the body of Christ to just the local church; rather he has in mind the universal church, the church throughout history. One way in which the universal church develops, shapes, and builds us up is through its historically developed theology. The resulting tradition of theology, usually called historical theology, shapes our identity in several ways.

The church's theological traditions structure our understanding of Scripture and the Christian faith. Historical theology transmits the collective wisdom of the Christian community. The great creeds and theological writings of the past have stood the test of time and offer more penetrating insights into the reality of God's Word than what we are able to perceive on our own. By dialoguing with them—but always subjecting everything to the Word of God—we enhance the process of faith-seeking understanding and can escape some past missteps.

In addition, this theological tradition structures the church's mission. Christ has commissioned the church to go to the ends of the earth with the gospel. This mission, however, cannot be narrowly conceived as just evangelism. As Charles Malik insightfully noted:

> The problem is not only to win souls but to save minds. If you win the whole world and lose the mind of the world, you will soon discover you have not won the world. Indeed it may turn out that you have actually lost the world.[17]

The church's mission is to convert the whole world, heart and mind. Here again, theology is indispensable for shaping our identity in the world.

Theology, we have argued, represents the basic work of every believer. It is necessary for interpreting Scripture, evaluating the contemporary world, and shaping our identity as Jesus Christ's disciples.

The subsequent chapters in this section examine the key biblical categories framing a Christian worldview. And in the final section we will illustrate how Christians have organized these doctrines in various ways to deal with the challenges they faced.

For Further Reflection

1. Evaluate this claim arising from general revelation: "The liberation of Eastern Europe and the demise of Communism are the work of God."
2. What are the implications of grounding the Christian worldview solely in our ability to demonstrate that this worldview is the most consistent and comprehensive one to date?
3. If the Bible includes both testaments, why do we have editions of the Bible with just the New Testament? Are we guilty of being Marcionites? If all of Scripture is inspired and if the purpose of all of it is to "show forth Christ," why do some Bibles print the quotations of Jesus in red letters?
4. Is it important to confess the plenary verbal inspiration of Scripture?
5. Dan Wakefield's book *Returning* (New York: Penguin, 1989) provides a retrospective account of God's interventions in his life, though at the time he did not usually realize it. Read Wakefield's book to see how he discerned God's activity in his life, then see if you can identify some events where God was active in your life.
6. What biblical arguments can you make to question the "German Christian" interpretation outlined above?

For Further Reading

Allison, C. FitzSimons. *The Cruelty of Heresy.* Harrisburg, Pa.: Morehouse, 1994.

Bruce, F. F. *The New Testament Documents: Are They Reliable?* 5th ed. London: Inter-Varsity, 1960.

Charry, Ellen T. *By the Renewing of Your Minds.* New York: Oxford University Press, 1997.

Demarest, Bruce A. *General Revelation: Historical Views and Contemporary Issues.* Grand Rapids: Zondervan, 1982.

Hill, Andrew E., and John H. Walton. *A Survey of the Old Testament.* 2d ed. Grand Rapids: Zondervan, 1999.

McGrath, Alister. *Understanding Doctrine.* Grand Rapids: Zondervan, 1990.

Metzger, Bruce. *The Canon of the New Testament.* New York: Oxford University Press, 1987.

———. *The New Testament: Its Background, Growth, and Content.* Nashville: Abingdon, 1983.

Packer, J. I. *Fundamentalism and the Word of God: Some Evangelical Principles.* Grand Rapids: Eerdmans, 1958.

Sproul, R. C. *Explaining Inerrancy: A Commentary.* Oakland: International Council on Biblical Inerrancy, 1980.

Wenham, John W. *Christ and the Bible.* Downers Grove, Ill.: InterVarsity, 1972.

four

Setting the Stage:
The Creation of the World
and Human Beings

hen you come into this class on evolution, leave your religion outside the door!" Perhaps you have heard of such a mandate or even experienced this scenario in a high school science class. It is a common attitude, and one we should not be surprised to hear of; in fact, in some settings it may be the only time where "religion" is ever mentioned. Such an encounter fulfills the prophecies of Sunday School classes, youth groups, and Christian camps that often warned that science was pitted against the biblical view of creation. Unfortunately, that is about all many of us understand about the biblical view of creation!

Too often Christians view the doctrine of creation as only a fighting point against the theory of evolution. Actually, the doctrine of creation is much more important than just a point of debate with contemporary science. Some of its significance can be seen by opening the beginning pages of Scripture. While the Bible concentrates upon God's redemptive work culminating in Jesus, it does not begin there. God creating the world stands at the beginning. This is because the God-creation relationship sets the stage for understanding the universe, human purpose, the problem of evil, and God's remedy in Jesus Christ. Through our discussion in this chapter we will discover that the biblical understanding of this relationship fundamentally distinguishes our Christian family's worldview from other non-theistic worldviews on the scene.

God Alone Is the Source of All That Is

The Bible makes it clear that *all* things were made by God (see Gen. 1:1; Ps. 33:6, 9; John 1:1–3; Col. 1:15–17; and Heb. 11:3). In fact, eight times in Genesis 1 we read the refrain, "And God said, 'Let there be. . . .'" That is to say, all things were created by the Word of God alone. God is not a carpenter who shapes preexisting materials. God is *truly* creative! He created everything that exists, even the fundamental elements of the universe. Theologians have referred to this as *creatio ex nihilo*: through an act of his purposive will God brought the world into being *out of nothing*—simply by speaking the world into existence.

This thesis implies that the Christian worldview is incompatible with any kind of pantheism. *Creatio ex nihilo* rules out *creatio ex deo* ("creation *out of* God"). The universe is not some extension of God's being, as emanation theories suggest. There is no blurring of the distinction between God and the world in the Christian worldview. A line is drawn between the Creator and the creation. God is not the world, and the world is not God. God prohibits idolatry—that is, worshiping the creation in contrast to the Creator—precisely so we will not confuse the two.

The Christian worldview is also incompatible with any kind of eternal dualism. The biblical record insists that there is no eternal reality apart from or alongside of God. Rather, creation bears the marks of being created and dependent on God for its very existence: "In his hand are the depths of the earth" (Ps. 95:4). Because God created the universe from nothing, at any moment it could sink back into nothingness if He chose not to preserve it. Consequently, the universe is not independent of its Creator, but radically dependent upon God, who alone is self-sufficient.

Because God created this world, He owns it and has the right to rule it (Ps. 95:3–7). Since everything that exists finds its source ultimately in God, God is not a slave to his creation or its history. He does not have to answer to the universe. He is under no obligation to it other than that which he imposes upon himself. Nor is God limited by something outside himself. God cannot be finally impeded by his creation or its history. When we sing, "He's got the whole world in His hands . . ." the message rings true, for the believer can have peace and confidence that evil will finally be vanquished!

Because *all* things are dependent on God for their very existence, *nothing* in creation is worthy of our worship. It is all finite, partial, transitory. If it came into existence and is sustained in its existence by the Word of God, it can just as easily be called out of existence by the same Word. God must constantly uphold creation's existence and prevent its decay into nothing. It is radically dependent on the self-sufficient God who preserves it (see Col. 1:17: "in him all things hold together"). Therefore, only this life-giving Word is worthy of our worship.

It does not even make sense to worship this creation, since our world and our existence are contingent. That is, our universe did not have to be. Sometimes, only traumatic and tragic events can open our eyes to this feature. If you were one of the many who witnessed via TV the explosion of the space shuttle *Challenger*, you probably shared a common reaction. It shocked us into realizing reality is not as solid and secure as it appears on the surface. It was a very visible and sobering reminder that forced us to confess that nothing finite can be held on to for ultimate security; for nothing created is necessary or self-sustaining.

Our existence is not something that we generated or even control. We did not choose to be born. Our continued existence is precariously dependent upon air and food; it is absolutely dependent on other things. But let's take it one step further. If the whole universe is composed of contingent beings like us, then what accounts for the existence of this particular universe? It simply cannot account for its own

Bernard Ramm (1916–1992)

A significant twentieth-century evangelical who dealt with the relation between historic Christianity and science was Bernard Ramm. Ramm was a seminary professor and worked with organizations such as Young Life and World Vision. In all of this, his lifelong mission involved finding ways of addressing contemporary issues while remaining faithful to orthodox Christianity in the Reformation tradition, but succumbing neither to fundamentalism nor modernism in the process.

Relating Scripture and modern science was one of the areas in which he did this, especially in his book *The Christian View of Science and Scripture* (1954). Ramm became interested in physical science while studying weekly with a Russian playmate and his engineer father. Because of their conversations about relativity, atomic theory, and chemistry, Ramm decided to spend his life in science and prepared to set a course of study in math and science. But before entering the university he was converted to Christ in a profound way which led him not only to graduate work in the philosophy of science, but also to seminary education.

Ramm found his models for integrating the Bible and science among late nineteenth-century evangelicals who respected the facts of science and the data of Scripture, demonstrating with integrity that they are in harmony. On the other hand, Ramm lamented certain twentieth-century evangelicals whose fear and "narrow bibliolatry" buried the earlier tradition and resulted in science's reciprocal rejection of fundamentalist Christianity. With provocative insights, Ramm dealt with integration issues in astronomy, geology, biology, and anthropology. He concluded in his 1954 study that "if the theologian and the scientist had been careful to stick to their respective duties, and to learn carefully the other side when they spoke of it there would have been no disharmony between them save that of the non-Christian heart in rebellion against God."

existence. No matter how many contingent beings are added together, a necessary or self-sufficient reality is never the sum of the equation. Either there is no ultimate reason for this universe (a possibility difficult to live with), or there is something outside of this universe upon which the whole depends.

This way of thinking is often used in Christian apologetics (i.e., the defense of the Christian faith), but our point here is simply that the theistic belief that God created the world *ex nihilo* and all that that implies is more than simply a belief. It accounts for and shapes the way we experience the world.

God Chose to Create the World Freely and with Purpose

The first verse of the Bible indicates that God intentionally chose to create the world. He did not have to create this world or any other world. He could have remained the only reality in existence. He was perfectly complete and self-sufficient without a creation. But in his wisdom he created *this* world out of all the other possibilities that he considered. We can praise God, then, not simply because he redeemed us, but first because he created us freely and intentionally.

Several implications follow from this. First, naturalism is ruled out. In the beginning was God (John 1:1). God was not out of the picture in the eternal past; the world was. Furthermore, because God created purposefully and intentionally, the resultant creation is not simply a bundle of physical occurrences that occur randomly, as naturalism argues. Having been created according to God's wisdom, the world is ordered in law-governing ways that reflect the wisdom and purposes of God; it has an intelligible uniformity about it. Perhaps this was in the mind of the author of Genesis as he narrated the story of creation in a very orderly seven-day sequence. It certainly seems to be implied in the text when God makes cosmos out of chaos, particularly when he separates the waters and gives them boundaries (Gen. 1:9–10), since in the Jewish mind unbounded waters or turbulent seas represented a threatening chaos that needed to be confined.[1]

Second, it is this orderliness that makes possible the disciplines that are studied in a liberal arts institution—from the natural sciences (which depend on orderly occurrence in nature to conduct research) to the arts (which depend on orderly mathematical values to produce harmony in music or consistency in pigments which ensure that the painter's product remains the same from day to day). All these enterprises presuppose orderly occurrences. If there were no laws, or if these laws were always changing, we could never arrive at any enduring findings, except that everything is absurd.

"It is either not knowing or denying the createdness of things that is at the root of the blackness of modern man's difficulties. Give up creation as space-time, historic reality, and all that is left is what Simone Weil called uncreatedness. It is not that something does not exist, but that it just stands there, autonomous to itself, without solutions and without answers." (Francis A. Schaeffer, *Genesis in Space and Time*, 30)

As recent scholars have demonstrated, it is precisely this Christian conviction about God's purposefulness in creating the world that has laid the foundation for modern science.[2] Prior to the rise of a Christian worldview, a Greek understanding dominated. The Greeks viewed matter as irrational and unintelligible and so never attempted to investigate the whole universe. Nor did the Greeks encourage an empirical investigation of reality. For they assumed that we have access to the intelligibility of nature through reason (*logos*), apart from experience.

The Christian worldview led to the realization that if a wise God created the whole world, matter may also be intelligible. Furthermore, Christianity recognized that since this particular world is due to the decision and will of God, it did not have to be. Its existence is contingent, even its specific set of scientific laws. To understand how this world operates, we must empirically investigate creation itself. Indeed, the Christian sees the world laden with possibilities that can be explored and developed by the sciences, the humanities, and the arts.

One caution is in order at this point. Because the world's purpose and intelligibility is *derived* from God, we must avoid idolizing the world. The Christian's goal is not to "save the planet" for the sake of "Mother Earth." The goal is to "save the planet" so that it can glorify the one who made it worth preserving in the first place. Christians ought to be at the forefront of environmental concerns, but not always for the same reasons as those who hold different worldviews.

All Creation Has Value Derived from Its Creator

In Genesis 1, after every day but the second, God declares that what he has made is "good." In fact, when he is finished and everything is together in the right order, he sees that it is "*very* good."

The Christian perceives God as the source of the moral law and its values. While humans attempt to blind themselves to God's specific commands, no one can escape the language of "good" and "bad" or appealing to some standard of right and wrong.[3] While some attempt to explain morality as a human creation that expresses our hopes, does that really explain what we mean when we refer to the moral law? For the consciousness of the moral law includes a sense of obligation, the duty to obey, not simply the desire and hope that others will follow. Here, the Christian sees the imprint of the holy and just God upon his creation. This sense of obligation and duty reflects a higher being who is impressing his will upon us and who is not subject to our whims and desires.

And God's declaration that creation is good is his evaluation of *all* of his creation—the physical aspects as well as the spiritual. God did not create the world in such a way that only what is spiritual is valuable. To God, the physical is equally valuable.

This "very good" creation fell into sin shortly after God brought it into being. Yet God still finds great value in what he has made, particularly in his human creatures, sinful as they are. God invested in us by providing for our needs (even our bodily needs), he incarnated himself into this creation, he suffered to redeem and restore it, he actively remains Lord over it, and he will eventually re-create it (see Rom. 8:18–25). When Adam and Eve fell, God could have wiped the slate clean and started over again—but he didn't. It's a good creation and it's worth redeeming.

Thus, while the creation is not divine (contrary to what the pantheist thinks), it is *essentially good* as God made it. It is not intrinsically evil, to be shunned in otherworldly ways. In fact, ultimately the creation and evil are to be separated from each other.[4] Salvation is the restoration of the creation over against the evil that has intruded into it as a foreign object. The cancer will be excised; in the meantime, the creation groans (cf. Rom. 8:18–25; 2 Peter 3:10; and Rev. 21:1). So, the Christian worldview is not world-denying. It is world-affirming because Christians believe in a *world-affirming* God—a God who created this world very good and who is in the process of restoring it to its original condition.

Throughout its history the church has confronted groups who were world-denying. The Apostle Paul was one of the first. Upon encountering groups in some of his churches who denied the goodness of creation in a fundamental way, he dealt with them as heretics. Called Gnostics, these individuals held that this material world was evil. Consequently, these Gnostics considered salvation to be a flight away from this evil world by withdrawal and detachment. Writing against their prohibition of marriage and the eating of certain kinds of foods, Paul maintains that they have belittled God's good gifts "which God created to be received with thanksgiving by those who believe and who know the truth. For everything God created is good, and nothing is to be rejected if it is received with thanksgiving; because it is consecrated by the word of God and prayer" (1 Tim. 4:3–5).

Christians today must also acknowledge that all creation is good. How many times do we single out some part of the creation as the source of all

> "To be or not to be? That is the question. And it is decided by the way in which we answer the question: To give thanks or not to give thanks? The real human is the one who is thankful to God and he alone." (Karl Barth, *Church Dogmatics*, 3/2:171)

our problems? Just like the Gnostics, we often belittle God's good creation. In the process, we divert attention from the real problem, our rebellion against the Creator—a rebellion that was not part of God's original creation.

If God has made this world good and if he continues to see it that way despite the intrusion of sin, then this world is worthy of our careful, detailed, and devoted investigation.

Humans Are Part of the Created Order Made in the Image of God

As part of the physical and spiritual universe which God created, human beings were created as creatures with body and soul. While evangelical Christians have been good at emphasizing the God-given soul of each person, they have not always done as well in recognizing the body as part of God's good creation. But Genesis 1–2 makes it clear that God thought the body of a human being was important: he created it, clothed it, and protected it. And it is our body (i.e., our whole person) that God wants us to present to him as a living sacrifice, which is our acceptable worship (Rom. 12:1).

Perhaps even more significant than the fact that God made us to be physical-spiritual beings, Genesis makes it clear that the Lord created us to be relational beings (see 1:27; 2:18, 21–24). If nothing else, this is what it means to be made in the image of God.

This relationality is first of all God-directed. We who are made bearing God's image need to be centered in God. Our highest end is not found within us, but outside of us—in God. Jesus' statement that the greatest commandment is to "love the Lord your God with all your heart, and with all your soul, and with all your mind" (Matt. 22:37) is not simply a command, but it is reflective of the way in which we were designed.

Pascal is credited with saying that there is a God-shaped vacuum in the human heart. It can be filled by God alone. Another way to put it is to say that humans are incurably religious creatures. We need to be related to some infinite concern, even if it is an "infinite" of our own making. We cannot live without a god, even if it is a god made in our own image.

"Assuredly there is but one way in which to achieve what is not merely difficult but utterly against human nature: . . . It is that we remember not to consider men's evil intention but to look upon the image of God in them, which cancels and effaces their transgressions, and with its beauty and dignity allures us to love and embrace them." (Calvin, *Institutes* 3.7.6)

Human behavior in the ordinary everyday world reflects this infinite chasm, the deep longing for something more than anything finite can provide. We are constantly striving to find something to feed our hungers. We buy a new outfit, get a "make-over," go on a trip, even change neighborhoods or social cliques, but the hunger is never satisfied. In fact, the desire seems to intensify. We crave more and more, simply because finite things lack ultimate significance.

Our relationality is also directed toward other humans. When God made us in the image of his trinitarian being, the text specifies that he made us male and female (Gen. 1:27). That is to say, to be created in the image of God is to be created a social being; to be fully human the way God intended for us to be is to be a human-in-relationship. We were not created to be alone (Gen. 2:18). We were created to be with other people in all sorts of healthy relationships. Again, the second greatest command, "to love your neighbor as yourself" (Matt..22:39), reflects the way we were designed from the beginning.

Humans need to be in personal relationships with others. At every stage of life the evidence for this abounds. Infants need intimacy and fellowship. When one of us had a foster son, Donnie, placed in our home, it was after he had spent his whole life (seven months) in an incubator in the hospital. He did not even recognize persons as different from things: when he was held his eyes were constantly searching, never resting. His chronic illnesses were symptoms of a failure to thrive. Donnie's personhood was drawn out and developed by tickling him, kissing his neck, tossing him into the air (and catching him), and verbal play.

The need to connect continues among adolescents where the power of peer pressure is bolstered by this built-in need to belong. And when adults recall the high points of life, it is not usually as solitary creatures, but in partnership with others. Clearly, we are created for community.[5]

The Christian worldview runs headlong against the individualism that pervades our society. We affirm that community life and social institutions are necessary for people to live as image-bearers of God. Being a self-made person is foreign to the Christian worldview. Being a person who can achieve maturity and perfection only in the company of others who are committed to the same project is precisely what Christianity is all about (see Eph. 4:15–16).

Furthermore, Genesis makes it clear that humans were made to be in relation not only with other humans, but also with the animals (see Gen. 2:19–20) and the rest of nature. This is poignantly stressed in the unfolding drama of the story in Genesis as the writer repeatedly calls our attention to the connection between the first human beings and the ground: humans come from the ground (2:6–7); they are to tend the ground (2:15); their sin results in the cursing of the ground (3:17–19); and the ground cries out when human blood is spilled on it (4:11–12). That is to say, human destiny is bound together with nature's destiny—something that the author of Genesis knew long before twentieth-century environmentalists.

God's Purposes for Humankind

The first "earthkeepers" were the man and woman in the Garden. God commanded the pair to "have dominion" over the earth (Gen. 1:28–30, NRSV; cf. Gen. 2:15, 19–20; Ps. 8:5–8). Human beings were delegated to exercise God-given powers over the rest of creation (symbolized in the naming of the animals—an act of power in the ancient mind). God assigned us the role of participating in his care for the creation.

Eden was not a vacation site where our first parents simply sunbathed on the beach of the Euphrates and enjoyed their privacy. While idyllic and perfect, Eden was a place where humans explored and developed God's creation. The command to cultivate (or subdue) the creation is called the creation or *cultural mandate*. For the word "culture" originates from the Latin verb "to cultivate." To cultivate suggests not simply farming, but developing the intellect, the body, indeed, all dimensions of life. The result of this development of knowledge, skills, and arts is a culture. The subsequent chapters of Genesis show how humankind responded to this mandate.

We are to have dominion over all things created, not to exploit them for selfish purposes, but to be God's designated agents to till the gardens of nature and human culture in such a way that the whole thing flowers. We're to till these gardens to maximize their potential for growth and beauty, in such a way that nature and culture redound to the glory of the Creator. This mandate was God's first command to the human pair, and it has never been rescinded. To be obedient to God as a human creature means that we must be involved in the entire created order. Living faithfully now means caring for God's entire creation. To do anything less

This Is My Father's World

This is my Father's world,
And to my listening ears
All nature sings, and 'round me rings
The music of the spheres.
This is my Father's world:
I rest me in the thought
Of rocks and trees, of skies and seas—
His hand the wonders wrought.

This is my Father's world:
Oh, let me ne'er forget
That though the wrong seems oft so
    strong,
God is the Ruler yet.
This is my Father's world:
The battle is not done;
Jesus who died shall be satisfied,
And earth and heaven be one.

(A hymn by Maltbie D. Babcock)

is not only contrary to the Christian worldview; it is disobedience. Simply put, it is sin.

God has created a wondrous universe which bears his imprint! The cultural mandate, for instance, is possible only because this creation is structured with an intelligible order and meaning. God structured his creation with purpose so that his commands and his institutions cohere with the way in which he created us. And through revelation, the Maker has defined our purpose and goal, the *why* of our existence. Our own meaning and purpose will be enduring only insofar as we live within this God-given order.

For instance, the Ten Commandments' prohibition of adultery and prescription for sex only within marriage are not arbitrary. Sex has the psychological potential for renewing the unconditional transparency, acceptance, and trust established by the marriage covenant. But outside of that context, sex produces anxiety over performance and ability, not unconditional acceptance and trust. Such characteristics explain why God placed sex within the marriage relationship. In other words, there is a coherence to reality. The world is not alien to us. Rather, if we follow God's order and laws, it is meaningful and purposeful.

God Remains Actively Involved in His Creation

The God revealed to us in Jesus Christ is not the God of the deist who winds things up and lets them run on their own. In the Christian worldview God does not stop with creation; he continues with *providence*. He provides for his creation, the ultimate expression of which is the Incarnation.[6] He has our hairs numbered. The particulars count with God.

And it is not the case that he simply "watches from a distance," as Bette Midler sang to reassure us during the Gulf War. In fact, a deistic God who from afar simply watches human beings destroy over 200,000 lives is not a very reassuring deity in which to place much confidence. Calvin said it best when he insisted that the Christian doctrine of providence has to do not just with God's "eyes," but also with his "hands." God does not just watch us. He gets involved. He gets his hands dirty (literally). True, he does not constantly intervene with miracles. (As C. S. Lewis put it, that would be like playing chess and changing the rules with each move.) But he does not abandon his creation to constant chaos, either.

The Christian worldview holds that God is immanent in the world at the same time that he is transcendent over it. God made the world, he values it, he has entered into it, and he is currently reshaping it. He is very active—here and now. And he invites us to join him.

For Further Reflection

1. Did God create AIDS? Explain your answer.
2. Do you think the progress that the Western world has made in technology is due to the Christian doctrine of creation and the "cultural mandate"? Might sin somehow be involved in the West's technological progress?
3. What does "having dominion" over the rest of creation really mean? Can we hunt animals for fun? Should we kill pests and predators? Are animal rights activists off the wall? Should we encourage population control?
4. How should we pursue the cultural mandate today in music? In law? In biology? In your major discipline or area of interest?

For Further Reading

Gilkey, Langdon. *Maker of Heaven and Earth*. New York: Doubleday, 1959.

Schaeffer, Francis. *Genesis in Space and Time*. Downers Grove, Ill.: InterVarsity, 1972.

———. *Pollution and the Death of Man*. Downers Grove, Ill.: InterVarsity, 1970.

Thielicke, Helmut. *How the World Began.* Philadelphia: Muhlenberg, 1961.

Van Dyke, Fred, et al. *Redeeming Creation: The Biblical Basis for Environmental Stewardship.* Downers Grove, Ill.: InterVarsity, 1996.

five

After the Fall:
Sin and Its Consequences

hough God created the world good and still finds value in it, it is not now what it used to be nor what it one day will be. We live in a fallen world. The sin of Adam and Eve radically changed the world, plunging it into chaos and decay. The result is so catastrophic that the term "world" takes on the connotation of evil in Scripture: "The whole world is under the control of the evil one" (1 John 5:19). As a result, the Christian's worldview is as much shaped by the consciousness that sin is an inescapable reality this side of heaven as it is shaped by the belief that we live in God's created world. In fact, sin has a way of affecting our worldview that keeps us from properly viewing this world as God's creation.

What the Fall Did to the Original Creation

Sin Distorts the Truth about Us

The basic truth about us, as we have seen, is that we have been created in the image of God and are good, not that we are sinners. The basic truth about us is that we were created to glorify and serve God, not that we were born to be slaves to ourselves. But because we are caught in a web of sin, we fall prey to the same mistake that our first parents made: we believe a lie.

Sin began with a lie—with a distortion of the truth. The serpent tempted Eve by distorting what God had said: "Did God really say, 'You must not eat from *any* tree in the garden'?" (Gen. 3:1, emphasis added) For one thing, God had only said that of *one* tree. For another thing, Eve was enticed to focus on the one thing that God had *prohibited*, rather than on the abundance that God had *permitted*. This is the way sin often begins: we listen to distortions of the truth, and we focus on prohibitions rather than on the lavish permissions of God.

And then comes the lie that questions what God has said—the thought that distorts truth by calling into question the Word of God: "You will not surely die. . . . For God knows that when you eat of it your eyes will be opened, and you will be like God" (Gen. 3:4–5). The implication is that God is simply mistaken in what he said. If anything, God is miserly and selfish, since he just wants to deny humans the opportunity to actualize themselves—to become gods. So the lie is heard and believed and acted upon, and an entire life is built on distorted vision.

The non-Christian worldview sees the fallen world as normal or natural. But the Christian worldview sees the fallen world as "not the way it's supposed to be" and not what it will be; the Christian worldview pictures the fallen creation as *abnormal*. This is a significant difference because it explains in part why secular people call certain behaviors and lifestyles normal (such as homosexuality or selfish accumulation of wealth) while Christians call them "sin." We have gotten so used to the lie that what *should* be seen as abnormal looks perfectly normal. In fact, this view of the fallen world is so shaped by the media, schools, and popular culture that it is difficult to disagree with the accepted "politically correct" notions about certain activities and behaviors without being labeled a reactionary or neurotic. It is a bit like the world and main characters that Southern writer Walker Percy's novels portray. The question posed by his books, such as *The Thanatos Syndrome, Lancelot,* and *The Second Coming,* is this: Why would you want to adjust to a world that is neurotic? And if you refuse to adjust to what is called normal, you are the one who appears neurotic to the rest of the world.[1]

This lie simply will not let go of us. We keep trying to be what we were not made to be. We buy into the lie that material possessions will fulfill our lives. We live by the lie that security consists of having stockpiles of weapons to blow up our enemies. We have built our lives and our societies on lies. Just as the image of an object is distorted by being immersed in water, so sin twists and bends the truth about us so that even our view of reality is misshapen by it. The truth is, as we have seen, that we were created in the image of God. We are to mirror God and thereby redound to his glory. But

> Sin is "to live as if we are or can be authors of our own stories." (Stanley Hauerwas and William H. Willimon, *Resident Aliens*, 27)

the image is warped, as in the curved mirrors in a funhouse.[2] And what God sees and what we see in each other is not exactly that which God created. Of course, there is hope. In the one who is "born again," the image is being re-created by Christ, and the fallen creature is freed from sin's enslavement to become fully human again—to become like Christ, the sinless one (cf. Rom. 5:12–21; Eph. 4:24; Col. 3:10).

But in the meantime, sin is inevitable. We are born slaves to it. In fact, the biblical language is stronger than that: we are dead in sin (Gen. 2:17; Rom. 6:23). Sin has penetrated the whole of our existence, and we are beyond human repair. Put simply, we are in very bad shape!

Sin Is Pervasive and Infects Everything—from Individual Acts to Entire Economic, Political, and Social Systems

The penetration of sin into every fiber of our existence is what some theologians have referred to as "total depravity." Total depravity does not mean that we are as bad as we possibly can be, nor does it mean that we commit every sin. What it means is that every aspect of our being is tainted by sin. Total depravity is like a drop of ink that tinctures the whole glass of water. And the water cannot remove the tincture by itself, just as sinners are unable to change their fundamental bias toward sin into a love of God (Matt. 7:18; John 8:34; Rom. 8:7–8; 1 Cor. 2:14).

If we take Scripture's indictment seriously, namely that all our actions are tainted by sin, then we should be suspiciously scrutinizing our own worldview and its interpretations. This attitude is seldom evidenced by Christians. Too often the world's own doctored version of the struggle against good and evil sets the agenda for us. In the political arena, we often sit in smug judgment against Middle Eastern terrorists, maintaining that the West alone holds the moral ground. However, this bias was explosively exposed when Americans initially reacted to the Oklahoma City bombing by pointing the finger at foreign terrorists, for, as it turned out, the "enemy" was us!

Sinfulness is something that is akin not only to foreign enemies. Scripture says *all* humans are sinful, regardless of nation or tribe. There is none that is righteous, not even one (Rom. 3:10). The Lord's Prayer commands believers to ask daily for the forgiveness of our sins. Believers are not sinless and never will be, until glory! Accordingly, we must examine *our own* motives more critically and try to discern their sinful, distorted biases. If sin is fundamentally pride—humans desiring to rule themselves, and not be obedient servants of God—we should begin by asking whether even our own political and social stances are possibly rooted in pride and self-interest.

For example, conservative Christendom is committed to an antiabortion position. But Jesus tells us to look for the log in our own eye, before we expose the speck in the other's. Honestly, cannot support for the pro-life cause be motivated by a pride in one's own chastity? In C. S. Lewis's *Screwtape Letters*, Wormwood learns that appeal to pride is a multifaceted and extremely effective instrument in the tempter's toolbox. And isn't there evidence that this may be the case, given the fact that very few of us are willing to take responsibility for these unwanted babies after they are born? The popular joke about former President Reagan's policies—that he believed life began at conception and ended at birth, since he tried to cut programs which benefit children—should be applied first of all to us. How many of us show by our concrete actions that we are concerned about the born as well as the unborn?

Typically, when people think about sin's effects they think about personal sins—lying, stealing, adultery, murder. Certainly one should not minimize such individual sins, but sin's presence is far more pervasive and insidious. It includes powers and principalities that oppose God's agenda (Eph. 6:12)—the entire created order, including our political, economic, and social structures.

That sin is both personal and social pervades all Scripture. The Old Testament prophets condemned those who participated in the evil institutions of Jewish society. Speaking to the house of Israel, Amos declares, "You trample on the poor and take from them levies of grain" (Amos 5:11, NRSV). Isaiah attacks the rebellious nation of Judah, demanding repentance and that they "seek justice, encourage the oppressed. Defend the cause of the fatherless, plead the case of the widow" (Isa. 1:17). These judgments are directed at the nation as a whole; its institutions are evil. The prophets unambiguously declare that if these overtly evil and unjust institutions are not remedied, judgment will come upon all the participants. Participation in institutions which foster and fortify racism—even if one is not a bigot personally, even if one never uses a racist slogan—is just as sinful as a consciously willed act of racism. The Bible teaches that involvement with institutions that foster and fortify injustice and oppression—even if one loudly proclaims how much he or she is concerned for the oppressed, even if one has never owned a slave or hired a maid at low wages—is just as sinful as a consciously willed act of oppression.

Sin and evil even work through the good stuff. The serpent was "more crafty" (Gen. 3:1) than any other wild animal God had made. But that trait

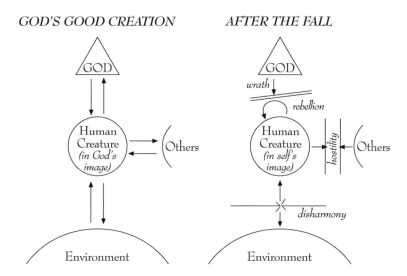

became the instrument of evil. As we have seen, the same can be true of our bodies and our minds.

When we come into this world we are born into a sinful nexus—a web of sin that has been spun out of everything from our personal behavior to our systems of commerce, military organizations, and governmental agencies. There is nothing human that lies entirely outside the web. The consequences of the Fall were of *cosmic* proportions (see Eph. 2:1–3), such that the effects of Christ's reconciling work must be of *cosmic* proportions (see Rom. 8:18–25), leading to the restoration of the whole person and the *whole* creation (see Col. 3:10; 2 Peter 3:10; Rev. 21:1).

The wide scope of the Fall's effects can be seen in the Genesis story itself. Genesis 3 indicates that profound changes took place in the whole created order as a result of Adam's and Eve's fall. Vertical and horizontal relationships, which are intricately connected, were affected.

The most obvious result of the Fall was *spiritual*: the relationship between God and human beings was no longer what it had been (Gen. 3:8–12). After the Fall, God's relation to the original sinners changes to condemnation and wrath. Indeed, it must. As sinners, humans are in a state of guilt before God, liable for punishment. God, who is holy, must rectify injustice. That is precisely what wrath guarantees. As a result, Adam and Eve are excluded from this loving relationship with God. And judgment comes: the ground is cursed, the first couple is expelled from the Garden. But this only foreshadows a greater judgment to come (Rom. 2:5).

Sinful humans are correspondingly unfriendly and even contentious toward God. Instead of seeking God's love and fellowship, Adam and Eve,

Corrie ten Boom (1892–1983)

It might be said that the Holocaust was the Super Bowl of sin! Few events in the twentieth century have been as graphic in reminding us of the depravity and fallenness of human beings. And that's just the trouble—it was human beings who launched and executed this atrocity.

Corrie ten Boom lived through it with her Dutch Reformed family in Haarlem (a town in the Netherlands). The ten Boom family chose to hide Jews in their home. In 1944 they were arrested by the Gestapo. Corrie and her sister Betsie were interred at the death camp, Ravensbruck. Despite the evils they endured (forced labor, rats, lice, cold, sickness, abuse), Corrie and Betsie ministered to fellow prisoners with the love of Christ. Betsie never made it out of the camp; she died. But Corrie was released on a "fluke" and spent the next three decades telling the story of God's faithfulness in the midst of sin's devastation.

Corrie's greatest test came when she returned to Ravensbruck and encountered a guard whose face was engrained in her memory. Sometimes sin and evil are not as difficult to deal with when they remain abstract, theoretical, or reduced to a matter of academic discussion. But when sin has a face, then comes the test of God's faithful love and our response. In Corrie's case, the forgiveness of the cross won, though it was not reflexive. It rarely seems to be this side of heaven.

after the Fall, dread and fear God. While guilt, fear, and shame can be good sometimes, in this case they were experienced as a result of the broken fellowship with God that sin precipitated. As Walter Brueggemann put it: "Perfect love casts out fear. But the man and woman in our narrative learned another thing. Perfect fear casts out love."[3] The uninhibited and close fellowship that they had with their Creator had become a threatening presence in a daily stroll. Scripture portrays them as hiding themselves from the presence of God (Gen. 3:8). Paul describes the sinner's state of mind in more belligerent terms: "the sinful mind is hostile to God" (Rom. 8:7). Nor does the sinner want to please God; the sinner unashamedly seeks to be the king and ruler of his or her own life (Phil. 3:19).

Intimate *human relationships* were damaged by the Fall. Instead of living in love and harmony, now enmity and malice arise. Genesis narrates that right after the Fall Adam attempts to excuse himself from blame: "The woman you put here with me—she gave me some fruit from the tree, and I ate it" (Gen. 3:12). Attempting to pin blame upon another in order to excuse oneself is a manifestation of anger and hatred. The relationship between husband and wife was no longer one of mutuality. God's judgment was that the wife would have a distorted desire for her husband and the husband would rule over his wife (see Gen. 3:16). However, this is a curse, not a command. And it manifests itself as early as Genesis 3:20 when Adam names his wife (an act of power). It is interesting to note at this point that Adam and Eve each became subservient to the sources of their created being as a consequence of the Fall—Eve, to the man, and Adam, to the ground. The curse is to be reversed in the kinds of relationships we experience in the church, where there is no male nor female in Christ, but the wife and husband are to be subject to each other (Gal. 3:28; Eph. 5:21).[4]

The succeeding chapters of Genesis outline further consequences—narratives of murder, greed, theft, and oppression. Indeed, two humanities arise, as the line of Cain and Lamech is pitted against the line of Abel and Seth (e.g., see Gen. 4:9–12, 19, 23–24). We refuse to be our "brother's keeper." Instead, the farmer is pitted against the rancher (or the American against the Iraqi, the African-American against the Hispanic-American against the Asian-American against the European-American, and on the list goes).

Physical and ecological problems followed the first sin. Eve is told that her pain in childbirth will be increased (Gen. 3:16). Certainly the diseases that we experience today, from various forms of cancer to AIDS, are the results of sin—either sinful behavior on our own part or genetic structures that have developed over periods of time. This has implications for our understanding of alcoholism and homosexuality, as well as other predilections, if they are genetic.

The adverse environmental effects of sin are also mentioned: weeds grow up. Work becomes a burden. The ground is resistant to the attempts of human beings to till it and to live off of it (cf. Gen. 2:15 with 3:17–19). These words remind us of so-called natural evils—those purposeless events of nature which harm humankind, such as sickness, death, tornadoes, earthquakes, and floods. While called natural evil, these perils of creation are not really natural, but unnatural events, the result of the Fall. Scripture reflects this; the Gospels speak of physical handicaps and sickness as Satan's work (Matt. 12:22; Luke 13:11, 16). Death, the principal natural evil, is again not a natural phenomenon, but a perversion of God's original intent for humankind. Scripture is clear: Sin brings forth death (Rom. 5:12; James 1:15).

The first human pair fell out of harmony with a garden that we have tried to recapture and re-create ever since. But not only can we not seem to re-create that harmony, our behavior continues to destroy the environment in which we live.

Nothing was immune from sin's pollution. And the pollution has spread—all from one original sin, as theologians refer to it. Perhaps we can be helped if we understand what that sin really was. In defining the original sin we will have a better knowledge of the enemy that thwarts our attempt to be human in the way God intended for us to be. What is the *essence* of sin?

What the Fall Was

Before we examine the original sin in the world of humans, we should remember that the primary adversary of God's rule in the world throughout Scripture is not sinful men and women, but Satan. Adam and Eve did not initiate the rebellion; they were tempted and led astray by the evil one. Scripture assumes that the forces of rebellion are under the control and direction of this evil one, or Satan (2 Cor. 4:4; Eph. 2:2). This is also reflected in Jesus' temptation, when Satan offers Jesus all the kingdoms of the world, on the condition that he would disobey God's will (Matt. 4:8–10). He is a malignant reality, always hostile to God's rule and people.

Furthermore, the principal mark of Satan's activity is manifest whenever and wherever creation does not reflect God's original intent. Thus even though death is God's punishment for sin (Gen. 2:17; 3:19; Rom. 5:12), Scripture attributes it first and foremost to Satan. In fact, Satan is described as being the murderer (John 8:44). Death reflects Satan's rule in this world.

All of that said, the Fall of Adam and Eve still devastated creation. The first human act of sin was momentous. Theologians have defined this original sin in various ways. We will mention three of these, all of which are correct. It will be the last, however, which seems to capture the very heart of what sin is.

Disobedience

The first sin was a simple act of disobedience to God's will (see Gen. 2:16–17; cf. Rom. 5:19; 1 John 3:4). It was an act of rebellion that involved thoughts and behavior directly contradicting what God had proscribed. Sin is always thinking or doing what God tells us not to. It can be that simple.

Worldliness

Sin has also been described as worldliness or concupiscence (see Gen. 3:6; cf. 1 John 2:15–17). This is misdirected love. We should love God and our neighbor. We should take delight in God. Our desire ought to be to do his will and to love what he loves. But we delight in that which we should not—forbidden fruit. Or we love that which we should not—material possessions, even ourselves. Some of these things that we love are actually good in themselves, but our love of them can be inordinate. We do not keep them in proper perspective, and we assign them a value that they should not have. For instance, work is good. However, we can love our work so much that we try to find in it what we should find only in God—namely, fulfillment and life's meaning.

Pride

Closely related to the previous understanding of sin's essence is pride or self-centeredness, for this is nothing but the inordinate love of self. But it goes deeper than that. It is *taking the place of God*. This is the real heart of all sin. To be autonomous, to be one's own god, to have the prerogative of saying what is good and evil, as Eve was tempted with (Gen. 3:4–5; cf. Rom. 1:21–25), is precisely what lies at the root of all sin.

From the time of the Fall human beings have wanted to be more than they are. They have sought to deny their creaturely status to worship and serve the creation. They have wanted to be in control—to become the self-appointed judges of what is right and wrong, good and evil. They have done this on the individual level and, most graphically and disastrously, they have done this on the national level. To center the world around one's self—whether that self is a person or a corporation or a nation or a time period—is to live in sin.

We were created with our true center in God. Our true center is not found within us but outside of us. But when we try to center our lives on ourselves, we are really off center, and everything around us spins out of control as a result—marriages, businesses, the affairs of nations, and so on.

This is the ultimate misuse of God's gift of human freedom. We were created as free creatures to live in God's world with God's other creatures on God's terms. But, like the prodigal son, we take the gift without the Giver, and we refuse to live as we were created to live. As Brueggemann points out, the irony is that whether we live in or out of the Garden, we still finally must live on God's terms.

Furthermore, the story of the Fall makes it clear that in trying to be what they were not, the first humans lost what they could have become. And millennia later we still have not learned this lesson. In attempting to play God we lose even our humanity. We become beasts, as C. S. Lewis dramatized with the dragon-like metamorphosis of Eustace in his *Voyage of the Dawn Treader*. When individuals or nations take the place of God, they end up treating others "in-humane-ly," and in the process they dehumanize themselves.

In essence, we create a new god who informs and shapes our understanding of who as humans we truly are. We become transformed into the idols we worship. If material possessions form the ultimate purpose for living, then we conceive of ourselves and others as simply objects, not per-

"Pride too strives to appear as though it was high and lofty, whereas you alone are God high over all. . . . And laziness seems to be looking for rest; but what sure rest is there except in the Lord? . . . Luxury would like to be called plenty and abundance; but you are the fullness and the unfailing supply of a sweetness that is incorruptible. . . . So all men who put themselves far from you and set themselves up against you, are in fact attempting awkwardly to be like you." (Augustine, *Confessions* 2.6)

sons. We evaluate others in relation to their bank account and their potential value to us. If sexual pleasure forms our god, again we conceive of self and others in simply those terms. Focus is concentrated entirely upon fulfilling our own lust, with no place for developing the full relationship of one human being to another. If security is our god, again we evaluate ourselves and others in those terms. Are they potentially dangerous to our security or not? In each case, we have lost the meaning of what persons created in God's image entails. Indeed, we are blinded to how God created us and even to the way our humanity has been lost.

Since the sinner evaluates others in these impersonal terms, and not from the perspective of God and being made in his image, the sinner really is not concerned for their well-being.

> Once a person, be he or she oppressor or oppressed, whether dressed in silk or sprawled in a Calcutta slum, is perceived as a thing or in terms of a commodity, he or she is thereby rendered replaceable. The fetus is a "blob of protoplasm." The criminal becomes "scum and vermin," the brain-damaged are "vegetables." The poor are "like animals." The Red Chinese are "the enemy." The wealthy or the police become "pigs." The "enemy" is an obstruction—quantifiable, repeatable, manipulable, expendable, the legitimate object of our hatred and violence.[5]

The other is no longer our neighbor, created in God's image, who we must treat with integrity and respect. The simple truth is that sinners are unable to love others because their real love is for themselves and their gods.

It is clear from the Decalogue (the Ten Commandments) that pride, self-centeredness, or taking the place of God is the root of sin, for the first commandment is to put nothing before Yahweh (Ex. 20:2–3). And if we do not get it at the front end of the Ten Commandments, then the final proscription puts it another way: "You shall not covet!" (Ex. 20:17) Do not insist on having that which is not properly yours as a creature of God. Be *the* creature that God meant for you to be. Don't try to be what *you* are not, for in doing so you are playing God.

The Christian family's worldview now has two poles: a good creation and a spoiled creation. It reminds us of a limerick we once heard:

> God made the world in the beginning;
> humans spoiled the creation by sinning.
> We know that the story
> will end in God's glory.
> But at present the other side's winning.

It does indeed seem that victory is nowhere in sight. How is it that the Christian family can be so confident that God will be glorified in the end? The whole story begins to come together in our next consideration: the person and work of Jesus Christ.

For Further Reflection

1. Read Genesis 3 in one sitting as if you were reading it for the first time. What things do you notice? What does the chapter have to say to you as an early-twenty-first-century reader?
2. In the Genesis account of the Fall, the serpent encourages analysis of what God says. Is this always bad? What makes it bad here? Are there times when knowledge comes at too high a cost?
3. Note the pronoun that is prominent in Genesis 3:10–13. What do you make of this?
4. Are there signs of God's grace even in the account of the Fall? (Gen. 3) Is there grace involved in God's prohibitions? Consider the Ten Commandments. Why do they begin not with a commandment (Ex. 20:3), but with a statement about the Exodus? (20:1–2)
5. If sin can be on a corporate as well as an individual level (as we have tried to show at various points in this chapter), how might that affect the way that Christians and the church think about and deal with sin in this world? And what effect(s) might sin have in the pursuit of a liberal arts education? What about in the pursuit of economic well-being for a nation?

For Further Reading

Berkhof, Hendrikus. *Christ and the Powers.* Scottdale, Pa.: Herald, 1977.

Brueggemann, Walter. *Genesis*. Atlanta: Westminster John Knox, 1982.

Colson, Charles, with Ellen Santilli Vaughn. *Kingdoms in Conflict*. Grand Rapids: Zondervan, 1987.

Gilkey, Langdon. *Shantung Compound*. New York: Harper and Row, 1964.

Kavanaugh, John Francis. *Following Christ in a Consumer Society*. Maryknoll, N.Y.: Orbis, 1981.

Plantinga, Cornelius, Jr. *Not the Way It's Supposed to Be: A Breviary of Sin*. Grand Rapids: Eerdmans, 1995.

six

Hallelujah, What a Savior: God's Salvific Work in Jesus Christ

niversity student Stella Zoblinski is an avid fan of talk shows, both TV and "talk radio." A recent TV show topic about God and spirituality particularly grabbed her attention. One religious expert portrayed Christ as the great therapist for recovering our self-esteem and healthfulness. Another interpreted Jesus as the guru of gurus, aiding us in our own independent search for the God within. Still another authority had encountered Jesus in a near-death experience where he announced to her that all religions are roads to God, with the common exhortation to love everyone.[1] The talk show hostess expressed relief at that news; now she knew that Jesus was a "cool cat"!

Of course, during her days in Nigeria and at the university Stella has encountered many moral non-Christians. While raised in a Christian home, she is now wondering what is so distinctive about Christianity and Jesus in particular. Wasn't the whole focus of Jesus' life and teachings to show us that God is love? Wasn't his purpose to bring people together, not to divide them?

Jesus Christ the God-man

A worldview is Christian only if its defining center is Jesus Christ. But who is Jesus? The answers vary today, as "channel surfing" the contemporary talk-show circuit reflects. But in each case, Jesus is interpreted by an independent and predetermined understanding of God and humankind. As a result, Jesus is shaped by that cultural scheme and thus has many confusing and contradictory faces. In fact, Jesus ends up looking a lot like the confessors' own reflections!

But there is a more subtle and consequential move that needs exposing here. When one interprets Jesus from a more ultimate point of reference, what or who exactly has the highest authority here? Certainly not Jesus. Jesus' place as Lord has already been subverted. Jesus' own claims regarding his unique and exclusive relationship with the Father (Matt. 11:27; John 14:6) have already been dismissed. Whenever one attempts to interpret Jesus by a prior and more ultimate point of reference, he is confined and pressed to fit that more ultimate framework. Jesus thus becomes just one amongst many windows into God.

In our pluralistic society where the words "In God we trust" are plastered everywhere, we have to ask *which God*. For the Christian, it is the God revealed in Jesus Christ. To know Jesus is to know God. Without Jesus as the definitive revelation of who God is, we would only have our own sinfully warped projections. The contemporary culture would like to give God a 1990s makeover so that he is just as nice (i.e., "nonintrusive" and retiring) as we are: He never takes offense. But Jesus breaks those stereotypes. When Jesus drove out the money changers from the temple, it was not to rearrange the furniture; it was because of the serious misconceptions people had about God.

Jesus did not come to confirm our prior thoughts about God and the cosmos, but rather to challenge them. When Jesus boldly proclaimed the presence of the kingdom, he was not providing insight into an immanent law of history or some intuition previously accessible. Rather, he was announcing God's unique and supernatural intervention in him alone. In this man God himself was overcoming and reversing the Fall, changing the very destiny of creation. Jesus is not simply a way to God; he claimed to be the one and only way! (John 14:6) To treat him as any less is to question Jesus himself.

This is precisely the purpose for the church's confession that Jesus is *fully God* and *fully man*. It is not a wooden thesis without implications for life, but the only way to affirm personally that Jesus is the truth-and-life way.

To confess Jesus as *fully God* means that if you want to know who God is, then you need only to look at the one in whom "the fullness of the Deity lives" (Col. 2:9). Philip asked Jesus, "Show us the Father and that will be enough for us" (John 14:8). And Jesus replied, "Anyone who has seen me has seen the Father" (John 14:9). That is, as we might say, Jesus is "a chip off the old block"; like Father, like Son. For this one who assumed flesh is God the Word, the creator of heaven and earth (John 1:1, 14).

> "None other could make a mortal being immortal, but He who is life itself, our Lord Jesus Christ." (Athanasius)

Jesus is the definitive revelation of God (Col. 1:15). We are not to give him a makeover in our image. We must get to know him as the God who weeps when someone hurts, who goes out of his way to dine with sinners, who, like Lewis's Aslan, "isn't safe, but He's good." *That* is God. He risked his reputation and even his life to reveal himself to us! When we know Jesus, we know God. When we believe in Jesus, we believe in God. When we worship Jesus, we worship God. But also, when we reject Jesus, we reject God himself.

As we will mention in chapter 9, the church did not agree on a way to say that Jesus is fully divine until the fourth century, when a church council gathered in 325 to formulate the Nicene Creed. By the time this creed was amended in a subsequent meeting of the minds in 381, Christians possessed a full-blown definitive statement that the one God exists in three persons—Father, Son, and Holy Spirit. In the creed's language, the three are "one substance" (*homoousios* in Greek). In making this claim, the church was insisting that the Son is the very same God as the Father.

Why is this important? As the fourth-century bishop Athanasius pointed out, only the God who created us could redeem us. No creature can repair the damage done by sin, because the *entire* creation is in need of salvation. Not even a "half-god" can save us, as the heresy *Arianism* suggested (a heresy named after Arius, the opponent of Athanasius). The Arian god could neither reveal who God is nor redeem what humans had become. Only God—the One who created all things—had the power and the authority to save us. And that same God, who existed before anything else existed, is the one we see in Jesus.

Indeed, God became a real human in Jesus of Nazareth. This is what the Incarnation is—the "in-fleshing" of the God who created the universe. Jesus Christ was fully human at the same time that he was fully divine. Yet we must go further. He was a particular human born of a young peasant girl named Mary. His "bio" sheet read—gender: male; residence: Palestine; occupation: carpenter and itinerant preacher; religion: Jewish. He had a specific height and weight, eye and hair color, and shoe size. He had a birthday once a year, perhaps snored when he slept, and played with the neighborhood children when he was a boy. He "grew in wisdom and stature" (Luke 2:52) and "he learned obedience from what he suffered" (Heb. 5:8).

Because he was also fully divine, there has always been a tendency to deny the full humanity of Christ. John addressed this tendency (a religion called Gnosticism, something like New Age) in his first letter when he insisted that "that which was from the beginning . . . which was with the Father" is the one "we have heard, which we have seen with our eyes, which we have looked at and our hands have touched" (1:1–2). "Every spirit that confesses that Jesus Christ has come *in the flesh* is from God, and every spirit that does not confess Jesus is not from God" (4:2–3, NRSV, emphasis added). In other words, because there were heretical Gnostics who denied that God could come into contact with a material world—let alone become incarnate in matter—John insisted that the true God was so "fleshy" in Jesus Christ that he and others had actually seen and touched *God!*

The denial of Jesus' humanity is called *Docetism*, a term that comes from the Greek word meaning "to seem" or "to appear." A docetist claims that God only seemed to be human or only appeared to be a man. There is a hint of it in the popular Christmas carol, "Away in a Manger," when we sing of the baby Jesus: "no crying he makes." No doubt, when God was a human baby—like all babies—he cried when he was hungry, wet, or tired. Unfortunately, we perpetuate this slightly docetic picture of Jesus when we sanitize our Christmastime stories and manger scenes.

Another heresy that denied the full humanity of God incarnate was *Apollinarianism*. This third-century view (espoused by a bishop named Apollinarius) argued that Jesus was a combination of a human body and the divine Logos (or Word). The divine Logos, according to Apollinarius, had to replace the human spirit or mind of Jesus, because, for one thing, the possibility of sin resides in the human mind. A contemporary rendition of this heresy was witnessed by one of us in a church new members' class. The pastor was trying to explain what it meant for God to stoop to becoming a human being. He used the analogy of a human being who wanted to communicate with dogs, but could only do so if he became a dog and spoke "dog language"—a helpful beginning illustration. But then the well-meaning pastor went on to explain that to do this the dog's brain would be removed and replaced by the human one. Though it certainly is not easy to explain how, to be truly "orthodox" the analogy should have had the human brain and the dog brain coexisting in the same dog. Any view that hints at denying any aspect of the humanity of Jesus borders on heresy and leads to a view of salvation as replacement rather than redemption of what is human. Thus, long ago the church asserted against Apollinarianism that Jesus was fully human, and to be fully human means having a human mind or rational soul.[2]

It was necessary for Jesus to be fully human, for sin so twists our perceptions that we no longer fully understand what it means to be human. As we saw in the last chapter, what God calls unnatural or inhuman is what we often label natural or normal behavior. By becoming a human, God reveals to us what we were meant to be. The first Adam fell from his true humanity; the second Adam has come to show us how far we have fallen and to re-create us in his image (Rom. 5:17–19; 1 Cor. 15:45–49; Col. 1:15; 3:10–11). So if we want to know what it means to be fully human, again we must look at Jesus. There we will find a man without sin (2 Cor. 5:21; 1 Pet. 2:22), for to be fully and truly human is to be without sin. To be human the way that God created us is to be completely obedient to the Creator. Sin is not a part of our created essence; it is a disease that eats away at our being. In fact, by his selflessness and the sacrificial giving of his life, he demonstrated that our self-centered lives are a distortion of our true nature. To be fully human is not to live for self; it is to live for others and for God in perfect obedience to the One who made us.

The Kingdom of God

New believers often first encounter the God-man Jesus by studying the Gospels. However, much in the Gospels presupposes some understanding of its Old Testament background. Jesus' language regarding the kingdom of God consequently seems foreign and strange. Some of his decisive actions are obscured. But Jesus insisted (Luke 24:27) that the Old Testament is crucial to understanding who he is and what he accomplished. In this section we will include a "fast forward" through the Old Testament in order to provide the proper framework for understanding Jesus' message and work in the New Testament.

The Old Testament Promise of the Kingdom of God

As we noted in prior chapters, God our Creator is the King of the universe. However, humanity has rebelled against God's rule. Satan is the *de facto* ruler of this world, frustrating and corrupting all dimensions of human life—spiritual, social, and environmental. But even while Adam and Eve were rebelling, God was seeking to mend this broken relationship, defeat Satan, and reclaim what is rightfully his. At the Fall God promised that he would reassert his legitimate authority over the universe and establish salvation by prophesying to Satan: "I will put enmity between you and the woman, and between your offspring and hers; he will crush your head, and you will strike his heel" (Gen. 3:15). God has taken the initiative in redeeming a sin-devastated creation by entering into our world and fundamentally reordering creation so that it will ultimately become obedient to him.

In the Old Testament, in fact, God developed this promise of salvation through announcements and enactments of his covenant, beginning with that original promise (the so-called *protoevangelion*) to Adam and Eve and culminating in Jesus Christ.[3] After humanity's failure upon failure (Gen. 1–11), Abraham became God's chosen instrument for starting his program of reversing Satan's earthly control and bringing all of creation into proper relationship with himself. In revealing himself to Abraham and promising that he would become the father of a mighty nation in Palestine, and that through him "all peoples on earth will be blessed" (see Gen. 12:1–3), God overcame some of Satan's destructive work within the *spiritual sphere*. For it is God who came to Abraham and promised him reconciliation—"to be your God, and the God of your descendants after you" (Gen. 17:7)—despite his sinfulness. But the road to becoming a person who trusts solely on God is rocky. God led Abraham to migrate from Ur, a city on the Persian Gulf, to Palestine. Abraham repeatedly trusted in himself instead of God when troubled by the Pharaoh, Abimelech, and even Sarah's barrenness. Finally, when commanded to sacrifice Isaac, Abraham began learning to fear God and to obey him at all costs (Gen. 22:12).

God's promise that Abraham would form a great nation passes through Abraham's son Isaac to his grandson Jacob, who fathered the founders of the twelve tribes of Israel. When famine gripped Palestine, Jacob and his sons migrated to Egypt. Here the Children of Israel eventually became slaves. But demonstrating his covenanted promise, God rescued the Children of Israel from bondage through a runaway Israelite named Moses and miraculous events.

At Mt. Sinai God renewed his promise through the Mosaic Covenant and advanced the plan for bringing all creation under his reign. Liberating the Jews from bondage made it possible for them to worship God in purity and righteousness as a *nation*. This covenant included more instructions or stipulations regarding God's will for the *social* sphere, so that among all nations the Israelites would "be my treasured possession, . . . a kingdom of priests and a holy nation" (Exod. 19:5–6). God desired to redeem the *social* sphere, in addition to the *spiritual*.[4] Thus, an overriding purpose was to produce a nation of social justice. Note God's heart for those easily victimized and the oppressed:

> You shall not wrong or oppress a resident alien, for you were aliens in the land of Egypt. You shall not abuse any widow or orphan. If you do abuse them, when they cry out to me, I will surely heed their cry; my wrath will burn, and I will kill you with the sword, and your wives shall become widows and your children orphans.
>
> If you lend money to my people, to the poor among you, you shall not deal with them as a creditor; you shall not exact interest from them. If you take your neighbor's cloak in pawn, you shall restore it before the sun goes down; for it may be your neighbor's only clothing to use as cover; in what else shall that person sleep? And if your neighbor cries out to me, I will listen, for I am compassionate (Exod. 22:21–27, NRSV).

Athanasius (ca. 293–373)

Much of orthodox Christianity grew up in North Africa. One of the most prominent theologians in that region of the world was Athanasius, often called the "Father of Orthodoxy," for he helped establish the Christian doctrine of the Trinity that resulted in the Nicene Creed (325).

Athanasius eventually became the bishop of Alexandria, one of the three leading centers of the church in his day. Before becoming bishop, Athanasius struggled with others to put the "pure gospel" in the context of Greek culture and language. When he was about twenty-five years old he produced a classic—*On the Incarnation of the Word*. In this small treatise he argued that the Christian belief in God's incarnation was both true and reasonable.

The rationale for Athanasius's insistence that God became a human in Christ is the doctrine of salvation. Working with the Greek Christian notion that God planned our salvation to restore the image of God in us, he insisted that only God—the one who created us in his image in the first place—could repair the damage and redeem us. Our salvation required one who was as closely related to the Father as possible (a relationship he expressed with the Greek word homoousios—"of the same substance"). His major opponent, Arius, argued that the one changeless God cannot incarnate himself in a human; therefore, Jesus was only a man who was promoted to "sonship." Arius's "savior" was an inspired human, not an incarnate deity.

In making his case, Athanasius used both Scripture and reason, for he believed that reason, when rightly used, confirmed revelation (since human reason was fashioned in the image of God). Though he used Platonic philosophy when helpful, he jealously guarded the full divinity of Christ, using Old Testament Scripture against the Jews and rational arguments against the Greeks. But against both Jews and Greeks, the crucial issue was the same: "The unfittingness or incongruity (as it seems to them) alike of the cross and of the Word's becoming man at all."

C. S. Lewis wrote of Athanasius: "It is his glory that he did not move with the times; it is his reward that he now remains when those times, as all times do, have moved away."

And in the spiritual sphere, the stipulations regarding the tabernacle, the priesthood, and their sacrificial system pointed more clearly to Jesus' future work. For through these sacrifices, God's people not only learned to trust in his promise, but also came face to face with the gravity of sin, whose penalty is death.

This Mosaic Covenant set the stage for God's administration during the next thousand years in their Promised Land, Palestine. But again and again the Israelites failed to live as a "holy nation" and rebelled against God. From the period of the judges, through the establishment of the monarchy, the division into the two kingdoms, the fall of Israel, and Judah's exile and return, the people constantly resisted and defied God. God brought judgment to force recognition of who he is and raised up a judge, king, or a prophet to call the people back to himself. God judges his people, but he never deserts them. (See Ps. 78!)

But this constant rebellion shows that evil must be vanquished once and for all. And from the monarchy onward, God began taking another step with the promise of the New Covenant. First given to David and then reiterated and expanded by Isaiah, Jeremiah, and other prophets, this covenant promises that the Messiah will establish salvation in a final way. In this kingdom, God will rule forever, and all creation will be transformed. The Messiah will eradicate evil within the social sphere, upholding it with righteousness and justice from that time on and forever (Isa. 2:4; 9:7). The environment will be entirely renewed and transformed, eliminating all natural evils. "Then will the eyes of the blind be opened and the ears of the deaf unstopped" (Isa. 35:5). Death itself would be conquered (Isa. 25:8). The earth will be restored to the garden that was once lost (Isa. 35:6–7). So productive will be the earth that "the one who plows shall overtake the one who reaps" (Amos 9:13, NRSV).

Finally, redemption in the spiritual sphere will be perfectly established. The administration of the New Covenant will succeed where the other failed.

> But this is the covenant that I will make with the house of Israel after those days, says the LORD: I will put my law within them, and I will write it on their hearts; and I will be their God, and they shall be my people. No longer shall they teach one another, or say to each other, "Know the LORD," for they shall all know me, from the least of them to the greatest, says the LORD; for I will forgive their iniquity, and remember their sin no more. (Jer. 31:33–34, NRSV)

Not only will God judge sin in a final way, but he will also place the law in our hearts so that believers possess a new power of obedience and knowledge of God. Sin—even its possibility—will be eradicated once and for all (Ezek. 36:25–27). This obedience to God's rule will characterize not simply the Israelites, but all nations (Isa. 2:2–3).

The Jews referred to this promise as the *kingdom of God*. However, the *kingdom of God* here refers not to a place, such as the Magic Kingdom (at Disneyland) or the kingdom of Monaco, but the situation where God actually reigns and rules over an obedient creation (Matt. 8:11; 13:31–32; 24:14; Luke 13:29). Perhaps this phrase is better translated the kingship of God, for it refers to the circumstances in which God is truly acknowledged as King—when and where the will of God is done on earth (see Matt. 6:10). The Jews, however, knew that this kingdom was totally future and even distinguished between the present age and the age to come, when the kingdom would arrive. When the Israelites returned from exile, still subject to an occupying force, they pleaded for this promise. Throughout the intertestamental period, when foreign control changed from Persian to Greek to finally Roman, the Jews looked desperately and prayed for the coming Messiah and this kingdom.

Jesus' Ministry and the Kingdom

It is precisely this kingdom message that lies at the heart of Jesus' ministry. As Mark narrates, "Jesus came into Galilee preaching the gospel of God, and saying, 'The time is fulfilled, and the kingdom of God is at hand; repent, and believe in the gospel'" (Mark 1:14–15, RSV). Everywhere the kingdom of God was on Jesus' lips and manifested in his deeds.

Nor was Jesus just reiterating the prophets' hope. At the beginning of his career Jesus entered the synagogue of Nazareth and was asked to read Scripture (Luke 4:16–21). He read the messianic prophecy from Isaiah 61:1–2. Here Isaiah prophesies that the Messiah would preach the good news: the good news in an Old Testament context referred to the proclamation that the kingdom of God had arrived and that the Messiah would vividly demonstrate that God's kingdom had arrived by releasing the captives, giving sight to the blind, and freeing the downtrodden from Satan's grasp. As every Jew knew, these events would occur only in the end times. But after reading this passage, Jesus declared, "Today this Scripture is fulfilled in your hearing" (Luke 4:21). The promised future kingdom of God had now invaded our time. Jesus insisted that he is the fulfillment of this promised New Covenant, that he has established this kingdom now!

Jesus claimed that the kingdom of God had entered into history through his coming, but not in all its glory and fullness. That is why his disciples were to remain alert (cf. Matt. 25:13) and pray for its coming (Matt. 6:10). Only in the age to come would God's rule be consummated—that is, completely established throughout all creation. Nevertheless, Jesus insisted that the prophecies concerning the kingdom of God in all its dimensions—spiritual, social, and environmental—are being fulfilled in *part* now.

Jesus liberates people from the control of Satan by empowering a reversal of their ways, so that they obey and follow God. Because he has come to "give his life as a ransom for many" (Mark 10:45; cf. 14:24), Jesus forgives sins (Mark 2:5–12). One becomes a member of the kingdom only by responding to Jesus' message, turning from sin and choosing in a decisive way to give allegiance to the King. For one listener mentioned in the Gospels, that meant giving up wealth; for others, it meant something entirely different. For all people it means turning aside from whatever has been valued too highly and choosing without reservation to honor Christ, the King (Luke 17:7–10). This is the point of the Zacchaeus story (Luke 19:1–10) and the parable of the merchant finding a great pearl (Matt.

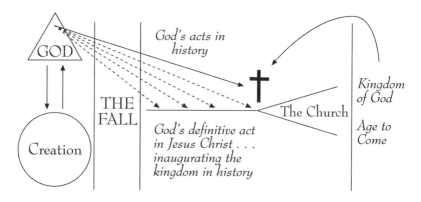

13:45–46). In both instances, the advent of the kingdom overturns their past and projected future.

Moreover, Jesus' actions were consistently directed toward the social dimension of the kingdom of God. His love for and fellowship with Zacchaeus the tax collector, the prostitutes, and the women who followed his band of disciples publicly demonstrated that he viewed these individuals as having equal value with everyone else in society. Within his own group of disciples he united Matthew the tax collector and Simon the Zealot—members of two groups that intensely hated each other. Through his parables Jesus frequently portrayed what the kingdom of God would involve socially. One recurring image is that of a banquet (Matt. 22:1–14), which represents a time of joy when men and women have all that they need and everyone is accepted. In brief, there would be a radically new society—a utopia where no hostility or injustice exists.

Jesus established the kingdom in the environmental sphere through his miracles. Miracles such as calming the storm or healing the leper represent Jesus' battles with Satan, overthrowing the devil's power, and reclaiming this world for God. In addition, they represent invasions into the present by the promised future kingdom of God. And so they are signs and foretastes of God's future consummated rule. Jesus raising the dead was not just a spectacular miracle, but a victory over the kingdom of Satan and a demonstration that death will be forever eliminated in the age to come. Jesus casting out demons signaled that God has bound Satan and that evil's final annihilation is certain. In sum, Jesus' miracles were integrally tied to his preaching of the kingdom; they were anticipations of what the consummated kingdom will be like in its spiritual, social, and environmental dimensions. Through these actions we have a glimpse of what the "age to come" will be like, when creation will be whole again and not distorted.

But how is Jesus and his work any different from what was narrated in the Old Testament? Jesus' miracles do not appear to be much different from the Old Testament variety. How, then, can he assert that the promised king-dom is present now and was not before?

The unique and distinguishing feature of Jesus' ministry centers around his conflict with Satan (Matt. 12:22–29; Mark 3:23–27; 9:14–26). According to Jewish expectations, only the Messiah at the end of time could bind Satan. So Jesus' claim in Matthew 12 that he can cast out demons because Satan is bound is significant: "How can one enter a strong man's house and plunder his goods, unless he first binds the strong man? Then indeed he may plunder his house" (Matt. 12:29, RSV). Jesus' point was that his work of casting out demons indicated Satan has been bound; therefore, the promises concerning the future kingdom of God are present now.

Similarly, in Luke 10 after the disciples had returned from their first missionary journey, they were amazed at their power. "The seventy-two returned with joy and said, 'Lord, even the demons submit to us in your name'" (Luke 10:17). Jesus explained why: "I saw Satan fall like light-ning from heaven. I have given you authority . . . to overcome all the power of the enemy" (Luke 10:18–19). Falling from heaven refers to Satan's loss of power and authority from that which he previously had. Jesus claimed that this power to "overcome" the enemy, Satan, reflects his authority.

All these verses indicate that in some sense Satan has been bound, dis-armed, or defeated. The advent of Jesus means that Satan's power is no longer supreme here on earth. This obviously does not mean that Satan has been rendered powerless. The devil is still a power in the world, but in some sense his power has now been limited. This is a difficult idea; it takes faith even to imagine that it is true, for it is not readily apparent from look-ing at history. But this is something that the New Testament consistently proclaims. Listen to Paul:

> Having disarmed the powers and authorities, he [Jesus] made a public spec-tacle of them, triumphing over them by the cross. (Col. 2:15)
> [God] raised him [Christ] from the dead and seated him at his right hand in the heavenly realms, far above all rule and authority, power and dominion, and every title that can be given, not only in the present age but also in the one to come. And God placed all things under his feet. (Eph. 1:19–22)

Paul's point is that through the cross and resurrection, Christ defeated Satan and his principalities and powers; Jesus triumphed over them so that they no longer have humankind in their grasp. This is the center of the New Testament message: *the kingdom has arrived!*

But if the kingdom has arrived, even in part, why does Satan appear to be so active in history today when he is supposedly bound and defeated?

> "Since the coming of Christ, the key to history is to be found in his death and res-
> urrection, and the proclamation of the gospel places humanity face to face with
> only one alternative—Christ or Antichrist." (C. René Padilla, *Mission Between the
> Times*, 127)

How can history appear so bleak to the people of God if Jesus has disarmed
Satan? One popular explanation among New Testament scholars uses a
military image. In World War II, the Normandy Landing on June 6, 1944,
(D-Day) represented the decisive battle and turning point because the Allied
Forces established a beachhead in France and put the German troops on
the run. At that battle, the war against Germany had been won in principle, even though mopping-up actions were still necessary and a peace agreement with Germany was not signed until a year later (V-E Day). Similarly,
through the life, death, and resurrection of Jesus, the decisive battle
between the forces of God and the forces of Satan has been fought. Satan
has been decisively defeated. The final outcome is secure. The rest of history consists of a mopping-up action: subduing the scattered forces of Satan.
Certainly, Satan is vicious today, but his fate is sealed. The end is near! D-
Day came with the death and resurrection of Jesus; V-E Day will arrive at
his second coming.

Accordingly, Jesus' message is that in his own person and mission God's
future promises have become a reality in human history. God has triumphed over evil, even though the final deliverance from evil will not
come until the end of this age. Because of Christ's work, creation itself
"waits in eager expectation" (Rom. 8:19). "The whole creation has been
groaning as in the pains of childbirth" (Rom. 8:22), anticipating with certainty the consummation when the Garden will be reestablished, when
social justice and love will reign among humans, and all creation will obey
God. For Jesus has established the kingdom of God now (albeit in part) in
all of its dimensions—spiritual, social, and environmental!

As the followers of Christ, our calling is not simply the cultural mandate. Jesus changed the destiny of history by defeating the principalities
and powers and establishing the kingdom of God. And as the disciples of
Christ, we are called to be instruments of Christ's work of redemption. The
kingdom of God identifies the goals and objectives for the Christian's mission. We must be combating Satan's perversion throughout creation and
redirecting culture toward its true Lord and Savior, Jesus Christ. His kingdom is our pursuit!

Jesus' Incarnational Pattern

But how is the Christian to carry out this task? What strategies are appropriate? What virtues and values are essential in pursuing this mission? Here again, Jesus sets the norm and pattern for the Christian's life. In this section we will outline the pattern of Jesus' incarnational work and discover how he establishes the model for Christian character and action today.

Jesus Christ Is the God Who Reveals Himself by Humbling Himself to Our Level

Frank Sinatra's enduring classic "My Way" may be paraphrased as a theme song for the human race—for we inevitably attempt to do things in our own way. We so comprehend reality that we think we must take the initiative, find God, and save ourselves. Others are at best just gurus, spiritual guides who help us pursue a journey for which we alone are responsible. Salvation in the strictest sense is our achievement, for and by us alone. Not only is this strategy arrogant, but in the end isolating, since in the end we don't need the other person.

But the opening pages of the Gospel accounts present a contrary narrative of God's action. That baby Jesus, born inconspicuously in Bethlehem 2,000 years ago, was God. This is an incredible claim, in some ways not much different from George Burns's portrayal of God visiting us in the movie *O God.* In the last scene Burns appears as a groundskeeper, spearing pieces of trash in the community park. Is it any less incredible that a carpenter who once lived in a small village called Nazareth was indeed God visiting us? It is nearly unfathomable.

Yet Scripture reiterates that in Christ, God was with us on our level. John 1:14 says that "The Word became flesh and dwelt among us" (rsv). The Hebrew background for the word "dwelt" in this verse is the tabernacle in the wilderness that was God's presence among his people. In other words, when God came to us in Jesus he "tabernacled" among us. He pitched his tent with us.

The beautiful hymn that Paul records in Philippians 2:6–11, describing God's condescension to our level, expresses the humility of God in becoming human. In fact, he became a slave of those who were themselves slaves—that is, slaves to sin. Remember that this is what it means to be great in God's kingdom—to serve all, even the slaves (cf. Mark 10:45). He met us at our lowest level. As someone once put it, "The greatness of God consists in the fact that he condescended so low."

In fact, what is amazing is that Jesus did not just attempt to pull humanity out of the mudhole of its selfishness while daintily lifting up his trousers by his fingertips.[5] He got his hands dirty. He wrestled with us in our own mud. People who did not understand who Jesus was or what he was all about put it this way: "This man welcomes sinners and eats with them" (Luke 15:2). We must ask ourselves a hard question. Could the same accusation be made of evangelicals today? But in obedience to the Father, Jesus risked his good name and his reputation, even his life, to be with the undeserving, the sinful, and the unworthy.[6]

The fact that sinful humans still insist upon discovering God by themselves uncovers how prideful we actually are! Salvation is not something we can do by ourselves. God must come to us and act in our history. Even more important, God's process of salvation does not give us permission to hide in seclusion. Since the Gospel is historical and others do not know it unless they are told, we are commanded to go to them, proclaiming the good news. And so Christ's self-abasing love becomes the pattern of our lives, as we obey his command to witness this Gospel of God's mercy (Matt. 28:18–20). This process of salvation is the Lord's way of sanctifying us and bringing us together as the new people of God.

Jesus Is God the Judge Who Was Judged for Us

Our disposable society is blind to the claims of justice. It seems that only those who are living (and voting) possess rights. No one cares for the dead victim—except God! God is holy; he will punish those who have rebelled against his rule (Isa. 3:11; Matt. 25:31–46), rectify all wrongs, and reestablish his good and righteous rule (Rom. 2:5–11; 12:19).

Of course, our society refuses to hear this, for it imagines that love is diametrically opposed to wrath. But as the psychologist Rollo May once noted in his book *Love and Will,* the opposite of love is not hate; it is apathy.[7] A mother who gets angry with her daughter for running across the street without looking does so not because she hates the child but precisely because she loves her so much. If she did not love her daughter, she simply would not care if she played in the streeet.

Similarly, because God loves us he is jealous of anything that stands between us and him. He is deeply concerned about any thoughts, actions, or emotions that will get us into trouble or hurt us. So God's anger toward sin reveals the depth of his concern for us. God's wrath means that God has drawn so near to humanity that he is affected and even wounded by our actions. It is because he loves us that he expresses his wrath. By contrast, a God of an ever condoning pardon is tantamount to a God of indifference.

When we are living a lie it hurts for someone to tell us the truth about ourselves. It is hard to admit that we have made a wrong turn. Anyone who has gone through a 12-step program knows that the most difficult first step toward recovery is the admission that something is wrong. The addicted person has been lying to self and others, refusing to believe what friends have been telling him or her. Sometimes when confronted we will even attempt to destroy the truth-tellers because it hurts so much.

God assumed human nature in Jesus to reveal how far we had gone in the wrong direction. He demonstrated by his life what we were supposed to be and how addicted we had become to the lies that fed our egos. It hurt so much to admit he was right that we tried to silence him. We thought that executing this rabble-rousing truth-teller would allow us to settle back into the comfort of our self-delusions. We see ourselves there in the Sanhedrin's response to Christ, blinding ourselves to the truth of who Jesus is; in Judas' selfish action, seeking a quick buck; and finally in Pilate's unwillingness to take the initiative and put his neck on the line and right the situation. Jesus' crucifixion exposes us all as sinners. Before the cross there are no innocent parties. The cross of Jesus cannot be turned into a battering ram for some against others. For we are all guilty; "there is no one righteous, not even one" (Rom. 3:10).

But while humans were killing this righteous one, God had other plans. Through its various images,[8] Scripture reveals that at the cross Jesus suffered God's wrath for our sin and established reconciliation with God. Those who trust in Jesus are no longer viewed by God as sinners, but in terms of Jesus' righteousness (Rom. 3:25).

On the cross God demonstrated both his wrath and his love. The Judge, God himself, was judged for our sake. When Jesus died on the cross, God the injured party took the initiative to restore the broken relationship (Rom. 5:8; 1 John 4:19). Though his law has been transgressed and though his love for us has been offended, God takes the first step and reconciles us to himself. God demands that a sacrifice must be made to atone for our sins, then he sacrifices *himself!*

This should serve as a model for us. When we are injured we are tempted to sulk or hold a grudge. The last thing we think about doing is to go to the person who has offended us and seek reconciliation. Pity parties feel too good for that. But as those who look at things from Christ's perspective, unless the circumstances are abusive or highly unusual, we should take the initial steps toward a resolution of the conflict. This is not to say that no response is necessary from the offender, but hopefully it will be just that—a response to our initiative.

Jesus of Nazareth Is the Perfect Human through Whom God Restores Wholeness to Human Nature and Creation

In our culture, where history appears to have no goal and no ending, we naturally attempt to "grab all the gusto" we can. For this is it, isn't it?

By contrast, the decisive truth about Jesus Christ is that he changed the very destiny of creation itself, and in him we know history's ultimate goal.

In Jesus of Nazareth God became a real human being and in so doing revealed what true human nature is and established what we can become. As Paul notes, the first Adam fell from his true humanity, but the Second Adam has come to show us how far we have fallen and to re-create us in his image (Rom. 5:17–19; 1 Cor. 15:45–49; Col. 1:15; 3:10–11). It was not enough for Jesus just to *reveal* what true human nature is. Such an education would leave us miserable and despairing. Our human nature must be restored, along with the rest of creation (see Rom. 5:12–21; 8:21–25). And so Jesus came preaching the kingdom, defeating Satan, casting out demons, healing the disabled, and in so doing constituting new powers of righteousness and obedience available through him alone. Jesus is the Second Adam, "a life-giving spirit" (1 Cor. 15:45).

We know that Christ has conquered Satan and reestablished a new reality, obedient to God, because of the resurrection. Though silence reigned for three days as the disciples waited in fear and despair, the resurrection turned them around. The day Jesus rose from the dead the universe changed: Jesus is now Lord over all.

Jesus died on the cross, *totally*. This was no mere swoon. And God raised Jesus from the dead *bodily*. The last enemy, death itself, has been defeated! Jesus did not escape from his humanity, but he renewed it through the kind of resurrected body that we shall have when our salvation is completed (see Luke 24; John 20; 1 Cor. 15:42–44). Our resurrected bodies will be like Christ's; that is our hope. Like Jesus, our bodies will not be replaced, but resurrected—like a caterpillar that enters the tomb of a cocoon and comes out a butterfly.

Jesus is *now* Lord of *all* creation (see Matt. 28:18; Eph. 1:20–21; Phil. 2:9–11; Rev. 17:14). It may not seem like it sometimes, but one day everyone will acknowledge this truth when the war is finally over. In the meantime, we confess his lordship over all creation with the eyes of faith—with a Christian worldview that looks at the world and everything in it from this side of the cross and resurrection. That means that no area of life is to be excluded when it comes to our responsibility in living out the lordship of Christ. We are to testify to it not just in our evangelism, but in our daily work, our recreation, our ministry to people's bodily needs, our care for the environment, and our personal relationships.

Because we know the end of history, we can selflessly expend our lives participating in his plan of reconciliation (2 Cor. 5:18–21) for the meaning of our lives and even history itself does not depend on us "pushing our own agenda." Jesus is Lord—now. And to reflect his lordship, we should sacrifice our lives for his purposes. But to live faithfully now, we need to examine the context for life in the kingdom. So now we turn to the church.

For Further Reflection

1. What do you think should be the Christian's primary responsibility today, fulfilling the creation mandate or pursuing Jesus' kingdom of God? Why?
2. What implications does the kingdom of God have for the Christian's action toward the social problem of poverty?
3. Think about Luke 15:2. Could people actually accuse you of this? If not, does that bother you? Why or why not?
4. Is your view of life affected by your understanding of the incarnation, the cross, and/or the resurrection? For instance, does the incarnation provide you with a model for your involvement with non-Christians? Does the cross affect the way you respond to your enemies? Do you live your daily life as if the resurrection really decided the power struggle between God and the forces of evil? Take some time to do an inventory here.
5. Respond to the pluralist's charge that the orthodox interpretation of Jesus as the only "Way" contradicts his teachings regarding love.

For Further Reading

Guthrie, Shirley. *Christian Doctrine,* 2d ed. Atlanta: Westminster John Knox, 1995.

Ladd, George E. *A Theology of the New Testament.* Grand Rapids: Eerdmans, 1974.

McGrath, Alister. *Understanding Jesus.* Grand Rapids: Zondervan, 1990.

Stott, John R. W. *The Cross of Christ.* Downers Grove, Ill.: InterVarsity, 1995.

seven

Already but Not Yet:
The Church and the Kingdom

fter Jesus instructed his followers to be his witnesses on earth (Matt. 28:19–20; Acts 1:8), he ascended into heaven. This was a visible sign to the disciples that he would no longer be appearing to them in the same way that he had during the previous forty days. Now he would be present to the world through his body, the church (1 Cor. 12:12–20; Eph. 4:4, 11–16). Luke makes this point in a subtle way at the beginning of the second half of this two-volume work, Luke-Acts: "In the first book [Luke's Gospel], O Theophilus, I have dealt with all that Jesus began to do and teach, until the day when he was taken up, after he had given commandment through the Holy Spirit to the apostles whom he had chosen" (Acts 1:1–2, RSV). That is to say, what Jesus began in his incarnate ministry would now continue through the church.

Now we are right back where we started, with the Christian family, that is, the church. They are the people of God who continue Christ's incarnate ministry by being his representatives in the world. It is an ominous task: to us has been entrusted the Gospel message and the ministry of reconciliation (2 Cor. 5:20). Being entrusted with all the precious gems in the world couldn't be as unnerving as this responsibility. Thus, we had better have a good understanding of what the church is in order to be in the world effectively. To live faithfully as messengers of reconciliation, we must understand our place in God's role first.

The Church is Rooted in the History of Salvation

The church is not just a parenthesis in history between the first and second comings of Christ, nor is it simply a holding tank for Christians to give them something to do while they await "the rapture." It is part of God's history of redeeming his people and establishing his lordship over all creation, which began with his covenant promise to Adam and Eve (Gen. 3:15), continues with Christ's inauguration of the kingdom, and will be fulfilled when the kingdom of God arrives in its fullness.

The presence of these kingdom or eschatological realities (i.e., realities of the end times or the age to come) is the source of the Christian's joy and confidence. We do not just blindly hope for a better day and a new reality. Instead, we experience in the here and now the realities that Jesus established in all the dimensions of life—spiritual, social, and environmental. As a result, we know that the destiny of history has been changed.

This kingdom—God's rule over an obedient cosmos—is worth any effort (Matt. 13:44–46; Luke 18:18–28). It is the priceless treasure for which we will sell all to obtain. The kingdom is not intended for people who are just well-meaning or who want to be part of the crowd. It is meant for those who desperately crave God's kingship above anything else. It is for people who are willing to enter it "violently" (Luke 16:16, RSV). Since Jesus tells Pilate that his kingdom is not established by the sword (John 18:36), "violently" must be used figuratively here. That is to say, entering the kingdom violently refers to the total rejection of our past ways and the radical new future that the kingdom provides.

Baptism is a good symbol of this, even though we usually treat it as an insipid ceremony. It symbolizes a violent death—a death to the world that is as traumatic as a drowning, but crowned by being snatched up out of the water to a resurrected life. Flannery O'Connor's short story "The River" and her novel *The Violent Bear It Away* graphically portray this significance of baptism.[1] In each case a boy who is baptized drowns. O'Connor wants to shake us up—to see our entrance into the kingdom as an act that is traumatic and *literally* life-changing. Yet we usually find it less interesting than entering Disney's Magic Kingdom.

But that is not all! Now Christ is working to complete his kingdom and his lordship over all. With the resurrection and ascension, God has raised Christ "and seated him at his right hand in the heavenly realms" and "appointed him to be head over everything"; and now Christ is working through his "body," the church, which "fills everything in every way" (Eph. 1:20–23). We have been given a mission—we are the instruments through which Christ now works. Through the church Jesus Christ is now confronting the powers of evil and working to bring all creation to voluntary submission under his lordship.

God's salvation history is moving swiftly into the future. Those who are baptized into the church are jumping onto a moving train that is charging through a landscape littered with the forces of evil, death, and destruction. This is an exhilarating ride, but it is not for people who want to sit back and be waited on in first class![2]

The Church and Jesus' Kingdom

From Peter's claim at Pentecost that this advent of the Spirit fulfills Joel's prophecy (Acts 2:16–21) to the Hebrews description of believers as tasting "the powers of the coming age" (Heb. 6:5), the New Testament writers consistently and repeatedly note that the new realities in the church fulfill the Old Testament promises. But the church is more than simply the location for these kingdom realities. More accurately, it is the training ground for Christ's kingdom people. The church exists "to prepare God's people for works of service" and thereby "become mature, attaining to the whole measure of the fullness of Christ" (Eph. 4:12–13).

Unfortunately, many Christians separate saving faith in Jesus Christ from participation in the church. But in the New Testament "church" translates the Greek term ecclesia, which refers to a meeting of people who have been called together. The *ecclesia* of God is a specific type of people, one that God in Jesus Christ has called into existence by his work (Acts 20:28). When one accepts Jesus' offer of salvation, one is now "in Christ" (Gal. 1:22; 1 Thes. 2:14), part of his "church" (Eph. 5:23), a member of the "body of Christ" (Eph. 4:4, 15–16). In fact, our English term "church," which is related to the Germanic word *kirche* and the Scottish *kirk*, has an etymology that originally meant "of the Lord" (from the Greek *kyrios*). We who were not a people, are now a people "of the Lord." That is our primary identity.

Of all these biblical descriptions of the new relationship between Christ and the believer, the *body* is a particularly profound image. Jesus Christ, as Paul explains, is the *head* of this body (Eph. 4:15–16; Col. 1:15–20; 2:19).

> "And he gave some as apostles, and some as prophets, and some as evangelists, and some as pastors and teachers, for the equipping of the saints for the work of service, to the building up of the body of Christ; until we all attain to the unity of the faith, and of the knowledge of the Son of God, to a mature man, to the measure of the stature which belongs to the fulness of Christ." (St. Paul, Ephesians 4:11–13 NASB)

Paul's point is not merely that Jesus is the authority over the church. Rather, just as a stream is the *head* or *source* of a river, Jesus is the source of the believer's nourishment, strength, and life. The head provides life for those in the body (Col. 2:19). Simply put, Christ's body—the church—is where we access Jesus and his kingdom realities.

In addition, the church is to equip and nurture believers so that they "grow up into" Jesus, the head, and attain "the whole measure of the fullness of Christ" (Eph. 4:13). The goal is not to placate or even pacify believers, but to enlist them in Christ's kingdom purposes for history. Jesus makes this point in his final farewells to his disciples: "You will be my witnesses . . . to the ends of the earth" (Acts 1:8; cf. Luke 24:44–48). In the New Testament, the concept of a witness is defined in terms of Jesus' work. Only those who salvifically know Jesus and become part of his kingdom are his witnesses, not those who simply report secondhand information. And as witnesses, their lives must incarnate the new realities that Jesus has established. Simply put, believers are saved to serve Jesus as Lord "to the ends of the earth."[3]

There is another interesting implication of this image of the church as Christ's body. It means that Christians do not exist as "lone rangers," but first and foremost as part of this organism, the church. As part of this body, believers are interdependent upon each other (1 Cor. 12:12–31). Although the body consists of many parts, all "form one body" (1 Cor. 12:12) so that the foot needs the hand and the eye the ear. Paul further explains that while maturity in the Christian life originates from Jesus, it occurs only insofar "as each part does its work" (Eph. 4:16). Other believers are indispensable to developing and maturing us as believers.

In our individualistic culture this is an overlooked theme. Unfortunately, the only church many think the believer needs is Bedside Baptist with Pastor Pillow. How is the church essential to our Christian faith? Perhaps the answer is to examine how the body is crucial to the development of these eschatological realities in the individual believer. How are the spiritual, social, and environmental realities of the kingdom linked to and cultivated by the church?

Old Testament Prophecy	New Testament Fulfillment
. . . Spiritual Sphere . . .	
Joel 2:28-32	Acts 2:14; Eph. 2:22: presence of the Spirit among all believers Heb. 6:5: Christians taste the powers of the coming age
Jer. 31:31-34	2 Cor. 5:17; Col. 2:11–15: new hearts, made alive Rom. 3:21–26: our wickedness forgiven once and for all
Ezek. 36:25-28	Rom. 6:5–6: no longer slaves to sin Eph. 2:10: can do righteous acts James 1:25: this is the law that gives freedom, enables us to obey
. . . Social Sphere . . .	
Isa. 9:7	Acts 2:42; 4:32–34: unity and fellowship of believers as expressed by the sharing of possessions Eph. 2:14–16; Gal. 3:28–29: unity and social equality among believers
. . . Environmental Sphere . . .	
Isa. 35:5-6	Acts 5:12–16: apostles healed many; natural evils overcome
Isa. 26:19	1 Cor. 15:16–20: hope for life after death established by Christ's resurrection

The Church As the Locus[4] of Eschatological Realities

The Spiritual Realities of the Kingdom

As prior chapters have explained, sin constitutes the human problem, and it entails a "double whammy." The Fall corrupts human nature so that we now choose our egocentric good, rather than God's good. "The heart is . . . desperately corrupt" (Jer. 17:9, RSV), even enslaved to sin. God's holy standards shatter any human pretensions to righteousness. From God's perspective there is no inherent difference between us and any other: "There is no one righteous, not even one" (Rom. 3:10). Moreover, the sinner is subject to God's judgment, which is as great as the One against whom the sin is directed. Since sin is first and foremost a rejection of God, the penalty, like the One whom sin rejects, is infinite.

Despite this bleak predicament, God promised in the New Covenant that he would forgive our wickedness and remember our sins no more, create a new heart in us by giving us his Spirit, and move us to follow his laws (Jer. 31:33–34; Ezek. 36:26–27). In Jesus Christ, God has fulfilled these promises through the realities of justification and sanctification.

Justification

Jesus' life and death was a vicarious and substitutionary sacrifice for us. His cry, "My God, my God, why have you forsaken me?" (Matt. 27:46) is that of the holy and merciful Judge, the "Lord of glory" himself, accepting the punishment due us (1 Cor. 2:8). God imputes Christ's satisfaction and righteous life to all who believe in Jesus. As Paul proclaims:

> But now a righteousness from God, apart from law, has been made known, to which the Law and the Prophets testify. This righteousness from God comes through faith in Jesus Christ to all who believe. . . . God presented him as a sacrifice of atonement, through faith in his blood. He did this to demonstrate his justice . . . at the present time, so as to be just and the one who justifies those who have faith in Jesus. (Rom. 3:21–26)

Justification is the fulfillment of the forgiveness promised in the Old Testament. It is a declaration by God, our true Judge, that the believer in Jesus Christ is righteous and without guilt, even though still a sinner. We can know now that God will judge us as righteous (Rom. 3:21–22; 5:9; Eph. 4:32). Simply put, in Jesus Christ God forgives and embraces us with his love, despite who we are.

This message of Jesus' work—that Jesus has come to be and do what we have failed to be and do before God—is the essence of the Gospel. It is the good news; it constitutes the church's *kerygma* or preaching. Through the proclamation of the church we personally encounter God in Jesus Christ, as the one who is calling us, the sinner, to himself. Trust in Jesus Christ is the only access to these kingdom realities. So evangelism is indispensable. But this kerygma is not simply for gathering disciples into the kingdom. The kerygma must be heard repeatedly, for even the believer constantly sets up her own culturally shaped views.

Sanctification

Of course it takes supernatural faith to perceive our sinful predicament and the reality of Christ's benefits. Or as Jesus bluntly states, only those who are "born again" can "see the kingdom of God" (John 3:3). The Spirit's reviving moves us to repent and trust wholly upon Jesus Christ as Lord and Savior. Once we were "dead" in our sins, but now God has made us "alive" in Christ (Col. 2:13)! This internal work of God, making us holy, is called sanctification.

God's work not only breaks the bondage of sin, it claims us for Christ's kingdom purposes in history. Salvation entails a basic reordering of our priorities and a reorientation of our perspective on life, all in the light of Christ's kingship. This is what Jesus means in Matthew 6:33 when he instructs his disciples to seek the kingdom first. We are not to think of ourselves first as Democrats or Republicans, capitalists or socialists, red, yellow, black, or white. Jesus Christ and his kingdom must reorder our thoughts and actions; to put anything else in that position is idolatry.

Under God's rule, believers are called from self-interest to self-sacrificial service for Christ (Rom. 12:14–21). While we cannot earn or merit God's forgiveness, our actions demonstrate that "we are God's workmanship, created in Christ Jesus to do good works" (Eph. 2:10) and so evidence the new kingdom realities. In fact, if we are truly "in Christ," we must do good works for "every good tree bears good fruit" (Matt. 7:17).

The Zoblinskis have recurrently showed us the role that family plays in shaping our personality and character. Just as their family context shapes every child, so those who have been "born again" need the church's social support and training. This cultivation is imperative since Christ's kingdom contradicts the desires and expectations of this world. That is why Scripture places so much emphasis upon the spiritual disciplines by which we replace the habits of sin with the habits of righteousness by following the example of Christ (Gal. 5:22–26). Scripture outlines a twofold pattern for the lifelong process of sanctification: crucifying the old nature and rising with Christ to a developing life of holiness (Col. 3:5–10; Rom. 12:1–2).[5] Imitating Jesus Christ and thereby being remade in his image is not an individual pursuit. The church exists to hold us accountable to Christ's commands. That is why Paul and Peter wrote their letters to various churches. Actually, this is every believer's responsibility. All are called to "teach and admonish" (Col. 3:16) and even "carry each other's burdens" (Gal. 6:2). And the explicit context for both passages is discipline—shaping the praxis and understanding of other believers!

The various means of grace in the church offer an immensely rich and indispensable context for sanctification. Bible studies, catechism or new believer classes, and preaching are the *didache* (teachings) that map out the new intellectual landscape for the believer. And perhaps nothing educates like teaching itself—to which all believers are called (Col. 3:16). Teaching a Sunday School class or leading a youth group are God's internships for believers.

Other church activities also cultivate this new knowledge through praxis. In worship believers praise God without any thought of a reward, but simply because God is worthy. Worship "re-centers" our attention on God's

"It is impossible for any that have it, to conceal the religion of Jesus Christ. This our Lord makes plain beyond all contradiction, by a two-fold comparison: 'Ye are the light of the world: a city set upon a hill cannot be hid.' . . . Your holiness makes you as conspicuous as the sun in the midst of heaven. . . . So impossible it is, to keep our religion from being seen, unless we cast it away; so vain is the thought of hiding the light, unless by putting it out! Sure it is, that a secret, unobserved religion cannot be the religion of Jesus Christ." (John Wesley, *Wesley's Standard Sermons*, 1:388–89)

glory instead of on ourselves (Rom. 12:1–2). As Søren Kierkegaard pointed out, the audience in worship is God—in other words, the one who should be clapping when the music is finished is the Lord. In the sacrament of the Lord's Supper, Christ is spiritually present with believers through his redemptive work and enjoins them to demonstrate his love to others and physically offer themselves for furthering his kingdom (1 Cor. 11:27–32). This end is cultivated through the church's *diakonia* (service). This is not serving at arm's length through alms giving, but following Jesus' practice of face-to-face service to "the least of these" (Matt. 25:40). In doing this we learn to reflect Christ's love, by serving others unconditionally and gladly, even making ourselves expendable for God.

The Social Realities of the Kingdom

The Old Testament promised that the age to come would establish social justice and overcome all natural evils within the environmental sphere. In the New Testament it is the church which exemplified these realities. Note the *koinonia*—that fellowship of love, equality, and family bonds between believers—in the earliest church in Jerusalem. They ate together in one another's homes, treated others with open and sincere hearts, and were of one heart and mind. Their communal practices and lifestyle were even more startling. "All the believers were together and had everything in common. Selling their possessions and goods, they gave to anyone who had need" (Acts 2:44–45, NIV:ILE). "There were no needy persons among them" (Acts 4:34).

At one time, these verses were embarrassing to many American believers. For those of us who grew up during the Cold War, this smacked too much of the dreaded Communism. We knew all too well the best interpretive diversions: "Of course, this communistic practice is why the Jerusalem church was so poor, needing the financial support of other churches (1 Cor. 16) and ultimately failing!" But such eisegesis (reading into the text) had missed the whole point of Jesus' work. These practices reflected the social love and justice of Christ's kingdom. How else could one better testify to Jesus' work of reconciliation among people?

This concern for community and social justice is a constant and yet often troublesome theme throughout the New Testament church. The church's original Jewish context made it difficult to understand the radical implications of Jesus' work for the Gentile. In fact, it demanded that Gentiles must first follow ethnically Jewish practices, including circumcision and the dietary laws, in order to be eligible for believing in Jesus (Acts 11; 15; Gal. 2:3–5). While Peter knew firsthand through his encounter with Cornelius that God "accepts those from every nation" (Acts 10:35, NIV:ILE), he later refused to have table fellowship with Gentile believers in Antioch (Gal. 2:11–13). But Paul understood that Jesus "has destroyed the barrier, the dividing wall of hostility" between Jew and Gentile and created "in himself one new man out of the two" (Eph. 2:14–16). The kingdom unites as a community all races and peoples (Col. 3:11).

Paul developed other social implications from Jesus' kingdom message. In contrast to the existing social hierarchies, Paul encouraged believers who are one in Christ to submit to each other, despite their social station, gender, or race (Gal. 3:28; Eph. 5:21). Writing to Philemon, a slave-owner, Paul charged that Christians must recognize that their believing servants can no longer be treated as such. Since Onesimus belongs to Christ's family, he must be treated "better than" a servant; indeed, "as a dear brother" (Philem. 16).

These decisive insights in the early church illustrate why our life together (koinonia) in the church cannot be limited to just our age, ethnic, or social group. The cultural context of these restricted groups automatically shapes our understanding of the Christian life. For example, when we in the West read Scripture's attacks on the wealthy (Matt. 19:23; Luke 6:24; James 5:1), do we immediately exclude ourselves if we don't occupy the highest social strata in American life? From the perspective of the third-world Christian, however, most Western believers sit at the very highest levels of the social and economic ladder!

Sharing life with believers different from ourselves allows us to become aware of these cultural and social blind spots. And through this process, Jesus Christ—not these distortions—can become the one and only thing that is decisive for us.[6]

The embodiment of love and reconciliation is not only for believers. Christ calls his disciples to the "ministry of reconciliation" (2 Cor. 5:18) through evangelism and service to others. This body of believers is called to follow Christ to the lost, the oppressed, and the outcast.

Already but Not Yet: The Church and the Kingdom

The Environmental Realities of the Kingdom

Finally, Christ's kingdom promised the end of natural evils. Indeed, the disciples showed the firstfruits of Jesus' kingdom by their miracles and healings (Acts 5:12–16). Above all, though, Jesus' resurrection from the dead establishes that death itself has been defeated and his resurrected body represents the firstfruits of the reality that we can expect (1 Cor. 15:16–20). As a result, Christians can live this life in a confident self-sacrificial service to Jesus, since they know what their future holds.

Following Jesus' kingdom message, we must also oppose natural evils. To those suffering from nature's terror, from hurricanes and earthquakes to the ravages of mental illness and terrifying diseases, we must bring Christ's love and message of hope. And perhaps nothing demonstrates the reality of the kingdom more than when Christians, at great danger to their own lives, help those whom society considers to be expendable. Being tangible witnesses of Christ's redemption in the world is integral to the process which transforms us into his image. Such actions demonstrate the integrity of our witness to Jesus Christ. It permits us to sing Isaac Watts's hymn "Joy to the World!" without embarrassment or apology: "No more let sins and sorrows grow, *nor thorns infest the ground;* He comes to make His blessings flow *far as the curse is found.*"

So the church is the place where our Christian identity and the prom-

John Perkins (1930—)

Born into a poor black Mississippi family, the violence and injustice inherent in racist systems shaped John Perkins's life. After his conversion in 1957, he returned to bring the Gospel to those with whom he had grown up. Through this work Perkins realized that Christian ministry must be holistic and confront the economic and political expressions of sin. For "Jesus' strategy [is] to rescue whole people, and to enlist both their bodies and spirits in his kingdom." So Perkins and his wife, Vera Mae, developed educational, health, and housing programs as integral parts of their ministry; and their mission expanded beyond Mendenhall Ministries, to the Voice of Calvary Ministries (Jackson, Mississippi) and to Harambee Christian Family Center (Pasadena, California).

At the core of Perkins's comprehensive vision for the local church are three Rs. Through *relocation* believers live among the needy and begin to experience their anguish and distress. "After meeting some real needs, you can begin to communicate through these 'felt needs' to the deeper spiritual needs of a person." Being Jesus' agents, the local church must also demonstrate that his *reconciling* love bridges all racial, social, and economic barriers. And the local church must obey Christ by sharing with others in need, that is, *redistributing* not simply goods but our knowledge and skills so that the cycle of poverty is broken. "And as we commit ourselves to just redistribution in terms of creating a new economics in broken communities, we can see how Jesus, through us, offers himself."

ised eschatological realities are developed. The church is God's family (Matt. 12:48–50) where his children are nurtured and trained to be his disciples.

The Church's Mission

The church exists "between the times." On the one hand, the kingdom has *already* come. Jesus' lordship over all creation was established through his advent, but it will not be a completed reality until every creature acknowledges him as Lord. So the kingdom is not yet here in all its fullness. The "already" aspect of the kingdom makes our struggle against the forces of evil possible, while the "not yet" aspect makes our struggle necessary. What are the implications for the church living in tension between these two poles?

Members of the Church Are Citizens of Two Cities

Saint Augustine argued that believers are at the same time citizens of both the earthly "city of man" and the heavenly "city of God." With this dual citizenship Christians feel the tension of living in these in-between times. We are not really at home in this present world, but we are not yet in that eternal world in which we will dwell ultimately and eternally. We live in this world, yet as "aliens and strangers" (1 Peter 2:11). The church is to be groaning "inwardly as we wait eagerly for our adoption" (Rom. 8:23). We're not supposed to feel comfortable under the present earthly circumstances; we are to be anxiously aching for our redemption.

People who feel this tension are not satisfied with the status quo. They are the ones who suffer with the rest of creation as it moans under the present evil conditions. They are believers who get involved in this world to proclaim the Gospel, never satisfied with how far the reforms have taken us in society, but always looking for the revolutionary overthrow of those powers that stand in the way of the kingdom's coming.

Members of the Church Are People of Expectation Whose Lives Are Directed by That Goal

God's goal—the end of history as we know it now—is the establishment of his kingdom. *Everything* that the members of the church think, say, and do is to be judged and evaluated in the light of the coming kingdom. As one little girl rightly put it: "The Bible begins with Genesis and ends with Revolution!" Christians are radical people who are out to turn the world they live in upside down (Acts 17:6). The French sociologist and theologian Jacques Ellul put it powerfully:

> This, then, is the revolutionary situation: to be revolutionary is to judge the world by its present state, by actual facts, in the name of a truth which does not yet exist (but which is coming)—and it is to do so because we believe this truth to be more genuine and more real than the reality which surrounds us. Consequently it means bringing the future into the present as an explosive force. It means believing that future events are more important and more true than present events; it means understanding the present in the light of the future.[7]

Christians are people whose activities are not so much determined by their past as by their future.

In the same way that every December our children's thoughts and behaviors are dictated by their eager anticipation of Christmas, so Christ's disciples should be consumed by their confident expectation that God will finish what he has started. That is the hope by which our lives are to be governed. Just as our kids cannot contain themselves once we pass Thanksgiving, so it should be for members of the church. We are not here to keep the good news of the kingdom to ourselves. We are to live it out in our daily lives, to make it a present reality in our environment, and that includes every aspect of life—our schooling, our work, our home life, our political existence, our economic structures, our care for the earth, and our ministry to other people.

As aliens and exiles whose true home is the coming kingdom, we are to live as *pointers* to what is on the way—as *witnesses* to a reality that is a fact, but is not yet acknowledged by all. We live in *anticipation* of that day, praying down the kingdom and groaning for it until the ultimate destruction of all the powers of evil is accomplished and the re-creation of this universe is completed (Rom. 8:18–27). If Jesus is Lord now, it must be manifest in our lives now. Otherwise we are contradicting the present reality of Christ's lordship over all.

The Church Must Not Mistake Itself for the Kingdom

While Jesus proclaimed that the kingdom had arrived, we got the church! And that has led to confusion regarding the identity of the church and the kingdom. However, the church cannot be equated with the kingdom because it is never completely obedient to God's rule. In this life the church is always a mixed fellowship, wheat and tares, even as it was among Jesus' own disciples! (Matt. 13:24–30) But the church does *witness* to the coming kingdom. As a witness, the church points to the kingdom which is different from itself, yet it cannot be divorced from it either for the church *anticipates* what the kingdom will be by its life.

Perhaps it is best to see the church as the instrument—much like a rake or a hoe—through which Christ works in the fields of this world. As a result, the church has no power in and of itself, but only that mediated by Christ. The church will not even bring in the consummated kingdom. That is Christ's own work, as Paul makes clear in 1 Corinthians 15:25: Christ must reign "until he has put all his enemies under his feet," and then comes the end. In Revelation Christ conquers the remaining forces of evil (Rev. 19:11–16). Consequently, the end of history does not directly depend upon the church. The kingdom will be consummated by Jesus alone.

If we get the idea that it is the church's job to bring in the kingdom, then, as Hans Küng warned, we will be led "to an intolerable glorification of the church," forgetting "that the church is composed of . . . sinful men."[8] History repeatedly tempts the church to control the kingdom and even bring it to completion. But in attempting to impose its rule on others by political and social means, the church abandons its role as a witness and even usurps Christ's place.

The Church Witnesses Now to the Coming Kingdom

The church does not exist to serve itself but to witness to Jesus' kingdom work (Matt. 28:18–20; Luke 24:44–48; Acts 1:8). At all times and everywhere we are to be confident witnesses to Christ's lordship in our daily tasks. There must be evidence of this in the way that we get along together in the church (see John 13:34–35; 17:20–21). There must be evidence of it in our society. For if our priorities and perspectives have changed, then there will be social consequences. We will find ourselves being more responsible, not less responsible, for the reordering of the conditions of this present life.

Christ did not issue his Sermon on the Mount as instructions to his followers for some ideal world. His commands are for this world. Praying "thy will be done" does not refer to "pie in the sky, by and by"; it means that we are to adopt the Nike motto and "just do it" now in every context of our lives. Praying "thy kingdom come" is not to ask God to do something to the world while we stand by as mere spectators. It is a petition for us to accept the will of God for our lives and world, to pay the price of its acceptance, and to clear away anything that hinders that acceptance. This is no petition for people who want to remain the way they are.

We live in a fallen world in which its redemption and Satan's overthrow is possible because of Jesus' work. And we are called to that work, combating Satan's reign in the world and redeeming creation from its perver-

> "We can only act within a world we can see. Vision is the necessary prerequisite for ethics. . . . A vision of the inbreaking of a new society. . . ." "That explains why, in the church, a great deal of time and energy are spent in the act of worship: In worship, we are busy looking in the right direction." (Stanley Hauerwas and William H. Willimon, *Resident Aliens*, 84, 95)

sion. This entails two distinctive tasks: first, denouncing Satan's perversion of creation, and second, redirecting culture toward its true Lord and Savior, Jesus Christ.

Jesus Christ changed the destiny of history by defeating the satanic principalities and powers, that is, the sinful structures, customs, the elements within our daily life (Col. 2:15). Because Christ has judged and defeated these sinful structures, they should no longer enslave us. So the task of the Christian is to denounce them when they have become supreme and thus demonic. Nothing is or should be absolute except Christ alone; he alone is our Lord. Thus, we are called to identify how an absolute allegiance to our nation, our own race, or our own lifestyle, instead of submission to Jesus, is demonic, distortive, and inherently disruptive.

In addition, the church is to demonstrate that we have been freed from Satan's bondage and that we evidence the firstfruits of the age to come. As the new community established by Jesus, we must evidence his work of reconciliation and love for the lost. The church exists to be an instrument of Christ's offer of grace wherever Satan still hangs on to power. The church must stand for justice, love, and healing in a world full of injustice, pain, and suffering. The church must share Christ's eschatological realities with all those for whom he died.

Conclusion

But what actually is the state of the church in North America? Does the church perceive herself as a witness to God's work in Jesus Christ? Perhaps we betray our answer when we mistakenly talk about "going to church" on Sunday mornings. We do not go to the church; we are the church. The church is not a building; the church is people. Too often we have confused the church's existence with what it does inside her buildings. We often forget that "the church" goes to a building to worship on the first day of the week so that its members can "re-center" their focus on the King and his kingdom once again and then go out as "the church" into the world for the remaining six days, until we regroup the following Sunday.

The church exists twenty-four hours a day. Sometimes it does so inside four walls, praising God and being confronted by his Word. But most of the time it exists in neighborhoods, businesses, schools, families, city streets, suburban malls, parks—in other words, anywhere the church has dispersed after the pastor gives the signal to "Charge!" at the benediction on Sunday morning. Then we go where Christ goes—into the blighted and dark places of the world, where people are addicted and alienated and diseased and dying, where spiritual powers oppress and enslave people, and where social conditions perpetuate idolatry, classism, racism, and sexism—bringing the good news of the kingdom.

For Further Reflection

1. What are the responsibilities of the church as outlined in this chapter? (Rom. 8:18–39; 1 Cor. 12; Eph. 3:14–4:16) Evaluate your local church from this perspective.

2. Given what Paul says in Ephesians 3:14–4:16, how important is the community of the church for the individual Christian's spiritual growth? Is it possible for Christians to witness to the coming kingdom without the church?

3. Discuss this statement: "No Christian can serve a world human community in a religious spirit that thrives chiefly inside a church building" (Donald Shriver, *The Lord's Prayer: A Way of Life* [Atlanta: Westminster John Knox, 1983], 61).

4. Discuss this statement: "No nation, denomination, government, or culture on earth deserves the unrestrained, unconditional respect of Christians. We are first human beings created by God to be free from subservience to any human to be free to serve all humans" (Donald Shriver, *The Lord's Prayer*, 50).

5. Evaluate: "Evangelism, that is, the proclamation of salvation in Jesus Christ, is the sole biblical mission of the church. For evangelism was the only purpose for Jesus' reconciling work on the Cross. The greatest and the most enduring benefit to the world's needy flows from lives made new in Jesus Christ."

6. In your vocation—accountant, chemist, musician, engineer, homemaker—how can you use these skills and activities for Christ's kingdom?

For Further Reading

Abraham, William J. *The Logic of Evangelism.* Grand Rapids: Eerdmans, 1989.

Ellul, Jacques. *The Presence of the Kingdom.* Colorado Springs: Helmers and Howard, 1989.

Foster, Richard. *The Freedom of Simplicity.* San Francisco: Harper and Row, 1981.

Hauerwas, Stanley and William H. Willimon. *Resident Aliens: Life in the Christian Colony.* Nashville: Abingdon, 1990.

Kraybill, Donald B. *The Upside-Down Kingdom.* Scottdale, Pa.: Herald, 1990.

Küng, Hans. *The Church.* New York: Doubleday, 1967.

eight

Back to the Future

any Christians have written off eschatology ("the study of last things") as curious and eccentric. Bumper stickers that warn, "When the rapture occurs, this car will be driverless," the absolute certainty and precise predictions offered by radio preachers, and the constantly revised biblical interpretations which fit every new political crisis into their prophetic scenario certainly provide little assistance in its defense. However, eschatology cannot be so easily dismissed.

As we have seen in the previous chapter, one's vision of the future shapes one's involvement in society and culture. Having parents who articulated a Christian vision of the future that highlighted Jesus' promises of justice and love, especially for the outcast, powerless, and unwanted, helped us to see things differently. Where these ideals were neglected—as in the case of shut-ins without any family or the aged wasting away in a nursing home without any visitors—we were inspired and even impelled to act. This vision provided a reference point for evaluating and ranking our actions. And the certainty of this future supplied the resolve for facing life's terrifying and repulsive moments. In a parallel way, the bitterness and stridency in American politics probably derives from a pervasive secular worldview, which realizes that if "we don't get it here, we won't get it anywhere." So eschatology is important for our view of society and culture; it shapes our actions, attitudes, and expectations.

124

Evangelical Essentials on Eschatology

While there is diversity within evangelical circles regarding the precise order of events at the end, we are agreed on the big picture. As evangelicals, we confess that Jesus Christ has established the kingdom of God in part and that we await the kingdom's future consummation. At the end Christ will bring these eschatological realities to completion. All enemies will be conquered. All humanity will be raised to answer to Christ, the final judge, and pass into either heaven or hell (Matt. 25:31–46; John 5:24–29). Then, God's rule will be "all in all" (1 Cor. 15:28) as Jesus Christ will personally reign as King over a new heaven and new earth. This framework coheres with our basic beliefs regarding Jesus' work, and it outlines the mission for Christ's disciples. Thus, a quick review of whence we have come in recent chapters is important.

First, the kingdom we look forward to is already present in part. Jesus Christ demonstrated that he is the Messiah by changing the destiny of history and establishing these qualitatively new kingdom realities. If Jesus Christ did not establish the kingdom in part, what distinguishes his work from that of any other prophet? Our belief that the kingdom is present now is tied to the absoluteness and deity of Jesus Christ.

Second, the kingdom is *not yet* fully here. We look forward to the future when evil will no longer confront us and when the kingdom will be consummated. This "not yet" aspect of the kingdom permits us to distinguish between the church and the kingdom of God. Indeed, as Scripture repeatedly notes, the church will always be a collection of wheat and tares (Matt. 13:24–30). As the previous chapter noted, this expectation of the future outlines the church's mission: to bear witness to the kingdom.

Third, because of Jesus' work, our hope for the future is not just a blind hope; it is grounded upon and foreshadowed by Jesus' life, death, and resurrection. Despite our present struggles and defeats, we know how history will end. And because we know what our future holds, we can actually carry out Jesus' imperative: "Those who would come after me must deny themselves and take up their cross and follow me" (Matt. 16:24, NIV:ILE). Jesus' response to a lost world was to humble himself and suffer for our sake. He boldly preached the good news of the kingdom in the face of death itself. Similarly, because our future is assured our concerns should no longer revert to ourselves, but reflect Christ's kingdom and its goals—for we have been guaranteed a utopian existence and are experiencing its firstfruits right now. We must evidence that we are Christ's disciples by selflessly participating in his plan of reconciliation (2 Cor. 5:18–21), even at the price of our lives.

The Second Coming of Jesus Christ and the Millennium

More controversial in evangelical circles is the timing of Jesus' second coming, as well as the nature of the millennium. The millennium refers to the period, explicitly mentioned only in Revelation 20:1–10, when Christ reigns for a thousand years.[1] This period occurs after Satan has been thrown into the abyss and is unable to deceive the nations. As a result, the millennium is usually conceived of as a time of unparalleled righteousness, peace, and prosperity for earth. At the end of this period, however, Satan will be released. Once again he deceives the nations in a period of tribulation and is defeated and thrown into the lake of burning sulfur, which finally seals his fate.

The labels for the different eschatological positions in evangelical circles arise from the question: When will Jesus' second coming occur? In evangelical circles the answers are:

1. Jesus' second coming will occur before the millennium and after the tribulation; this is called *premillennial posttribulational eschatology.*
2. Jesus' second coming will occur before the millennium and before the tribulation; this is called *premillennial pretribulational eschatology.*
3. Jesus' second coming will occur after the millennium; this is called *postmillennial eschatology.*
4. There is not a specific millennial period per se; this is called *amillennial eschatology.*

Premillennial Posttribulational Eschatology

Following a straightforward reading of Revelation 20, this position understands Christ's second coming as a single event that occurs at the height of the tribulation. At this time Christ destroys the Antichrist and his forces at Armageddon. All believers are then raised to reign with Jesus during the millennium. With the end of the millennium God's plan reaches completion with the final judgment and the creation of a new heaven and new earth.

A major question facing this position concerns the purpose of the millennium, since it will be occupied by nonbelievers and believers reigning with Christ. These advocates note that the millennium represents a new advance for the kingdom from its status during the church age. In some way Satan will be less active than he was previously during the church age, and Jesus will now be reigning *visibly* instead of invisibly in heaven. During this period, when Satan is locked up and unable to deceive the nations, this sinful world is as perfect as possible. Yet humankind still rebels against

God at the end, after Satan is released. Such a scenario clearly shows how sinful humans are and how eager they are to rebel against God. It demonstrates that the root of sin cannot be attributed to environmental or social conditions, but to a rebellious heart. This graphically demonstrates that salvation requires a new creation; the old cannot be just refurbished.

This position was the historic position of the early church fathers until about A.D. 400. Its strengths include biblical support as well as its recognition of sin's depth that only Christ can reverse.

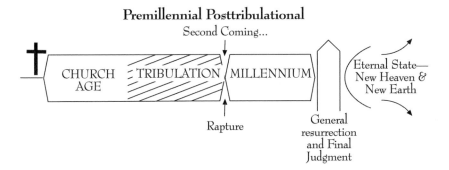

Premillennial Pretribulational Eschatology

This view divides Christ's second coming into two phases, one for the church that occurs before the tribulation and a second for Israel that occurs during the tribulation. Jesus' return begins with the rapture of the church (the parousia), prior to the tribulation. At this first phase of his return dead believers will be raised, and living Christians will meet Christ in the air and triumphantly go to heaven. This spectacular event prompts Jews to recognize Christ as their Messiah, and many are converted during the subsequent period.

The tribulation follows this, when the Antichrist attacks Israel. This world ruler will be defeated at Armageddon by Jesus Christ and his heavenly forces (Rev. 19) during the second phase of his second coming. At that time the dead saints and the tribulation martyrs will be raised, and Christ will reign for 1,000 years on earth with Jerusalem as the capital of his kingdom. This will be a time of peace and righteousness, with evil held in check. The purpose of this millennial period is to fulfill the Old Testament promises given to Israel. God had promised Abraham that his descendants would possess the land of Canaan (Gen. 12); that they would have a privileged and prosperous place in the world (Ps. 72); and that one of David's descendants, the Messiah, would rule over the Israelites (Isa. 11). Then Satan will

Premillennial Pretribulational (Dispensationalism)

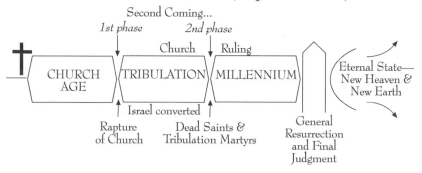

be loosed, and there will be wars on Jerusalem. This is followed by the "Great White Throne" judgment and the creation of the new heaven and new earth.

Closely tied to "dispensationalism," this view dominated evangelicalism much of this century. However, recently it has begun losing support. A key issue is whether the Old Testament promises can be so sharply disconnected from the realities that the church experiences. The New Testament appears to insist that the Old Testament promises are now being fulfilled within the church (1 Peter 2:9).

Postmillennial Eschatology

In this view, Jesus' second coming will occur after the millennium. Jesus bound Satan during his earthly life (Rev. 20:2–3; cf. Matt. 12:29; Luke 10:18), and he has not only commanded the church to extend his rule throughout the whole world (Matt. 28:18–20), but even promised that nothing will resist the church's onward march (Matt. 16:18). Consequently, there will be an unprecedented revival in the church preceding Christ's return. Through its preaching and acts of self-sacrificial love, which bring social justice and improving conditions, the church is extending the kingdom of God. Christian values are pervading the world, transforming the ills that beset society (such as slavery, injustice, sickness), and progressively bringing the world under the rule of God.

Simply put, the millennium is not a visible reign of Christ on earth, but an invisible spiritual reign of Jesus through the power of the church. The church brings about the millennium, not the visible presence of Jesus Christ! At the end of the millennium Satan will be unleashed for a little while (Rev. 20:7–8) and the tribulation will occur (1 Tim. 4:1–3; Matt. 24:14, 27), though believers will survive. Then, at Christ's second coming, the dead

Postmillennial

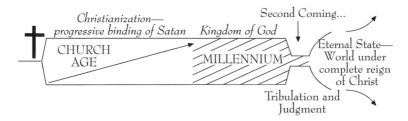

will be raised and the final judgment will take place. The world will finally be under the complete reign of Christ.

Postmillennialism was the dominant view of some conservative Protestants in the nineteenth century. Affirming God's goal to restore creation to its original perfect state through evangelism and social action, it motivated many to take up the cause of abolition, women's rights, and care for the poor. In recent times, with the perception of worsening conditions in the world, postmillennialism has fallen out of favor. Opponents also charge that it fails to do justice to Scripture's pessimism about the human condition (Mark 13) and some biblical prophecies (Rev. 20).

Amillennial Eschatology

Amillennialism is not as unduly optimistic about the future as postmillennialism. This position insists that we are *now* in the so-called "millennium," since Christ bound Satan, established the kingdom in part, and now reigns in the church and the hearts of the redeemed. Simply put, we are in the "last days." As we get nearer the final end there will be increasing wickedness (tribulations). The church, however, eagerly looks forward to Christ's second coming. At that time, all living believers will meet Christ in the air and will return with him to earth. Then the world will be under the complete reign of Christ; that is to say, the consummated kingdom will finally exist.

This view has been popular from the fourth century on, especially after Constantine was converted and made Christianity a legal religion. Christianity subsequently gained popularity and ascendancy, and the church viewed itself as making the kingdom present. It has been especially popular with many in the Reformed tradition, which stresses the transformation of the present world until Christ comes again.

Critics suggest that amillennialism diminishes evil's destructive power. This view usually denies that the end of time involves a destruction of the

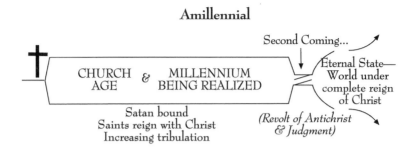

Amillennial

creation and its re-creation. Rather it envisions creation being released from the perverting powers of evil. For example, a contemporary amillennialist, Richard Mouw, in *When the Kings Come Marching In*, suggests that in Isaiah's vision of the end:

> There is no need to read the negative passages as insisting that these pagan entities as such will be destroyed. . . . My own impression is that the judgment that will visit the ships of Tarshish is of a purifying sort. . . . The judgment here is meant to tame, not destroy. . . . It is not, then, the ships as such that will be destroyed; it is their former function that will perish (Isa. 23:14).[2]

Assessment: The Future and the Church's Mission

Many of the Christian's attitudes about society, the church's role in the world, the value of education, involvement in the culture, and interest in political processes reflect his or her eschatological views. Certainly these millennial views directly affect the church's understanding of her mission in the world. For instance, the predominance of pretribulational premillennialism among evangelicals has had the effect of stimulating financial assistance for modern-day Israel, since those who hold this view believe that the current nation is to be the recipient of God's Old Testament promises. (The perhaps unintentional side effect has been the near neglect of Palestinian Christian brothers and sisters in the same region.)

The indictment of premillennial dispensationalism for its pessimism about the church's ability to shape society is well-trod. However, this may be due more to early dispensationalism's spiritualized view of the kingdom for those in the church than a problem inherent in premillennialism itself. Admittedly, if one's "only hope" is the Second Coming, then one may not be eager to get involved in social action. As we heard from pulpits when growing up, "Getting involved in social action is like rearranging deck chairs on the *Titanic*." So the emphasis is on "saving souls." The popular movie *A Thief in the Night* illustrates this position well; the sole concern of Christians in the film is that people not be left behind when Jesus comes unexpectedly. While this position often discourages attempts to transform society on political, economic, and social levels, it places a strong emphasis on the Christian's hope and his or her future in Christ. On the other hand, amillennialists and postmillennialists are frequently praised because they stress the church's role in evangelizing and transforming society (the two going hand-in-hand).

It is important to note that any assessment of eschatological views is making an implicit judgment regarding what constitutes effective action. For instance, postmillennialists and amillennialists value working through the system, that is, through the normal political and social means. But doesn't the pervasive and systemic nature of sin question that assumption? If evil has a stranglehold on the world, including its political, economic, and social structures, don't these structures shape our understanding of the problem and even blind us to other alternatives, perhaps more moral ones? Contemporary historical studies have shown how Christians active in missions and social action have frequently carried out the American ideology, class structure, and racism of the establishment.

If Jesus' consummation of the kingdom will establish a qualita-

Eschatology and Slavery

Eschatology has been a "hot topic" among twentieth-century theologians. But James Cone rightly points out that in their sermons, prayers, and songs African-Americans were talking about eschatological hope long before contemporary discussions: "The vision of the future and of Jesus as the Coming Lord is the central theme of black religion" (Cone, *God of the Oppressed,* 129).

Black slaves fed their struggle for freedom in this world with a vision of the coming of Jesus and the New Jerusalem. Jesus was the one who would return, liberate the oppressed from slavery, and take them home to glory. The vision of heaven gave black slaves a new identity that contradicted the value system of the slave owners who treated them like cattle. As Cone puts it, "The future reality of Jesus means that what is contradicts what ought to be" (p. 131).

The hope of justice and vindication is vividly portrayed in "The Judgment Day," one of seven plantation sermons of black preachers set into poetic verse by James Weldon Johnson (1871–1938) and published as *God's Trombones* (Viking/Penguin, 1990). This sermon graphically envisions "one of these mornings" when God calls for Gabriel to blow his silver trumpet and "wake the living nations": "God's a-going to rain down fire" and divide the sheep from the goats. The former, "who've come through great tribulations," will enter into God's kingdom wearing starry crowns and silver slippers, holding harps, feasting on milk and honey, singing new songs of Zion, and "chattering with the angels." But the goats will fall headlong like lumps of lead for seven days "into the big, black, red-hot mouth of hell, belching out fire and brimstone"; and "God will stop his ears." Then, "with a wave of his hand God will blot out time, and start the wheel of eternity."

tively new reality, different from this corrupted world, shouldn't his people be working for goals that the system does not expect? Herein lies some of premillennialism's strength. The premillennialist's expectation of a new heaven and earth, qualitatively different from the present, means that they are not bound to the system and have suggested radically new ideas. Premillennialism originally envisioned and provided the motivation for the worldwide missionary initiative in modern times. At the turn of the century, premillennialists were leaders in evangelizing and providing social help to those the political establishment had already discarded—the alcoholics and prostitutes.[3] The dispensationalist W. E. Blackstone (1841–1935) was a political visionary, in an isolationist and jingoist America, who vigorously worked for a land for persecuted Russian Jews and advocated an international court of justice where national disputes could be justly settled. His advocacy significantly aided the Zionist movement in America, as well as President Wilson's promotion of a World Court.

On the other hand, some argue that while premillennialism takes Scripture seriously and literally (e.g., *really* 1,000 years), it has often led to a wooden interpretation of the Bible such that there is an unwillingness to be surprised by unexpected ways in which prophecy might be fulfilled. After many people who took the Jewish Scriptures quite seriously missed the first coming of Jesus, one cannot be too careful about being too careful! At the same time, we must note that some of the leading proponents of social action and evangelism in the nineteenth century (such as Charles Finney) were committed postmillennialists.

Regardless of where one "plants" oneself on this issue, all the views presented affirm that Jesus Christ is Lord of history and that history is going somewhere—that it has meaning. God's purposes are ensured!

For Further Reflection

1. In one sitting, read Romans 8:21–28 and Revelation 20–22. What are your observations? What do these passages say about the future?
2. If you had to choose between the four views of the millennium presented in this chapter, with which would you side? Why?
3. Take some time for personal inventory: How have your views about evangelism and social action been influenced by your ideas about the return of Christ and the end of the world as we know it?

For Further Reading

Clouse, Robert G., ed. *The Meaning of the Millennium: Four Views.* Downers Grove, Ill.: InterVarsity, 1977.

Ellul, Jacques. *The Presence of the Kingdom.* Colorado Springs: Helmers and Howard, 1989, chapter 7.

Grenz, Stanley J. *The Millennial Maze: Sorting Out Evangelical Options.* Downers Grove, Ill.: InterVarsity, 1992.

Part 3

Living Faithfully Now

nine

How the Family Got Its Start: The Early Church

he Zoblinski family has had a long heritage. Pasted into their family album are photographs of grandparents and great-grandparents and great-great grandparents. Tucked away in the pockets are yellowed, tattered documents that go back two hundred years to when the family was in Poland. Stories have been passed down from generation to generation, and although these stories have been embellished as time has gone on, they communicate certain family traits, some of which have been passed on and some of which are merely memories of bygone days. In fact, the present family members often enjoy a good laugh as they recall the ways in which their ancestors did things and related to others around them. But just as often the modern-day Zoblinskis detect many resemblances between the attitudes and behaviors of their forebears and those of their own.

That is the way it is with the Christian family too. We have a rich heritage that goes back many centuries. Recounting the ways in which *our* forebears viewed the culture and behaved in society conjures up all kinds of sentiments in us: remorse, embarrassment, pride, joy, satisfaction, curious wonder, and so on. It all depends on which branch of the tree we happen to be sitting on and which branch we are looking at (including how far down the tree we are looking). Like the Zoblinskis, we learn much about ourselves when we look at our varied past. We find out what it means to be on our particular side of the family tree, we become aware

of how we differ from the attitudes and behaviors that have characterized other sides of the tree, and we learn how we can do better in the
future.

Each generation of the Christian church has interpreted and applied the
biblical categories of a Christian worldview (which we looked at in part 2)
in various ways. As a result, the manner in which the church related to the
society in which it found itself has differed. We are heirs of these differences, and as we look at the history of our family, focusing on its attitudes
and actions relative to the culture, you should come to a better understanding of who you are and where you fit in. Which grandparent do you
and your church resemble the most, and what are the features that you
recognize in these old snapshots?

We will begin this part of the book with a general typology of the church's
varying relationships to the prevailing culture. Then we will continue with
an examination of the early church's relationship to its culture, focusing
on the first three centuries of Christianity, up to about 312. Enjoy thumb-
ing through your family album!

Being a Faithful Witness to Christ in this World

Every Christian exists as a witness of Jesus Christ in a specific culture.
The Apostle Paul addressed his letters to the saints who were in Rome,
Corinth, Ephesus, or some other specific city (see Rom. 1:7; 1 Cor. 1:2; Eph.
1:1). These letters to people in specific places help us pose the central question facing every believer: How are we to live in this world—specifically,
our part of the world—and be obedient witnesses of Jesus Christ? What
stance should we as Christians take toward the prevailing culture within
which we live? Throughout its history, the church has developed four par-
adigmatic ways of relating to the prevailing culture as a witness of Jesus
Christ.[1]

The Church as Antithetical to the Prevailing Culture

Many Christians have insisted that the lifestyle, values, and even the
institutions of a specific culture are detrimental to confessing Jesus Christ
as Lord and obediently following him in all areas of life. Motivated by the
desire to distinguish the values of the Gospel from those of the prevailing
culture, they tend to *withdraw* and *separate* from certain cultural involvements. The youth pastor who burns rock albums, for example, is one expression of separatism or antithesis. But withdrawal assumes different forms.
The monks in the early church *physically* separated from their culture and

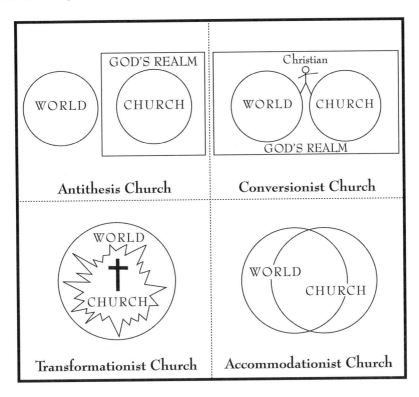

took up residence in remote locations because their prevailing culture distracted them from obedience to Jesus Christ. Amish communities are separated not only physically, but also *socially* from other Americans. Fundamentalist Christians at the turn of the century were integrated with some aspects of American culture; in other respects, they presented an alternative to the prevailing order, *mentally* withdrawing through their Christian conception of reality, truth, and values, which was evident in their family practices and religious and educational institutions.

The Church as Converting Individuals within the Prevailing Culture

Some Christians insist that the sinful structures of this world will never be rectified until the Second Coming, when Jesus Christ re-creates this cosmos. Christ's work in this period "between the times" concentrates solely upon the individual's personal guilt and need for reconciliation to God and neighbor. As a result, the church's mission is to convert individuals. Certainly believers will demonstrate the lordship of Christ in their thoughts and actions, especially by challenging the distorted political and social values in the culture around them and by demonstrating a self-sacrificial love to others. But Jesus does not call the church to a political or even social agenda. The church as an institution is to debate the culture, but not to be engaged in political actions to try to better it. Simply put, this view says save souls, not society.

The Church as Transforming the Prevailing Culture

After the Roman emperor Constantine became a Christian (A.D. 312), many church leaders attempted to establish a Christian society. Jesus, they insisted, called the church to better society—to rectify social institutions so that they are obedient to God. Christian values, they argued, should dominate society. The degree of success differed in the various historical settings in which the transformation view was put into practice. In some localities, the Medieval and even the Reformation church imposed Christian *values* and even a specific confession upon all members of society. Those resisting this belief were expelled or in some other way eliminated. With freedom of religion, this type of domination is no longer feasible in the Western world. But some proponents from the Religious Right, a contemporary example of the transformation model, apparently would be content to impose Christian *values* on American culture by political and legal means. Still other groups, such as many evangelical liberal arts colleges, are just as eagerly striving to transform society, yet with more subtlety in their use of media, educational, economic, and social institutions.

The Church as Accommodating and Adapting to the Prevailing Culture

Throughout the church's history, many Christians have perceived no great tension between their commitment to Christ and being in the world. They see this world as God's creation and the Lord as still being active in the purest aspirations and desires of culture. As a result, they work by conforming, modifying, compromising, and accommodating themselves to the values of society. They maintain that the culture's search for truth and its movements for social change and justice all reflect God's activity. Jesus Christ and his acts of love and justice are the supreme exemplification of God's universal work throughout his cosmos. Consequently, the church is to be active in all aspects of culture and should aid the recognition of God's work wherever it is found.

Which Way Is Best?

The question "What stance should I as a Christian take toward this prevailing culture?" is complex and difficult precisely because it is so far-reaching. As the above four different models illustrate, each answer assumes many theological decisions. Your answer necessarily makes assumptions regarding the effects of sin (Is sin personal or structural?), the nature of social institutions (Are the political and economic orders the instruments of Satan or God's authoritative means for keeping order?), the church (Is the church a political agent or simply a fellowship for believers?), Jesus Christ and his work (Is Jesus an example, a Justifier of our sins and a Sanctifier, or the King of the universe now?). Yet every believer, knowingly or unknowingly, answers the question of cultural stance in some way or another.

As we said, in this part of the book we will present historical examples of these varying models. By examining these differing models, you will begin to see the interconnection between differing theological stances, as well as the implicit assumptions you may have already made. The purpose, of course, is to help prepare us so that we can faithfully confess Jesus as Lord in our culture today.

The Early Church in Its Jewish Religious Context

Sometimes we forget that the earliest Christians were Jewish—in their religious practices, worship, Scriptures, and ethical behavior. In fact, at first they were considered a sect of Judaism. They differed from other Jews primarily in their belief that Jesus of Nazareth was the Messiah and that he was coming again very soon. But that did not necessarily make them less Jewish. In fact, they sometimes argued that they were more Jewish—the true Israel in a new age, the age of the Spirit (see Joel 2:28; Acts 2:16–21).

But as Christianity spread outside of Judea, questions arose about the status of Gentiles (non-Jews) who were confessing Jesus as Lord and joining the Jewish-Christian communities. At the same time, because the Jewish-Christian church existed in and evangelized in a Greek culture it was not always easy to keep the influences of the culture out of the church. This created tensions in the church: they were united when it came to their belief in Jesus, but they were divided over many other issues.[2]

The church was able to compromise at one crucial point (see Acts 15). A council of leaders met at Jerusalem, the mother church, to hear the testimony of different factions. It was decided that Gentile converts should be recognized as full members of God's covenant people, even if they were not circumcised (which was the Jewish sign of membership in God's covenant community). The only requirement was that they abstain from a handful of practices that Jewish Christians would find particularly offensive. This was a daring decision made by the Jewish Christians in Jerusalem. They must have recognized that it would mean being ostracized by their Jewish neighbors. That is precisely what happened, and these magnanimous Christians suffered economically as a result. (This is why during his later missionary travels Paul collects money for the Jerusalem church; for example, see Romans 15:25–27, where Paul mentions the debt the Gentiles owe the Jerusalem saints.) These early Jewish Christians were willing to sacrifice their own success for the expansion of the Gospel to the Gentile world.

Eventually, Christianity was severed from its Jewish roots and was no longer considered a sect of Judaism. This happened in stages. In A.D.70 the Romans smashed Jerusalem and the temple in response to Jewish revolts (66–70). More than a million Jews were killed or sold into slavery. In the midst of this there was some Jewish antipathy toward the Jews who were Christians, and Christians began to distinguish themselves from the Jews (such as by meeting on Sundays instead of Saturdays). After the Jews had instigated a second revolt against Rome, Emperor Hadrian published an edict in 135 that ordered the expulsion of all Jews (including Jewish Christians, even though they had not participated in the revolt) from Judea. The result was that Jerusalem became a virtually Greek city with a completely Gentile-Christian church, and the center of Christianity shifted from Jerusalem to Antioch and, especially, Rome. The future of Christianity would now be in Gentile hands, as the new religion spread throughout the Mediterranean world.

The Early Church in Its Hellenistic Intellectual Context

Hellenism was the policy established by Alexander the Great in the fourth century B.C. in order to share the benefits of Greek civilization with those he had conquered. By New Testament times it had unified the world in language and culture. Hellenistic thought and patterns of life affected both Judaism and Christianity. This could not be avoided in the latter's case, for Christianity grew up on Greek soil.

The most telling point at which Greek culture influenced Christian thought involved the application of the concept of Logos to Jesus Christ. It involved an attempt by the church to relate the Gospel to the culture by packaging the message in cultural terms.

The Logos concept was used by the Apologists.[3] These were Christian writers from about 120 to 220 who made a reasoned defense of Christianity to people outside the church, particularly to Greeks and Jews. Appealing to the equivalent of twentieth-century "yuppies," these Christian intellectuals sought to show that Christianity was politically harmless and culturally superior to paganism. They dealt with popular misunderstandings and slanderings of Christianity that arose from pagan philosophy and Jewish objections.[4]

Part of the challenge facing the Apologists was this: How do you explain Jesus Christ to someone who reads and loves Plato? They decided that the best way to do this was to borrow contemporary philosophical ideas to present Christianity to an intellectually sophisticated Greek culture in a systematic and intelligible fashion. Christianity adapted well in their capable hands.

As implied above, a favorite ploy of these Apologists in answering Greek intellectuals and Jewish objectors was to refer to Christ as the Logos of God. In Greek thought, the *Logos* (which is translated as "Word" in our Bibles) was the universal principle that permeated and governed everything. It gave order and unity to the universe. Jewish thought had employed a similar concept (using the Hebrew *dabar* instead of the Greek *logos*), though it was conceived as the mediator of God's creative activity (Ps. 33:9) and his special revelation to humans (Deut. 4:13; Jer. 1:9). One philosopher with Greek and Jewish roots, Philo, combined these two concepts. With good precedent, namely John's writings (John 1:1, 14; 1 John 1:1; Rev. 19:13), the Apologists argued that the Logos that created and sustained the universe and that permeated everything had come to us in the flesh in the person of Jesus the Messiah.

But unlike John, the Apologists did not argue that this Word "shines in the darkness, but the darkness has not understood it" (John 1:5). In fact, the very opposite conclusion was crucial to their apologetic strategy. Not only did the Apologists insist that the noble insights of Greek philosophy originate from the Logos, but that Socrates (ca. 470–399 B.C.) was a Christian! Their conception of Jesus, called Logos Christology, downplayed the significance of his historical particularity. They argued that one can know the Logos, and even have salvific communion with God, outside of knowing Jesus Christ. While the Apologists' strategy did help overcome their culture's resistance to Christianity, in the end their theology tended to simply sanction their culture's prior understanding of the cosmos.

The Early Church in Its Roman Political Context

Christianity was born heir to the *pax Romana* that had brought peace and stability to the Roman Empire under Caesar Augustus (27 B.C.–A.D.

14). The empire stretched over an immense geographical area, was highly organized, touted a sophisticated civilization, and was unified under the leadership of an absolute ruler, the emperor, who often claimed the status of divinity. Still, the empire was never without its social and political problems.

For the first thirty years of its existence, the Christian church was thought of as simply a part of Judaism and enjoyed the legal protection that was given to Judaism by Rome. Rome respected Jewish monotheism as one of the religious options permitted in the empire under the rule, "one people, one religion." The Romans tolerated religious cults provided that they did not encourage sedition or weaken public morality. Since the worship of the emperor helped to maintain unity and stability throughout the empire, no religion would be tolerated if it posed a threat to the imperial cult. Beyond that, Rome was very tolerant. She believed that her military success was due largely to her piety in worshiping all the gods in the empire. It was thought that a state could prosper only through the favor of the gods, and Rome thought she had her bases covered and her bets hedged.

But the tide turned for the Christian church in the 60s, as the state turned from protector to persecutor.[5] For several decades there was no settled Roman policy regarding Christians. Some local governors actually protected Christians. Much depended on imperial whims and pretensions to divinity. In fact, Roman officials probably did not take Christianity all that seriously until the third century when it was realized just how far and wide it had spread as a new religion. (For example, by the end of the second century, Christianity had reached the upper strata of society.) Before that time, the persecutions of Christians were limited and inconsistent.[6] And the persecutions that did occur spurred church growth, such that the third-century theologian Tertullian remarked, "The blood of the martyrs is the seed of the church."

Why did the state turn persecutor? At least three categories of reasons can be given.

First, there were *religious* reasons. The Romans feared the displeasure of the gods and the threat this posed to the security of the empire. All people were expected to make some sacrifice to the gods to forestall harm or to insure victory in battles. Along with this, they were to worship the emperor. But the monotheistic Christians refused. They worshiped one God, and their allegiance to this God could not be compromised. As the Romans began losing to the barbarians in the third century, they suspected it was due to the Christians' hostility to the ancient gods, who had assured Rome's earlier victories.[7]

Second, there were *political* reasons for the state's persecution of Christians. Church members were seen as subversives and unpatriotic citizens. They would not burn incense to the emperor, since they pledged allegiance to God alone. For them, since Jesus was Lord, Caesar could not be. Christians refused to participate in warfare or to endorse capital punishment, because they believed it was wrong to kill. They would not engage in some professions and businesses, such as the theater. All of this led to a repeated accusation: Christians were charged with "hatred of the human race." But to their credit, though they were largely uninvolved in Roman political and social life, their lives and their deaths were strong witnesses to the integrity of their faith.

Finally, there were *social* reasons for Rome's antipathy toward Christians. Through misunderstandings and rumors, fueled by Christian practices such as prudently worshiping in secret, calling each other brother and sister, baptism, and Communion, early Christians were often accused of incest, child sacrifice, and cannibalism at nocturnal meetings.

It got worse for the church before it got better. The earlier persecutions had been sporadic and of varying intensity. At its worst, for example, Nero had used Christians as human torches for illuminating the imperial gardens. Many Christians were thrown to the lions or burned on crosses to entertain the Roman populace. Nevertheless, a more subtle persecution was constant: the Christians were treated as social outcasts and deviants. Christians regularly risked their property and even their lives to confess the name of Christ.

In the third century, harsh persecution became more comprehensive and systematic, though still dependent on the emperor's personal attitude toward the church. In the mid-200s, for example, Decius attempted the systematic extermination of Christianity. The last great persecution of the church was instigated by Emperor Diocletian (284–305). He had good intentions as a ruler. After decades of anarchy, inflation, political instability, and invasions, he reorganized the empire into halves (East and West) and tried to establish a kind of state socialism. He was worshiped by Roman citizens and was considered to be the earthly embodiment of the god Jupiter. In his efforts to unite the empire and enlist the aid of divinities who could ensure the success of the Roman military, he consulted an oracle that revealed to him that Christians were responsible for bad relations and poor communication with the gods. He responded by issuing an edict that ordered the destruction of all churches, the surrender of all Bibles and liturgical books, the confiscation of sacred vessels (such as communion cups), and the cessation of all worship meetings. A few months later a second edict ordered the arrest of all clergy; however, since the prisons could not hold them all, a general amnesty was eventually given to all of those who offered a sacrifice to the gods. Finally, in 304 all Christians were required to sacrifice to the gods. Refusal meant death.

To prove one had made the required sacrifice, one had to obtain a certificate that provided the evidence that a sacrifice to the gods had been made. Some Christians complied, bought a certificate, or hid. These were often referred to as the "lapsed." Those who refused were imprisoned or executed. The prisoners who survived were later called the "confessors"; those who died were the "martyrs."[8]

Aliens in a Pagan World

In this hostile context, the earliest Christians naturally regarded themselves as aliens in the prevailing culture. But this opposition was grounded in their faith in the Lord Jesus Christ, whose impending second coming, they believed, would bring about the destruction of this sinful and rebellious world. This perspective enabled them to see with clarity that service to Jesus Christ must be sharply distinguished from alliances with this world, and this in turn motivated them to oppose this world.

A believer writing around 180 described the life of Christians:

> They live in their own countries, but only as aliens. . . . They marry, like everyone else, and they beget children, but they do not cast out their offspring. They share their board with each other, but not their marriage bed. . . . They busy themselves on earth, but their citizenship is in heaven. They obey the established law, but in their own lives they go far beyond what the laws required. They love all men and by all men are persecuted. They are unknown, and still they are condemned, they are put to death, and yet they are brought to life. They are poor, and yet they make many rich, they are completely destitute, and yet they enjoy complete abundance. . . . They are reviled and yet they bless.[9]

Christians took quite literally Jesus' statement that one cannot serve two masters, God and mammon (Matt. 6:24). Not only did they refuse worship of the Roman emperor, but any form of service that could not be engaged for the sake of Jesus Christ. As Tertullian (200) put it,

> There is no agreement between . . . the standard of Christ and the standard of the devil, the camp of light and the camp of darkness. One soul cannot be due to two masters—God and Caesar.[10]

Actually they resisted any entanglement which could compromise their obedience to Jesus Christ. The enticements of this world—its ostentatiousness, frivolity, sensual gratifications—were refused. Tertullian articulated the argument: "Will the neck that wears a necklace bow before the ax of the executioner? Will the ankles adorned with bracelets submit to the pressure of the screw?"[11] The church must refuse luxury, not simply because it excites lust for more, but because it strangles absolute obedience to Jesus Christ, even to the point of death.

Conversion consequently involved a complete break from the pagan world to a new life in Christ. Indeed, baptism was the sign that one had renounced Satan and his evil ways and was now consecrated to Jesus Christ. The sign of the cross, representing their Lord's sufferings by which he conquered Satan, was placed on their forehead, marking every believer as a soldier of Jesus Christ (*milites Christi*) against the kingdom of Satan. The sign of the cross began every day, marked even every transaction, and displayed trust in Christ's victory and a self-sacrificial service to others. The pattern of Jesus' death and resurrection shaped the Christian's week. Friday was partially set aside for following the crucified Christ—by fasting and repentant prayer—in order to crucify the old man. Sunday was exempt from all signs of penance, such as kneeling or fasting, in order to celebrate the risen Christ who had raised the sinner to a life of fellowship with God.

Life among Christians was qualitatively different from that of Roman society. Unlike the class system ordering Roman culture, Christians accepted each other as equals. Slaves were recognized as brothers and sisters by other Christians; no one refused to give the kiss of fellowship. These Christian congregations freely shared among themselves to relieve the needs of the poor and sick believers. As the *Epistle of Barnabas* (120–140) comments:

Martyrdom of Polycarp (ca. 69–ca. 155)

He stepped forward and was asked by the proconsul if he really was Polycarp. When he said yes, the proconsul urged him to deny the charge.... "Swear by Caesar's fortune; change your attitude; say: 'Away with the godless!' ... [E]xecrate Christ."

"For eighty-six years," replied Polycarp, "I have been his servant, and he has never done me wrong: how can I blaspheme my king who saved me?"

... retorted the governor, "I'll have you destroyed by fire, unless you change your attitude."

Polycarp answered: "The fire you threaten burns for a time and is soon extinguished: there is a fire you know nothing about—the fire of the judgment to come and of eternal punishment, the fire reserved for the ungodly. But why do you hesitate? Do what you want."...

When the pyre was ready... Polycarp prayed: "O Father of thy beloved and blessed Son Jesus Christ, through whom we have come to know thee, the God of angels and powers and all creation, and of the whole family of the righteous who live in thy presence; I bless thee for counting me worthy of this day and hour, that in the number of the martyrs I may partake of Christ's cup, to the resurrection of eternal life of both soul and body in the imperishability that is the gift of the Holy Spirit...."

When he had offered up the Amen and completed his prayer, the men in charge lit the fire, and a great flame shot up.

You must share all things with your neighbor and must not say that they are your own property; for if you are sharers in that which is incorruptible, how much more in that which is corruptible?[12]

Congregations even collected funds for unknown believers who were imprisoned because of their faith. Requesting funds for Christians held for ransom in another locality, Cyprian, the Bishop of Carthage, pleaded, "We cannot regard the imprisonments of our brethren but as our own, nor their sufferings but as ours, since we are united with them in one body."[13] Rejected by society, the church became believers' new family and the center of their fellowship, lives, and hopes.[14]

Although socially ostracized, Christians responded like Christ, with a love for their enemies. When an epidemic devastated Carthage in 254, the fear of infection prompted many to discard the dead and dying in the streets. Cyprian charged his church to rectify the situation by tending to the sick and burying the dead.

If we merely show kindness to our own people, we do no more than publicans and heathens; as genuine Christians we must overcome evil by good, love our enemies as our Lord exhorts us, and pray for our persecutors. Since we are born of God, we must show ourselves worthy of our origin by imitating our Father's goodness.[15]

Christians, Cyprian noted, "do not speak great things, but live them."[16] Simply put, the church expected Christians to be like Christ. Salvation must bring a life of righteousness and love.

Conclusion

The church often experienced ambiguity and tension in relation to the Jewish religious, Hellenistic cultural, and Roman political contexts in which it was immersed. In general, though at times the early church chose not to participate in the prevailing culture and at times it was forced to go underground, it nevertheless continued to witness to its vibrant faith, whether by its apologetic literature, its loving communal existence, its prayerful concern for the culture in which it existed, or its martyrdoms.

But all of this was to change. Ambiguity and tension would more often be found *within* the church when the political context in which it existed dramatically changed. For that part of the family's history we must now turn to the Middle Ages.

For Further Reflection

1. Consider the four Christ and culture categories. With which of these does your denomination or church tradition most closely identify? Which one makes the most sense to you personally? Why?
2. Do you think the early church was right in using a secular philosophical idea (the Logos) to make Christianity relevant to their contemporaries? Are there dangers in doing this?
3. Is it harder, easier, or about the same for us to be Christians in our world today (over against the early church)?

For Further Reading

Chadwick, Henry. *The Early Church*. New York: Penguin, 1967.

Niebuhr, H. Richard. *Christ and Culture*. New York: Harper and Row, 1951.

Troeltsch, Ernst. *The Social Teachings of the Christian Churches*. Vol. 1. Trans. Olive Wyon. Chicago: University of Chicago Press, 1976.

Weaver, Mary Jo. *Introduction to Christianity*, 2d ed. Belmont, Calif.: Wadsworth, 1991.

Webber, Robert E. *The Church in the World*. Grand Rapids: Zondervan/Academie, 1986.

Wells, William W. *Welcome to the Family*. Downers Grove, Ill.: InterVarsity, 1979.

Williams, D. H. *Retrieving the Tradition and Renewing Evangelicalism*. Grand Rapids: Eerdmans, 1999.

ten

A Mixed Marriage: The Medieval Church

*T*hough the state had been hostile to Christianity, the empire and the church's response would soon make a 180 degree turn. The church's relation to the world profoundly changed when the state ceased its hostility to Christianity. Most Christians no longer remained aloof from the world, as they had when the state was their persecutor. What changed all of this was the decision of an emperor.

The Conversion of Constantine

After the persecution instigated by Diocletian, the next emperor, Galerius, was forced to admit that such a policy had not achieved its goal of wiping out the Christian church. Consequently, Galerius issued an edict of toleration in 311. It contained an admonition to the Christians to pray for the empire—sort of a "you-scratch-my-back-I'll-scratch-yours" deal.

After that, there were struggles for succession to the imperial throne, due in part to Diocletian's reorganization of the empire. In order to gain sole power of the western half of the empire, Constantine marched against Maxentius in Rome in 312. On the way to the battle, Constantine is said to have had a vision of a cross in the heavens under which he was to fight. Here is how the fourth-century historian Eusebius described it:

Accordingly he besought his father's god in prayer, beseeching and imploring him to tell him who he was and to stretch out his right hand to help him in his present difficulties. And while he was thus praying with fervent entreaty, a most incredible sign appeared to him from heaven, the account of which it might have been hard to believe had it been related by any other person. . . . He said that about noon . . . he saw with his own eyes the trophy of a cross of light in the heavens, above the sun, and an inscription CONQUER BY THIS attached to it. . . . then in his sleep the Christ of God appeared to him with the sign which he had seen in the heavens, and commanded him to make a likeness of that sign which he had seen in the heavens, and to use it as a safeguard in all engagements with his enemies.[1]

This vision turned him to the Christian faith. So, Constantine had the chi-rho (a combination of the first two Greek letters in *Christos*—XR) placed on all of his military standards (and later on his coins). He marched into battle against Maxentius at Milvian Bridge and defeated him. With Licinius, emperor of the eastern half of the empire, he issued the Edict of Milan in 313.[2] This promulgation guaranteed religious freedom for *all* people, including the Christians.

Was this an attempt to enlist the favor of whatever gods there might be? Did Constantine have a genuine conversion? (His mother was a devout Christian, though his father worshiped the sun god.) Was his conversion simply an expedient political move to cement the empire (much as politicians today might curry the favor of religious leaders)? Did he even have a vision or dream? No one today knows for sure, and historians continue to debate the issue. We shall probably never know, but we do know what effects his edict had on the Christian church. Its significance cannot be overemphasized, changing the church's role in culture.

For the first time in history, the emperor of Rome favored Christianity. Constantine even gave the church special assistance. For example, he restored church property, aided in the production of Bibles, gave certain exemptions to clergy, and built new church buildings at imperial expense. But the new toleration and the emperor's favoritism did not proscribe paganism. In fact, certain aspects of monotheistic sun worship were confused with certain aspects of Christianity (such as the institution of *Sun*day as the Christian day of worship and celebrating Jesus' birth in December at the same time as the pagan festival for the sun god). Whether this began a healthy amalgamation of church and culture is still debated today. Nonetheless, the legalization of Christianity enabled the church to participate directly in the shaping of Western culture during the next 1,000 years.

Christianity did not prove to be as good a "cement" for Constantine's empire as he might have hoped. There were controversies about the legitimacy of certain churches and bishops, as well as heated debates over the burgeoning doctrines of the Trinity and the person of Christ.

The Nicene Creed

We believe in one God the Father Almighty, Maker of heaven and earth, and of all things visible and invisible;

And in one Lord Jesus Christ, the only-begotten Son of God, begotten of the Father before all worlds, God of God, Light of Light, Very God of Very God, begotten, not made, being of one substance with the Father by whom all things were made; who for us men, and for our salvation, came down from heaven, and was incarnate by the Holy Spirit of the Virgin Mary, and was made man, and was crucified also for us under Pontius Pilate. He suffered and was buried, and the third day he rose again according to the Scriptures, and ascended into heaven, and sitteth on the right hand of the Father. And he shall come again with glory to judge both the quick and the dead, whose kingdom shall have no end.

And we believe in the Holy Spirit, the Lord and Giver of Life, who proceedeth from the Father and the Son, who with the Father and the Son together is worshiped and glorified, who spoke by the prophets. And we believe one holy catholic and apostolic Church. We acknowledge one baptism for the remission of sins. And we look for the resurrection of the dead, and the life of the world to come. Amen.

Theology and Politics

Almost immediately after Constantine became emperor the church was embroiled in a dispute about the Son, the preincarnate Jesus Christ: Was he God himself or a part of the creation (albeit a special part of the creation)? The issue was a difficult one, for Christians had been worshiping Jesus—this one who prayed to God the Father during his incarnate ministry—yet they were monotheists (believers in one God). How could they affirm the deity of the Son and the unity of God at the same time? It is important to realize that this doctrinal issue arose out of the church's confession and liturgy. Theological issues were not treated as armchair speculation for members of the early church. They were literally matters of life and death.

To settle the issue Constantine called an ecumenical council. Church leaders from all over the empire were invited to debate and resolve the issue at the Council of Nicaea in 325. They lined up on the sides of a presbyter named Arius or a bishop named Alexandria and his underling Athanasius. Arius believed that Jesus was the first of God's creation, through whom God made everything else. After all, Arius could argue that Colossians 1:15 indicated that Jesus was the firstborn of all creation. At best, the Son is like God—of a similar essence (*homoiousion*). Athanasius eventually led the way for the opposition, claiming that the Son must

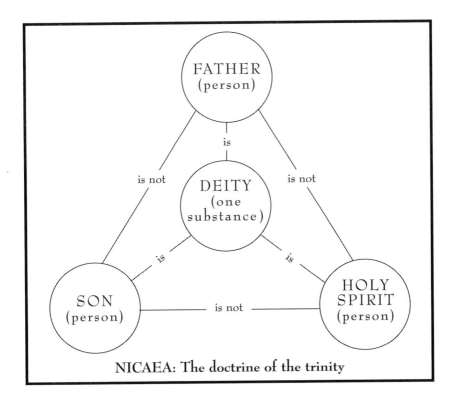

NICAEA: The doctrine of the trinity

be of the same substance or essence (*homoousion*) with the Father. For one thing, if that were not the case, to worship the Son would be idolatry. For another, that the Father begat the Son did not mean that the Father created the Son; God begets God, but God creates non-God. More importantly, in his treatise *On the Incarnation of the Word,* Athanasius argued that if the Son is not God then we have no self-revelation of God; we would be left without a true knowledge of God. But the ultimate issue is our salvation: if the Redeemer is not one with the Creator—that is, if the Redeemer is not God himself—then we are still in our sins, for no creature can redeem us. After another fifty years of discussion, the church championed Athanasius' position in the final version of the Nicene Creed— the Christian church's formal statement of the doctrine of the Trinity. The Nicene Creed summarizes the church's biblical stance that God is three persons in one essence. This does not explain it all, but it does draw boundaries around what we can say about God and still remain within the Christian church.

Once the divinity of Christ was established, the next major issue that was settled with an ecumenical creed was the question of the relation

Definition of Chalcedon

Therefore, following the holy fathers, we all with one accord teach men to acknowledge one and the same Son, our Lord Jesus Christ, at once complete in Godhead and complete in manhood, truly God and truly man, consisting also of a reasonable soul and body; of one substance (*homoousios*) with the Father as regards his Godhead, and at the same time of one substance with us as regards his manhood; like us in all respects, apart from sin; as regards his Godhead, begotten of the Father before the ages, but yet as regards his manhood begotten, for us men and for our salvation, of Mary the Virgin, the God-bearer (*Theotokos*); one and the same Christ, Son, Lord, Only-begotten, recognized in two natures, without confusion, without change, without division, without separation; the distinction of natures being in no way annulled by the union, but rather the characteristics of each nature being preserved and coming together to form one person and subsistence, not as parted or separated into two persons, but one and the same Son and Only-begotten God the Word, Lord Jesus Christ; even as the prophets from earliest times spoke of him, and our Lord Jesus Christ himself taught us, and the creed of the Fathers has handed down to us.

between the divinity and humanity of Christ. How can God assume the form of a human being? (John 1:14) How can Jesus be 100 percent divine and 100 percent human? The numbers do not seem to add up. The church rejected Apollinarianism—which united a divine Son with a spiritless human body—as a docetic (not fully human) understanding of Christ (see chap. 6). If Christ has not taken upon himself a human soul—the seat of sin—then he cannot heal our souls. But the insistence on a divine nature and a *full* human nature can go too far in the other direction if, with an early church patriarch named Nestorius, one ends up with two persons. In that case we are left with little more than *our* relationship with God: a Jesus who voluntarily unites himself in close union with God until the two enter into an *ethical* union. But Scripture portrays Jesus not as a man trying to be like God, but God's own act and personal presence (John 1:14). Then again, it is just as wrong to do what another church leader named Eutyches did—namely, make an overcorrection in the direction of collapsing the distinction between the natures so that only one hybrid nature results after the incarnation. Both natures (human and divine) retain their integrity in Jesus Christ: the one who cried and died is God himself! Again, an ecumenical council "settled" the issue in 451. The resulting Definition of Chalcedon made it clear that Christians confess a Christ who is one person in two natures.

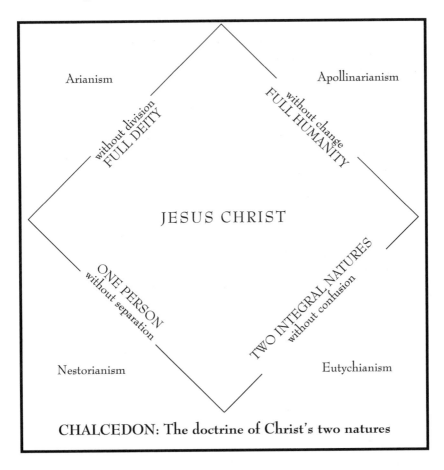

CHALCEDON: The doctrine of Christ's two natures

These major creeds—the Nicene and Chalcedonian—along with the Apostles' Creed are accepted by evangelicals as true and faithful summaries of Scripture's understanding of God and Christ. Evangelicals still use them to articulate the most basic Christian doctrines. In fact, to deny them would be tantamount to placing oneself outside the Christian church.

What we have skipped in this account of the development of these creeds and the councils that produced them is the political intrigue that was involved at each step. Emperors and empresses not only called councils, but church officials sometimes played dirty pool and gained influence at court to sway doctrinal decisions at these meetings. These were no four-day theology conferences at the "Nicene Hilton." It was becoming painfully obvious that the church and the world were mutually affecting each other in a new synthesis, but not without a protest from monks.

The Apostles' Creed

I believe in God the Father Almighty, Maker of heaven and earth,
And in Jesus Christ his only Son, our Lord, who was conceived by the Holy Ghost,
born of the Virgin Mary, suffered under Pontius Pilate, was crucified, dead, and
buried; he descended into hell; the third day he rose again from the dead; he
ascended into heaven, and sitteth on the right hand of God the Father Almighty;
from thence he shall come to judge the quick and the dead.
I believe in the Holy Ghost; the holy catholic Church; the communion of saints; the
forgiveness of sins; the resurrection of the body; and the life everlasting. Amen.

Monasticism—Protest Against a Worldly Church

When the state stopped being hostile toward the church, certain elements of the church became "worldly." Christianity was being secularized as it enjoyed prosperity and patronage. Doctrinal and political strife became more common. There were mixed motives for holding public office and for becoming a Christian (much like Russians after the downfall of Communism who now found it "fashionable" to be seen going to worship on Sundays).

The monastic movement arose in part as a reaction to all of this. It became a kind of reform movement and a protest against the world and a worldly church—a "culture church." It was a way of saying that the church did not receive its definition and mandate from the secular state. It was a witness to the fact that the kingdom of this world is not coterminous with the kingdom of God and that the meaning of the Christian life is not exhausted by life lived in the secular world. It was a reminder to the church that the "last days" had not yet come, that the kingdom of God is not of this world, and that there is still a tension between this age and the age to come.

The monastic protest began in the desert, particularly in Egypt. These early hermits practiced monastic disciplines or *asceticism*—acts of self-denial and self-renunciation (e.g., fasting, silence).[3] By giving up small things, they believed, greater things could be had. Some went too far with all of this, such as the Stylites who sat for long periods of time on poles set high in the air. The idea behind it all was to achieve a full Christian life—perfection—that was thought to be unattainable in existing churches and in contact with a despotic, pagan, and immoral Roman culture. Some sought to do this in monastic communities (such as the Benedictines), balancing their cloistered lives in acts of work, study, and prayer, over against the unbalanced outside world.

Monasticism became an early expression of one option that the church took in relating to the secular culture that surrounded it—namely, withdrawal. But this did not lessen its influence, for monasticism has profoundly impacted the Western world. These monks were the major missionary arm of the church during the Medieval period, and Europe was won to Christianity largely through their efforts. Monastics also copied, studied, and preserved the great books of Western culture. They taught people how to read them as well; monastic schools were the great educational institutions during the first half of the Middle Ages. In fact, many of the great Medieval scholars and theologians were monks, such as Augustine, Anselm of Canterbury, and Thomas Aquinas.

Monasticism would take on a different flavor by the thirteenth century with the rise of friars and the mendicant orders. Instead of cloistering together, the friars served society by moving into the new growing cities. One of the most famous was Francis of Assisi, who gave away his wealth and devoted himself to a life of preaching and service to the needy. He eventually had a growing band of followers, who are known to this day as the Franciscans (or Order of Friars Minor). Other mendicant orders (such as the Dominicans) also arose at this time.

The Growing Synthesis of the Church and the World

Monasticism was by no means the option that most Christians chose in response to the prevailing culture during the Middle Ages. At the beginning of the fifth century the Roman Empire lay in shambles. Internally it had been weakened by immorality, paganism, despotic rulers, famine, disease, and a weakened economy. Externally it had been invaded by the Visigoths. As we mentioned in the previous chapter (see chap. 9, n. 7), Augustine (354–430), a bishop in North Africa, had written *The City of God* to exonerate Christians from the blame that had been heaped upon them for the demise of the Roman Empire. The explanation was to be found in Rome's sinful history. And that history was just part of the drama of a much larger history that had been set in motion since the creation and Fall and which would conclude with the final establishment of God's kingdom.

In the meantime, Augustine argued that Christians are members of two cities—the city of this world and the city of God. Each city is a community of people who are united by a common love. The former love themselves, the flesh, the devil, or sin; the latter love God. These spiritual loyalties cut across lines of church and society. That is, not all of those who live in the visible church are members of the city of God; lovers of the world and lovers of God coexist in the visible church. Members of the city of God must coexist in secular society with those who are members of the city of this world. Someday there will be a final separation of these two communities, but for now there is a mixture.

During this age, before the return of Christ, Christians must try to influence society as much as possible, extending the boundaries of the church to embrace more and more of society. While Augustine argued that the state should not have control over the church, he insisted that Christians should serve the state as God's instrument to maintain order, encourage goodness, and punish evil. The church governed affairs of the spirit, but the state was equally necessary in this life for governing the affairs of the material world.

Integrally linked to this transformational and even domineering stance was Augustine's revision in eschatology. Augustine discarded the early church's expectation of a future millennium which Jesus alone would establish by conquering the forces of this world. Rather, he argued that Revelation 20 referred to the present age (amillennialism). Satan was bound by Jesus, and saints are reigning now with Jesus Christ through the activity of the church. Augustine's proposal meant that the church was not looking toward the future with as much expectation as before, nor could it as sharply distinguish between the kingdom of Satan and the kingdom of Christ. Attached to the prevailing culture, the church can hardly avoid being shaped by the culture's conception of the viable values, goals, and means for change.

Augustine's vision of God's sovereignty over society and the Christianizing of the state through the work of those in the city of God helped to shape the growing synthesis of church and culture that was made possible by the "legalization" of Christianity during the reign of Constantine. A look at three significant popes in the Middle Ages will give us some idea of the historical development of this fusion in which the Western church finally controlled both church and state and pieced together a new empire out of the ashes of the old. This will help us to see how a very different church-world relation arose out of Medieval Christendom than that lived out by monastics. First, however, we need to say something about the rise of bishops in the early church in order to fully appreciate the impact of these popes.

The Emergence of Bishops and the Growing Power of the Pope

Circumstances surrounding early church life gave impetus to the rise of bishops. For one thing, as we mentioned in an earlier chapter, the canon of Scripture had not been finally settled until the fourth century. In the meantime, spurious books claiming apostolic authority circulated among the churches. Furthermore, even when local churches were using the same books of Scripture, interpretations varied, and certain people claimed special insights handed down from the apostles that were not in their writings. Who could arbitrate these matters, especially when some of the ideas generated from these interpretations and special "revelations" led to heresy? Bishops like Clement of Rome and Ignatius of Antioch (early second century) and Irenaeus (late second century in Lyons, France) argued that the bishop must be the supreme authority in the church. This would guarantee unity in the church and safeguard the purity of doctrine. The guarantee of unity and purity extended to the actions of the church, so that the sacraments of baptism and the Lord's Supper were considered invalid unless done or approved by the bishop; this laid the groundwork for the medieval sacerdotal system in which the sacraments that dispensed saving grace were inextricably bound up with the authority of the priests and bishops. Additional weight was added to this claim as early as the second century when a succession of bishops could be listed, tracing an unbroken chain back to the original apostles. Though the rosters were not always identical, this was particularly significant when Roman bishops made the claim that the baton they were passing on was first handed to them by Peter—the rock upon which Christ would build his church (Matt. 16:18).

Power plays between the bishops of Rome, Carthage, Antioch, and other sees centered on issues of church discipline in the third century. The early church taught that baptism brought with it the forgiveness of past sin. But what about post-baptismal sin, particularly of a heinous nature, such as murder, fornication, or apostasy? Some bishops argued that there was no hope of restoration—no "second washing." Excommunication from the church was the consequence for such grave sins. This was serious, for all agreed with Cyprian that "outside the church there is no salvation." But as time went on, the arguments of two Roman bishops in particular won the day over those who were more strict: Callistus and Stephen, in successive eras, argued that sincere penitents might be restored to Christian fellowship and reenter the ark of the church, no matter how serious the sins. Confession, contrition, and acts of penance were required before readmission was granted. But even with these conditions, some groups in the early church, such as the Novatians and Donatists, thought that the church had become worldly and morally lax. Again, in each case Rome was on the winning side in these arguments. This was just the beginning of her dominance over other Christian centers in Western Europe as she carried the banner for the faith throughout the Middle Ages.

Gregory the Great (540–604)

Gregory the Great, called the "father of medieval papacy," found Rome in shambles when he became pope (bishop of Rome) in 590. Furthermore, Rome's position as the leader in the church was being threatened by competing claims of superiority in Constantinople.[4] The time was ripe for an able administrator to reestablish Rome's place in the world, and Gregory did just that. Through shrewd political alliances and treaties, he took the place of the secular power and secured the temporal power of the papacy. This had the added effect of spreading the power of Rome's bishop throughout the Western world.

We should mention that at the same time he did not neglect the needs of the church. In fact, Gregory was instrumental in evangelism and church renewal; he helped get the church back on its feet. Through his efforts Rome unleashed a great missionary movement, using monasteries as the beachheads for a Christian assault which eventually succeeded in evangelizing Europe. Without Rome's vision and perseverance, many of us would still be worshiping Thor, Odin, and Frigga, hanging sacrificial animals and humans on trees in sacred groves, participating in drunken orgiastic rites, and identifying right and wrong only in view of our tribe's endangerment. On the other hand, Rome's success at evangelization had the added effect of further spreading its ecclesial and political power throughout the Western world.

Leo III (d. 816)

Leo III did his part to help create the "Holy Roman Empire" when he crowned Charles the Great (Charlemagne) as its first emperor. In a church building on Christmas Day, 800, Pope Leo III dropped the crown on the head of Charles, coronating him as the "Roman Emperor" and leading the onlookers in the salute, "Hail Charles Augustus!" Charles had already expanded the empire in the name of Christianity, and this seemed to be his reward, endorsed by the church's highest authority. Whether the pope and the new emperor had carefully orchestrated the crowning moment or not, the event meant at least three things for church-state relations. First, the pope, acting as head of the church, recognized Charles as the legitimate ruler of the Western world. Second, the coronation implicitly signified that the king derived his powers from the pope, even if this had been done unwittingly. Charles retained wide powers, even over pope and papal domains, but he had strengthened the pope's hand. Third, the papacy became an office of increasing political power. As a result, Christianity became a political entity with a visible emperor, backed by the spiritual and political power of Rome's bishop who would soon assert himself over the civil power.

During this period two significant documents were forged to back the growing influence of the pope in the secular domain: the "False Decretals" and the "Donation of Constantine." The former, said to have come from early bishops of Rome, claimed that the clergy should not be subject to civil courts and that any priest might make appeals to Rome when accused of a crime. The latter purported to be Constantine's bequest of the whole Western empire to Rome's bishop in thanks for curing him of leprosy. The Roman church would use this to gain political power during the Middle Ages, and the document's validity was not questioned until the first half of the fifteenth century by Lorenzo Valla, when it was found to have been a forgery. But for some time these documents emphasized the rights of the Roman church over the civil power, enhancing papal claims to universal jurisdiction.

Thus, by the early 800s, the state had become partially sacred and the church had become partially secular. As the papacy became a political office of sorts (the pope had his own standing army and police force and collected taxes), the pope and emperor became political rivals. Papal claims continued to grow, with more and more power shifting into the pope's hands, particularly under the "two swords theory." The pope claimed the right to unsheathe the two swords of power—that of the church and that of the state.[5] This was forcefully brought to bear on several controversies, such as those involving the right to empower church officials (over against secular rulers who had claimed that right) and the

Anselm (1033–1109)

Toward the height of the medieval synthesis, one of the greatest figures of the church was Anselm. Born in North Italy, Anselm became a Benedictine abbot at Bec and later the archbishop of Canterbury.

Anselm followed in the shoes of Augustine, particularly in his theological method. At the beginning of his famous ontological argument for God's existence, Anselm stated: "For I do not seek to understand in order that I may believe, but I believe in order that I may understand. Unless I believe I shall not understand." Indeed, his very rational argument for God's existence is couched in the context of a prayer. In many ways, some contemporary movements among evangelicals echo Anselm's approach.

Anselm did not believe that the mind could fully comprehend the mysteries of the faith. But he did believe that the mind can give necessary reasons for them—why they are true. To that end, Anselm wrote *Why God Became Man*, a logical proof of the "fittingness" of the incarnation. His confidence in reason was based on an understanding of the way God put things together in the universe. God himself was largely rational and had reasons in his mind for all that he has done—reasons which we can understand.

Well liked by many, Anselm cared for the poorest of his people and was one of the first to stand as an opponent of the slave trade. It is "fitting" that in Dante's *Paradiso* he is found among the spirits of light and power in the sphere of the sun, next to St. John Chrysostom.

right to overstep the jurisdiction of secular courts whenever the church wanted to do so.

Innocent III (1160–1216)

Innocent III represented the height of papal power over secular rulers during his papacy (1198–1216). He used the "weapons" of excommunication and the interdict (the equivalent of excommunicating whole regions of people). These were formidable, since baptism, marriages, communion, last rites, and the like were denied to the excommunicated. One's daily life and eternal salvation were in the hands of the church. In true medieval style, the pope acted like the lord over his fiefs, which just happened to include all of Western Christendom. In fact, the pope's realm even extended into countries outside of the empire with which he dealt.

In the bull (papal decree) *Venerabilem*, Innocent claimed the right to bless, coronate, and invest the emperor. He retained the power to veto the choice of emperor if he did not like the one who was elected and to select his own candidate. These rights were claimed because the pope insisted he was responsible for the Roman Empire.

In fact, Innocent was the first to use the title "Vicar of Christ," indicating that the pope's office lay between God and humans and declaring that "no king can reign rightly unless he devoutly serve Christ's vicar." Supplemented by the two-swords theory, Innocent insisted that the emperor was to the pope as the body was to the soul and as the moon was to the sun. In other words, the pope's position over the secular ruler was built into the very structure of the universe.

This pope claimed to be a "Melchizedek"—the priest-king who would bring a *centralized Christian society* into being, embracing all of Western Europe. And for a brief time Innocent III did. A Christianized Europe was a reality until the synthesis began to break down in the next century.

The Theological Framework for the Medieval Synthesis

Just as the papacy coalesced power to itself, the church's theology was systematically concentrating salvific authority around the clergy.

Religious Authority

The threat of heresy in the early church had consolidated religious authority around the clergy. The medieval theologians further reinforced and developed this idea. The church, they argued, had preceded the Bible.

After all, the apostles were members of the church long before they wrote the Scripture. When the New Testament books were written, the church had guarded those writings. In time, the canon of the Bible was formulated and transmitted by the church. Moreover, Christ established the church hierarchy to interpret Scripture and even apply it to the contemporary scene. Otherwise there would be not one standard for belief and practice, but many conflicting interpretations. As a result, ultimate authority resides in the church hierarchy which authenticates, interprets, and expounds the Bible for individual Christians.

A Sacramental Conception of Salvation

The *sacramental system* provides the classic Catholic answer to the question, "How can I be saved?" According to medieval Catholic theology, the work of Jesus Christ possesses an infinite salvific power and efficacy. It overcomes human disobedience and guilt and establishes salvation. However, God conveys this grace to men and women only by means of the sacraments, the special rites which are guarded and administered by the church hierarchy. Through the sacrament of baptism the stain of original sin is washed away and the baptized person enters into the church and the process of salvation. This and other sacraments, such as the Eucharist or the Mass, penance, and confirmation, infuse into the believer a justifying grace that enables one to become more and more just. Here justification is construed as a process that changes the very character of the believer so that one comes to share the moral character of God, justness, and righteousness. God's acceptance of humans depends upon one's interior character, for God cannot commune with the unrighteous.

Ordinarily, justifying grace does not automatically elevate the believer to a new level of righteousness. The sacraments mediate only the possibility of a new stage. This new power does not become actualized unless and until it is acted upon and thereby becomes a part of one's character. The believer must make this justifying grace his or her own by doing good works. These good works are worthy of God's acceptance and thus merit more justifying grace at the next sacrament. Through this process, the believer becomes pleasing and acceptable to God. In fact, that is the goal— to become completely just and righteous internally, a saint.

This salvific process guaranteed that one would eventually arrive in heaven, if no mortal (deadly) sins were committed. But it did not guarantee that one would enter heaven *directly* after death. Unless one had attained the level of a saint, additional cleansing would be necessary after death in a place called *purgatory*.

Sacerdotalism

The Medieval church sharply distinguished between the clergy and the laity, relating them hierarchically. The sacramental system ensured this. When a bishop ordained a priest, he bestowed on that man the power to perform the sacraments. Except under extremely unusual circumstances, only a priest was allowed to baptize or to celebrate the Eucharist in a Catholic church. Simply put, the new life that Jesus offered (salvation) was transmitted *only* through the sacramental actions of the ordained clergy. This is a full-blown sacerdotalism: the clergy are the sacred conduits (*sacerdotal* = "to make sacred") of Jesus' grace and thus indispensable mediators.

Conclusion

When the world has extended its invitation to the church to become a recognized, legitimate part of society, should Christians smell compromise and withdraw for the sake of purity, or should they take advantage of the situation and attempt to dominate the culture, knowing that they will end up looking a lot like the culture in the process? Those were the medieval options: monasticism and the Holy Roman Empire. But they would not be the only options for long. The Reformation would see to that.

For Further Reflection

1. How would you answer the question posed in the final paragraph of this chapter? How would the churches with which you have been affiliated answer?
2. Can Christians who get involved in the political process and try to dominate the culture with Christian values remain unaffected by the values of the culture? Is a trade-off or some degree of compromise inevitable?
3. How are movements like the Religious Right similar to or different from that of the medieval papacy?

For Further Reading

Bell, David N. *Many Mansions: An Introduction to the Development and Diversity of Medieval Theology West and East.* Kalamazoo, Mich.: Cistercian Publications, 1996.

Gilson, Etienne. *Reason and Revelation in the Middle Ages.* New York: Scribners, 1938.

Knowles, David. *Christian Monasticism.* New York: McGraw-Hill, 1969.

Southern, R. W. *Western Society and the Church in the Middle Ages.* New York: Penguin, 1970.

eleven

From Protest to Revolution: The Protestant Reformation

*C*s a doctor of divinity, a university professor, and a priest, Martin Luther was widely regarded as a reform leader in the church by the late 1510s. But by the beginning of the next decade his life appeared forfeited as he was charged with heresy. Now on April 18, 1521, he had been summoned before Emperor Charles V and his Imperial Diet at the city of Worms and commanded to recant his writings. Luther resisted:

> Unless I am convinced by the testimony of Scripture . . . my conscience is captive to the Word of God. I cannot and will not retract anything. . . . I cannot do otherwise, here I stand, may God help me. Amen.[1]

In retrospect, Luther's courageous defiance which resulted in the Protestant Reformation stands as one of the decisive turning points in church history.

The Reformation still shapes American evangelicalism. In fact, the term "evangelical" became prominent during this period. Due to his emphasis on the *euangelion*, the good news of Jesus Christ, Luther was called an evangelical, a term Lutheran churches proudly use to this day. In a broad sense, evangelicals are those who remain faithful to the central insights of the Protestant Reformation. However, Protestantism itself is now over 400 years old and split into various denominations. The Reformation cry is a constant challenge and imperative: *ecclesia reformata semper reformanda* (the reformed church must always be reforming)! In this chapter we will review both the historical context for the Reformation as well as its central theological developments.

Context for Reform

The Institutional Church

During the Middle Ages the church became an integral part of society, indistinguishable from the world. The church calendar mandated over 150 holidays and even governed the diet. The church oversaw much of the education and sanctioned what was permissible to read. Its courts taxed as well as legislated, and it possessed the spiritual and political means to enforce its laws. At the highest institutional levels, the papacy struggled for power with Europe's political leadership. Pope Alexander VI (1492–1503) was intent on advancing the careers of his children as a cardinal, duke, princes and princesses. Pope Julius II (1503–1513) led his troops into battle to rid Italy of foreign powers. All the popes in this period furthered Rome's splendor as the artistic and cultural capital of the world. Though politically weakened, the pope and his bishops retained their regal ways and trappings as true princes of the world.

Like any institution, Rome was preoccupied with its increasing budgetary demands. The Roman church possessed great wealth and material resources. As the greatest landlord in Europe, many church positions were benefices, that is, funded by income from Rome's holdings. Usually a benefice was a good investment and so attracted many bidders. Frequently the winner was not equipped for the priesthood, and so another would be hired to perform the duties at a fraction of the annual income.[2] Thus the local parish was deprived of proper spiritual counsel, and money flowed up the hierarchy and eventually to Rome.

Those at the top acted primarily as worldly rulers rather than priests, and many at the parish level did not take their ecclesiastical duties very seriously either. The requirements for the priesthood were low. Not only were many priests barely literate, few possessed more than minimal knowledge about the Bible. Moral requirements were even more appalling. Though forbidden to marry, priests often kept concubines. Before his career as a Reformer, for instance, Zwingli was public about his own sexual failings. But that did not exclude him from candidacy for the position of priest at Zurich; in fact his key rival was said to be the father of six.

In short, the church had conformed to the world. Much of the populace was affronted by the wealth, corruption, and immorality of the clergy.[3]

The Religious Situation

The medieval theological system, in which salvific authority coalesced around the clergy and its sacramental work, accentuated these problems. The grace of Jesus Christ available through the sacraments was justifying, that is, it ensured one's final destiny in heaven and could make one more just and righteous. This power was indispensable since Rome taught that only the holy and virtuous—the saints—were wholly pleasing and acceptable to God.[4] So through good works and other activities the devout would make this justifying grace their own and thereby attain a proper standing before God. Otherwise, they would be purified of their corruption in purgatory. Of course, many other institutional options to good works existed. Catholic theology also taught that the Mass was a meritorious work which the priest could say on behalf of a patron, whether present or not. So the wealthy often endowed a position for a priest which guaranteed that a number of future masses would be said for them. Emperor Charles V left provision for 30,000 such masses, and Henry VIII ensured these meritorious works "while the world shall endure."[5]

In addition, by the late Middle Ages Rome taught that the good works of Mary and the saints had exceeded their own requirements; their extra merits accumulated in a "treasury of merit" which the church could distribute to others. Such transfers were effected by issuing "indulgences." Those who went on crusades, for example, might receive total remission of sins through an indulgence. During the fourteenth and fifteenth centuries, the requirements were gradually lowered until forgiveness could be obtained for an appropriate donation. In 1517 one of the great hawkers of indulgences, the Dominican Johann Tetzel, was journeying throughout Germany. Tetzel's enticing jingle, "As soon as the coin in the coffer rings, the soul from Purgatory springs," helped complete St. Peter's Church in Rome, but also pushed Luther to nail his "Ninety-five Theses," an offer to debate indulgences, to the church door at Wittenberg.[6]

Even though life at this time was thoroughly intertwined with the religious, fear and anxiety increased. The fragility of life and the constant cycle of the plague accentuated the preoccupation with death and judgment. Yet the dominant sacramental conception of salvation was spiritually problematic; these external actions did not satiate the religious quest. But since the length of one's stay in purgatory was unknown, religious activism spiraled. The incessant attempts to earn merits multiplied the external forms of religion—indulgences, masses for the dead, veneration of relics, pilgrimages, and self-flagellation. New options increasingly fused the sacred and the secular, evidenced by the proliferation of minor saints with the purported power "to cure everything from sore throats to hemorrhoids."[7] Spiritual confusion prevailed.

Few questioned the need for reform and spiritual leadership. Luther stood in a long line of reformers. His discovery in Scripture that faith in Jesus alone provides salvific communion with God became spiritually electrifying for tens of thousands.

Defining Protestant Beliefs

Justification by Faith Alone

Like others in the Medieval period, Luther was asking, "How can I win God's favor?" Luther had been taught that justice referred primarily to God's holy character and his determination to reward the righteous and punish the sinner. This was a frightening concept which the sacramental system sought to resolve.

However, the Medieval Catholic penitential system did not allow Luther the monk to find the peace with God that he craved. While acknowledging its impetus for good works, Luther argued that the spirituality which lived through these achievements fails on one of two counts. If these good works become a ladder by which one attempts to merit closer fellowship with God, the problem of sinful pride has not been rectified. In fact, here piety is simply elevated to a smug self-righteousness. On the other hand, if one never attains these standards, anxiety over continuing sin cripples and paralyzes the believer. And that was Luther's predicament, as he confessed:

> If ever a monk could get to heaven through monastic discipline, I was that monk. . . . And yet my conscience would not give me certainty, but I always doubted and said, "You didn't do that right. You weren't contrite enough. You left that out of your confession." The more I tried to remedy an uncertain, weak and troubled conscience . . . the more I daily found it more uncertain, weaker and more troubled.[8]

In the presence of God's holiness, Luther knew that none of his works were pleasing.

Through reading Psalms and Romans, Luther began to understand that justification is not an ethical power which enables one to become righteous. As Luther studied Paul's letters, he saw that Jesus Christ has already met God's demand for righteousness and satisfaction for sin. And God

"The Christian lives not in himself, but in Christ and in his neighbor. Otherwise he is not a Christian. He lives in Christ through faith, in his neighbor through love. By faith he is caught up beyond himself into God. By love he descends beneath himself into his neighbor." (Martin Luther, *On the Freedom of the Christian*)

imputes Christ's righteousness to those who have faith, even the wicked (Rom. 4:5).

Salvation is God's achievement; it is God in Jesus Christ coming to us and offering a personal relationship. Jesus personally encounters us, saying, "I justify the wicked through faith in me! I have come to save, not the righteous, but sinners." Luther insisted that this offer is not contingent in any way on one's ability to meet God's demands. For sinners—even sinful believers—are totally incapable of meeting God's standards. So the believer flees to Jesus, trusting upon Christ and what he has accomplished. Because of Jesus' atoning sacrifice and righteous life, those who have faith in Jesus know that they can stand in the presence of God without the fear of being punished. Reconciliation between God and the sinner is established. Salvation is an act of God's grace, a free gift.

Justification is by faith alone, simply by trusting upon Christ. This conception of salvation undercut the Catholic church's insistence on the priests' sacramental work and believers completing their own salvation by becoming righteous. Luther countered that the sacraments do not bestow grace simply by the priests doing their work. Rather, the sacraments are signs of God's promised salvation which is appropriated through faith alone. Faith in Jesus alone provides salvific communion with God. Nor are good works necessary for attaining a proper standing before God, for Jesus Christ has provided all!

Knowing God's continued acceptance and forgiveness, despite who we are, means that the Christian life is one of joy. But there is also an activism inherent in justifying faith. Because life's most troublesome problem— one's relationship to God—has been solved, a gratitude to God breaks forth in a spontaneous love toward God and others. Since salvation is complete and their destiny assured, Luther insisted that believers can turn from a concern for their own inherent righteousness and serve their neighbor, taking no account of personal loss or gain. We have been changed through faith in Christ, and we see the evidence of it in our love to others. Indeed, we are empowered by the same love that Christ has shown us. The task of the Christian then is to implement and demonstrate the salvation which has been given.

Sola Scriptura

The Roman Catholic church had insisted that the interpretations and decisions made by the church hierarchy had equal authority with Scripture. Rome, of course, had her reasons. The authority of the church was necessary to protect the truth of the Christian message from perversion through misinterpretation. And this was the church's responsibility, for the church preceded the Bible. Without the church's pronouncement and decision, the Bible as a literary composition would not exist.

Luther's rediscovery of the gospel, however, permitted him to see how church tradition easily distorts and imprisons Scripture's message. This should be expected, since believers inevitably bring their sinful ideals and attitudes to their interpretation of Scripture. Through the pope's sanction, this sinful interpretive tradition then became authoritative. The papacy had effectively precluded any possible reform by arrogating final authority to itself. Luther labeled Rome's authority as tyrannical, even calling it a "Babylonian Captivity."

Rejecting Rome's claim to an equal authority with Scripture, Luther insisted that Jesus Christ is the sole head and authority of the church. Jesus creates and nourishes the church through his Word, now found in Scripture. The norm for the church then is the Word alone. The "alone" is indispensable, for it precludes church tradition as an equal authority.

While acknowledging that the church was older than the New Testament, Luther noted that this is not relevant to the issue of religious authority. For God's Word has been transmitted in a variety of ways: written, oral—even by a donkey and stone tablets! In some form or another, God's Word of promise has always preceded the church. It is this Word that calls into existence believers and thus the church.

> The church has no power to initiate and institute divine promises of grace. . . . For the church was born by virtue of her faith in the Word of promise, and by that promise she is both fed and maintained. In other words, she was instituted by God's promises, not God's promise by her. . . . She is a created thing, and being such, has no power to institute, to ordain, or to make; but only to be instituted, to be ordained, and to be brought into being. No man can beget his own parents or settle the author of his own being.[9]

Consequently, the church is subordinate to God's Word of promise and grace.

Today, God's Word is written in Scripture. Believers know that this is God's Word, not by the declaration of the church hierarchy but as the Spirit

The Printers

While Luther and Zwingli are justly remembered as the courageous Reformation figures, their associated army of forgotten printers and pamphleteers was just as instrumental in the Protestants' success. Taking advantage of the latest technology—movable type—the presses poured out inexpensive books for the interested public, small enough so they could be easily transported across Europe. They printed Bibles in the vernacular, commentaries, sermons, and popular diatribes reinforcing cardinal Protestant themes. One scholar estimates that by 1550 Protestants had produced as many as 10,000 different titles. A common type of pamphlet attacked the deceit, wealth, and greed of the papacy, complete with satirical woodcuts that literally portrayed the Catholic church fleecing its sheep (the laity). Others would contrast as polar opposites the lifestyle of the papacy and Christ. Another attacked the authority of the church's tradition by contrasting it with Christ's declaration, "I am. . . the truth" (John 14:6). These popular works encouraged the laity's skepticism toward the church and helped undermine the priests' elevated status in the medieval world. As a result, the laity became more vocal in rebuking the church by the norm of Scripture.

speaks through the text assuring them that this message is God's. Then the believer's

> mind is so laid hold of by the truth itself. . . . The mind is unable to judge the truth as such, although it is compelled to say, when entirely confident, "This is true."[10]

Scripture's self-authenticating authority is comparable to other first truths, such as the taste of bitterness, the visual distinction between light and darkness, and mathematical truths.

> For example, the mind declares with infallible assurance that three and seven make ten, and yet it cannot adduce any reason why that is true, although it cannot deny its truth. The fact is that, rather than being itself the judge, the mind has been taken captive, and has accepted a verdict pronounced by the Truth herself sitting on the tribunal. Similarly by the illumination of the Spirit . . . the church possesses a "sense" whose presence is certain, though it cannot be proved . . . (1 Cor. 2:15).[11]

Scripture then is the norm, the "Lydian stone by which I can tell black from white and evil from good."[12]

Luther recognized that certain passages in the Bible are difficult to understand. But contrary to Rome, he maintained that any person illuminated by the Holy Spirit could understand Scripture's basic message, the promise of salvation through faith in Jesus Christ. So the Scriptures are "clear"

"A Christian is a perfectly free lord of all, subject to none. A Christian is a perfectly dutiful servant of all, subject to all." (Martin Luther, *On the Freedom of the Christian*)

to the believer; they are not obscure and in need of clarification by the church.

While the church must bear witness to the fact that the Bible speaks with the authority of God, the church does not and cannot bestow that authority. John the Baptist witnessed to Jesus, but that did not make him superior to Christ. In the same way the church points to the Bible. Consequently, the canon is merely the church's recognition that the Bible is the Word of God. The Bible's authority, then, does not depend in any way upon the decision of the church.

This principle of *sola Scriptura* (Scripture alone) not only overturned the church's tyranny and the laity's "servile dependence," but also provided Luther with a critical perspective on the history of the church. The teachings of the church are helpful, but only as a servant; they never sit in judgment on God's Word. Rather, Jesus speaking through Scripture is the church's final authority.

The Priesthood of All Believers

The Roman Catholic church was grounded solely through the priesthood. They alone were the apostles' successors and thus possessed the authority to dispense sacramental grace. In this system the laity, on the other hand, were qualitatively different, ever dependent on the clergy for grace and communion with God.

Luther, however, envisioned the church as a community. For Jesus Christ is the church's head, and all believers are united with Christ. Through faith all that is Christ's is bestowed upon his bride, the church.[13] Jesus as the High Priest (Heb. 5–9) shares his rights with everyone who believes in him. So believers are priests in Christ (1 Peter 2:9). As adopted children, Christians have a standing invitation to enter into the Father's presence (Heb. 7–10). As priests, we are worthy to appear before God (Eph. 3:12; Heb. 9:14; 10:10). No other human intermediary is necessary, not even the clergy.

The position of priesthood, however, is not one of privilege as the Romanists assumed, but of service. The church is the body of Christ, united in fellowship with him; as we fellowship and participate and support each other through Christ's work we grow up together into one body. So we are called to act as priests to other members in the body. Just as Christ prayed for the disciples, so we must pray for each other. Just as he taught God's Word of Law and Gospel, we are to proclaim that to each other. Just as Jesus gave himself in service to his disciples, so also we must participate in our neighbors' situation in order to know their burdens and serve them. Luther succinctly observed:

> Although the Christian is free from all works, he ought in his liberty to empty himself, take upon himself the form of a servant, be made to the likeness of men, be found in human form, and to serve, help and in every way deal with his neighbor as he sees that God through Christ has dealt and still deals with him. This he should do freely, having regard for nothing but divine approval.[14]

Simply put, all believers have the responsibility of acting as priests to neighbors.

This concept of the "priesthood of all believers" is the third basic element of Protestant theology. In fact, the idea of the priesthood of believers is inherent to the Protestant understanding of salvation. Insofar as salvation is complete and assured through justification by faith alone, believers can freely serve their neighbor, taking no account of personal loss or gain.

The Protestant Reformations

Luther's courageous stands and writings were indispensable to the birth of Protestantism. His basic insights—justification by faith alone, *sola Scriptura,* and the priesthood of all believers—outline the foundations of an evangelical Protestant theology. However, the Protestant Reformation was not a single event nor a homogeneous movement. Divisions quickly arose as different Protestants developed these principles in varying ways. Let's take a closer look at some of the branches of the family tree.

The Lutheran Tradition

Justification by faith alone stands at the heart of Lutheranism. In Jesus Christ Luther found freedom from anxiety of sin, the law, and death. God in Jesus Christ has entered into our world, lived a righteous life, and made satisfaction for sins. This righteousness is now imputed to the believer, even though still a sinner. The individual's standing before God is Luther's primary concern. Certainly salvation has ramifications in society, as gratitude breaks forth in love to others. But Luther's understanding of justification did not mandate a social reordering. Furthermore, Luther's hands were tied politically. Luther was subject to a prince, who protected the fragile

Protestant movement against an emperor committed to rooting out this heresy.

While Luther was hiding after the Diet of Worms (1521), some radicals in Wittenberg seized hold of the *sola Scriptura* principle and demanded an immediate and thorough reformation of the church. They immediately began reforming worship, outlawing the pictures and statues of the saints in churches. Fearing an unraveling of the social order, Luther immediately returned to quash this radical turn. Theologically, Luther rejected this quest for perfect obedience to Scripture as not only impossible, but as a new form of legalism. The Christian always remains a sinner in need of forgiveness: the believer is completely just and sinful at one and the same time (*simul justus et peccator*). As a result, freedom is found only in Christ's perfection and his forgiving grace. This forgiveness for sin allows an accommodation to the social order as long as it is not contrary to Scripture. Utilizing that principle, Luther's attitude toward worship was very conservative; he retained many Roman practices, including candles, pictures, and the crucifix. A few years later, when the peasants demanded justice and rebelled against their oppressors, Luther's social conservatism became even more pronounced. He denounced any revolt as a rebellion against God's order; he called for the political authority to crush these rebels as one would a "mad dog."

Luther's political supporters requested a meeting between the German and Swiss Reformers at Marburg (1529) so that a united front could oppose the emperor's reinvigorated attempts to suppress German Protestants. But instead of ironing out theological differences, the issue of Christ's physical presence in the Lord's Supper proved an insurmountable stumbling block. Luther insisted that Jesus' words, "This is my body," must be interpreted literally. The issue was not simply Scripture's authority, but the incarnation, namely, that God in Jesus Christ is truly present as God and man to the believer in communion. Luther attributed to the Swiss a "different spirit," and thereafter Lutheranism sought to survive by itself. Eventually the German princes came to a political agreement, called the Peace of Augsburg (1555). Only Lutheranism and Catholicism were recognized, and the only legal religion was that of the ruler in that area. No other Protestant movement was permitted; even Calvinists were repressed, to the point of imprisonment and torture.

Thereafter Lutheranism consciously distinguished itself from Calvinism through the *Formula of Concord* (1577). This huge document (well over 100 pages!) explained, refined, further specified, and even went beyond Luther's key insights. The sacraments and predestination were divisive doctrines. All the magisterial Reformers affirmed "predestination." For salvation is free and gracious because it is grounded solely in God's act of bringing us to himself. Luther acknowledged a predestination to salvation and damnation, but highlighted the mystery of this electing act, explaining that what seems unjust now will be vindicated in the eschaton. By contrast, the *Formula of Concord* taught only a predestination to salvation, insisting that God desires all to be saved. It argued that Paul in his great chapter on predestination in Romans 9 had identified humanity's perverse will as bringing about damnation. Certainly God did not elect some to reprobation, otherwise there would be no need for him to have "endured with much patience the vessels of wrath" (Rom. 9:22, RSV). This became an important distinction from the Reformed tradition, which emphasized a double predestination.

The Reformed Tradition

At the same time Luther was attacking Roman abuses in Germany, Huldrych Zwingli (1484–1531) had already acknowledged the authority of Scripture over the church's traditions.[15] When called to pastor the Great Church in Zurich, Switzerland, he set about reforming it directly. As he came to see that an aspect of life did not accord with Scripture, he would expound the biblical perspective from the pulpit. Zwingli used the principle of *sola Scriptura* to eliminate anything that was not expressly commanded and to reorder life. The Swiss republican tradition allowed a more extensive reform effort. Like the Old Testament kings, Zwingli thought that the magistrates were responsible for enforcing God's law. And the city council in Zurich would usually follow his guidance and ensure that life conformed to God's Word. As a result, the Reformed tradition extended Luther's work. It sought to remove all "papist" remnants from the church and thereby make Christ Lord in every dimension of life, hence the name Reformed.

Central to Zwingli's theological vision was the qualitative difference between the sovereign God and creation. Nothing must encroach on God's glory. Rejecting Rome's emphasis on humanity's cooperation with God in attaining salvation as prideful arrogance, he countered that humanity is utterly dependent upon God's sovereign choice at every point in life. Moreover, Zwingli's greatest fear was idolatry, which allowed creaturely images to intrude between God and ourselves. Humans were created in the divine image; as a result, the only thing that can arouse true love is the Word of God, not anything created. But sinners clothe themselves with images to appease their anxieties, turning their attention from God. So Zwingli banned from worship all the Roman ceremonies and decorum—imagery, burning candles, incense, and the special locations for the rulers. Here one stood only before God's Word. He even rejected the traditional view that the elements of the Lord's Supper were the means of Christ's communion with the believer. Instead, he celebrated it as a "memorial of Christ," in which the congregation is the active party by declaring their loyalty to Jesus.

Zwingli's work was cut short when he was killed on the battlefield, trying to impose a Protestant vision on some Catholic cantons. About that time a brilliant young French law student, John Calvin (1509–1564), experienced a sudden conversion to Protestantism. At twenty-six he published the first edition of his *Institutes of the Christian Religion*, prefaced with a defense of the Protestant cause to the king of France. The perils for a Protestant in Catholic France forced Calvin's exile; as he was passing through Geneva he was asked to stay and help in the Protestant movement that had just been established there.

Although continually faced with opposition, Calvin sought to establish a Swiss city that was obedient to Scripture in all areas of life. Through his leadership, Geneva became the intellectual center of the Reformation movement. Refugees across Europe made their way there and studied in Geneva. And when the opportunity allowed, they would return home to pursue the Reformation in their own countries. Calvin's influence extended across the continent, from Scotland (John Knox), England (the Puritans), through France (the Huguenots) and Holland, to Eastern Europe. Geneva became the training ground for pastors to these regions. And in time the United States received and nurtured Calvin's ideas and the Reformed tradition from its Puritan, Presbyterian, and Baptist immigrants.

Calvin was a second generation Reformer with an irenic mind-set who possessed a great ability to synthesize. He continually reworked and supplemented his *Institutes* so that it became the most significant theological text of the Reformation. In contrast to Zwingli, Calvin defended the Lord's Supper as a sacrament, a means of sanctifying grace. Even though not physically present, Christ bestows his grace through this means, which the believer apprehends through faith alone.

Extending Zwingli's attempts to Christianize the community, Calvin structured the church offices so that discipline would be effectively administered. This demand to reform all life shaped Calvin's understanding of the relationship between salvation and good works. The Catholics had repeatedly attacked the Protestant notion of justification by faith—where God declares the unjust righteous, without changing them internally—as producing persons who did not serve the moral law and do good works (antinomians). While that was a clear misrepresentation, Luther's contrast between the law that damns and the gospel that frees could suggest an indifference to good works. Calvin maintains that in salvation we receive all Christ's benefits: justification, sanctification, and regeneration. In other words, Christ justifies no one whom he does not also make holy. And since Jesus is the embodiment of obedience to the law, believers will love the law and desire to live in obedience with God.

Like Zwingli, Calvin confessed predestination but set it within the context of salvation. The believer, acknowledging his or her own pride and blindness, readily confesses that salvation is due solely to God's prior act. Calvin believed that God's salvific action is grounded in his election and love for some and his damnation of others. In the next century, controversy marked this understanding of double predestination. The Synod of Dort (1618), which rejected the Arminian stance that salvation is grounded in God's foreknowledge, proved to be just the opening shot in these ongoing debates.

The Anglican Tradition

John Wycliffe's (1330–1384) constant appeal to Scripture's authority to challenge Rome's distortions predated Luther by more than a century and prepared England for the acceptance of Protestant ideas. But reform in the Church of England was initiated by a political decision, when Henry VIII created an independent English church so he could divorce and remarry. But during the king's lifetime there was little change in the church. Henry's published religious views favored Rome, and the church's episcopal structure remained intact. The key difference was that the king was now the church's supreme head instead of the pope. And since the monarch was the head of the Anglican Church, religion in England became even more intertwined with support for the state. Under Henry's son, Edward VI, the liturgy became decidedly Protestant. Not only was English used, but the *Book of Common Prayer* reflected Protestant understandings of justification by faith, the sacraments, and the priesthood.

Groups representing both Rome and Geneva attempted to redirect the church toward their ends. In the subsequent century both sides had their turns, and both exposed the dangers of their respective theological perspectives to national unity. Queen Mary (1553–1558) attempted to reestablish Catholicism, but her bloody persecution of the Protestants aroused the people against her. The next monarch, Elizabeth I (1558–1603), was decidedly Protestant. Pope Pius V excommunicated her and released the English from any allegiance to her, making Rome a challenge to national unity and thus no longer a viable religious option for the English.

During Mary's reign many Protestants took refuge in Geneva and returned with Calvin's vision of a Reformed church. They advocated complete obedience to God's Word—in all matters, from Sunday observance to a non-episcopal church structure. The influence of this "Puritan" party eventually led to the English Civil War (1642). While the Puritans were militarily successful, the beheading of King Charles I (1649) and Cromwell's subsequent reign provoked a backlash that was fiercely royalist and Anglican. These events exemplify how the Reformed vision of bringing all life under God's Word is often at odds with the elevation of political unity and nationalistic concerns.

The above snapshot briefly shows the origins of one branch in the Christian family. Clearly, the historical and political context has shaped the Anglican Church. Doctrinally it is broad and inclusive, as it consciously took the middle way between Rome and Geneva. While confessing Scripture as its preeminent authority, church tradition and reason were crucial interpretive guides. In fact, the most influential and enduring theologians in the Anglican Church have attempted to establish the reasonableness of the faith by showing that Christianity completes and fulfills the natural order.

The Anabaptists

The prior forms of Protestantism worked within the "system," that is, in tandem with the political authorities, and thus are called the "magisterial Reformation." But Luther's revolt unleashed many other voices who radicalized his complaints. The Anabaptists were the evangelical wing of this "radical Reformation." The Anabaptists presented a trenchant critique, targeting not only Rome but even the mainline Protestants: in the end, they argued, both groups spiritualized Christianity instead of demanding a radicalized life of discipleship to Jesus Christ. Even the Reformed vision accommodated to a strategy of slow and gradual reform, in league with the political authorities.

For instance, some of Zwingli's disciples at Zurich realized that the New Testament had reserved baptism solely for those who confessed faith and obedience to Jesus. When they began preaching against infant baptism, the town council reaffirmed the long-standing custom of baptizing infants. This practice reflected a basic assumption that Christians had held for a millennium, namely, that state and church should work together in order to create a Christian society; in fact, to be baptized in the church was, at the same time, to have one's existence recorded for the state's purpose. But Conrad Grebel and his associates saw that the test of Christian faith was obedience to Jesus in all his commands. Thus, at a prayer meeting he rebaptized Georg Blaurock, and thereby the group was known as "Anabaptists," meaning "re-baptizers."

This incident reflects some of the core ideals of the Anabaptist movement. The Christian life must be one of discipleship to Jesus Christ, expressed in a life of holiness without any compromise. Whereas the magisterial Protestants assumed that the state and church should work together in order to create a Christian society, the evangelical Anabaptists saw these "worldly" institutions as the source of evil and compromise. The governmental imposition of religious beliefs, its use of violence and warfare, and its demand of one's allegiance (the oath) were all contrary to Christ's commands. Furthermore, the social order where many "go about in silk and velvet, gold and silver, . . . ornament their house with all manner of costly furniture," while others are poor and hungry, is contrary to Jesus' command to love others as oneself. Menno Simons admonished the magisterial Protestants, "Where is the power of the gospel you preach? . . . Where are the fruits of the Spirit you have received? Is it not all hypocrisy that you preach . . . ? Shame on you for the easygoing gospel!"[16]

The Anabaptists upheld true faith as a voluntary act of obedience to Christ alone. Jesus commands his disciples to follow solely him and his path of nonresistant love. So the Anabaptists separated from such compromises by reinstituting the New Testament vision of the church, a voluntary community consisting only of Jesus Christ's faithful disciples. This church is a disciplined community whose members evidence a qualitative difference from the world. Underlying this vision is a distinctive view of Scripture's authority. In contrast to the traditional stress on the continuity between the testaments, the Anabaptists affirmed the normativity of the New Covenant established by Jesus Christ. The New Testament does not simply fulfill the Old. Jesus' kingdom is radically new; it overturns the compromises of the past and establishes a new law of nonresistance and self-sacrificial love.

By repudiating infant baptism, and even inverting baptism to denote an individual's repudiation of a culture, the Anabaptists were making a revolutionary statement. Even the term "Anabaptist" was a pejorative label, concocted by their opponents to brand them as traitors to the religious-political unity of European society.[17] When the evangelical Anabaptists separated from political institutions and denied the government any right to enforce a uniform religious practice, they were persecuted as revolutionaries. Within a year of Blaurock's baptism, Zurich began drowning Anabaptists. Their early history is a tragic tale of martyrdom by drowning, fire, the rack, and beheadings. These Reformers were hated, feared, and persecuted by both Protestants and Catholics!

However, the Anabaptists survived, often in secret. Two early and enduring groups are the Mennonites and the Hutterites. Menno Simons (1496–1561) pastored Anabaptist groups throughout the Netherlands and Northern Germany. A commitment to discipleship and specifically Jesus' way of the cross guided his life and thought. Many German and Swiss Anabaptists fled to Moravia where they found refuge. Through the influence of Jacob Hutter (d. 1536) these groups repudiated private property in order to share their goods and live together as one economic community.[18]

Conclusion

As this overview illustrates, early Protestantism assumed very different stances toward culture. While these are variations of previous positions, in the hands of these Protestants they became important theological proposals that still shape us today. In the following chapters, we will explore and evaluate these different stances toward the prevailing culture to better enable us to live more faithfully now.

For Further Reflection

1. For what belief would you risk your career, family, or life? Compare your answer to the Protestant Reformers. What is the source of their religious courage and boldness?
2. How could Luther use the doctrine of justification by faith alone to evaluate and critique contemporary evangelical piety?
3. How does the Anglican tradition understand the authority of Scripture differently from the Reformed? From the Anabaptists? Which conception of biblical authority do you think is correct? Why?
4. How does Luther's understanding of the priesthood of all believers relate to your life?

For Further Reading

Bainton, Roland H. *Here I Stand*. Nashville: Abingdon, 1950.

Dillenberger, John and Claude Welch. *Protestant Christianity Interpreted through Its Development*, 2d ed. New York: Macmillan, 1988.

George, Timothy. *Theology of the Reformers*. Nashville: Broadman, 1988.

McGrath, Alistair. *Reformation Thought: An Introduction*. New York: Blackwell, 1988.

Ozment, Steven. *Protestants: The Birth of a Revolution*. New York: Doubleday, 1992.

twelve

Anabaptists:
The Church Living
in Antithesis to the World

For some Christians, the pervasiveness of sin in culture precludes confessing Jesus Christ as Lord in all areas of life. During the Reformation the Anabaptists argued that since Christians are called by Jesus to righteousness, they must resist any sinful compromise and intentionally live in opposition to culture's sinful structures. The Anabaptists called for Christians to separate and establish a community that faithfully heralds Jesus Christ. At the center of this alternative world is the church, the community of Jesus Christ's faithful disciples evidencing their qualitative difference from this sinful world. While actively persecuted by Christendom and dismissed as eccentrics and even as failures, the Anabaptists measured success not by their influence or impact on society but by their conformity to Jesus Christ. For in the end, that alone counts.

The Anabaptists' Theological Vision

The Anabaptists' distinctive theological vision of Christian mission builds on their understanding of sin, Jesus' radical work, and the church.

Creation and Sin

God created a perfect world for humans to live in love and obedience. Humans were to place their "hope and comfort" on God alone, the source of all good, and "seek diligently to please Him"; they were not to trust the structures of politics, possessions, and family that constitute human society and culture.[1] But humans rebelled and sought "salvation, comfort and help apart from God," through the state, a "wife, child, house, farm, money, goods or even himself."[2] These structures of God's good creation usurp the place of God. They demand *absolute* allegiance, claiming that salvation and hope are found only in *this* state or *this* family and not any other. To ensure this idol's triumph, no human action or sacrifice is prohibited, for this state, family, or individual determines what is just and right. There are myriad contemporary examples: the Bosnian Serbs contort "patriotic nationalism" into "ethnic cleansing"; Planned Parenthood rationalizes abortion as "free choice"; the Gay Lobby exonerates its "alternate lifestyle" as "the way God created us"; and the CEO justifies laying off thousands of middle-aged employees, without regard for their family or future, as "helping the bottom line."

Simply put, at the Fall the world and its structures succumbed to Satan's rule (1 John 2:15–17). Even humanity's noble aims—justice, righteousness, and peace—are warped and prostituted to the sinner's own endeavors. The Old Testament recognized evil's present and invincible reality and looked forward to the Messiah's advent and his defeat of evil. As a result, the Mosaic Law could only place restraints on evil and this through compromise. While the Law prohibited unjust retaliation, such as a life for an eye, it sanctioned proportionate retaliation (Deut. 19:21). Its toleration of warfare, divorce, and not loving one's enemies all reflect the incorrigibility of evil. The New Testament similarly describes creation as under the "dominion of darkness" (Col. 1:13), where the "evil one" (1 John 5:19) is its "prince" (John 12:31). These sinful structures with all their "abominations" and "adulteries," the "haunt for every evil spirit" (Rev. 18:2), constitute Babylon (Rev. 17:4–5).

Jesus Christ and His Kingdom

In the midst of this sinful world, God in Jesus Christ has supernaturally invaded Satan's realm, disarmed these principalities and powers (Col. 2:15), and established his own kingdom. This kingdom is not simply a spiritual experience of forgiveness, a foretaste of some glorious future, or a sociopolitical program for bettering humanity. Christ's kingdom offers a whole alternative to Satan's kingdom, opposing it at every level. Jesus not only

OLD TESTAMENT	JESUS' ETHIC
Divorce permitted (Deut. 24:1–4)	Divorce prohibited (Luke 16:18; Matt. 19:8)
Do not love your enemy (Deut. 19:21; Ps. 139:21ff)	Love your enemy (Matt. 5:43ff)
Heretics and false prophets should be put to death (Deut. 13:5)	Shun heretics, but commit their judgment to God at the end of the age (Matt. 13:25–30, 36–43)
Believers active in government	Christians must not be magistrates (1 Cor. 5:12)
Partake in this sinful world	Separate from Babylon (2 Cor. 6:14ff)

Anabaptist Interpretation of Jesus' Ethic

defeated evil's power for his followers, but established a new ethic that is alien to the compromises of this sinful world. This kingdom exists now and fully in the church.

However, the radicalness of Jesus' advent and ethic is seldom recognized. Even Christendom mutes Jesus' radical ethic by viewing him as simply deepening and extending the intent of the Old Testament law. But the Anabaptists counter that the Sermon on the Mount (Matt. 5–7) reveals the qualitative newness of Jesus' work and kingdom. For here Jesus replaces the Old Testament law with his kingdom's ethics. Matthew 5:38–39 poses a classic contrast: "You have heard that it was said, 'Eye for eye, and tooth for tooth.' But I tell you, Do not resist an evil person." According to the Anabaptists, Jesus startles the audience by setting aside the Old Testament law of retaliation and establishing a totally new standard: do not avenge evil. Throughout the Sermon on the Mount and in many other passages, Jesus sharply contrasts and even sets up an opposition between the Old Testament prescriptions on divorce, warfare, religious authority, and his own ethic. Rejecting the old law, Jesus insists upon an absolute ethic of righteousness without compromise and love without retaliation.

As the table above indicates, the Anabaptists interpreted Jesus' distinctive ethic as antithetical to the Old Testament law. Why this sharp contrast between the Old and New Covenants? Anabaptists affirm that both are God's Word. However, they interpreted the Old Testament as looking forward to the advent of something radically new, the Messiah, Jesus Christ. During the Old Testament period, the Messiah had not yet arrived. Only the Law was available; and it is "a yoke of bondage, doing nothing but . . . demanding."[3] As a result, evil remained a present and invincible reality, so that compromises with evil—retaliation, divorce, oaths, not loving one's enemies—were permitted.

But with the coming of Jesus Christ, the "new age" has arrived. Jesus has triumphed over Satan's reign and established his own kingdom of righteousness and holiness. Now "something better is come, that is, the covenant of God is more clearly and perfectly revealed and come fully to the light"; and as a result, "that which is dark and imperfect must cease and come to an end."[4] Unlike the Old Testament period, God now prohibits evil and makes absolute demands upon his people. Jesus has revealed a new ethic for his people; "the law [is] our schoolmaster until we are in Christ."[5] Compromises are no longer permitted; the New Covenant has displaced the Old.[6] Warfare, arrogance, and selfish ambition must be abandoned. Jesus demands obedience to a new set of values: humility, righteousness, no divorce, love for one's enemies, separation from Babylon.

Jesus' life consistently proclaimed his kingdom's demands. Jesus conquered evil by entering sinful structures and unmasking their idolatrous pretensions and resultant evils. He challenged idolatrous Jewish pride and its related stigma toward tax collectors, adulterers, and other outsiders in Jewish society. Despite a life of threats and suffering, Jesus did not take the path of human rebellion and retaliate. He "loved everyone without measure" (Luke 6:27–36).[7] Nor did he coercively impose his kingdom through military power. Using the sword would only have elevated allegiance to temporal powers above trust in God, reintroducing idolatry. Rather Jesus conquered through the cross by "entrust[ing] himself to him who judges justly" (1 Peter 2:23).

In conquering evil Jesus instituted an alternative life of love and righteousness. Christ's kingdom embodies those people who are empowered by his Spirit to live in obedience to his standards and not the world's. And this kingdom exists now in the church. Presently, though, Christ's kingdom exists in a hostile environment, the kingdom of Satan. This world is Satan's territory and his reign will cease only at the Second Coming.[8] In his original proclamation, Jesus accentuated the ineradicable opposition between Satan's and his own kingdom: "Repent, for the kingdom of heaven is near" (Matt. 4:17). The Greek word for repentance, *metanoia*, entails an about-face, a repudiation of the past. Similarly, Jesus' demand for repentance poses an "either-or" decision: Satan or Christ. There are no other options and no room for the lukewarm. For sin so pervades the cosmos that unless the world's values and structures are consciously opposed, obedience to Christ is inevitably compromised. That is why Paul exhorts believers not to "conform any longer to the pattern of this world, but be transformed by the renewing of your mind" (Rom. 12:2). This is the narrow road that alone leads to life (Matt. 7:13–14).[9]

The Church

The Church as a Covenanted Community

Seeking to fulfill Jesus' command to "be my witnesses" (Acts 1:8), the Anabaptists reconstituted the idea of the church on the model of Christ's kingdom. The church is conceived as a qualitatively new reality in history, the only place where Christ now rules. As a result, Jesus' disciples must reflect Christ's life and standards, not Satan's. In addition the Anabaptists contend that Babylon's grasp can only be resisted if the church separates from the world's sinful structures.

The need to separate from the structures and values of the prevailing culture resound throughout the Anabaptist writings. Note the first Anabaptist confession at Schleitheim (1527):

> A separation shall be made from the evil and from the wickedness which the devil planted in the world; . . . we shall not have fellowship with them [the wicked] and not run with them in the multitude of their abominations. . . . For truly all creatures are in but two classes, good and bad, believing and unbelieving, darkness and light, the world and those who [have come] out of the world . . . and none can have part with the other.[10]

They viewed separation positively as the way to enhance one's piety and obedience to Jesus Christ. For this sinful world can quickly divert our allegiance to Jesus Christ, even without our recognition, unless the church vigilantly cultivates discipleship.

In addition, the church is differentiated from the world because her members have *freely* covenanted to follow Christ. The Anabaptists detached religion from political power, for Christ rules inwardly, through the Spirit's work, not through physical coercion. Nor is religion a solitary quest in their view. The church is a brotherhood, a community that intentionally disciples and guides the believer. The Anabaptists maintained that Christians were to live in opposition to society, not as individuals or hermits, but in *Gemeinde* or community—true church. Jesus' work established a new order, which overcame the sinner's pride and selfishness. As a result, believers have been transformed so that they can put others ahead of themselves and thereby love each other with a self-sacrificial love. Jesus set down the criterion of brotherly love: "By this everyone will know that you are my disciples, if you love one another" (John 13:35, NIV:ILE). Simply put, the church is the people of God, a voluntary brotherhood and a fellowship which reflects Christ's love.

According to classic Anabaptist teaching, *believer's baptism* was the rite of "entry into the holy church." In this ceremony the adult believer publicly confesses that he or she has died to this world and has surrendered the self to Christ through the church and "pledges to live and to die according to His will."[11] To ensure that their communities imitated Christ's righteousness, the Anabaptists maintained a strict discipline. Those who did not display a Christian life were disciplined. At the extreme, this could mean exclusion from the community (Matt. 18:15–17). The banned could be readmitted, but only if they demonstrated their repentance through godly lives.

The result is a church that is sharply distinguished from the prevailing culture. This is what sociologists call a "sectarian church," one that seeks no worldly sanction and separates itself as much as possible from the world's sinful compromises.

The Church as Christ's Kingdom

Christ is not only the Savior for sinners, but also their Lord and thus the norm for every aspect of life. As a result, the Anabaptists define the true church through four criteria derived from Christ's life.[12] The first is *holy living*. Christ has established a church that has no "blemish, wrinkle, or any such thing, but [is] pure and holy, as He, himself, is holy."[13] The Anabaptists explicitly reject the traditional move in the church's history to spiritualize Christ's kingdom by incorporating all that are sacramentally graced or have faith without regard to whether they live righteously. Faith must be evidenced by fruit: Jesus' disciples must "live unblamably in His holy commandments."[14]

Second, the believer's life must be one of *self-sacrificial* love or servanthood. Jesus' disciples must put themselves last and serve the other (Matt. 20:25–27; Phil. 2:3–5). As a result, the ways of the world—pride, selfishness, retaliation, and even coercion—had absolutely no place among the Anabaptists. Attempting to evade all forms of "self-seeking," they even prohibited Christians from "eating and drinking the sweat of the poor (that is, making one's own people and fellow-creatures work so that one can grow fat)."[15] Nor could possessions be used solely for oneself, for the disciple of Christ "was not the lord but only the steward of His goods." The Anabaptists' acts of generosity and love for fellow believers as well as the stranger were renowned, a heritage that continues to this day.[16]

Third, *the way of the cross* is not only Christ's calling, but his disciples' calling as well: "Those who do not carry their cross and follow me cannot be my disciples" (Luke 14:27, NIV:ILE). Bearing the cross refers to Jesus' nonretaliatory suffering resulting from his social nonconformity. Through the way of the cross Jesus conquered Satan (Col. 2:15). In his servanthood (Phil. 2:3–11), Jesus denied the sinful powers their claim to absolute allegiance by trusting entirely in God (1 Peter 2:23). The disciple of Jesus shares in this same destiny (2 Tim. 3:12; 1 Peter 2:21; 4:1, 12–16). In the times of insult, persecution, or death, Anabaptists regarded the "holy cross of Christ" as their "highest shelter and shield," as "we have surrendered with holy patience (not obliged or forced patience) to overcome all our enemies in the victory of Christ."[17] So by bearing the cross, the disciple trusts in Christ's victory over the powers of this age.

Finally, Christ's Great Commission was every disciples' charge. Anabaptists traveled throughout Europe to preach, live, and suffer for Christ's sake. Even more crucial, the Anabaptists understood a *witness* not as one who simply believes or proclaims a message, but as one who embodies this message in the face of hostility from the world, even at the price of martyrdom. Indeed, the Greek term for witness (*martys*) is the origin for the English "martyr" and means bearing testimony at the expense of oneself. Similarly, they embodied Jesus' life and teaching, offering an alternative kingdom in this world.

The Church as an Alternative Culture

While insisting that the church must separate from the prevailing culture, the Anabaptist is not suggesting that Christians hide from the world. One is separated in order to be known and recognized as qualitatively different from the world. The Anabaptist community of believers *visibly* demonstrates that Jesus is the Lord of life. The church is an "assembly . . . gathered and led together by the Holy Spirit . . . so that they want only to be like Christ, to partake of his nature, and diligently to do his will."[18]

Offering an alternative, even a counterculture, is the church's mission. As Peter Rideman recounts, the church is

> a lantern of righteousness, in which the light of grace is borne and held before the whole world, that its darkness, unbelief and blindness be thereby seen and made light, and that men may also learn to see and know the way of life. Therefore is the church of Christ in the first place completely filled with the light of Christ as a lantern is illuminated and made bright by the light: that his light might shine through her to others.[19]

The church's mission is simply to exist, to be a beacon in the world, showing the world that sin's power no longer controls her and that Christ's kingdom has arrived.

Rejection of Christendom as the Compromised and Apostate Church

Christendom (institutionalized Christianity that prevails in a culture) has resisted the Anabaptist's conception of the church living in opposition to the prevailing culture as too radical and disruptive to the social order.

The excuses are well-rehearsed: Jesus' lifestyle of humility and nonresistance is unpractical; the world just does not operate like that. But Jesus challenged that response, "No one can serve two masters" (Matt. 6:24).

The Anabaptist interpretation of the church's history supports this contention. Beginning with the Constantinian period, the church exchanged the image of itself as a community of saints for an institution integrally coupled with the broader society. The church and society formed an organic whole which in turn shaped the church's own self-understanding. Church attendance became a civic duty, supported by the state's coercive power. Of course, not everyone who attended was a believer. As a result, theologians proclaimed that the true church was invisible. And, since believers were known only to God, all "pew warmers" had to be treated *as if* they were Christians, even if they showed no signs of faith.

The Anabaptists rejected this spiritualized or invisible church. Jesus commands that the church visibly bear his witness (John 13:34–35; Acts 1:8). Peter similarly envisions the church as "a chosen people, a royal priesthood, a holy nation, a people belonging to God, that you may declare the praises of him" (1 Peter 2:9). If the church is identified with society, then the existing social and political order defines the adjectives "chosen," "holy," and "belonging to God." And in the end, doesn't this mean that Christ's demands are equated with the status quo?

The Constantinian church did in fact curtail Jesus' absolute demands so they were within the reach of their culture. The bonds of fellowship and nonresistant self-sacrificial love, by which the apostolic church offered a welcome alternative to pagan society, were soon eclipsed.[20] Instead of following Christ's command that his disciples be servants to all, selfish ambition and its trappings pervaded the church. Hierarchy and social status replaced community. Even the emperor's political arrogance entered the church. Rather than willingly suffer martyrdom for Christ's sake, now the church sanctioned the state's own restricted notion of justice and the state's demand for the ultimate sacrifice. In only a matter of time the church began employing political power for its own ends. This scenario has been repeated throughout church history. This betrayal of Jesus' commands, the Anabaptists conclude, is inevitable when the church collaborates with the world.

The Reformation did not escape such compromise. The magisterial Protestant Reformers, the Anabaptists charged, proclaimed faith in Christ but without any moral demands. As Menno Simons derisively observed, "They strike up a Psalm, . . . 'Snapped is the cord, now we are free, praise the Lord' while beer and wine verily run from their drunken mouths and noses. Anyone who can but recite this on his thumb, no matter how carnally he lives, is a good evangelical man and a precious brother."[21] The Anabaptists conclude that as long as the prevailing culture shapes our values, the church will be little different from the rest of society.

The Christian's Mission: The Church Living in Opposition to the World

This theological vision provides the framework for exploring the Anabaptists' conception of the Christian's mission.

Jesus Is Lord over All

Only if Jesus is our sole norm, judging every other aspect of reality, the Anabaptists insist, is he truly Lord over all. While Christendom typically supplements and thereby moderates Jesus' commands with cultural or practical concerns, the Anabaptists demand that Jesus' ethic must define every other obligation. As a result, the church replaces sinful institutions.

Believers Must Separate from Sinful Structures

Obedience to Jesus Christ necessitates separation from the prevailing culture and its domineering values and expectations, for the social reality in which one is most rooted shapes one's values and priorities. The church, consequently, must provide an alternative context for nurturing disciples of Christ strong enough to resist the system of the world. Similarly, believers are not responsible for coercively transforming the sinful structures of this world, but demonstrating their own freedom from Satan's enslavement and the reality of Christ's kingdom.

Certainly this understanding of the church's mission allows believers to evade the controlling confines of certain sinful structures. Take, for example, participation in the ordinary social and political hierarchies. Throughout the centuries, Christians have adorned their superior positions in society—as politician, administrator, magistrate/lawyer—with Christian values. But the Anabaptists reject this option as a compromise. How can a magistrate wield power in managing society yet at the same time obey Jesus' command that his disciples must be last, even a slave to others? (Matt. 20:25–27) For in the end—no matter what rhetoric is employed, whether "law," "justice," or "individual rights"—the use of even legal power entails imposing one's views upon others. Or take, for example, the administrator, bureaucrat, or the so-called "civil servant"—those who apply institutional rules to particular situations. Are those "servants" as Christ demands—"to the least of these" (Matt. 25:40, 45)—or as the institution prescribes? Who actually is their lord?

Moreover, social hierarchies are symptoms of a whole system of disobedience. As the parable of the Pharisee and the tax collector portrays (Luke 18:10–14), haughty arrogance is an irresistible temptation accom-

> "It does not befit a Christian to be a magistrate: the rule of the government is according to the flesh, that of the Christians according to the spirit. Their houses and dwelling remains in this world, that of the Christians is in heaven. Their citizenship is in this world, that of the Christian is in heaven." (Schleitheim Confession, art. no. 6)

panying social achievement: "I made it to this place; you could as well, if you'd only work at it!" The disciples' fight for the seat nearest to Jesus (Mark 10:35–45) shows the powerful lure that more status and a higher position on the social ladder holds for us all. The problem is not simply prideful desire, but the distorting effect of reciprocity on morality. In our sinful world if you scratch my back, I'll scratch yours. Likewise, if you stab me, watch out! A tit for a tat is inescapable, and it quickly escalates to more violent forms of retaliation. By contrast, Jesus commands his disciples to return good for evil.

The way of the cross is not an Anabaptist strategy for transforming the world. They never claim that innocent suffering will shame this evil world or that the acceptance of suffering allows one to succeed in life. The way of the cross simply reflects trust in and obedience to Jesus alone. The resulting disengagement from the prevailing culture frees the Anabaptists from the world's idolatrous temptations.

Through Servanthood, Believers Show Victory over Sin

Not even the Anabaptist can evade every aspect of our sinful world, for these structures form human life. The political order, for example, provides a peaceful civil order necessary for a stable life. While refraining from active participation in certain structures, some passive involvement is inevitable. But how could the Anabaptist participate without being affected by that idolatrous structure?

The Anabaptist stance toward governmental powers provides an important case study and illustrates their response. The Anabaptists insist that the political order—the state and its power of the sword—was ordained by God in order to restrain evil only after the Fall. Since those in the kingdom of Christ evidence the new reality of Christ's righteousness, believers do not need the sword for restraining evil. Like the Old Testament law, the state's authority and coercive power is God-ordained only where evil is invincible. Simply put, the governmental authorities exist only for the wicked, not for the saved.

Christians must obey Jesus' command, "Do not resist an evildoer" (Matt. 5:39, NRSV) and so must not actively participate in political institutions or carry out their decisions. In the words of the Schleitheim Confession, the government is "outside the perfection of Christ."[22] But the Anabaptists were not naive about evil; the sword is necessary, but only nonbelievers should employ its power.

On the other hand, Anabaptists accepted Paul's counsel, "Let everyone be subject to the governing authorities" (Rom. 13:1, NIV:ILE). They supported political institutions, giving them "what we owe them before God according to divine testimony . . . be it taxes, interest, the tithe, service . . . whatever does not contribute to the destruction of man."[23] But severe restrictions are placed upon governmental power. The state can never stand in the way of obedience to God. If the state crosses this line, the Christian must refuse its demands, but then accept the penalties imposed. Again, Jesus' command to not resist evil must be obeyed. As in the early church, the Christian must refuse to worship Caesar, yet submit to Caesar's persecution.

While participating indirectly in the political structures, the Anabaptists refused to conform to its sinful values. By witnessing to the lordship of Jesus Christ and embodying his self-sacrificial love, they repudiated and even subverted the prevailing ethos. Similarly, when they were condemned because of their obedience to Jesus Christ, Anabaptists saw their submission to the state's penalties as following the way of the cross. For despite political threats and suffering, they trusted on God's final victory, and denied these structures their claim to absolute allegiance (1 Peter 2:23).

Evaluation

Christianity is deeply indebted to the Anabaptists. In an age when no one conceived of the possibility of a stable government without the church's involvement and endorsement, they proposed and implemented religious belief apart from political entanglement. Moreover, few Christians have taken more seriously the absolute authority of Jesus. Their lives of righteousness, self-sacrificial love, and freedom from the prevailing social expectations have always shamed mainline Christianity. Living in opposition to the prevailing sinful structures, the Anabaptists possess keen insight into evil's operation in the world. As a result, they have always played a necessary prophetic role within Christendom. In the contemporary period where the church flirts so readily with the world, the Anabaptist strategy of the church living in opposition to the prevailing culture is frequently caricatured and attacked. However, their understanding of the church's disciplining nature can provide an effective counterweight to the pervasive influence of culture on Christians.

Their strategy of opposition to the prevailing culture is more controversial. In fact, it is traditionally read as mandating a reactionary withdrawal and repudiation of society, like the Amish who use horse-drawn carriages instead of cars or kerosene lamps in place of electric lights. But throughout church history opposition to the world has assumed many forms, ranging from withdrawal to heralding. The monks in the early church *physically withdrew* from their culture and took up residence in remote locations, because the prevailing culture distracted them from obedience to Jesus Christ. Amish communities are not physically but *socially withdrawn* from other Americans, insofar as they do not actively seek to engage American society. Many Anabaptists, however, represent another option. They are not physically or socially separated, but *worldviewishly separated* in view of their distinctively Christian conception of reality, truth, and values. In addition, they have sought to challenge society by establishing an alternative institution—the church—that *heralds* Jesus Christ. When they were not being martyred by the Protestants and Catholics, the Anabaptists embodied the Great Commission. Modern groups representing the Anabaptist vision, such as the Jesus People U.S.A. community in Chicago, reflect this same *heralding stance*. They are not separated physically or socially, but worldviewishly. The alternative institutions they have established in this urban setting—ranging from roofing companies to a youth magazine—*herald* Jesus Christ and challenge cherished American values.[24]

Despite these strengths, several important criticisms are directed toward the Anabaptist proposal. First, is it really possible to live in complete opposition to the kingdom of Satan? Can one so separate from the prevailing sinful structures that any compromise, any entanglement with evil is precluded? Admittedly, the Anabaptists do not actively engage in governmental power, but aren't the political authorities and their sinful violence supported indirectly by their taxes? While they do not actively use their neighbor for gaining wealth, doesn't their participation in business and commerce allow others to do the same? Doesn't their indirect participation enable these sinful structures to endure and even thrive? As a result, is not the Anabaptist guilty by complicity? Complete separation is impossible because we live in a world in which we are necessarily in a relationship of interdependence with others.

In addition, living in *total* opposition to the sinful world is impossible because Christ's kingdom is now present only in part. While Christ has freed us from Satan's slavery and enables us to act righteously, this righteousness is attainable only in part. But the rhetoric of the Anabaptists often suggests that perfection is possible in this life: Christ's church is "pure and

Jesus People U.S.A.

Who would ever take note of a few strung-out hippies, a young man searching for his sexual identity, and several other social drop-outs? No one, except Jesus Christ! In the early 1970s, Jesus called these castaways together to be his disciples and witnesses, especially to the urban poor. The result is "Jesus People U.S.A.," a thriving evangelical Christian community, located in the Chicago neighborhood known as Uptown.

Jesus People U.S.A. (JPUSA) emphasizes discipleship to Christ, that is, putting him first in every area of life. Their communal life, which includes sharing material possessions and income, is crucial to the process of discipleship—as it was for the New Testament church (see Acts 2:44–47, 4:32–35). Meeting daily for meals, fellowship, prayer, and work requires mutual openness, honesty, and discipline. Not only does the community provide nourishment and oversight for the individual, but it also provides encouragement and wisdom in living out Christ's call in everyday life, such as figuring out how to be the neighbor who consistently and truly loves the homeless one who smells like urine and liquor, curses at them, and defecates on the floor.

Members of JPUSA strive to live out the full Gospel of Jesus Christ. They realized that bringing others to Jesus, who is Lord and life itself, is part of a "seamless garment" with other issues, such as protecting unborn human life, providing adequate housing and food for the poor, and politically opposing those powers aligned against the poor. Jesus highlighted these connections in his own teaching: ". . . as you did it to one of the least of these my brethren, you did it to me" (Matt. 25:40, RSV).

Unlike so many other communal groups, JPUSA does not attempt to escape the city, but is vitally involved through its businesses (contracting, painting, roofing) and political activity. Witnessing to the poor involves living in close identification with the poor—being in the same location, existing at the same standard of living, using public health care. JPUSA views this call as an *honor*. For Christ is demonstrating through them (like he did with the original disciples) that ordinary people, by pooling their resources, can accomplish extraordinary things. JPUSA produces a major Christian magazine (*Cornerstone*), has an internationally known band (REZ), feeds 200 street people daily, annually organizes the Cornerstone Festival (the leading Christian arts and music festival in the U.S.), and ministers in youth homes, hospitals, and jails.

holy, as He, himself, is holy."[25] Correspondingly, the Anabaptist's depiction of Christendom is often shrill and demeaning, and reflects more than just a hint of self-righteousness: the "assembly of the unjust and sinners, . . . adulterers, brawlers, drunkards, the covetous, selfish, vain and all those who lie in word and deed . . . belong not to Him."[26] This consistent demand for perfection suggests a legalism or a form of salvation by works. Paul, however, is clear; we are all sinners. God in Jesus Christ justifies the wicked (Rom. 4:5), not the godly! Believers still battle Satan; complete obedience and freedom awaits the future.

Finally, if complete opposition is naive, then perhaps we should recognize our interdependence and necessary involvement in the wider world and strive to bring about the lordship of Christ not just in our church, but in the world at large. The following chapters will examine such attempts at living faithfully now, taking Christ into the prevailing culture.

For Further Reflection

1. Why would the Anabaptist conception of the church be threatening to those in the Middle Ages?
2. Why do the Anabaptists claim that separation from the prevailing culture is crucial to the Christian's identity? What related arguments does Jim Wallis (see appendix B, p. 279) make regarding our contemporary prevailing culture? Evaluate these.
3. Does the Anabaptist separation from the culture contradict the concept of the incarnation or the Christian understanding of the good creation?
4. Is there an underestimation of sin in the Anabaptist tradition? Or does it take sin more seriously than the other options?
5. Are God's standards known only through Jesus Christ? Does this position seriously underestimate the general knowledge of God among all people?
6. How would an Anabaptist stance look in the contemporary American pluralistic environment?

For Further Reading

Bender, Harold S. *The Anabaptist Vision*. Scottdale, Pa.: Herald, 1944.

Hershberger, Guy F., ed. *The Recovery of the Anabaptist Vision*. Scottdale, Pa.: Herald, 1957.

Jackson, Dave and Neta. *Glimpses of Glory: Thirty Years of Community. The Story of Reba Place Fellowship*. Elgin, Ill.: Brethren, 1987.

Kraybill, Donald. *The Upside-Down Kingdom*, 2d ed. Scottdale, Pa.: Herald, 1990.

"The Schleitheim Confession," in John Leith, ed. *Creeds of the Church*, 3d ed. Atlanta: John Knox, 1982.

Yoder, John Howard. *The Politics of Jesus*. Grand Rapids: Eerdmans, 1972.

———. *The Royal Priesthood: Essays Ecclesiological and Ecumenical*. Ed. Michael G. Cartwright. Grand Rapids: Eerdmans, 1994.

thirteen

Martin Luther:
The Conversionist Church

R ejecting the Anabaptists' counsel of separation, Martin
Luther (1483–1546) countered that God has not abandoned this world to Satan. Through his "left hand" God
rules this sinful world. He restrains evil and establishes law
and order in the world for all—believers and unbelievers.
Yet the inevitable religious options arising from our troubled world—either
a prideful works righteousness or a cynical despair—can only be resolved
by God's "right hand," Jesus Christ and his Gospel of grace apart from
works. In fact, Christ's spiritual kingdom and his church exist for the sake
of this sinful world. The believer, then, cannot follow the Anabaptists' counsel of separation without abdicating the Christian's responsibility to his
neighbor.[1]

To use Luther's distinctive language, the Christian has responsibilities
in both kingdoms, the temporal and the spiritual. The sinful structures of
this temporal world will never be rectified until the Second Coming, when
Jesus Christ re-creates this cosmos. Christ's work in this period "between
the times" concentrates solely upon the spiritual kingdom, the individual's
need for reconciliation to God and neighbor. As a result, the church's mission is to convert individuals. Certainly believers will demonstrate the lordship of Christ in their thoughts and actions, especially by challenging the
distorted political and social values in the culture around them and by
demonstrating a self-sacrificial love to others. But Jesus does not call the

church to a political or social agenda. The Christian's mission is to save souls, not society.

Luther's Theological Vision

The Orders of Creation: The Temporal Kingdom

At creation, God structured life through certain hierarchical relationships that bind humans together. These political, economic, and social structures form the fabric of human life. These "orders," along with their own authorities, values, and norms, are rooted in the way in which God created us. And through these structures, the "hidden" God directs and preserves human culture, as Luther put it, through his "left hand."

For instance, God created humans as social creatures and the political order for establishing civil peace. He even created humans with the fear of the sword and punishment so that these political authorities could effectively rule. Scripture explicitly affirms as much:

> Let everyone be subject to the governing authorities, for there is no authority except that which God has established. The authorities that exist have been established by God. Consequently, whoever rebels against the authority is rebelling against what God has instituted, and those who do so will bring judgment on themselves (Rom. 13:1–2, NIV:ILE).

Similarly, the social structures of the family and marriage cohere with our created social and sexual needs and God's command to "be fruitful and multiply" (Gen. 1:28, RSV). This created order has its own established authorities; as Scripture states, "Honor your father and your mother" (Ex.

	Political Order	Economic Order	Social Order
God's rule is exercised through	Officers of the state	Trade, economic forces	Parents over children
Using the human motive of	Laws and external power which punishes the wicked; fear of the sword	Desire to survive, need to sustain life	Social companionship; sexual desire
Purpose	Produce civil peace (Rom. 13:1-4)	Cultivate creation (Gen. 1:28)	Be fruitful and multiply (Gen. 1:28)

Luther's Conception of the Temporal Kingdom

20:12). Likewise, the economic structures of trade and commerce—which cohere with our need to survive and sustain life—were established by God for the purpose of cultivating the creation.

But with the Fall, sin has perverted these structures and thus the whole fabric of human life. Evil always accompanies the good ends that these structures make possible. Nationalistic pride and suspicion of others is interwoven with the political order. In his refreshingly blunt style, Luther has no illusions regarding political authorities.

> From the beginning of the world a wise prince is a rare bird indeed; still more so a pious prince. They are usually the greatest fools or the worst knaves on earth; therefore one must constantly expect the worst from them.[2]

Similarly, marriage is inherently entangled with lust. Greed, selfishness, and even deceit are part and parcel of the economic spheres.

The pervasiveness of evil can be illustrated in another way. Humans are historical creatures; consequently, our lives are inevitably constructed and forged through the sins of our ancestors. Insofar as we accede to these specific historical structures, we must also bear some complicity in these evils. For example, some years ago both of us purchased homes in Wheaton, Illinois. While Scripture sanctions the ownership of property, just like any other creation structure, private property is tainted and intertwined with sin. In our area of Illinois, private property exists only because these lands were stolen from Native Americans. Just examine the property deeds! Thus, buying these homes implicitly sanctioned those great seizures of land from Native Americans by force and deceit.

However, Luther insists that God has not abandoned these institutions, but still works through these structures to preserve and direct them. Paul knew firsthand the sinfulness of the Roman government, yet he could write that "there is no authority except from God, and those that exist have been instituted by God" (Rom. 13:1, RSV). In part Paul is referring to the rulers' use of the sword for restraining evil and preserving peace. Without the sword, Luther warns, "men would devour one another, and no one could preserve wife and child, support himself and serve God; and thus the world would be reduced to chaos."[3] Similarly, even though sexual intercourse has lost its purity, marriage does channel lustful desires and in so doing reflects God's rule.

Luther's theological perspective also maintains that in and through these creation orders God reveals his requirements for humans. Everyone—from the daughter, husband, employer, to the lord—have a station in society related to those above and below. These structures bind us together as a community and impel us to serve and love each other. Both unbelievers and believers know their obligation toward their neighbor: "Love your neighbor as yourself" (Matt. 22:39). No society could exist except by recognizing in some form this maxim, which finds concrete expression in the second table of the Ten Commandments (i.e. Laws 5–10). The Christian sees this as confirming that God has "written" on everyone's hearts "the requirements of the law" (Rom. 2:15).

Luther's point is that God has imprinted the temporal sphere with meaning and purpose. Consequently, the Christian cannot abandon the temporal sphere, despite its sinfulness. Separation would abnegate the Christian's responsibility to his neighbor. In any case, since the fabric of human life and its development is intertwined with these structures, abandonment is impossible. The Anabaptists, for instance, pridefully and naively claimed to be righteously separated from the world, while their taxes indirectly financed the sword.

Despite God's work in the temporal kingdom, Luther holds little hope for substantially lessening evil. Evil so pervades human life that we can never succeed in following God without exacerbating our sin. Even believers exist as completely righteous yet completely sinful at the same time (*simul justus et peccator*). Until the eschaton, "we cannot obey God without at the same time giving the devil his due."[4] Even the most laudable social reforms are morally ambiguous and inevitably bring more harm to the innocent.

Luther's point is important, yet often slighted. Typically we view injustice simply in terms of the harm done to just one side, ignoring the complicity of both in this evil and the consequences resulting from its rectification. Take, for example, the Gulf War with Iraq. Americans often view this as a paradigmatically just war, where the innocent defeated evil. But was it? The war between Iraq and Kuwait was fought over a common boundary that the West had imposed at the turn of the century. By siding with Kuwait, the U.S. propped up a dictatorial monarchy that was more concerned for the royal family than the good of all who lived in Kuwait. While this war allowed Kuwait to retain ownership of its oil-rich lands, and thus help quench the West's thirst for oil, did it actually establish justice? Not in Kuwait; the monarchy is still as autocratic and anti-Christian as ever. And in Iraq, Saddam Hussein still sits smugly as dictator. Meanwhile, thousands of Iraqi children have died from diseases because the United States decimated the Iraqi infrastructure.

The point is that politics offers no real hope for our world. When social and political change occurs, it usually hurts the defenseless. Evil continues to exist, but under another guise. According to Luther, these social evils will not be redeemed until the eschaton. As a result, Luther counsels believers not to place their hopes in changing the structures of creation. And since God established these orders of creation, set up their authorities, and through them still rules today, popular rebellion is *always* wrong.

Jesus Christ and the Spiritual Kingdom

The inevitability of sin in the temporal sphere reflects sinful humanity's incessant yet futile attempt to establish meaning for and by itself. If the temporal sphere encompassed all reality, life would terminate in only two options—a prideful works righteousness or a hopeless despair. But God in Jesus Christ has graciously established a spiritual kingdom that promises redemption of this fallen world. This is God's "revealed work," the activity of his "right hand." The sole purpose of the church is to proclaim Christ's work and offer his salvation to the world. God achieves this end through the preached Word and sacraments, which the Spirit's internal work makes effective.

Jesus Christ, the only righteous one, has paid the penalty for our sin and conquered sin, death, and Satan for eternity. Through faith in Christ, all that he accomplished becomes ours. God brings about this salvation through the Law and the Gospel. The Law crucifies the believer's prideful smugness by showing that his or her actions never meet God's standard. In the midst of this resulting despair comes the Gospel message, namely, that in view of Christ's alien work God loves the ungodly. Faith and trust is now directed to Christ alone; the sinner's turn toward self is broken. With life's most troublesome problem resolved, gratitude to God in Jesus breaks forth in a spontaneous love toward others as Christ's witness. Only those whose future is secure can expend themselves in such selfless love to others. "From faith in Christ flows forth love . . . that serves one's neighbor willingly and takes no account of gratitude or ingratitude, or gain or loss."[5]

Christ indicates that his kingdom is not of this temporal world. It concerns the soul, not the body; it is internal, not external; it is a spiritual, not a temporal order. But just as the soul cannot exist without the body in this life, so also the spiritual kingdom needs the temporal order. The church could not proclaim the Gospel and produce piety without some social order restraining sinners' natural inclination toward anarchy. Even believers in this life constantly struggle against the flesh and its principalities and pow-

God's rule is exercised through	Preachers in the church
Using as spiritual instruments	Word, sacraments, the Spirit's internal work
Purpose of	Salvation: the forgiveness of sins, and new motives of unselfish love and righteousness.

Luther's Conception of the Spiritual Kingdom

ers. Christians still need the Law and the "left hand" of God revealed through the temporal order. Simply put, the Christian lives in the interim. While Christ defeated Satan in principle, and believers evidence now the firstfruits of his kingdom, they still await his final victory at the eschaton. So the temporal order is as necessary as ever, but at the eschaton this will change. Then evil will end, and even these temporal structures will evidence their provisionality. Thus, in heaven there is no marrying (Matt. 22:30), and love rules without the law.

The Relationship between These Kingdoms

In contrast to the Anabaptists' attempt to displace the temporal with the spiritual kingdom, Luther sees these two spheres as complementary, representing the two hands of God's governance in the world. The spiritual kingdom needs God's work of preserving the temporal order in order to accomplish its goal. Similarly, the temporal order needs the church to correct its distortions regarding the orders of creation and to hear God's offer of salvation, the only answer for the inevitable pride and despair this life produces.

These two kingdoms, however, must not be confused or allowed to exceed their limits. The political authorities, for example, must not interfere with questions of faith. The authority of the temporal kingdom extends "no farther than to life and property and what is external upon earth." In any case, how could a temporal power change the soul? "For no matter how much [temporal authorities] fret and fume, they cannot do more than make the people obey them by word and deed; the heart they cannot constrain, though they wear themselves out trying."[6] When temporal powers encroach the spiritual kingdom, at best only a feigned or deceitful obedience ensues. Only God can regenerate the sinner's heart.

In addition, the church should not interfere in matters proper to the temporal kingdom, such as offering a political program for society. Jesus never sought to be an ayatollah.[7] He did not provide a blueprint for the ideal political or economic system. Admittedly, the Gospel provides basic principles which individual Christians must apply to their specific historical and cultural setting, but even these attempts are shaped by sin and are necessarily imperfect.

More importantly, the spiritual kingdom must not coercively impose on unbelievers its moral vision of a Christianized temporal order. Such a theocratic undertaking forgets that only God can change the soul. The spiritual kingdom can employ only spiritual—not physical—means to destroy the forces of evil. God alone is the final judge, and he will bring Satan's perversion to an end only at the eschaton.

The Christian's Mission: Believers Converting the World

Recall that the Anabaptists counseled separation to retain obedience to Jesus Christ amidst this sinful world. Luther also emphasized evil's pervasiveness as well as Christ's command that his disciples be holy as God is holy (Matt. 5:48). How did Luther resolve this tension? What is the Christian's mission and responsibility in the world?

Jesus' Work Frees the Believer for Action

Luther maintained that Jesus' salvific work dealt with the inevitability of sinning in this fallen world by atoning for all our sins—past, present, and future—on the cross. That is precisely what justification by faith alone entails. God judges us, not in terms of who we are internally, but in terms of who Jesus is. Because Jesus Christ has paid the penalty, the sins in which we inevitably partake should not terrify and paralyze us from acting. Despite the necessity of sin and compromise, Christ's work of salvation frees us for service in the world. Or as Luther characteristically put it, "Be a sinner and sin boldly, but believe and rejoice in Christ even more boldly, for he is victorious over sin, devil and the world."[8]

Moreover, through conversion Jesus Christ creates in believers a new heart, reflecting his humility and self-sacrificial love for others. Luther identifies the Sermon on the Mount's values as central to Jesus' teaching: the moral ideals of love for your enemy, forgiveness, placing the interests of others above your own, and even non-retaliation. The Christian's mission is to demonstrate Christ's love and proclaim the Gospel, bringing spiritual healing to society.

Unlike the Catholics and Anabaptists, who often separated and isolated spiritual and temporal callings, Luther maintained that whatever the station—whether a prince, judge, farmer, or hangman—every Christian is called to witness Christ. Christ has freed believers for action and given them a mission, whatever their place in society. With Luther, the spiritual kingdom becomes the force and presence of individual Chrsitians throughout their varying offices and positions in the temporal kingdom.

The Believer's Responsibility in Both Kingdoms

Doesn't the Christian's membership in both kingdoms necessarily entail conflicting allegiances? How could a Christian prince "not resist an evildoer"? Here Luther deftly employs his two kingdoms theory to argue for different rules depending on the kingdom involved. For example, the Sermon on the Mount and its ethic of forgiveness and non-retaliatory love is normative for the Christian's relationship to other individuals, but cannot be elevated into a principle governing the temporal kingdom. Jesus "is not tampering with the responsibility and authority of the government, but He is teaching individual Christians how to live personally, apart from their official position and authority. They should not desire revenge at all."[9]

Luther's general argument regarding Jesus' controversial command in Matthew 5:38–45 regarding non-retaliation provides further insight into his basic proposal and its contemporary implications. This command, Luther argues, does not eliminate the temporal order and its authorities, for Jesus recognizes its legitimacy when instructing believers to "give to Caesar what is Caesar's, and to God what is God's" (Matt. 22:21). The Christian sins if non-retaliation impacts his temporal obligations to "some other person, whether under him or over him or even alongside him, like a lord or a lady, a wife or children or neighbors, whom he is obliged, if possible, to defend, guard, and protect."[10] Moreover, disaster would ensue if non-retaliation were applied to all structures of society.

> [It] would be like a shepherd who should place in one fold wolves, lions, eagles, and sheep together and let them freely mingle with one another and say, Help yourselves, and be good and peaceful among yourselves.[11]

When Jesus says, "Resist not evil,"

> it is this, that a Christian should be so disposed that he will suffer every evil and injustice, not avenge himself nor bring suit in court. . . . For others, however, he may and should seek vengeance, justice, protection and help.[12]

The Christian values of love and forgiveness are not meant to overthrow, but to operate within the structures of creation. The Christian can be present in all sectors of society, witnessing to Christ's Gospel and the new love his grace makes possible. The believer's unique mission is not diverted toward a specific political or social agenda, but focuses on witnessing to the Gospel of Jesus Christ and saving souls.

Examples

Christian businesspeople, for instance, must permeate their work with Christian values. If Christians gave away all that they had and forgave all their debtors, they would no longer be businesspeople, but beggars. They could no longer provide the necessities for their employees or their families. Instead of promoting the common good of society, they would hinder it. But while operating within economic structures, Christians must effectively embody Christ's self-sacrificial love and forgiveness to others. Chris-

Martin Rinkart (1586–1649)

There are more hymns in German than in any other language. In fact, hymn-singing as we know it—popular lyrics praising God and sung by congregations in public worship—was born with the German Reformation and in particular with German Lutherans. For that reason, the Lutheran church has been called "the singing church." (Martin Luther himself composed many hymns and once commented: "He who sings prays twice.")

One of the best known and most loved German hymns is "Now Thank We All Our God." It was written by Martin Rinkart, a seventeenth-century German pastor and archdeacon in Eilenberg of Saxony during the infamous "Thirty Years War." Eilenberg, a walled city, became a place of refuge for the homeless and hungry. As a result, it soon became overcrowded and unsanitary. Famine and disease followed. During its worst pestilence in 1637, death or desertion of clergy and officials left Rinkart alone to care for the dead and dying. At times he conducted forty to fifty funerals a day. Eventually, the dead were so numerous that they had to be buried en masse without a funeral. In all, Rinkart oversaw the burial of more than 8,000 people—including his own wife. Foreign sackings and levies of tribute followed. Through all of this, Rinkart's services were received with little gratitude, and in later years he was even harrassed by city authorities. Out of money and exhausted, he died at the age of sixty-three.

The amazing thing is that during the worst of the crisis in Eilenberg, Rinkart's faith in God was so strong that he was able to compose this hymn of thanksgiving. This is most evident in the second stanza:

> O may this bounteous God through all our life be near us,
> With ever joyful hearts and blessed peace to cheer us,
> And keep us in His grace, and guide us when perplexed,
> And free us from all ills in this world and the next.

Originally, the first two stanzas were meant to be sung around his household table at mealtime. The first expresses *praise* and looks *back* to the goodness and providence of God. The second expresses a *prayer* and looks *forward* to God's grace and guidance in the days to come. The third stanza was added later as a Trinitarian doxology.

tian love will be evident amidst the selfishness and greed in the sinful structures. The Christian eagerly lends and gives to the genuinely poor, "that is, to the one who really needs it."[13] "If you see that it is a genuine seeker, open your hand and lend it to him if he can pay you back. But if he cannot, then give it to him free, and call the account square."[14] The Christian is "poor in spirit" (Matt. 5:3) and does "not set his confidence, comfort and trust on temporal goods . . . and make Mammon his idol."[15] The believer is free with his or her possessions. When faced with political fraud or when interference and legal remedies are impossible, the believer must be willing to suffer this injustice. The Christian's goal, then, is not to change social structures, but to be a witness of Christ's love in these sinful structures.

In Luther's era, the common person could not effect social and political change. But his basic theory does suggest an outline for contemporary Christian political involvement. The Christian will not attempt to impose through coercive means his or her moral vision on the political order, for only God can change the soul. But since God is active in the temporal order, revealing the requirements for justice, the Christian politician can persuasively employ reason and the evidences of general revelation to form a broad social consensus on moral values that even nonbelievers can accept. Christians will work for the betterment of society, while recognizing the moral ambiguity of their lot. Compromises are inevitable. Structural evils will remain until the eschaton. Moreover, the political goals of peace and justice must never supplant the believer's distinctively spiritual task of proclaiming Christ and his Gospel, which alone brings about salvation and overcomes despair.

Evaluation

Historically, Luther's proposal represents an important advance in understanding the Christian's responsibility in the world. Rejecting the medieval view, where the church ruled over all the temporal orders, Luther provides a framework in which the political order exists independently of the church. By affirming that God is Lord over the entire creation, even the temporal order, Luther provides an important corrective to the Anabaptist view. God has not abandoned any part of creation to Satan. Luther's positive view of creation—as fallen but still God's—paved the way for Christians to engage the secular order directly. Adaptations of this view dominate the contemporary evangelical church.

Luther keenly recognized the historical and structural dimensions of sin: we are always making sinful compromises and sanctioning prior evil acts. Jesus' gracious work does not establish a new legalism. Rather, Christ's salvific work of justification liberates the Christian for action in this sinful world! The Christian—who is never perfect in this life, but completely sinful and righteous at the same time—is called to work individually within the structures of society and make Christ's healing love and witness a reality. Luther's proposal means that Christians should consider their work—whatever their stations in life—as Christian callings and vocations. This model provides an especially creative response for the believer who cannot change the social and political structures. Consider believers a decade ago in a Marxist country or in apartheid South Africa: rather than being paralyzed by the fear of helping demonic forces which controlled those societies, this model frees them to show Christ's love individually to others.

On the other hand, important criticisms may be directed toward this strategy. In this model Christians must live in both the kingdom of Christ and the kingdom of the world at the same time, without any final resolution to the conflicting demands placed on them. As a result, this strategy is frequently labeled "the church and the world in paradox."[16] These tensions and conflicting obligations produce an unstable model that tends to strip away the necessary nuances of each kingdom or else promotes without qualification one kingdom in place of the other.

Assumptions supporting the authority of the temporal order in place of the spiritual are clearly present, for Luther stressed that the established temporal authorities are God's instruments and exercise his rule. Luther's insight regarding the pervasiveness of sin tended to undermine reform movements (since they always produce more evil) as well as the church's mission of challenging society. For doesn't sin color the church's proclamation of God's social ideals, rendering them morally ambiguous?

Moreover, what is the enduring incentive for good works, if justification is by faith *alone*? No value ever accrues to oneself, nor does good necessarily ensue. At best, the actions of believers are only a witness or opportunity that God may or may not use to convert others—since only God can convert the soul.

As a result, this strategy contains little impetus for changing the social and political structures. Frequently this model devolves into an implicit, if not explicit support for the status quo, the current shape of society. For example, early in his ministry, Luther attacked the German princes for their abuse of the peasants. But when the peasants rose up in revolt, Luther's true colors were uncovered. He brazenly championed the princes' cause: "Let everyone who can smite, slay and stab, secretly and openly, remembering that nothing can be more poisonous, hurtful, or devilish than a rebel."[17] The church's mission of challenging society was forgotten; supporting the temporal orders was all consuming.

Sometimes this fixation on the status quo results in two moralities, one for the nonbeliever and another for the believer. Since only God can change the heart of the unregenerate, mustn't morality be defined by the current standards in the temporal sphere? Luther's counsel to Philip of Hesse, a Lutheran German prince whose support was crucial for the Reformation, illustrates this. Philip was married, but constantly engaged in adultery. Unable to improve his conduct, he thought that polygamy might be a viable option. The Old Testament saints practiced it; the New Testament never expressly forbids it. And more importantly, there was a new seventeen-year-old beauty in his court! Luther eventually advised Philip that it would be better to marry and have two wives than to continue in adultery—but this second marriage must be kept absolutely secret. Eventually, however, word leaked out. The resulting black eye for the Reformation seriously damaged the Protestants' political power in Germany.

Against these tendencies, it must be emphasized that acquiescing to the status quo results only in more injustice. Doesn't the church sin in God's eyes, and doesn't the church cause more suffering by letting the injustice and genocide of the political authorities continue? If believers don't try to change these social structures, aren't they responsible for this injustice? All of these criticisms point to the lack of an enduring transcendent moral norm within the temporal order. In Luther's proposal, God is using these rulers and authorities. However, doesn't Scripture evaluate authorities in the temporal order from the perspective of God's kingdom? Perhaps this is the central element missing from this model of the church's relationship to the world.

Some variants of Luther's proposal take the other perspective, supporting the spiritual kingdom in place of the temporal. Thus, conversion or regeneration becomes the panacea for all social ills.[18] You've heard the refrains. "Society will not be changed until everyone is converted." "Evangelism is the only means for curing social evils." At the root of this move is Luther's thesis that only through justification and conversion can one love self-sacrificially.

While conversion is indispensable, does this stance fully recognize the extent of the Christian's sinfulness? Just because an individual is converted does not mean that one perceives his or her sinfulness clearly. In fact, certain sins are very subtle, especially social sins. The various social groupings that shape our existence—whether cultural, national, political, racial, or sexual—impact us. We naturally put the aims of our group first. As a result, we are often unaware of how prideful or prejudicial we actually are. The blatant racism practiced by some Southern white Christians against African-Americans has been and continues to be a sad testimony to deep-seated prejudice untouched by the love of Christ. If we are honest we must admit that, in some form or another, we all are blinded and prejudiced by our social grouping. The sins of racism, sexism, and nationalism do not grow up in a vacuum, but emerge from social structures and "family" groupings.

Ethnocentrism—the belief that one's own group is superior to others—is a natural and ever present temptation. Conversion does little to resolve these cultural blinders. Through dialogue with other social groups and perhaps even painful confrontations, we may begin to perceive the ways in which we have pridefully disregarded the other's concerns. In addition, limited governmental actions can also help overcome some of these persistent and grievous injustices. While the civil rights legislation during the 1960s did not end racism in our country, it did force many to recognize the problem as well as give African-Americans some political and legal power which they previously had been denied.

Given the problems inherent in this stance, some have argued that the church should assume a more active role in the temporal sphere and even articulate a vision for the social and economic order. To this proposal we now turn.

For Further Reflection

1. How does the Lutheran option escape some problems of medieval theocracy and Anabaptist separationism?
2. In what ways does Charles Colson's address (appendix C, p. 284) reflect a conversionist strategy—its strength and weaknesses?
3. Does the conversionist strategy underestimate human sinfulness? How so?
4. Does this strategy adequately account for all of Jesus' teachings and work? That is, do you think that the Sermon on the Mount only applies to certain contexts and not to others?
5. Luther strictly separates the duties and responsibilities of the temporal and spiritual authorities. Is this an adequate understanding of the church's mission?
6. How would the optimal conversionist stance look in our contemporary American pluralistic environment?

For Further Reading

Braaten, Carl E. "God the Creator Orders Public Life." Chap. 7 in *No Other Gospel! Christianity among the World's Religions.* Minneapolis: Fortress, 1993.

Colson, Charles, with Ellen Santilli Vaughn. *The Body: Being Light in the Darkness.* Dallas: Word, 1992.

Gritsch, Eric W., and Robert W. Jenson. *Lutheranism: The Theological Movement and Its Confessional Writings.* Philadelphia: Fortress, 1976.

Ozment, Stephen. *Protestants: The Birth of a Revolution.* New York: Doubleday, 1992.

fourteen

John Calvin:
The Transformationist Church

ome Christians are dissatisfied with the Anabaptist option of separation as well as with Luther's limitation of the believer's mission to just evangelism and helping the needy. Rather, they seek to transform the world's institutions and structures, so that the whole cosmos reflects Christ's lordship. Guiding this vision is Scripture's future goal in which Christ and his kingdom subdues Satan's rule and the effects of sin within the cosmos.

During the Reformation period, John Calvin (1509–1564) was a key proponent of this transformational strategy. Though a second-generation Reformer, he was not second-rate. He not only authored the most significant theological text of the Reformation, *The Institutes of the Christian Religion,* he also sought to ensure that life in Geneva was lived in obedience to Jesus Christ (see chapter 11). As a result, Calvin organized the church and state so that Christ worked through both to redeem this fallen world.

Calvin's Theological Vision

Temporal Kingdom

Like Luther, Calvin maintained that God created the political, economic, and social structures of human life. Government did not originate, for instance, as an afterthought to restrain evil following Adam's sin, as the Anabaptists assert. Rather, God created humans as social creatures; as a result, we are naturally bound together. Moreover, God instituted governmental structure and its coercive power for more than simply peace-keeping, as Luther claimed.

> Civil government has as its appointed end . . . to cherish and protect the outward worship of God, to defend sound doctrine of piety and the position of the church, to adjust our life to the society of men, to form our social behavior to civil righteousness, to reconcile us with one another, and to promote general peace and tranquility.[1]

Similarly, God's institution of the family with parental authority over the children "ought to be a step toward honoring that highest Father," God himself,[2] for "it is a father's duty to teach his sons what he himself has learned from God" and so "propagate God's truth."[3] Each of these temporal structures is responsible for promoting, in its own way, "a public manifestation of religion."[4] Christians are engaged in the temporal order out of love for neighbor and in obedience to God's aims.

Calvin's positive assessment of these temporal structures reflects his understanding of creation. Creation is obliged to God the Son (Col. 1:15–20): it is "proper that our life, of which He is the beginning, be directed to his glory."[5] Humanity, the pinnacle of creation, was created in obedient fellowship with God so that the Son's glory would radiate through Adam's righteous love of God and neighbor.[6] Similarly, human authorities are obliged to God. Since no person has an innate right to rule over another, God must ground these authorities. Calvin even labels these officeholders "God's deputies." Since God desires to reflect his glory, these human authorities are obliged to help his spiritual kingdom, the church. And they will have to answer for their actions to God himself.[7]

All of life, then, is under God's claim. Moreover, this world operates properly only when obediently related to him. Without obedience to God, "we do like him who would build a house in the air." If God does not "preside over and guide us," the whole course of life becomes "disordered."[8]

Fallen Creation

All of creation is fallen. Humanity rebelled against God, so corrupting the divine image that what remains is a "frightful deformity."[9] Adam's Fall brought estrangement from God and death to humanity. As a result, humanity is enslaved to sin and unable to obey God. This sin inevitably disrupts the whole of life. Disorder pervades the political institutions which were meant to establish social justice, civil order, and peace. The princes

> "Now it will not be difficult to decide the purpose of the whole law: the fulfillment of righteousness to form human life to the archetype of divine purity. For God has so depicted his character in the law that if any man carries out in deeds whatever is enjoined there, he will express the image of God, as it were, in his life." (Calvin, *Institutes* 2.8.51)

selfishly indulge their own wants and desires instead of following God's moral norms. They exploit the weak and despised. Similarly, the purpose of the economic sphere is to provide for the needs of life and thereby allow individuals to fulfill the cultural mandate. But it is distorted by greed, trickery, and plundering of the weak. While inequity should prod us to neighborly love, the rich get richer, the poor get poorer.[10] When God's intention for creation is not followed, chaos and disorder inevitably result.

Christ, His Church and His Kingdom

Fortunately, God did not wish to abandon his creation to this state of disorder. Yet who could "swallow up death" except "Life" itself? Who could "conquer sin" except "very Righteousness"? And who could "rout the powers of the world and air" unless "a power higher than the world and air"? So "our most merciful God, when he willed that we be redeemed, made himself our redeemer in the person of his only-begotten Son."[11] God in Jesus Christ is reestablishing his reign—the kingdom of God—throughout the cosmos. God in Jesus Christ was our Prophet in proclaiming his Gospel, our Priest in making perfect satisfaction for human sins and filling us with his holiness, and our King with "eternal power" protecting his church and providing us "with confidence to struggle fearlessly against the devil, sin and death" so that we may "bring forth fruit to his glory."[12]

Christ is the King of believers in the church. The church is indispensable to the advancement of Christ's kingdom. She is "the mother of all believers"; she does "regenerate them by the Word of God, educate and nourish them through their whole life, strengthen, and bring them at length to absolute perfection."[13] In this school she trains her children to a holy and perfect life. These descriptions clearly evidence Calvin's stress on the importance of a deliberate regimen of study and discipline for believers in the church. Or as he puts it, "as the saving doctrine of Christ is the soul of the church, so does discipline serve as its sinews." Discipline is "like a bridle to restrain and tame," "a spur to arouse," or "a father's rod to chastise mildly."[14]

This stress on discipline reflects a significant difference from Luther's understanding of the church and the Christian life. Contrary to Luther's single-minded focus on justification, Calvin maintained that Jesus Christ is our Savior and we receive all his benefits as a whole. As a result, Christ justifies no one whom he does not also sanctify.[15] Moreover, the goal of the Christian life is imitating Christ in all areas of life, for "we belong not to ourselves but to the Lord."[16]

Calvin organized the church government to implement this understanding. He extended church offices to four: pastors, teachers, deacons, and elders. Deacons were entrusted with the pastoral care and social work for the needy. Elders oversaw discipline among church members. Along with the pastors, the elders formed a council that evaluated the morals of everyone in the church. While they were not to be oppressive, but to call sinners to Jesus Christ, they did have the power to discipline by fining or even imprisoning individuals leading a disorderly life. Unlike the state, elders did not have the power of the sword.

The church does not set the boundaries of Christ's kingdom, for Christ is the King of the whole cosmos. Demonstrating his kingly rule, he casts down and destroys "the reprobate who decline to submit themselves to his obedience; thus making it manifest that there is nothing which has the power to resist his will."[17] Of course, creation is not entirely obedient to Jesus Christ now. But Christ is reestablishing his lordship and the renewal of creation now. Paul in Romans 8:19–23 points to creation's "eager expectation" and its "groaning as in the pains of childbirth." Creation is groaning in anticipation of the new thing that is being born—right now!

The church's mission is to help extend Christ's rule over the whole of society so that it is brought into conformity with Jesus Christ, for at his resurrection Christ was appointed "to be head over everything for the church, which is his body, the fullness of him who fills everything in every way" (Eph. 1:22–23). Calvin, of course, never expected the church to complete this task, for the kingdom will not be perfected until the eschaton. Similarly, Christ's kingdom cannot be absolutely identified with any particular historical enterprise; sin will pervade our world until the eschaton. Nevertheless, our actions can reflect this kingdom, which in turn bestows eternal meaning and purpose on these acts. As a result, Calvin exhorted believers to work for the progressive realization of God's kingdom in history.[18]

Relationship between the Two Kingdoms

Calvin champions both the temporal and spiritual spheres. Only those who naively imagine that Christians are perfect—"as can never be found in a community of men"—attempt to eliminate the temporal sphere and its respective authorities, including the state and its power of the sword.[19] Due to the pervasiveness of sin, the temporal sphere must direct humanity's outward life toward salvation by suppressing idolatry and preventing public offenses against God, including blasphemy. Since the authority and power of the temporal orders are grounded in Jesus Christ, who desires to extend his kingdom, these officeholders are obliged to help the spiritual kingdom, the church. But Calvin carefully preserves the church's supremacy and its independence from state control. The state cannot dictate its wishes to the church. Rather, the reverse is more accurate. For the church alone proclaims God's special revelation, which both the church and the state are obliged to serve.

The Christological Grounding of All Authority

While Luther strictly segregates the duties and responsibilities of the two kingdoms, Calvin does not. Rather, he envisioned a society where Christ reigns throughout. Jesus Christ, the eternal King, ought to be acknowledged as the ruler of both the spiritual and temporal kingdoms. In fact, this Christological ground limits these temporal authorities. This point gives Calvin's view a dynamic that is completely lacking in Luther. Calvin, for example, insists that the social order, specifically the family, is subordinate to Jesus Christ. The fifth commandment, to obey your parents, is not a law that must be blindly followed.

> Rather, parents are to be obeyed in the Lord. That is, parents must be obeyed as long as they don't command something contrary to God's law. If they do, then we must view them not as parents, but as strangers who are attempting to seduce us from obedience to our real Father.[20]

This Christological limitation applies to every temporal power.

With respect to the state, for example, if the princes forbid us to serve God, then they are not worthy to be regarded as princes or to have any sort of authority. For there is only one source for the power underlying the order and structures of creation, Jesus Christ. The state's authority is not autonomous, but was established by Jesus Christ at creation and remains obliged to him. If the exercise of that power is contrary to God's norms, then it is illegitimate. Unlike Luther, Calvin does not counsel Christians to be generally compliant and submissive to the political authorities. Rather, the Christian must first ask: Is the power of the political rulers being used legitimately? Do their commands accord with Jesus' norms?

The ethical norms established for the various social institutions are found in the Ten Commandments and summarized by Jesus as love of God and love of neighbor (Matt. 22:37–39). In general, the norm is a neighborly love grounded in true worship of God. Calvin insists on the interconnection between true worship and love of God and a neighborly love. For the worship of God as found in the first table of the Law is the "source and spirit because from it men learn to live with one another in moderation and without doing injury."[21] This moral norm obligates us to care for others and "be ready to benefit our neighbor with no less eagerness, ardor and care than ourselves."[22] Nor is the neighbor limited to those with whom we are tied by a visible bond, but the whole human race, even those who "more often engender hate than love, is our neighbor."[23]

For example, neighborly love within the social sphere will attempt to rectify social inequalities by giving the weak and powerless that which is essential for participation in society and community. Otherwise, exploitation and injustice exist. In the Old Testament, Exodus was the central event reflecting God's righteousness and justice, and by this action God demonstrates how we are to judge what is just today.

> Do not deprive the alien or the fatherless of justice, or take the cloak of the widow as a pledge. Remember that you were slaves in Egypt and the Lord your God redeemed you from there. That is why I command you to do this. When you are harvesting in your field and you overlook a sheaf, do not go back to get it. Leave it for the alien, the fatherless and the widow, so that the Lord your God may bless you in all the work of your hands. (Deut. 24:17–19)

It is this norm that Jesus' future kingdom will manifest fully.

Jesus and Non-retaliatory Love

Recall that the Anabaptists maintained that Jesus' non-retaliatory love on the cross is normative for believers. Calvin countered that Jesus' unique work as Savior must not be confused with our task as believers. Jesus died by his own choice in obedience to God's plan, a plan that only he could fulfill. God's plan demanded that Jesus not establish his kingdom by arms, but by dying. Because we are not saviors of the world, we must carefully distinguish what is normative in Jesus' life. Clearly, Jesus says—and his life sustains this fact—that we are not to avenge our own individual persecutors (Matt. 5:39). Instead, we must return love for malice (Matt. 5:44). But nowhere does Jesus state, nor does his life indicate, that we should remain passive while others are being exploited.[24]

Throughout his career Jesus exercised whatever power he had for others who were oppressed. Jesus used his power against Satan's slavery when he exorcised demons (Matt. 12:22–28). Jesus demonstrated his power over the temporal authorities who were profiteering from others, with his one-man show in the temple (Mark 11:15–18). Where was nonviolent love then? Jesus' rejection of the oral law was regarded as a hostile act by the Pharisees. His words of judgment and warning that the temple would be destroyed were regarded as hostile acts by the Jewish political leadership. His popularity, his miracles during his last week which heightened the people's expectations, and his triumphal entry into Jerusalem on a donkey were all hostile acts toward the Jewish political authorities. These acts disrupted their oppressive and ungodly control over the people. In all these ways, Jesus challenged the legitimacy of the power used by the Pharisees, the temple, and Jewish authorities. In fact, it was Jesus' use of this power that ultimately led to his suffering and death.

To expand and generalize Calvin's point, there is a power relationship in every social relationship. Jesus did not ask us to give up power for non-retaliatory love, but raised the issue of the proper use of power. Is power legitimate? Calvin's view acknowledges that power is a force throughout all social relationships and attempts to place Christ's norms upon it.

The Christian's Mission: The Church Transforming the World

Jesus' Work Frees the Believer for Action in the World

Calvin rejects the Anabaptist call to separate from and abandon the sinful temporal order as naive. God calls us to service within these institutions, as our existence and development as humans mandates. Like Luther, Calvin stresses the political implications of Jesus' salvific work. Since God has declared us just and righteous in view of Jesus' work, despite who we are internally, we are freed to participate in the world, even though compromise and sin are inevitable. In addition, Jesus Christ creates in believers a new heart, one which strives obediently to be his instrument and witness in the redemption of creation.

The Sovereignty and Rule of God

Contrary to Luther's vision, God is not currently engaged in a holding action, but is sovereign and actively involved in history. Calvin's point is not simply that creation is the "theater of God's glory"—a theater in which God still works so that not even a drop of rain falls unless he commands it—but that God is guiding and governing history so that his kingdom is reestablished. Calvin calls for believers to pray that God's kingdom will dissipate "the darkness of Satan and . . . abolish all iniquity by furthering his own righteousness" "until it reaches the summit of its power."[25] Moreover, Christians are responsible for the advancement of God's kingdom in all areas of life. As Calvin puts it, believers either work so that the temporal authorities honor God or else they are helping "to have Him excluded from our midst."[26] Calvin is confident that God's purposes cannot fail; creation will be redeemed. This knowledge of God's sovereignty gives Christians a

Harriet Beecher Stowe (1811–1896)

The daughter of one of America's Calvinist revivalists, Harriet Beecher Stowe knew that believers must be God's instruments for transforming society. But by 1850 she was confined to her home in Maine, raising six children. How could she advance the kingdom of God? She had helped fugitive slaves escape while living in Cincinnati. But now, so far from the border, she determined to use her literary abilities and persuade America that slavery was an intolerable evil. Her novel *Uncle Tom's Cabin* uncovered slavery's searing injustice; it became a best-seller in the North and galvanized many to action.

Stowe portrayed how slavery reduces humans to mere "things," only to be treated or disposed of in accordance with the owner's desires. As the malicious slave-owner Simon Legree declared, "I don't go for savin' niggers. Use up, and buy more, 's my way." Stowe described the full range of their treatment. Not simply were slaves sold—separating husband, wife, and even children—but, subject to their owner's arbitrary tyranny, they had to perform tricks like pets or were used as mere "breeders." Her realistic portraits of the slaves' personal lives—especially Tom's family, which is emotionally devastated by his sale—effectively countered the common prejudice that "blacks do not feel or think like whites." As Harley put it, "These critters ain't like whitefolks, you know, they gets over things." Stowe also demonstrated the way in which this system shaped the consciousness of the slave. The hours of unrelenting pressure to perform repetitive and monotonous tasks, such as picking cotton, produced "sullen, scowling, imbruted men," who callously discarded the weak. Despite the injustice and violence confronting Tom, this hero fixed his eyes on the future that Christ established and exemplified his Lord's courageous righteousness and love for enemies, even in the face of death.

confidence and boldness to go out and change the world. Not only are their actions in transforming creation meaningful, but God is on their side!

The Christian's Mission Begins with the Church

According to Calvin, the church is the beachhead for Christ's renewal of creation. In the face of political and economic injustice, the church's task is twofold. First, the church must establish the reality of a renewed creation within its own community. Calvin organized the church government with deacons and elders to oversee discipline and the care of the poor. As a preacher, Calvin was not afraid to develop the social implications of the Gospel: Since all things belong to God and we are the stewards of his property, how can believers who have experienced Jesus Christ's sacrificial love fail to be concerned for others? He even counseled wealthy believers to share their riches with the poor to show that God and not money was their object of worship.[27]

Second, after the church has established neighborly love and social justice within its midst, the church must challenge the governmental leaders

> "Where the glory of God is not made the end of the government, it is not a legiti-mate sovereignty, but a usurpation." (Calvin, *OS* 3:11)

to defend the weak and despised. For "where the glory of God is not made the end of the government, it is not a legitimate sovereignty, but a usurpation."[28] Unlike Luther, the church must strive to change the political and social structures so that social justice is established and evil is minimized.

The Christian and Resistance

With this strategy the possibility of a conflict between the church and civil authorities looms large. In these cases Calvin typically counsels the common believer to passive disobedience. That is, the Christian must not disobey God, even in the face of the state's punishment. Like Luther, Calvin insisted that the Christian should honor the institution of government. Since God has established this institution, it is impossible to resist the mag-istrate without at the same time resisting God.[29] Calvin never encouraged the common person to revolt. Nevertheless, the church must be vocal and prophetic in its proclamation. Calvin himself certainly did not shrink from criticizing political authorities. He dedicated the *Institutes* to Francis I, the king of France, who was martyring Protestants. In the preface Calvin warned that if the king did not relent, the Protestants would "await the strong hand of the Lord, which will surely appear in due season . . . to deliver the poor from their affliction and also to punish the oppressor."[30]

Calvin, then, did not sanction the status quo. He even suggested that those holding political offices have the right to resist wicked rulers.

> For if there are now any magistrates of the people appointed to restrain the willfulness of kings, I am so far from forbidding them to withstand . . . the fierce licentiousness of kings, that, if they wink at kings who . . . assault the lowly common folk, I declare that their dissimulation involves nefarious per-fidy, because they dishonestly betray the freedom of the people, of which they know they have been appointed protectors by God's ordinance.[31]

When God raises up a proper counterforce, led by lower officials, then the common person can legitimately enter into rebellion cautiously and as a last resort. At times, Calvin even hinted that popular rebellion is justi-fied. In his commentary on Daniel 6:22, he wrote:

> For earthly princes lay aside their power when they rise up against God, and are unworthy to be reckoned among the number of mankind. We ought,

rather, utterly to defy them [literally, "to spit on their heads"] than to obey them.[32]

Calvin's point is that power originates in Christ, who is Lord over all, and thus the use of power that does not accord with God's commands is illegitimate.

Other Reformed thinkers were less hesitant than Calvin in calling for revolt. John Knox, the Reformer of the church in Scotland, maintained that obedience was due to political authorities as long as God's law was upheld. But when God's law was violated, disobedience was justified and even necessary. John Knox insisted that it is "a sin—rebellion against God—not to kill an idolatrous sovereign."[33] This God-ordained desire to transform the social order is why Calvinists were influential in Cromwell's Revolution in England and in the American Revolution.

Evaluation

In this model, the church must engage in the restoration of all creation so that it is subject to Christ's authority and rule. Not only must the individual believer help the needy, the homeless, and the victimized, but the church must strive to change the social and political structures so that such injustice and oppression is finally eradicated from this world. These Christians do not simply hope for conversion, but for the transformation of society and creation.

This model properly pursues the demands of neighborly love, namely, that it is wrong to allow others to be exploited, when we have authority and power to resist that oppression. The transformationist approach sanctions social and political reform because it sees that all power in creation is under Christ's authority. In fact, it strives to transform all areas of life so that Christ is actually Lord over all.

This model has a long heritage in the church. After the Roman Emperor Constantine became a Christian, many church leaders sought to establish a Christian society. Jesus, they insisted, called the church to better society, to rectify social institutions so that they are obedient to God. During the medieval and the Reformation periods, the church in some localities attempted to impose Christian *values* and even a specific *confession* on all members of society. Those resisting this belief were expelled or in some other way eliminated. As we noted earlier, in the Western world, with its acceptance of freedom of religion, this type of domination is no longer possible. However, certain churches are just as eagerly striving to transform society. Their goals are usually not as religiously defined and detailed. For example, the Religious Right is seeking to impose Christian *values* upon American culture by political and legal means. Not to be outdone, the Religious Left also has its own agenda for dominating American culture.

Upon close examination, a number of serious problems emerge out of the transformational understanding of the Christian's mission. One important difficulty is its theocratic tendency. This model aims at controlling all public institutions so that the church's vision dictates life. In the medieval world this reality ended in the scandal and disgrace of the Catholic church. The Protestants likewise were no less capable of sinning. It was Cromwell's Revolution in England that killed the monarch. Even at Calvin's Geneva excesses abounded. The city government, supported by the religious authorities, burned the heretic Servetus at the stake. Further, the elders of the Genevan church took their oversight of church discipline very seriously. No one was exempt from their censures—including seekers of fortune-telling, disparagers of French Protestant refugees, those who claimed the pope was a good man, and even a seventy-year-old woman who planned to marry a man of twenty-five. Freedoms that we now take for granted in Western culture were denied.

A theocracy is theologically problematic. Church officials too easily assume that God's revealed will for society is obvious. Consequently they are oblivious to the possibility that their own interpretations may also be contaminated by sin. Furthermore, isn't the theocratic impulse to dictate and compel obedience contrary to Jesus' command regarding neighborly love? How can we love our neighbors as ourselves (Matt. 19:19), unless we treat them as rational beings who must be persuaded and not coerced?

Because this model seeks to transform all aspects of creation, even the economic, political, and social spheres, it tends to sacralize every good and beneficial act. Frequently in contemporary evangelical circles, marriage therapists who help families regain their lost fellowship and love, medical doctors who heal the sick, scientists who search for the cure for AIDS, and philosophers who debate the secularists are identified as kingdom agents who are redeeming this sinful world. But is Christ's work in the temporal sphere as indispensable as his spiritual work? Are all these activities of equal importance with bringing the Gospel message of Jesus Christ and a personal relationship with Jesus Christ to a lost world? Can every good and righteous act be considered kingdom work? If everything is kingdom work, hasn't the church lost its identity and its mission?

The Anabaptists have always insisted that once the church is actively immersed in this world's sinful structures, accommodation is inescapable. In seeking to transform society, doesn't this strategy almost inevitably assimilate the Gospel to that culture's intellectual and social parameters? For how else can the church achieve its social and political goals, except by employing that culture's accepted yet sinfully compromised means? Thus, the extreme rhetoric and mudslinging power politics of some religious groups is hardly surprising.

Could a similar devolution happen to the Gospel? For how else does the transformationist model propose to communicate the Gospel except by assimilating it to that culture's understanding of justice, goodness, and love? History is dubious about this enterprise. For instance, the Second Great Awakening in America, which was instrumental in converting thousands, unleashed many new social reform movements, all seeking to make America thoroughly Christian and bring about the Millennium. But fifty years later many of those reform organizations had lost much of their understanding of the necessity for conversion and had become secular movements. Indeed, it is difficult to retain over time the distinctive Gospel message in a sinful society. So the real question facing this strategy is: What is being transformed, the Gospel or the world?

On the other hand, some Christians have seriously defended the theological necessity of accommodating to the prevailing culture. This option was proposed during the Enlightenment, to which we will now return.

For Further Reflection

1. Do you see any points of contact between the model presented in this chapter and the government and society in the United States?
2. How does Mary Stewart Van Leeuwen's address (appendix D, p. 289) reflect a transformationist strategy—its strengths and weaknesses?
3. Does the transformationist model underestimate the Christian's sinfulness?
4. Does the Reformed option lead to potential compromise with secular culture?
5. What is the church's primary responsibility? Is it transforming the world?
6. How would the most optimal transformationist stance look in the contemporary American pluralistic environment?

For Further Reading

Leith, John. *John Calvin's Doctrine of the Christian Life*. Philadelphia: Westminster John Knox, 1989.

MacNeill, John T. *The History and Character of Calvinism.* New York: Oxford University Press, 1954.

Niesel, Wilhelm. *The Theology of Calvin.* Trans. Harold Knight. Grand Rapids: Baker, 1980.

fifteen

Slouching toward Secularism: Modernity and Accommodation

E vangelicals fondly recall the Protestant Reformation, not simply because of their spiritual ancestors and their attempt to bring all dimensions of life under Christ's lordship, but because it was a time when the Christian worldview was universally accepted in Europe. Humanity's sinfulness, the need for a divine-human savior, and the necessity of special revelation for a true knowledge of God were unquestioned.

That age, however, is now gone, dissolved by the Enlightenment and its ideology, modernity. The progressive development of modernity from the eighteenth through the twentieth century has produced a decisive and irreversible change in the political, social, and intellectual outlook of Western Europe. Society's religious moorings crumbled under the Enlightenment's impact. Revelation and religious values lost their influence in the culture. In this chapter we will take a close look at these catastrophic changes and their impact on the church.

The Enlightenment and Modernity

The period after the Reformation was a tumultuous time in intellectual history, particularly with regard to religious beliefs. The Roman Catholic church, having instigated its own reforms at the Council of Trent (1545–1563), became defiant toward Protestantism and reasserted papal control. The struggle for political control, incessant in any age, took on religious dimensions. Europe became the scene of constant military forays and intrigue as the great dynasties justified their expansionist desires with religion. Germany, for instance, suffered through a Thirty Years War between Lutherans and Catholics. When it ended in 1648, the population was decimated, declining from 16 million to 6 million, and indifferent to religion.

By the late seventeenth and throughout the eighteenth century, religion found itself in what has been called "The Crisis of the European Mind."[1] On the one hand, this was a time of unprecedented religious revivals in England and the American colonies. On the intellectual scene, however, religion was on the defensive, challenged by science and philosophy. Key thinkers characterized the Reformation as a period of "blind and bloody fanaticism, and barbarous credulity." They identified the claims to special revelation as the source of this problem. Believers had no need to ground their actions and beliefs in public reason, for "the holy spirit . . . is above the law."[2]

The Enlightenment rejected Christianity's appeal to revelation as a unique sphere of knowing and instead insisted that a statement could be accepted as true only if its proofs were universally or publicly grounded. The old authorities—the Bible, the church, and other authoritarian systems—were distrusted and replaced by human reason. Reason was elevated and honored as the protector from the subjectivism, prejudices, and fanaticism of the past. This was "humankind's coming of age," when humankind dared to think for itself, no longer blindly accepting tradition. This ideological vision to reestablish society and thought on an objective foundation in which everyone concurs is called modernity. Reason's critical scrutiny would provide the objective foundation for correct thinking about reality and accessing absolute truth, since all rational beings concur in reason. With this strategy, modernity offered the hope that humans could understand the cosmos, be reconciled to one another by establishing social peace, and attain their utopian vision of the future.

Driven by this new confidence, humanity freed itself from the old authoritarian and dogmatic patterns. Not only did modernity produce great cultural and social change, but it also posed a grave challenge to the Christian faith on several fronts.

The Challenges to Christianity

The Challenge from Natural Science

In medieval Christian Europe the Ptolemaic understanding of the universe had been brought into close connection with the biblical picture. This world picture was hierarchical both spatially and theologically: the highest and most inscrutable was God's abode, the lowest and most corruptible was hell, and at the center rested the earth. But Copernicus and Galileo, using the new empirical sciences, challenged these supposedly biblical ideas. The earth was neither motionless nor the center of the universe.[3] This Copernican view became scientifically irrefutable once Newton in 1675 demonstrated that his proposed laws of motion accounted for the orbits of the various planets and other scientific phenomena which had previously gone unexplained. Newtonian science discovered that what had previously been perceived as God's inexplicably mysterious acts was orderly and lawful. Moreover, these laws were experimentally verifiable. There were no hidden divine purposes to uncover; no other explanations were necessary.

The spectacular successes of the natural sciences enthralled the European mind. Humankind by the power of its own reason had discovered truth without dependence on God's revelation. Confidence in humanity's ability to unravel the mysteries of the universe quickly followed. Alexander Pope expressed this mood of the time more clearly:

> Nature and Nature's laws were hid in night,
> God said, Let Newton be! and all was Light!

Humans, by use of their reason, reveal the mysteries of this cosmos!

These spectacular scientific advances bolstered the scientific attitude: truth in the natural world could *only* be discerned through the scientific method, and must conform to general laws provable in theory to any rational person. As a result, biblical statements could no longer be automatically accorded the status of scientific or historical truth. The Enlightenment insisted that revelation must resign its claims on scientific and historical matters, unless established through their respective scientific methods.

Nor was this the only fateful impact of the scientific method on religion or the most consequential. Because science is a public enterprise whose findings are in theory universally testable, it necessarily assumes that all events are fundamentally uniform or similar. The scientist must explain occurrences in terms of ordinary causes that anyone in principle could observe with the proper scientific tools. If causes do not accord with this fundamental core of uniformity, they cannot be accepted as scientific.

For example, if you as a scientist were investigating the literary origins of this chapter, you would undoubtedly dismiss our claim that an angel had presented it on golden tablets. This is totally contrary to reality as you experience it. Instead, you would search for more "normal" causes. Simply put, there is no place to insert a totally different kind of cause, say a supernatural cause, within a scientific account. As a result, the scientist using the scientific method treats miracles and unique events as impossible.

Of course, not everyone has completely operated this way—not even Isaac Newton! Newton saw the universe as a machine of dead particles in motion, in contrast to the long-held Aristotelian view of animated objects that move because they are acting according to their God-given nature and purpose. But Newton was quite religious and inserted God into his mechanistic view of the universe at those points which he was unable to explain scientifically. For example, God was a convenient explanation for planets staying on course in their orbits, along with a kind of ether in which the planets floated. While his intentions were good, Newton's recourse to religious explanations had the effect of producing a "God of the gaps"—a God who was only needed to explain what scientists could not yet understand. Consequently, the more science has understood about the operation of the machine that we call the "universe," the less it has needed God. And insofar as science strives to provide an all-encompassing account of our cosmos, it poses fundamental challenges to the traditional Christian belief in miracles—and particularly the birth and resurrection of Jesus Christ.

The Turn to the Self in Philosophy and Theology

Science's great advances also shifted the grounding for human knowledge. Disturbed by conflicting and erroneous claims about truth, the French mathematician and philosopher René Descartes (1596–1650) proposed a method for attaining absolutely certain knowledge. Reversing the Aristotelian tradition in his book *Meditations on First Philosophy* (1641), Descartes took as his starting point the human subject and used reason to identify that which was so clear and distinct to the mind as to be beyond all doubt. His famous discovery, "I think, therefore I am," became the indubitable first principle of his philosophy. From this foundation he established other clear and distinct ideas and constructed an edifice of objective knowledge. While his resulting system supported the findings of the new sciences, Descartes played down any theological modifications, claiming to be a faithful Catholic.

In England John Locke (1632–1704) also sought to identify the limits and grounds for knowledge by beginning with the human subject. Employing an empiricist criterion instead of a rationalist one, he argued that experience in the form of basic sense data was the source of all our knowledge (in his *Essay Concerning Human Understanding*). From this base Locke challenged certain naive views regarding the cosmos, including the knowability of matter, yet he argued for the existence of God and other minds. Taking the next step, Locke boldly applied this method to theology in *The*

Reasonableness of Christianity, arguing that special revelation must be consistent with and supported by our knowledge from sense and reason. This was a fateful step; his premise meant that human knowledge now determined the acceptability of special revelation. In Locke's portrayal, Christianity was a true yet colorless moralism revealed by Jesus, the divine prophet.

The next step in the self-elevation of the rational subject was not long in coming. Countering Locke, the deists asked: How could God demand us to accept what we cannot rationally comprehend or verify? Isn't special revelation (which is limited to those who are historically privileged) inconsistent with a good and loving God? The deists insisted that religious truth must be universally available, just as truth is in other areas of life. So a year after Locke's *The Reasonableness of Christianity* (1695), John Toland published *Christianity Not Mysterious, or a Treatise Showing That There Is Nothing in the Gospel Contrary to Reason nor Above It, and That No Christian Doctrine Can Be Properly Called a Mystery* (1696). The Bible was no longer needed, except perhaps for its inspiring moralism. The deists espoused natural religion—a religion within the bounds of nature and human reason—which they thought would bring them out of the darkness of mystery (like the doctrine of the Trinity), superstition (like turning water into wine), and pedantic religious squabbles. Since revelation must agree with and support the findings of human reason, they emphasized toleration, morality, and the idea of human perfectibility.[4]

In the eighteenth century, David Hume (1711–1776) continued this preoccupation with the human mind, but with decisively different results. His *Enquiry Concerning Human Understanding* (1748) exploded the confidence that his predecessors had placed in reason and experience, along with their arguments for God's existence and even what happens outside of our minds. What Descartes and Locke thought they could affirm on the basis of reason and observation, Hume argued was simply the result of mental prejudices and habits that do not necessarily tell us anything about the real world.

Later, Immanuel Kant (1724–1804) in *Critique of Pure Reason* (1781) and *Critique of Practical Reason* (1788) essentially argued that what we know is a result of our mind's structuring the raw data it receives in experience. So, the individual can have no knowledge of things as they are in themselves (*noumena*), but only of things as one experiences them (*phenomena*). All rational minds structure experience in the same way through the categories of time, space, and causal connectedness. Newtonian science is therefore possible. But by the same manner, Kant denied that we have any knowledge of things that transcend experience, like God and the soul.[5] Rather, our awareness of God arises from the practical demands of our moral living. The sense of moral duty we all share presupposes that there is a judge who will hold us accountable in some afterlife. This belief in God

> "'Dare to know!' Have the courage to use your own understanding; this is the motto of the Enlightenment." (Immanuel Kant, *What Is the Enlightenment?*)

is at most a way of viewing the world, providing no knowledge of reality in itself.

The upshot is that Kant solidified the subjective turn in theology by identifying morality as the criterion for all valid theological claims. Consequently, religion becomes not much more than our sense of morality and the foundation of our ethical conduct. In his *Religion within the Limits of Reason Alone* (1793), aspects of the biblical revelation that transcend the region of morality, such as historical or scientific observations, are simply excised. Biblical statements that cannot be resolved into valid statements regarding humanity's universal sense of moral duty, such as Christ's uniqueness, are reinterpreted. Simply put, God's revelation must accord with what humans can accept regarding God. This thesis is appropriately called the principle of autonomy. The term autonomy—being composed of *autos* (self) and *nomos* (law)—means that no person can accept something as being true unless it is established as such by his or her own reasoning, that is, these laws of the self.

The New Sense of History

The scientific method not only assumes the uniformity of all events, but also their interconnectedness. All events stand in a continuous or interlocking connection within one another, so that anything which happens in this world—past, present, and future—is necessarily caused and conditioned by prior events.[6] Within a century, this recognition began to shape the way intellectuals conceived world processes.

One of the first to exemplify this new sense of historical development was Georg Wilhelm Friedrich Hegel (1770–1831). By history, Hegel is not referring to a mere chronicle of names and dates, but to the dynamic that motivated their very movement and development. In Hegel's view, spelled out in his *The Phenomenology of Spirit* (1807), Absolute Spirit is moving through history and evolving in a logical, dynamic, chartable process, leaving a pattern for all critical observers to see as it moves through civilization after civilization. Humankind gains new and deeper insights into the truth through this historical process in every area of life.

Even in religion, truth does not consist of some eternal verities handed down from on high, but is derived through this historical process. All religions possess at least some fragmentary insight into the truth, and all are necessary stages on the way. Nowhere in this historical world, not even in Jesus Christ, is there anything thought or done that somehow transcends this flux of interconnecting causes. So Christianity cannot boast to be the sole location of God's special revelation, for even it is formed through the historical process. As a result, Scripture is transmuted into a human and culturally limited insight into God, Jesus the God-man into a prophet, and God's free act of grace into an immanent historical process. Hegel did identify Christianity as the final culmination of these religious interpretations of reality—as the superior religion. That is, Christianity is not the truth in contrast to false conceptions of God, but the highest expression of the truth amidst other representations of this truth.

Breathing the same air of developmental explanations of human existence, Charles Darwin (1809–1882) marshaled facts and theories to support his thesis of evolution in biology. Precedent had already been set for the challenge that Darwin's theories posed to the Christian faith, such as Charles Lyell's *Principles of Geology* (1830), which taught that the earth was older than 6,000 years (as had been assumed on the basis of mistaken biblical calculations) and that Genesis was not trustworthy. In 1859 Darwin published *On the Origin of Species by Means of Natural Selection, or the Preservation of Favoured Races in the Struggle for Life,* where he explained how change can occur through purely natural and often brutal causes. Prior theories assumed that evolution was progressive and thus implicitly assumed God's providential care. In one bold stroke Darwin eliminated the need for that belief. William Hordern summarizes the impact of Darwin's proposal: "In place of the intelligent love of a Creator who gave each animal its shape and form, Darwin pictured a ruthless struggle for existence among life forms, with victory going to those best fitted to survive."[7] Darwin applied his theory to humans in the 1860s, finally publishing his theories in *Descent of Man* (1871). Many Christians concluded that if Darwin was right, central doctrines of Christianity would be in peril—God, the uniqueness of humans, a downward Fall, and redemption. Other Christians, however, tried to suggest alternative explanations of the data that were not so threatening to basic Christian beliefs. They argued that even though Darwin's theory has no need for God's activity, it does not necessarily preclude God's providential work.

From the end of the sixteenth century through the nineteenth century, much of what had happened in the natural and social sciences seemed to imply that the Christian religion had an outmoded view of the universe and human beings. This thesis became even more explicit in the thought of Sigmund Freud (1856–1939), who developed the science of psychiatry. He viewed religion as a form of wish-fulfillment—a childish refusal to face the hard facts of life that we cannot change, but that we wish the "gods" to change for us. We collect the gods into one supreme being onto which we project images of a father figure. We pray to such a projection of our minds when things do not go right (such as when there is a destructive hurricane); when the god does not seem to "answer" our prayers, we conclude that this father-god knows what he is doing and rest in his will. Freud argued in *The Future of an Illusion* (1927) that twentieth-century people need to grow up, throw off the illusion of religion, and accept the scientific understanding of our sometimes brutal world.

Biblical Criticism

The last intellectual challenge to the Christian faith that we will mention went for the jugular. It had begun with the critical examination of biblical texts during the Renaissance, a practice that had developed into a science and had resulted in better decisions about discrepancies in the ancient manuscripts and about vernacular translations. But as the seventeenth and eighteenth centuries progressed, the production and transmission of the biblical texts continued to be discussed, sometimes with the explicit intention of destroying the underpinnings of the Christian faith.

Each of the challenges explained above brought new pressures upon the authority and reliability of Scripture. The natural sciences not only challenged the verses traditionally used to support a Ptolemaic view of the universe, but also attacked the reality of miracles lying at the nucleus of the biblical narrative. The subjective turn in theology placed under scrutiny Scripture's purportedly morally repugnant elements. But it was the new understanding of history that became the greatest concern: it treated the Bible like any other piece of literature and searched for its literary origins.

Noting the stylistic peculiarities of the Pentateuch, some critics proposed that the books were composed by a number of authors. For example, look at the repetitions in Genesis 7:17–20. As one critic stated, is it not reasonable to suppose that if one and the same writer had been describing this event, he would have done so in far fewer words? These scholars concluded that the text of the Pentateuch is overlaid with a number of literary deposits. These questions and attacks were not new, but they were now being accepted as legitimate questions. Once that step was taken, the unity of the biblical narrative was also challenged.

Questions were raised regarding Jesus fulfilling the Old Testament prophecies, such as the use of Isaiah 7:14 in Matthew 1:22–23. As one critic argued, Isaiah does not refer to the "virgin" Mary and Jesus but to a "young woman" in the days of Ahaz, the King of Judah. Though the word *could* be translated as "young woman" *or* "virgin," naturalistic assumptions favored the former and ruled out specific predictions about Jesus of Nazareth coming in the first century.

> "The Gospel, as Jesus proclaimed it, has to do with the Father only and not with the Son." (Adolph von Harnack, *What Is Christianity?*)

But the capstone was the nineteenth century's search for the historical Jesus. Those active in this search rejected the possibility of a supernatural being and instead attempted to reconstruct a figure limited to the methodology of the historical sciences and human possibilities. To get at the "so-called" historical Jesus underneath the Gospels' portrayals of him meant peeling off layers of embellishment, miracle stories, and messianic claims. For example, Adolf von Harnack portrayed Jesus as a thoroughly human figure who proclaimed an ethical community of love that sought the moral advancement of humanity. This quest temporarily ended when Albert Schweitzer pointed out in 1906 that such searchers had looked down the well of history only to see their own reflection in the Jesus they had constructed. That is, they found what they wanted to find, superimposing their own values and images of reality on the findings.[8] But Schweitzer went on to argue that Jesus was a tragic figure who preached not an imminent ethical kingdom but an apocalyptic one, and who mistakenly thought that his death would hasten the kingdom's coming. Simply put, many scholars viewed the Bible as nothing more than ancient religious literature that included many misguided figures and reflected the cultural myths and illusions of that period.

The Secularization of the Western World

The cultural change accompanying the above challenges is usually called secularization. Secularization does not describe an intellectual critique, but religion's loss of influence throughout society including the daily lives of individuals. In a secularized society the institutions essential to a culture—science, technology, business, politics—exist without any religious support or connection.

Recall the history of the United States. For better or worse, the Puritans evaluated the whole of life from the perspective of revelation: they "thought that their own lives mattered only because they fit into the story of God's activity in history."[9] The covenant of the Massachusetts Bay Colony acknowledged their special role as God's people: "we shall be as a city upon a hill, the eyes of all people are upon us." Their communities camped around the church. Through their preaching and discipline the clergy ensured that Christian values were embraced by the local businesspeople and governmental leaders. Religion's role in American culture has changed greatly in the last 300 years. Currently religion is consigned to the private arena of the individual's life. If someone attempts to employ religion in the public arena, they are derisively labeled a "Waco Wacko" (referring to the unfortunate legacy of David Koresh and the Branch Davidians). The religious dimension of much American culture has been stripped away. If God matters at all to people, it is only because "he could be fit into the story of *their* lives."[10]

Why this cultural change? Why the collapse of religious influence? Sociologists have identified many causes. For one, the disestablishment of the church and the diversity of religious beliefs reshaped American society and signaled an end to the church's social domination. Today political institutions proudly emphasize their independence from any religious sanction or connection. John F. Kennedy gave a classic articulation to this separation when he assured Protestant ministers in Texas that his Catholic faith would not influence his presidential political decisions. He would be, as the old joke put it, "not religious enough to count." Whatever religious dimension that still remains within governmental institutions is confined to the ceremonial. Thus, Congress opens its sessions with prayer, and we pledge allegiance to "one nation under God."

In addition, the cultural dominance of science has demystified the cosmos. People of the Reformation era were dependent on God in part because so much was unknown about the physical world. Medicine, for instance, was the art of the barber. Luther's wife prayerfully attempted to cure him of kidney stones by filling him up with beer and then having him pulled by a cart over their rough roads! In the face of suffering, anxiety, and uncertainty, humans naturally pray. But due to the spectacular advances of science we now know how the cosmos works, and we can correct much of it when it goes astray. All our procedures and plans are carefully tested and controlled; nothing is left to chance. As a result, Christian practices and their focus on the "other world" appear less relevant to everyday life.

American mythic themes—those ideals and values that unify our culture—are no longer religious. Instead the inalienable rights to "life, liberty, and the pursuit of happiness" unify society. Individuals possess the freedom to realize their own dreams, as long as they do not infringe on the rights of others. Certainly anyone can pursue Christianity, but the social context of belief has now shifted. The primacy of individual rights has encouraged a narcissistic religion that emphasizes personal satisfaction. We believe because it makes sense to us, because it fulfills our needs and desires. As the recent slogan for the Unitarian Universalist church illustrates, "Instead of me fitting a religion, I found a religion to fit me."

Due to secularization, religion has not only lost its dominance within society, but the culture has begun to place limitations upon religion. American culture insists that religious beliefs be isolated from public life, and be pursued by individuals only in their own private sphere. Religion is privatized; it is acceptable only if it remains in the private realm. Marginalized and privatized, the choice of Christianity over other faiths has no more significance than one's preferring Ben and Jerry's "Chunky Monkey" ice cream over "Cherry Garcia." But when religion transgresses those boundaries and impinges upon public life it is considered offensive, or, worse, politically incorrect!

Responses to the Challenges of Modernity

How would the church respond to these challenges to her orthodoxy and influence? There were and are several choices. Should it meet them head-on? Should it acquiesce, lick its wounds, and go on making the best of it? Should it withdraw in reaction? In a sense, the branches of the Christian family did—and do—all three. Let's examine the last two of these historical responses to modernity. The first we'll reserve for the next chapter.

Withdrawal

The nineteenth-century Roman Catholic response was largely one of reactionary condemnation. In 1864 Pope Pius IX promulgated the *Syllabus of Errors,* a comprehensive attack on the errors of modernism, including eighty errors under ten headings. It condemned rationalism, pantheism, naturalism, toleration of other religions (including Protestantism), any ultimate authority other than Rome, separation of church and state, and modern liberalism. In reality, the pope was attempting to consolidate lost political power by drawing the line against the modern culture that seemed to be at the root of the papacy's lost influence. The sentiments of the *Syllabus* were rubber-stamped in a document entitled *Dei Filius,* composed at Vatican Council I. Convened in 1870, this council provided the principles upon which the Roman Catholic church would continue to stand against the infiltration of modernism well into the twentieth century. Not until Pope John XXIII, in the 1960s, called for the Catholic church to open her windows to the world would she reverse this stance through the sweeping changes growing out of Vatican Council II.

Accommodation

Others in the nineteenth century repudiated the Catholic strategy. They insisted Christianity was facing a life or death crisis. If the church is not relevant to modern life and if its claims are not perceived as valid, Christianity will soon be relegated to the dustbin of history. As a result, they responded by legitimating the Christian faith through a truth their culture already accepted. The ancient faith was reinterpreted through modern ideas; Christianity was adjusted or accommodated to the culture.

In every age, there are some who claim that Jesus legitimates the hopes and aspiration of their culture. They feel no great tension between being a disciple of Jesus and being at home in this world. This harmony between Christ and their culture may range from lifestyles and values to a theological reconception of the Christian faith. In all instances, though, the prevailing culture defines Christianity.

Protestant Liberalism: An Accommodationist Stance

Undoubtedly Protestant liberalism represents the most astute and convincing articulation of the accommodationist stance. These Christians immediately recognized that the modernist critique was simply too devastating to ignore. Many in society had already identified "Christianity . . . with Barbarism and culture with unbelief."[11] Attempting to reclaim these "cultured despisers," German theologian Friedrich Schleiermacher (1768–1834) courageously initiated a new method in theology. Over the past two centuries, this liberal experiment has continued and included some of the most creative Christian minds the church has ever known. As a result, liberalism remains an enduring, if not a dominant, force throughout the Christian world; this strategy cannot be ignored.

The Methodological Assumptions of Protestant Liberalism

Facing these critiques, Protestant liberals did not rebut these challenges, but readily conceded Scripture's discrepancies and its primitive (supernatural) outlook on the world. In part, this liberal move reflected their deep antipathy toward propositional revelation, that is, the thesis that God has acted and spoken to reveal his will regarding humans. Following Kant and much of modern thought, severe restrictions were placed on knowing truth claims. Protestant liberals precluded the possibility of God cognitively revealing himself.

This move also displays a defining assumption of the liberal enterprise—its fundamental respect for science and its findings. The very term *liberal* denotes open-mindedness and the freedom to follow modern scholarship and science wherever it leads. To demand total submission to Scripture's authority in the face of scientific findings is tantamount to intellectual suicide. A God who compelled such obedience would be a tyrant and dicta-tor. On the contrary, science must be allowed a free reign. It provides us with the truth; and certainly all truth is God's. So if Christianity really is true, why impede these challenges? For how could there be any final con-flict between human reason and the *true essence* of Christianity?

So Protestant liberalism sided with these modernist challenges and rephrased the question: How can Christianity, which grew up in a primi-tive age, be acceptable to modern men and women? There were only two possible options. If "the Gospel is in all respects identical with its earliest form" and that outdated worldview, then "it came with its time and has departed with it." Simply put, to identify Christianity with its revealed propositions dooms this religion. In the second option Christianity "con-tains something which, underlying differing historical forms, is of perma-nent validity." This is the classic liberal stance. Primitive Christianity must disappear so that true Christianity might remain.[12] According to Protestant liberalism, the essence of Christianity lies not in doctrine, but in a religious or moral spirit that doctrine presupposes.

The next defining move in Protestant liberalism was identifying the essence of religion. Following the modernist strategy regarding religion as outlined by Kant, liberals sought to ground the truth of Christianity in a universal religious experience, for then the faith would be attractive and acceptable to their world. Schleiermacher grafted Christianity onto a uni-versal experience, the pre-reflective feeling of absolute dependence—a con-sciousness that the entire universe owes its existence to something that lies outside of it or beyond it. Two other advocates of Protestant liberalism, Albrecht Ritschl (1822–1889) and Adolf von Harnack (1851–1930), were more dependent on Kant. In their own ways they insisted that the essence of the Christian faith was the ethical values it espoused—the ethics of the kingdom that Jesus taught. In both instances, Christianity had nothing to do with science or metaphysics, but the fulfillment of a universal human experience and the foundation for all religion.

This essence of religious experience becomes the norm or arbiter for determining Christianity's permanent and central values. Primitive views are eliminated, while the essence remains intact. This reinterpreted Chris-tian faith is thus compatible with the modern world.

For instance, even Jesus is subject to this external norm, though he is interpreted as its most perfect human embodiment. As a result, Jesus is received as the most godly man, or the most insightful moral teacher, or the one who always acknowledged his dependence on God. But in the end, Jesus is not the God-man, or even worthy of worship, but just a human pointer to the ideal.

Schleiermacher, in his epoch-making books *Speeches on Religion to Its Cul-tured Despisers* and *The Christian Faith*, redefined the concept of "miracle" so

"The cosmology of the New Testament is essentially mythical in character. . . . [The earth] is the scene of the supernatural activity of God and his angels on the one hand, and of Satan and his demons on the other. These supernatural forces intervene in the course of nature and in all that men think and will and do. . . . All our thinking today is shaped irrevocably by modern science. A blind acceptance of the New Testament mythology would be arbitrary, and to press for its acceptance as an article of faith would be to reduce faith to works. . . . It would involve a sacrifice of the intellect which could have only one result—a curious form of schizophrenia and insincerity. It would mean accepting a view of the world in our faith and religion which we should deny in our everyday life." (Rudolph Bultmann, *New Testament and Mythology*)

that it no longer offended Newtonian science. A miracle is merely an event which occasions the religious experience, but for which one can find no historical explanation. Similarly, Schleiermacher was undisturbed by the critical attacks on Scripture's reliability. None of the critical attacks—whether directed at the creation story, Adam and Eve, God's wrath toward sin, Jesus Christ as the God-man, or even Jesus' resurrection—bothered Schleiermacher. The Christian faith was impervious to scientific attack, for its heart and ground was the "feeling of absolute dependence"—a prereflexive intuition that the entire universe owes its existence to something that lies outside of it or beyond it.

The Protestant liberals, in other words, made an end run around the challenges from the sciences, evolutionary historical thought, and biblical criticism. They accepted these criticisms and creatively grounded the Christian message on an experience that their culture could endorse. From their perspective, Christianity had escaped unharmed and was relevant to the modern world. Its "cultured despisers" could now accept the Christian faith.

Protestant Liberalism in America

While Protestant liberalism originated in Europe, it was not confined there for long. The challenges facing Christianity—from Darwin to the "search for the historical Jesus"—electrified the Western intellectual world. Furthermore, America had always sent her most promising biblical and theological students to Europe for the finishing touches to their divinity training. So by the late 1800s, theological liberalism had appeared in the United States and was being taught in several seminaries. By the turn of the century, many of the most important brilliant theological minds in America advocated liberalism. Some of the more notable figures include Shailer Mathews (1863–1941) at the Chicago Divinity School, William Adams Brown

Walter Rauschenbusch (1861–1918)

The most formidable mind among the writers of what came to be called the Social Gospel movement was Walter Rauschenbusch. He had been brought up in a conservative German Baptist tradition, but studies in Germany moved him in a distinctively liberal direction, influencing him to accept the critical approach to the Bible and a developmental (evolutionary) view of Christianity. He identified himself with the theological tendencies of Schleiermacher, Harnack, Ritschl, and others. He was deeply influenced by liberal scholarship yet grasped by a personally profound Christianity.

He found a burden for social ministry and read widely in the social literature of his day, but he could not find a theological understanding to undergird his social concerns. This search resulted in his life-long work and to a revision of much of his understanding of the Christian faith. He would later reflect that all of his scientific study of the Bible had been undertaken to find a basis for the Christian teaching of a social gospel. He found this basis in the important doctrine of the kingdom of God.

His mature work *A Theology for the Social Gospel* (1917) drew freely on the liberal tradition in theology. Rauschenbusch taught that the kingdom is humanity organized according to the will of God. It can be progressively realized as a historical force through family, economic organizations, the state, and the church. Its coming can be speeded up by shortening hours of work and raising wages, providing adequate housing, and so on. In Christ the kingdom got its first foothold in humanity; now the social gospel must be concerned about the progressive social incarnation of God. Sin is selfishness, but if people turn from self toward God and others, following Jesus' ethic of love, they will find salvation.

Rauschenbusch was not merely a theorizer. For a time he served the parish of "Hell's Kitchen" in New York City. Later he taught at Rochester Seminary. His ideas were significant in the intellectual development of Martin Luther King, Jr.

(1865–1943) at Union Seminary in New York, Harry Emerson Fosdick (1878–1969) at the First Presbyterian Church and the Baptist Riverside Church in New York City, and Walter Rauschenbusch (1861–1918) of Rochester Seminary, a leader in the Social Gospel movement.

Facing a conservative American culture, liberals used their great rhetorical skills to overcome the resistance of a "dogmatic orthodoxism" and revise Christianity in the light of new learning. While their terminology may appear traditional, the content of their theology was not. Scripture, they insisted, must be critically examined through scientific methods, free from dogmatic interference. Scripture itself was interpreted as the experiences of "men who had some perception of the Infinite" and authoritative only to the degree it coincided with contemporary religious experience. Christianity's paramount theme was God's immanent work through the evolutionary progress of history. Sin is not a universal debility, but a moral disease that can be cured through human self-control, reason, and service to others. Jesus was not

God's unique or supernatural action in history, but the human ideal for morality. God's goal is that the whole human race becomes like Christ and so be an "incarnation" of the divine. Jesus' death on the cross did not defeat Satan or pay the penalty for sin, but merely expressed God's readiness to love and forgive. The church's mission is not to witness to reconciliation with God through a personal relationship with Jesus Christ, but to promote a new social order by imparting "Christlikeness." Not surprisingly, then, many liberals readily admitted that this "Christian faith" could be found in the lives of believers from other religions and even agnostics.

Other Forms of Accommodation

Cultural relevancy is an alluring temptation in every period, but not all accommodationist strategies require discarding the traditional Christian confessions. Consider a late nineteenth-century example, the theologically evangelical Russell Conwell, who heralded *laissez-faire* capitalism as the gospel. In his sermon "Acres of Diamonds," which was preached across the country over 10,000 times, Conwell proclaimed, "To make money honestly is to preach the gospel."[13] The pursuit of hard and honest work develops Christian character, and with the resulting wealth one can help the community and "poorer brethren." But this "gospel" simply fulfilled American mythic themes: equal opportunity, the moral benefits of work, and stewardship. Certainly, he eased the working class's transition in an industrial urban America and produced much good. Under Conwell's energetic leadership, his church in a working-class neighborhood of Philadelphia became the city's largest Protestant congregation. His church integrated evangelism with self-help programs; it provided concerts, clubs, health care; and its night courses helped working people better themselves, eventually developing into Temple University. But is this the Gospel of Jesus Christ? Was Jesus persecuted for the sake of our prosperity? Did Jesus suffer crucifixion so that we might pursue a successful career?

This superficial Christianity and its popularity are symptomatic of the problem with every accommodationist stance: Christianity is not permitted to critique and evaluate the prevailing culture. Instead, culture simply domesticates and eventually circumscribes Christianity, allowing conformity in only one direction.

Conclusion

In whatever form, the accommodationist stance has already displaced Christ's lordship with some form of the prevailing culture. While accommodationists take the world's challenges seriously, they also prove that if Christ is not Lord over *all*, he is no longer Lord at all! As we mentioned, however, there was—and is—another option. It's found in the evangelical Protestant branch of the family tree. But where it branched off from the tree is not necessarily where it is now located as it continues to grow and develop. We will turn to that response to modern culture in the next chapter.

For Further Reflection

1. Do you find the criticisms of Christianity lodged by Kant, biblical criticism, and Darwinism to be threatening to your faith? How do you respond to such criticisms? By withdrawing in a manner similar to the Catholic church or by seeking some sort of accommodation like the liberal Protestants? Or is there a third option?
2. Have you thought of God as a "god of the gaps" when it comes to the interface between religion and science? Do you see any strength/dangers in that?
3. In what ways does Fosdick's redefinition of key Christian doctrines (see appendix E, p. 293) reflect the strategy and assumptions of Protestant liberalism?
4. In what subtle ways does secularization impact your own Christian faith?
5. In what ways does contemporary evangelicalism—even your own church—reflect an accommodationist strategy?
6. Do you think that the present climate of pluralism makes it easier to be a Christian in today's world than it was for the nineteenth-century heirs of the Enlightenment?

For Further Reading

Hazard, Paul. *The European Mind (1680–1715)*. New York: World, 1963.

Henderson, Charles P. *God and Science*. Atlanta: Westminster John Knox Press, 1986.

Hordern, William E. *A Layman's Guide to Protestant Theology,* 2d ed. New York: Macmillan, 1968.

Johnson, Roger A., et al. *Critical Issues in Modern Religion,* 2d ed. Englewood Cliffs, N.J.: Prentice Hall, 1990.

Kuhn, Thomas. *The Structure of Scientific Revolutions,* 2d ed. Chicago: University of Chicago Press, 1970.

Matthews, Michael R., ed. *The Scientific Background to Modern Philosophy: Selected Readings.* Indianapolis: Hackett, 1989.

Stevenson, Leslie. *Seven Theories of Human Nature,* 2d ed. New York: Oxford University Press, 1987.

Thielicke, Helmut. *The Evangelical Faith,* Vol. 1. Grand Rapids: Eerdmans, 1977.

sixteen

We Are Family:
American Evangelicalism
and Its Roots

$\mathcal{F}$inally, we arrive at the branch of the Christian family tree we Protestant evangelicals are sitting on. When we look down below, we can trace the growth of our branch. It is thicker at the bottom because many strands came together to form it.

The European challenges to the Christian faith that we discussed in the last chapter, along with the Protestant responses, had an impact on the development of conservative Protestantism in North America, though some of these challenges did not enter into the American picture until the latter half of the nineteenth century. The response to these challenges, plus a somewhat unique pattern of Christianity that grew up in the United States, form the backdrop to what has been labeled "American evangelicalism."

In general, evangelicalism grew out of fundamentalism. In fact, at times in the past it has been hard to distinguish between them. The roots of fundamentalism go back to revivalists in the pietist tradition, denominational conservatives in the Calvinist tradition (especially at Princeton Theological Seminary), and dispensational premillennialists. We will describe these as we go along, adding a few other strands to the lower portions of our branch. In tracing the family tree, we will look first at American revivalism, then at the rise of fundamentalism, and finally at the fundamentalist-modernist battles that significantly shaped both fundamentalism and evangelicalism in the twentieth century.

The History of American Revivalism

There are at least three discernible periods in the history of American revivalism, a history that will lead us up to some crucial movements between 1870 and 1920.

The Great Awakening (1735–1750)

The Puritans who settled New England shared a covenantal theology: God had entered into a system of covenants with the human race (one of works with Adam; one of grace with Christ). Good works were the sign that a person had been elected by God into the covenant of grace. ("By their fruit you will recognize them," Matt. 7:16.) Salvation could be determined in terms of the bent of one's life: Was it tending toward holiness?

With this theology, the Puritan colonies restricted the membership of their churches to the *proven* elect. By 1660 there developed a system of "evidences" to prove one's election, followed by a gradation of membership. There were full members (the baptized who professed the Christian faith), half-way members (those baptized but not professing the faith, yet still bound to God by the covenant), and children of half-way members. It was not the only reason, but such "hereditary religion" helped usher in the demise of primitive and vibrant Puritanism by 1710.

It was in this context of stale religion and spiritual apathy in Puritan New England (as well as in the Anglican South) that a revival swept through all of the colonies, striking all classes of people. In fact, it became one of the first inter-colonial events in American history and may have united the colonies more than any other event before the Revolution. (For this reason some historians argue that it even helped to make the Revolution possible.)

The beginnings of the revival seem to have begun in the 1720s in New Jersey with some Dutch Reformed and Presbyterian ministers who began to preach an evangelical gospel, call for a life of discipline, and hold private prayer meetings. One of these men would even found a "log college" in the 1720s to train such ministers that would eventually blossom into Princeton University.

While this took place in the middle colonies, a revival in New England was touched off by the experience of a church in Massachusetts, pastored by Jonathan Edwards, a Puritan Congregationalist educated at Yale. In the

"True religion, in great part, consists in the affections . . . in vigorous and lively actions of the inclination and will of the soul, or the fervent exercises of the heart. That religion, which God requires, and will accept, does not consist in weak, dull, and lifeless wishes, raising us but a little above a state of indifference. God, in his word, greatly insists upon it, that we be in good earnest, fervent in spirit (Rom. 12:11), and our hearts vigorously engaged in religion." (Jonathan Edwards, *Religious Affections*, 1.2.1)

midst of increasing immorality and Arminianism (a theology that emphasizes the human's ability to turn to God), Edwards witnessed what he called *A Surprising Work of God*. His account of the incident, published in a booklet in 1735, established the pattern for all other revivals.

Edwards was delivering a series of sermons on the doctrine of justification apart from works. He challenged the respectable townspeople to evaluate themselves in terms of God's standpoint, not society's. The result was that people began to take the judgment to heart and lean on the love of Christ for its intrinsic value. Within a short time God's Spirit swept through the town and brought life where there had previously been religious apathy and self-interest. Edwards claimed that never before had Northampton been so full of joy and love—especially love for one's enemies. As a Calvinist, Edwards saw all of this as the result of God's sovereign action. Since he believed that humans are dead in their sins, unable to help themselves, by definition a true revival was a miraculous work of God. Even though he had prayed for a revival for many years, Edwards was genuinely surprised by these events.

The most phenomenal figure of the Great Awakening was the Calvinist George Whitefield. The revival peaked in 1741–1742 with his preaching from Georgia to Maine. He preached to folks overlooked by the institutional church. Whitefield's preaching was masterfully intelligible to the most simple and was transparently sincere. He sought Christians with an experiential knowledge of the Gospel. He did not simply want people to know some historical data about Jesus, but to experience firsthand Jesus' love for the sinner, the joy of being accepted by God, and the desire for Jesus' holiness. The result was a religious revolution across the colonies. Like Edwards, Whitefield tied conversion to social action. He raised funds for a school for blacks and an orphanage in Georgia and he voiced opposition to oppressive slaveholders.

But decline began to set in after this period. Why? For one thing, while Whitefield was initially received by Yale and Harvard, by 1744 these two institutions, along with several ministers, began to link Whitefield and Edwards with an excessively emotional man named John Davenport, who sought emotional shows such as barking, jerking, and fainting. They warned that such preaching offended reason and harmed the peace and purity of the churches. Even though Edwards had blended emotion and intellect as a Puritan and Calvinist, the emotional side came to be emphasized as the revival went on.

Still, the revival had benefited the Presbyterians and Congregationalists, as well as Calvinist theology. Also, its emphasis on the *experience* of religious conversion and an experiential piety helped to set part of the pattern of revivalism in North America.

But it also established another pattern that would continue into the future. The Great Awakening did as much to promote controversy as it did to stimulate revival. Theological divisions and denominational splits ensued, particularly within Presbyterian and Congregational churches. At issue was the relation between religion and the emotions. The "New Lights" followed Edwards in claiming that without affection (such as love for God) there cannot be true religion, but one must carefully discern whether the source of an emotion is God or Satan. The "Old Lights" followed Charles Chauncey, who warned against the emotional display in treatises like "Enthusiasm Described and Cautioned Against" and favored a rationally staid religion.[1] Such controversies and divisions evidence the elevation of the laity at the expense of the clergy, which has shaped American denominationalism.

As the Great Awakening died down, the European Enlightenment hit North America. It was first felt in the importation of deism. College students were especially influenced by the deistic thought of Ethan Allen and Thomas Paine—ideas that were shared by the likes of Thomas Jefferson and Benjamin Franklin. By the 1780s interest in religion was significantly low. Estimates are that only 5 to 10 percent of the colonial population were church members.

The Second Great Awakening (1790–1820)

In the first half of the nineteenth century revivals became part of our national history. They were seen as a way for Christian churches to cope with the mushrooming population that was rushing to settle the "frontier."

They started with some minor revival fires in the East during the 1790s, especially at Yale University. There Yale president Timothy Dwight had instituted a mandatory four-year Bible curriculum, and once all had gone through the program, an awakening occurred on campus in 1802. As a result, some of the Eastern universities provided ministers for the Western frontier.

It was on the frontier that much of this second Awakening took place. Due to factors such as the nature of frontier life and the leadership taken by Baptists and Methodists, the emphasis shifted from the sovereignty of God (the Puritan Calvinist "waiting on God" in Edwards and Whitefield) to the human role in salvation—a democratic, Arminian, active seeking and coming to God. Conversion and holiness came to be seen as matters of individual choice more than divine action.

It has been said that the migrant, unlettered population that moved West "liked their whiskey straight and their religion and politics red hot." Consequently, effective evangelistic preaching had to be quick, limited in scope, insistent on a decision, and full of assurances and promises. After all, the pioneers might not be in the same spot tomorrow; they may have moved on or they may have died. Life was fast and precarious. Furthermore, frontier folks were not interested in aristocratic ideas like divine election nor in learned lectures on doctrine such as those preached in weekly sermon series in the more settled East Coast churches.

It was the Baptists and the Methodists who dished up religion "red hot." Their circuit-riding system and the extended camp meetings (which would later spawn the Bible camp movement, so crucial to the rise of fundamentalism) made it possible for these two denominations to relate to the unique needs and ethos of the frontier. In fact, by 1800 the Baptists became the largest denomination in the U.S. The Methodists were close behind and took the lead in 1820.

The Second Great Awakening helped to establish a peculiar brand of American Christianity that involved an active seeking of salvation; it was pro-revival, individualistic, and pietistic. It set the stage for the popular evangelists in the next era of American revivalism.

Before turning to that era, we should mention that the response to this awakening was similar to that of the first awakening. Again, there was a distaste for emotional excess, spawning countertrends such as the Transcendentalism of Ralph Waldo Emerson. Conservative reactions were varied; some, such as at Princeton Seminary, drew up statements that countered perceived democratic, unchurchly, and emotional aspects of revivalism.

Urban Revivalism (1840–1955)

The "creator" of modern revivalism was Charles Grandison Finney (1792–1875). He represents the transition from rural and small-town revivalism to urban revivalism. Finney perfected American revivalism into a technique that was especially suited for the city dweller. Though he would later become a professor and president of Oberlin College (Ohio), he started out as a lawyer, arguing the case for Christianity like a jurist. He introduced "New Measures"—innovative and controversial techniques for urban revivalism—that became a standard feature of American revivals for decades. These measures were very successful and included cottage prayer meetings, the "anxious bench" (seats up front for people expecting to be converted), protracted meetings, and a public invitation at the end with an "inquiry room." These techniques were thought to break down the resistance to revival and to induce a conviction of sin. In fact, over against Jonathan Edwards's earlier view of revivals as "a very extraordinary dispensation of Providence,"[2] Finney maintained that "a revival is not a miracle, or dependent on a miracle in any sense. It is a uniquely philosophical [i.e., scientific] result of the right use of constituted means."[3] Thus, the revivalist became a persuader who appealed to the popular will. By the mid-nineteenth century such revivalism had become the predominant style across the landscape of American Protestantism.

Additionally, Finney also insisted that faith in Jesus Christ must be evidenced through social and moral action. His stress on Christ's work of holiness or perfect sanctification unified evangelism with social work and community service and helped generate the great reform movements (e.g., anti-slavery, temperance, women's suffrage) of the nineteenth century that defined Protestantism. Characteristic of the Protestant leaders of that period, Finney optimistically held the postmillennial vision that through God's help and revivals the church would usher in a new world where poverty, crime, illness, and war would be no more.

In the second half of the nineteenth century, Finney's "New Measures" were refined, but this time through a businessman's mentality—namely, that of Dwight L. Moody (1837–1899), a Congregational layman and former shoe salesman. Moody organized revival campaigns in the style of a successful business venture. This fit in well with the industrializing ethos of the latter nineteenth century. He gained notoriety by 1873 (along with his song leader Ira D. Sankey), preaching a simplistic evangelical version of the Gospel that emphasized three "Rs"—"Ruin by sin, Redemption by Christ, and Regeneration by the Holy Ghost." By 1880, Moody had so completely dominated the American religious scene that for about seventy-five years revivalism was patterned after his example.

In fact, Moody even fit the profile of what would become the fundamentalists: a believer in biblical infallibility and premillennialism, and a promoter of holiness teachings ("victory over sin") and conservative ethical emphases. The only thing Moody lacked was militancy. He was absolutely opposed to controversy. He was, instead, what George Marsden calls a "pragmatic activist."[4]

Moody was also a precursor of fundamentalism in that he was a member of no denomination, but had good relations with most evangelical denominations. Fundamentalists at first had ties with denominations, but even before they dissociated themselves from these denominations, they tended to associate around specialized agencies, conferences, publications, or local churches. As Marsden puts it, "It was a religion structured according to the free enterprise system."[5]

What Moody especially foreshadowed in later fundamentalism was its ambivalent attitude toward the American culture—a culture that had largely been shaped by the American evangelical revivalist movement. Would fundamentalism be exclusive and militant over against the culture? Or would it foster an irenic spirit concerned with holiness and saving souls? On the one hand, Moody agreed with the latter: as we mentioned, he was a pragmatist and wanted nothing to get in the way of saving souls. On the other hand, he also came to adopt the former sentiment with his premillennial eschatology, which fostered a pessimistic view of the culture and a strong impetus to evangelism. To quote Moody: "I look upon this world as a wrecked vessel. God has given me a lifeboat and said to me, 'Moody, save all you can.'"[6] If one recalls the attitude of Finney, who insisted that revivalism went hand-in-hand with the abolition of slavery, one has to agree with Marsden's evaluation of Moody's attitude.

> This view that "the world" would "grow worse and worse" was an important departure from the dominant tradition of American evangelicalism that viewed God's redemptive work as manifested in the spiritual and moral progress of American society.[7]

So revivalism in America came to include an amalgamation of two traditions—pietism and Calvinism, or an emphasis on emotional intensity and highly intellectual theology. Furthermore, it had in its background the Puritan ideal of transforming the prevailing culture and creating a Christian society; though, with some ambivalence, it also came to posit the holiness doctrine of gaining victory over sin and radically separating oneself from the worldly and the apostates. Individualism, voluntarism (along with Arminianism), and piety were stressed—themes that fit in nicely with the latter half of the nineteenth century in America, when democracy, free enterprise, and the welfare of society were being emphasized. The revivalist movement out of which fundamentalism would grow was largely "in sync" with American culture—and vice versa.

Nineteenth-Century Leaders in Social Work

While many conservative Protestants endorsed and confirmed the prevailing values of middle-class America in the nineteenth century, many of them led the way in preserving the tradition of evangelical social work, including those in the dispensationalist and holiness movements. Conver-

Emma Whittemore (1850–1931)

The revivals in the second half of the nineteenth century stressed the necessity for conversion and holiness—that is, a Christian life totally consecrated to Christ and reflecting his love for the lost. The life of Emma Whittemore exemplifies the resulting social consciousness. Raised in a privileged New York City home, Emma was converted at an evangelical meeting as an adult and was called to minister to the "girls on the street." Rejecting the belief of many "who call themselves Christian" that these women are impossible to reclaim, she recognized that "heartless commercialism" and "human vultures" had betrayed these women, so that prostitution became their path for survival. Whittemore opened the first "Door of Hope" in New York City in 1890, where women received the Gospel along with refuge, food, clothing, medical care, and even occupational training. Whittemore's primary objective was evangelistic: social agencies might bring the girls "out of the dens of vice, but only Jesus can get the vice out of the girls." Obedient to her Master, she welcomed all women, even those who repeatedly stumbled. Through her leadership, hundreds were converted. And ministry in these "foul" places and the bitter rebuffs made her more dependent on Jesus' "inexhaustible love." When she died in 1931, over 100 homes across the nation were affiliated with the "Doors of Hope."

sion, they insisted, must be evidenced by Jesus' love for the lost, poor, and oppressed. Social work was connected with the revivalist enthusiasm of the early- to mid-nineteenth century, particularly with revivalism's assumption of egalitarianism (leading to support for the abolition of slavery and for nineteenth-century feminist causes) and with its pre–Civil War postmillennial hope of reforming society in preparation for Christ's return. One prominent example is the revivalist Finney, who believed that God would, with the help of the faithful, bring about the millennium. One could also cite the examples of Jonathan Blanchard, Theodore Weld, Oberlin College, Wesleyan Methodists, Phoebe Palmer, and others.[8] After the Civil War this emphasis continued in organizations like the YMCA and the Salvation Army (begun in the U.S. in the 1880s). The latter, for example, assumed that a hungry person had difficulty hearing any sort of Gospel and that an "act of charity was often the best form of evangelism."

By the 1880s we see in the holiness tradition and the evangelical descendants of the revivalists a stress on the sanctifying work of Christ in the believer's life which, in turn, provided a strong moral impulse to complement the zeal for the salvation of souls with social work. It was believed that a sincere faith should usher in some kind of voluntary good work. Some of these evangelicals were progressive in their politics. Many worked with the homeless, the alcoholics (through rescue missions), the immigrants (for whom they advocated better treatment), and the jobless (on whose behalf they advocated labor unions). They advocated the prohibition of alcohol (the "root" of the problem), the legal recognition of the rights of women, legislation on behalf of women and children in the workforce, and campaigns for world peace.

The record of evangelicals' social service in an era when social reform was not necessarily popular was as impressive as that of almost any other group in the country. Humanitarians like Andrew Carnegie used religion to foster a laissez-faire attitude toward economics, and liberals like Henry Ward Beecher even argued that people were usually poor because they deserved to be (i.e., because they were lazy). From at least 1870 to 1890, before the rise of the liberals' Social Gospel movement, holiness-minded evangelicals assumed leadership in American Protestant work among the poor. As an example, the International Christian Workers Association, reputed to be the most important of the era's Protestant social service organizations, had world-touring evangelist Reuben Torrey as its president in the 1890s.

By the 1890s, some liberal Protestants were beginning to move toward less evangelistically oriented reform efforts to found a more decidedly social "Social Gospel." But even after 1890, many conservative Christians who emphasized soul saving and personal piety and generally held a pessimistic view of society still worked to meet social needs.

The Roots of Fundamentalism

In the context of the late-nineteenth-century challenges to orthodox Christianity in the United States—particularly with the rise of Darwinism, biblical criticism, and liberalism (see the prior chapter)—we can trace some of the very diverse roots of what came to be called "fundamentalism" in the 1920s.

Dispensationalism

In the 1820s dispensationalism sprang from England and Ireland, particularly from one man, John Nelson Darby (1800–1882), whose views were propagated through a series of Bible prophecy conferences. Later, dispensationalism had an even more significant advocate in C. I. Scofield (1843–1921), the editor of the Scofield Reference Bible. This study Bible was the most influential disseminator of dispensationalism in North America. As has been said, people read the pages of this Bible from the notes up.

Dispensationalism, as the name implies, divides history into several ages or dispensations, and God judges according to the specific rules for each age. Basically dispensationalism bifurcates the people of God into two distinctive groups—Israel and the Church—with a different set of promises for each. The Old Testament promises Israel a future earthly kingdom centered around Jerusalem; the New Testament promises believers who are in the church a future spiritual kingdom in heaven. According to dispensationalism the world's future is on a downward slope and God's imminent judgment is looming (hence, they held to a premillennial eschatology). The next key events are the Tribulation, the Antichrist, and the rapture. The true church, then, is not any large denomination riddled with heresy, but that formed by individual Christians who could expect to be saved from the impending destruction. Darby encouraged people to pull out of denominations. Most dispensationalists stayed, however, for the time being. Few left before World War I. They heavily influenced denominations with their teachings, which were especially attractive to Calvinists in Presbyterian and Baptist circles. Also, their teachings were developed and disseminated through summer Bible conferences, such as the Niagara Conference that met annually between 1868 and 1900. Many of the founders of "fundamentalism" were Bible study leaders at this conference during the 1870s.

Because they were pessimistic about the world's future and expected the imminent judgment of God and return of Christ, the dispensationalists stressed the study of biblical prophecy. This also led them to a special concern for biblical accuracy, since the Bible must be exactly right with regard to the world's future. This would become significant for forging an alliance with the concerns of Princeton Seminary, an influential Presbyterian school.

In fact, a series of prophetic premillennial conferences was begun in 1878 with the first International Prophetic Conference. Attending this conference was a group of conservative Calvinists closely associated with Princeton Seminary. Though the Princeton theologians were not dispensationalists, they shared a concern for prophecy and especially for the Bible's truthfulness. This relationship brought together two important roots of fundamentalism.

Princeton Theology

The professors at Princeton Seminary combined a biblical Calvinism with an intellectual repudiation of both dispensationalism and Finney's revivalistic measures; however, they defended the value of personal religious experience. The seminary was founded in 1812 and included, among others, Charles Hodge (1797–1878), Benjamin B. Warfield (1851–1921), and J. Gresham Machen (1881–1937) on its prestigious faculty.

They thought of themselves as defenders of the doctrinal system contained in the Westminster Confession of Faith (1647) and the fundamental tenets of the Reformation. Their most important teaching in this respect was what they considered to be the orthodox idea of biblical inspiration. Three significant elements of this teaching countered the theological liberalism coming from Germany, with its acceptance of higher criticism and evolutionary theories of development: (1) *verbal inspiration* (every word of the Bible is inspired by God), (2) *biblical inerrancy* (Scripture itself teaches it is without error), and (3) *original autographs* (inerrancy applies only to the original documents, though God superintended the faithful transmission of the copies). A large part of the importance of this view of Scripture stemmed from the Princetonian concern for the salvation message.

A more critical analysis reveals that their concern also stemmed from certain presuppositions that were part of the nineteenth century itself. The Princetonians believed that theology must be pursued scientifically, using rationalistic methods that Charles Hodge compared to Newtonian physics. Using a kind of Baconian method of pursuing science (against the liberals' speculation), the idea was that *facts* in the inerrant Scriptures were there to be studied by anyone who wanted to find them, just as the scientist had only to look around him to discover the facts which he would collate into scientific laws. One needs only to formulate these facts into spiritual laws and doctrines in a scientific fashion. Thus, doctrine did not progress in some evolutionary way, any more than did the law of gravity. What is true as revealed in the Bible has always been true and was just waiting for the scientific theologian to systematize it. Contemporary evangelicalism has inherited much of this style of "doing theology."

Holiness Teachings

Another root of fundamentalism emerged during the last third of the nineteenth century in the "holiness" movement, basically out of Methodism, as well as out of nineteenth-century American revivalism. Many of these holiness teachers were evangelists and Bible teachers like Scofield, and were associated with the rise of dispensationalism. In fact, holiness teachings and dispensationalism stressed the same thing—namely, that this is the age of the outpouring of the Holy Spirit which had begun at the time of Pentecost.

There were several "brands" of holiness teachings that were everywhere in American revivalist Protestantism by 1870, expounded through various camp meetings and conferences. The "brand" associated with American fundamentalism came from England and took root at Keswick (New York) in 1875. Keswick teaching emphasized repeated "emptyings" by consecrations and "fillings" with the Holy Spirit (as "canonized" in Scofield's Bible). Moody and his Northfield Conferences became associated with the Keswick form of holiness teaching, eventually emphasizing the practical concept of "power for service," especially in missions and evangelism. This practical emphasis had social implications, as we shall see.

A Militant Opposition to Modernism

The roots we have looked at so far were part of a growing organized conservative movement in America against modernism. As noted in the previous chapter, modernism was the attempt to save the Christian faith by modifying Christianity to meet the intellectual standards and scientifc findings of the day; it stressed cultural adaptation, an optimism regarding human potential and progress, the immanence of God in the evolution of the human race, and a stress on ethics and natural religious feelings over against beliefs. Doctrinally, what emerged as fundamentalism emphasized those supernatural aspects which theological liberalism denied, including the supernatural character of the Bible. Along with this, emphasis was also placed on the historicity of miracles and the supernatural character of Christ's person and work (including his virgin birth, resurrection, and second coming).

Since liberalism had gone worldly with its German higher criticism of the Bible and its acceptance of Darwinian evolutionary theory, among other things, the emerging fundamentalists sought separation of the church from the world. The liberals had erased the line that distinguished the church from the world. Furthermore, these militants thought revivalism was the best means for radically separating the saved from the lost and calling the saved out of the world. This was reinforced by the maintenance of strict moral codes which forbade all participation in external signs of worldliness (e.g., smoking, drinking, dancing, card playing, theater attendance). Because these concerns tended to pit the burgeoning fundamentalists in opposition to the progressive and liberal politics of the Social Gospel's reform movement (which we will look at below), they began to align themselves with conservative politics.

The conservatives dug in for the fight against modernism in every facet of life. One of the most amazing attempts to influence all American Christians to adopt conservative points of view was the publication of twelve pamphlets entitled *The Fundamentals*. These were produced between 1910 and 1915 and included ninety articles written by sixty-four authors. Depending on the volume, 175,000 to 300,000 copies were sent free of charge to pastors and laypeople. They were subsidized by Lyman and Milton Stewart, the founders and chief stockholders of the Union Oil Company of Los Angeles. They were edited by Reuben A. Torrey, dean of the Bible Institute of Los Angeles (later Biola), and Amzi C. Dixon, pastor of Moody Church (Chicago)—both dispensationalists.

The doctrines that were defended in these pamphlets were eventually narrowed down to what have been called the "Five Fundamentals": (1) the inerrancy of Scripture, (2) the virgin birth of Christ, (3) substitutionary atonement, (4) the bodily resurrection of Christ, and (5) Christ's personal premillennial coming or the miracle-working power of Christ. In the popular mind these became identified with "fundamentalism." In fact, the first time that the term *fundamentalist* was used to identify a group of people was in 1920 when a man named Curtis Lee Laws spoke about those who were ready to wage warfare against the liberals for the "fundamentals".

The Fundamentalist-Modernist Controversy

Events leading up to World War I put Protestant evangelicals on the defensive. For one thing, immigration was breaking down the Protestant evangelical consensus. Though the optimism of the liberals was also being shattered by the events of the early twentieth century, they regarded the conservatives as a reactionary movement, and so the tension between fundamentalists and modernists increased.

Actually, the signal for the battle came from a liberal, Henry Emerson Fosdick, who served as a regular "guest minister" of First Presbyterian Church in New York City, in a May 21, 1922 sermon entitled "Shall the Fundamentalists Win?" (see appendix E, p. 293). Reiterating the liberal line, he insisted that the sciences demand a new interpretation and understanding of Christianity. Then, sounding the battle cry, he provocatively insisted, "Now the people in this generation who are trying to do this are the liberals, and the fundamentalists are out on a campaign to shut against them the doors of the Christian fellowship. Shall they be allowed to succeed?" His answer was "No!" A study in rhetoric, this sermon claims not to be directed against fundamentalism per se, but against the fundamentalists' exclusivism and intolerance of other Christian opinions. Yet throughout, Fosdick caricatured the fundamentalists' beliefs and their claim that the liberals' accommodation destroys the Christian faith. The sermon infuriated fundamentalists.

Just a few years later, these infuriated fundamentalists would find themselves fighting the battle against modernism on two battlefronts. In both cases they would lose.

The first battlefront was *societal* and involved the fight against evolution. The final skirmish took place at the Scopes trial in Dayton, Tennessee in

1925. Led by lawyers William Jennings Bryan (for the fundamentalists) and Clarence Darrow (defending the public school teacher Scopes, who had illegally taught evolutionary theory), this trial really marked the demise of fundamentalism in society. The press sensationalized the proceedings and poked fun at Bryan and the fundamentalists, making them look like anti-intellectual buffoons.

The second battlefront was *denominational* and primarily involved the Baptist and Presbyterian churches in the North. As the liberals gained strength, the conservatives sought to consolidate their position by focusing on central doctrines. Even though the Presbyterian General Assembly endorsed the "Five Fundamentals" three times, in 1924 some Presbyterian clergy met in Auburn, New York, and signed the "Auburn Affirmation," claiming that this was not the only way to see Christian doctrine.

J. Gresham Machen, then at Princeton Seminary, led the fight against the Auburn signers until control of the seminary shifted to the other side by 1929. Machen was put on ecclesiastical trial and defrocked in 1933 for going against the rules and unity of the church by setting up an independent mission board in 1933 to counter what Machen and some other conservatives perceived to be growing Presbyterian sentiment that Christian missions work jointly with other religions. In 1936, he and several others formed their own denomination (the Orthodox Presbyterian Church) and Westminster Theological Seminary.

Fundamentalism

After 1925, fundamentalists were no longer respected. During the next ten years, the fundamentalist movement retreated slowly and defensively from the Protestant mainstream. The liberals succeeded in ousting the conservatives from any control they may have had. This development was catastrophic for conservative Christianity.

What happened to these fundamentalists after 1925? Having failed to win control of the leading denominations and ousted from leadership, many of them separated from these institutions and then began to establish and build a whole new network of educational institutions, mission agencies, and publications. Fundamentalism became a vital religious movement on the American scene; during the depression era of the 1930s, twenty-six new Bible schools were founded! New fundamentalist empires were built paralleling most of the old denominational establishments.

Three important characteristics define these fundamentalist institutions. First, in order to preserve the integrity of their faith, they separated from important social institutions, including the prevailing intellectual culture.

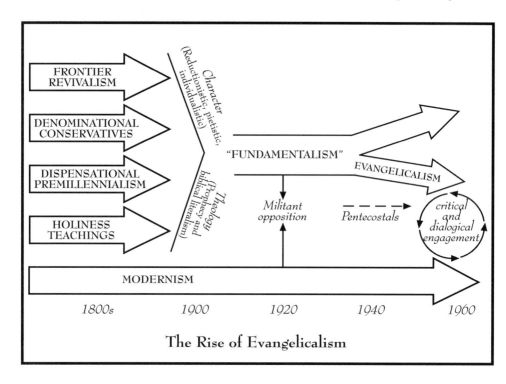

The Rise of Evangelicalism

For example, the mainline educational centers would not tolerate fundamentalist beliefs, so Christian colleges were formed to preserve the fundamentalist faith. Quite naturally, fundamentalists were opposed to the mainline ideas of evolution, biblical criticism, and the scientific method.

Many fundamentalists believed that any institution which refused to discipline theological liberals could not be seeking the truth and thus was not worthy of a Christian's loyalty. These fundamentalist leaders became militant separatists. They insisted that fundamentalists should separate themselves not only from liberals, but also from conservatives who compromised the Gospel by associating with liberals, the so-called doctrine of "double separation."

Second, fundamentalist institutions were generally dispensational in their theology. Throughout its American history, conservative Christianity had been predominantly postmillennial; it contended that the church was working to bring about the kingdom and that it would succeed. But the fundamentalists had just suffered a devastating defeat. They knew that history was not getting better; history was going downhill! This corresponded exactly with dispensationalism's view of the end: the next key event in human history is the rise of the Antichrist and the tribulation. Furthermore, it was the Social Gospel movement, Fosdick, and Rauschenbusch who were arguing that history was getting better and better. Thus, post-millennialism was rejected and equated with liberalism.

Third, this reversal on eschatology corresponded with a reversal on social action. There was a dramatic curtailment—almost a disappearance—of interest in social concerns among the fundamentalists. Why? Some of it had to do with shifts in theology, especially in eschatology. Premillennial-ism was gaining ground among conservatives, with its tendency toward pessimism about this world. Much of it also had to do with the reaction to the rise of the liberal Social Gospel movement after 1900.

The Great Reversal

According to George Marsden, there were two stages to this reaction.[9] First, from 1865 to 1900, the revivalist evangelicals' interest in using political means to promote the welfare of society (especially the poor and oppressed) diminished, but they still championed social concern, especially in the form of private charity. Second, from 1900 to 1930 the "Great Reversal" happened, when all progressive social concern, whether public or private, became suspect among revivalist evangelicals and was relegated to a minor role.

1865–1900

This period marks the transition from a basically Calvinist tradition to a pietistic view of political action. The former Reformed view saw the law as the expression of God's will in society. As we have seen, this was typical of the Puritan model of covenant and stewardship that was based on the Old Testament covenantal view of the identity of God's people with the advance of a religious-political kingdom. Even revivalists in this tradition like George Whitefield practiced philanthropy on this basis; Whitefield's orphanage in Georgia is a case in point. Such was the outward sign of the inner experience. In this view politics was seen as a means to advancing the kingdom of God on earth. The later pietistic view saw political action as no more than a means to restrain evil. In other words, one could see a shift in emphasis from Old Testament to New Testament models for understanding politics. Most importantly, one could see a shift from postmillennial to premillennial views of the relation of the kingdom of God to the present social and political order.

More specifically, the dispensationalist holiness tradition moved from an emphasis on law toward an emphasis on the personal experience of being filled by the Spirit (with the resulting *personal* power for service). Slowly a wedge was driven between Law and Spirit, Old Testament and

New Testament, involving a shift toward a more *private* view of Christianity in which the Holy Spirit worked in the hearts of individuals. As a result, social action came to be placed more and more in the context of private agencies as opposed to political and public agencies. In turn, politics became much less important.

Christians were not taught to remove themselves from the political arena altogether. Most saw government as ordained by God to restrain evil, so that politics in *this* way became a means to do good. And still there were those who urged quite progressive political reform (such as A. C. Dixon, Charles Blanchard, and James M. Gray).

1900–1930

Further changes in the interest in social concerns took place after 1900. Premillennial and personal holiness advocates did not abandon politics altogether. For example, they campaigned against evolution and Communism. In keeping with what we said above, they often discouraged Christians from being active in public welfare work, and they abandoned the view of Finney and other mid-nineteenth-century moral philosophers that the kingdom of God would be positively advanced by good laws. *In other words, they applied their reservations about political action quite selectively, disregarding them when they themselves became concerned with a public issue.*

As their views about social concerns dampened, the *crucial factor* in the "Great Reversal" was the fundamentalist reaction to the liberal Social Gospel movement after 1900. As their attacks on liberalism and modernism increased, their attempts to balance revivalism and social concern (à la Finney and others) decreased.

It was felt that the Social Gospel movement put almost all its weight on the support of private and public social programs over against the regenerating work of Christ which saved souls for all eternity, whereas, as we have seen, conservative evangelicals had viewed these as complementary. Conservatives saw the threat not in social concern itself, but in the emphasis on social concern in an exclusivist way that seemed to undercut the relevance of the message of eternal salvation through trust in Christ's atoning work, substituting the "social gospel" for the Gospel itself. Thus, they feared that traditional Christian beliefs were at stake. But in their conservative reaction, the fundamentalists would come to lose their social attitudes. Fundamentalists became fixated on prevailing political views of middle-class America of the 1890s, forgetting that up until then their predecessors had espoused fairly progressive social concerns in their day. According to Marsden, "By the 1920s, the one really unifying factor in fun-

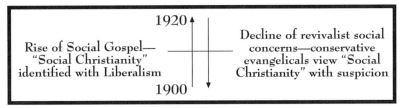

"The Great Reversal"

damentalist political and social thought was the overwhelming predominance of political conservatism."[10]

Evangelicalism

By the mid–1930s the more moderate fundamentalists began to part company with those who were more militant. Though they shared a legitimate concern to defend the faith, some attitudes were not acceptable to the moderates. For instance, since the fundamentalists had fought liberals on issues such as higher criticism and evolution, and since those were emphases in centers of higher education, fundamentalists tended to look down on and avoid the university. Furthermore, with their criticism of liberalism's overemphasis on the "social gospel," fundamentalists overreacted by denying the legitimate role of speaking out for justice and equality in society. Along with this, they were becoming fiercely conservative politically.

Was there a place for the centrists or moderates who liked neither liberalism nor strident fundamentalism? And what about groups that had never had a home in either camp, such as the recently emerged Pentecostals who were conservative Christians, alienated from the modern world but rejected by the fundamentalists as well?[11] Furthermore, some fundamentalists began to question the strategy of separation: "By remaining isolated, how can one challenge our culture and bring it to Christ?" A new generation of intellectually self-confident fundamentalists eventually emerged. They had been trained at the nation's best educational institutions and were now eager to transform American culture and bring it back to its Christian roots.

As the 1940s began, the answer for some of the moderate fundamentalists was to reclaim the more historic term *evangelical*. In 1942 the National Association of Evangelicals was formed to give organizational clout and voice to disorganized conservative Protestant groups, from fundamentalists to Pentecostals. In 1947 Fuller Theological Seminary was founded. In its early years its "dream team" of faculty included Edward John Carnell

Henrietta Mears (1890–1963)

The evangelical family's maturity may owe more to one woman's work than to the work of any other single individual. Dr. Henrietta C. Mears was Director of Christian Education at First Presbyterian Church in Hollywood, California. The Sunday School she orchestrated grew from 400 to over 6,000!

This was no "flash-in-the-pan" show which attracted such numbers. Mears carefully developed and maintained a graded curriculum that led children and teens through the entire Bible. Her mimeographed curriculum eventually grew into Gospel Light Publications, a leading evangelical publishing house.

Known simply as "Teacher," she also worked in the "trenches," teaching college students who would later become evangelical leaders, including Bill Bright (founder of Campus Crusade for Christ) and Richard Halverson (former chaplain of the United States Senate). Many became college and seminary professors, pastors, and missionaries, such that Mears's influence has extended throughout every part of the globe.

Mears also founded Forest Home Conference Center—a spiritual retreat that has featured leading evangelical pastors and educators as speakers.

Hundreds of Henrietta Mears's "children" have become the significant "players" in the development of this century's evangelical family.

and George Eldon Ladd, who had earned their Ph.D.s at Harvard. Under the editorship of Carl F. H. Henry, *Christianity Today,* founded in 1956, engaged the opposition, even liberals, by inviting them to debate key theological issues. Billy Graham's crusades in the 1950s helped refurbish the tarnished image of conservative Protestantism. Graham deliberately included on the stage with him religious leaders many considered to be "worldly" churchmen. The activities and institutions promoted by these moderates led to a decisive negation of fundamentalism's distinguishing marks, helping to define the resulting evangelical movement.

First, rejecting the defensive separatism of fundamentalists, evangelicals attempted to transform culture by involvement in the world. No more would Christian colleges merely be Bible colleges preparing students for missions and pastorates. From the mid–1950s on, the Christian college movement emphasized a Christian liberal arts education. The idea was to produce graduates who could work as professionals—lawyers, politicians, doctors, teachers, corporate executives, and the like—to transform the United States from within by working as Christians in the societal structures.

At the same time, a Christian presentation and defense of the faith, along with sophisticated articulation of the Christian worldview, was deemed a necessity. Groups like InterVarsity Christian Fellowship, schools like Fuller

"In past years we evangelicals have not given great importance to the Christ of the Gospels, the One who set up His tabernacle among human beings in order to live among them in fullness of grace and truth. We saw Him in the glory of the heavens, not so much in the glory of the manger and of the carpenter shop of Nazareth. We gave very little or no attention to the social and political implications of the conflict between Jesus and the religious leaders of his country. Nor did we emphasize as we should have that Jesus Himself was a sign of contradiction for those who were hungry for earthly power and who were ready to go to any length, even physical brutal violence to achieve or maintain it." (Emilio Antonio Nuñez, *Liberation Theology*, 237)

Theological Seminary, and publications like *Christianity Today* provided the means for training and expressing the evangelical Christian stance. These groups have encouraged many to return to or remain within the mainline denominations and work for renewal.

Second, evangelicals rejected dispensationalism as the only acceptable theological option. From its very beginning the National Association of Evangelicals welcomed all conservative Protestants. While the debate on speaking in tongues, a second work of sanctification, or the future status of the state of Israel could be heated, evangelicals consciously embraced a range of theological positions. And through this process, Darby's dispensationalism has seen its own doctrinal development and is no longer associated with its original militancy and anti-intellectualism.[12]

Third, rejecting social passivity, evangelicals have insisted on active Christian involvement in all segments of society. Evangelicals conscientiously worked for a more consistent and faithful social witness, beginning in the late 1940s with Carl F. H. Henry's lament and rebuke in *The Uneasy Conscience of Modern Fundamentalism*, continuing with Billy Graham's refusal to hold segregated evangelistic crusades in the South, and presently well represented in a number of organizations (such as Evangelicals for Social Action) and publications (such as *Sojourners*). Evangelicals are typically people who practice their Christianity in tangible expressions of justice and charity, though they have a long way to go regarding issues like racial reconciliation.

The Contemporary Scene

Contemporary evangelicalism is recognized as an important spiritual, social, and intellectual force. On the surface the original strategy to challenge and transform America by working within the structures appears to be a great success. But evangelicalism is not without her problems.

As we mentioned in chapter 2 and will elaborate in the next chapter, at the beginning of the twenty-first century the prevailing American culture has dramatically shifted. The 1950s Judeo-Christian consensus has evaporated; diversity of values and beliefs has become the defining societal virtue. Modernity's attempt to establish culture and life on a universal and objective foundation is being dismantled. American society is progressively being fragmented by an increasing plurality of ethnic, gender, and social worlds. Nothing dares to claim universality. Even science, which once held normative sway, is now viewed as just one research tradition among others.[13]

This fragmentation extends even to evangelicalism itself. The popular indicators suggest that evangelicalism's unique moral and theological inheritance is collapsing. The rising instances of adultery and divorce—even among nationally known figures—no longer startle us. Evangelicals increasingly look to the secular sphere, from politics to psychology, for answers to society's gravest ill.[14] But this crisis of identity is clearest in the evangelical academy. The old theological control-beliefs—such as the inspiration and sole authority of Scripture, Jesus as the God-man, the centrality of Christ's atoning work, salvation solely through a personal trust in Jesus Christ—are no longer defining.[15] Rather, the scientific method—and its precise form depends on the discipline—is often given priority over the claims of revelation.[16] Other ways of gaining access to salvific communion with God, outside a personal trust in Jesus Christ, are openly debated.[17] Clearly the particularity of Christ in our religiously pluralistic culture is the preeminent issue; it is beginning to provoke reflection on evangelicalism's identity and hopefully a return to her roots.[18]

How will evangelicals continue to maintain that Jesus is the only way to salvation and the unique self-revelation of God in a culture that treats religious convictions on a par with preferences for ice cream flavors? Already the refrain of our contemporary culture—toleration and civility—fills the evangelical academy.

What *does* the future hold for evangelicalism? Where is it headed? The final chapter will suggest one scenario and a call for action.

For Further Reflection

1. What roots of fundamentalism (e.g., features of revivalism, biblical inerrancy, emphasis on prophecy) do you recognize in your own upbringing or church background?

2. What, if anything, surprised you about the history of fundamentalism?
3. Why does the history of American revivalism tend to get marginalized in public education materials and classes?
4. After reading Carl F. H. Henry's address (appendix F, p. 299), indicate why you think he went to such lengths to recount the history of evangelicalism to Christian college students.

For Further Reading

Balmer, Randall. *Mine Eyes Have Seen the Glory: A Journey into the Evangelical Subculture in America.* New York: Oxford University Press, 1989.

Bloesch, Donald G. Foreword to *The Future of Evangelical Christianity: A Call for Unity amid Diversity,* by Mark Noll. Colorado Springs: Helmers and Howard, 1988.

Dayton, Donald. *Discovering an Evangelical Heritage,* 2d ed. Peabody, Mass.: Hendrickson, 1988.

Frank, Douglas W. *Less Than Conquerors: How Evangelicals Entered the Twentieth Century.* Grand Rapids: Eerdmans, 1986.

Marsden, George. *Fundamentalism and American Culture.* New York: Oxford University Press, 1980.

McGrath, Alister. *Evangelicalism and the Future of Christianity.* Downers Grove, Ill.: InterVarsity, 1995.

Noll, Mark. *The Scandal of the Evangelical Mind.* Grand Rapids: Eerdmans, 1994.

———. *A History of Christianity in the United States and Canada.* Grand Rapids: Eerdmans, 1992.

Sandeen, Ernst R. *The Roots of Fundamentalism.* Chicago: University of Chicago Press, 1970.

seventeen

Recommendations for the Family in a Culture against Christ

Richard Niebuhr's classic *Christ and Culture* set the agenda for discussions of the relation of the Christian church to culture, even though Niebuhr himself stood upon the shoulders of Ernst Troeltsch (*The Social Teachings of the Christian Churches*) and Etienne Gilson (*Reason and Revelation in the Middle Ages*). Niebuhr's legacy included an unflattering presentation of the position he labeled "Christ against Culture." Though he never used the word "Anabaptist" in his discussion of this paradigm, and though he only mentioned the Mennonites on one page,[1] this position has most often been associated with the Anabaptist response to culture. It comes as no surprise, then, to find Anabaptists and their sympathizers lobbing heavy artillery against what they consider to be Niebuhr's caricature of their stance.

The Anabaptist Model Revisited

The most recent defense of the Anabaptist position has come from Stanley Hauerwas and William H. Willimon.[2] At the end of an argument that begins with the insistence that Niebuhr wanted to ensure that the Reformed transformationist approach ("Christ the Transformer of Culture") would be viewed as the most worthy of his five paradigms in order to give a theological rationale for liberal democracy, Hauerwas and Willimon conclude that "the early Anabaptists had no desire to withdraw from the world."

> They were murdered by Calvinist, Lutheran, and Roman Catholic societies because they attempted to be the church. Their withdrawal came in an attempt to prevent people opposed to them . . . from killing their children. The Anabaptists did not withdraw. They were driven out.[3]

While the authors may overstate their case and argue for effect, and while they presume (though not without cause) that Niebuhr had in mind the Anabaptists, there is this kernel of truth in their diatribe: the centrist positions of the Lutheran conversionist model ("Christ and Culture in Paradox") and, especially, the Reformed transformationist model have been the dominant positions of most evangelical groups in the latter half of this century, particularly in their cozy relationship with Western liberal democracy. We will return to this theme in a moment.

Another defense of the Anabaptist position vis-à-vis Niebuhr—one which pays closer attention to the details of Niebuhr's argument (as well as to Niebuhr's other writings) and appreciates much of what he wrote—is the case presented by Charles Scriven in *The Transformation of Culture*.[4] Scriven's argument is worthy of a brief summation.

When Niebuhr argues in *Christ and Culture* that the "Christ against Culture" paradigm is "the one that uncompromisingly affirms the sole authority of Christ over the Christian and resolutely rejects culture's claims to loyalty,"[5] Scriven argues that Niebuhr *really* does not mean what he says because: (1) he would be contradicting himself (since he insists that even Christ himself participated in culture); and (2) his descriptions of the early church, Tertullian, monasticism, and Tolstoy recognize that they used and were heirs of cultural elements. So Scriven concludes that Niebuhr really must mean that these exclusionists were "not the enemy of culture as such, but the champion of a particular cultural option."[6] That is to say, if one reads Niebuhr closely, he does not deny that the Christ-against-culture church itself is a culture—a "withdrawn community," an "exclusively Christian community," "a new and separated community," a "new society" over against the old society. In the title "Christ against Culture," then, Niebuhr means by *culture* "the *dominant* [or *prevailing*] way of life"—broadly accepted patterns of behavior and modes of thought in which the Anabaptists refuse to participate due to their radical answer to the "Christ and culture" problem that allows no compromise between the way of Christ and the way of the world.

But this is only half of the problem in interpreting Niebuhr. Scriven cogently argues that when Niebuhr comes to the transformationist option he changes the denotation of the word *culture* to mean "life in the world"— the total process and result of human activity. This definition of culture makes it senseless to ask whether one should participate in cultural life. Certainly the Christian is called to the conversion of the culture in *this* sense. Because Christ is part of culture (he came into, lived in, and expressed himself through culture) and because Christ's authority has to be understood within the context of the general cultural life in which the Christian community exists, Christians value *cultural* existence positively, *but* they may be opposed to the way of life presently *dominant* in the culture. *This* is what Scriven thinks Niebuhr really meant to say.[7]

What gives sense to Niebuhr's theme of social transformation through Christ is his ascription of the Sermon on the Mount as a "new Law for Christians." Since Niebuhr's larger corpus does not allow for ahistorical reason (and therefore for some ahistorical rational laws), Niebuhr must accept the notion that general moral concepts have to be interpreted from the specific historical perspective of Christ—at least for the Christian. This is consistent with Niebuhr's "social existentialism" and his view that our lives are radically historically determined, which, for Christians, means that our selfhood is found in a communal life that is shaped by the story of Jesus of Nazareth. That is to say, given the heterogeneity of cultural life within which believers must have a relation to Christ, and given that all moralities are rooted in a shared story,[8] which in the Christian's case is Christ's story, Scriven's revision of Niebuhr's question is this: How can we be *in* the culture as loyalists to the cause of Christ? This is compatible with the original Anabaptist vision according to advocates like Hauerwas and Willimon.[9] And it would seem to be faithful to the demands of the New Testament. It certainly has been the central question thoughout this book.

The Changing Church

It seems fairly safe to argue that during the past four decades U.S. evangelicals have tended to fit into the mold of one of two Niebuhrian categories: the conversionist Lutheran position in which justified Christians live out their calling in a sinful culture through which God works, not to advance the kingdom, but to prevent degeneration and thereby allow Christians a place in which to evangelize the world; and the transformationist Reformed position which differs from the former paradigm only in its more positive attitude toward culture. Besides antinomianism, Niebuhr observes that the conversionist stance can lead to cultural conservatism—certainly observable in this century's evangelicalism.[10] Augustine's and Calvin's version of the transformationist stance falls short of envisioning the transformation of *all* humans and culture, since it stressed the conversion of only the elect and the reborn creation they will inherit. In fact, Niebuhr suggests that this is really a combination of the antithesis and transformationist positions.[11]

Thus, either position seems susceptible to the charge of Hauerwas and Willimon in *Resident Aliens* and the observations of John Howard Yoder that these paradigms promote the *support* of the dominant or prevailing culture rather than its *radical transformation*. But in a society that is ostensibly, if not deeply, Judeo-Christian in its orientation, this position would not seem unreasonable, and it certainly would not be thought of as problematic.

For instance, it has been argued by John Howard Yoder that all ethical thinking is provincial or particular. What a nation refers to as "natural" or "public" moral insight is really "the *dominant* [italics ours] moral views" of an "oppressive, provincial, or (to say it theologically) 'fallen'" known world. And the reason that so-called "natural law" sounds so much like a Christian ethic is because the former has been elaborated in a Judeo-Christian context.

The discussion of how to speak of "values" of a public nature usually takes place in the post-Christian West. The examples of not specifically churchly moral insight represent post-Christian Enlightenment values. These values are, though, largely derived from the Hebraic and Christian world vision. They do not, therefore, constitute tests of the possibility of accepting, as complementary or compatible with distinctively Christian views, insights with a complete different rootage.

> The real test of the accessibility of a common moral language "out there," more general than confessional language, must then not be the times we find ourselves agreeing with "men of good will" (especially not if they be Western humanists); it must be the capacity of this line of argument to illuminate meaningful conversations with Idi Amin or Khomeini or Chairman Mao.
> . . . the search for a public moral language is motivated rather by embarrassment about particularity.[12]

Yoder goes on to point out that the medieval concept of natural law worked because it was not meant to communicate with outsiders; it was developed in a milieu where there were no non-Christians.

To return to our immediate concern, one might offer the analogy that in the 1950s the United States resembled the consensus of medieval Christendom to a large extent (though not to the extent that it fit the "Christ above culture" paradigm—see appendix A, p. 277). A conversionist position was not unreasonable because the cultural ethos was largely Judeo-

Christian. And the conversionist could proceed on the assumption that the church and the culture used the same vocabulary with the same meanings. Radical transformation was not necessary. Rightly or wrongly, the prevailing culture was perceived as not that far removed from Christ.

But as this Judeo-Christian consensus has broken down in the U.S., a dramatic shift in the culture has taken place. As Hauerwas and Willimon put it, "Sometime between 1960 and 1980, an old, inadequately conceived world ended, and a fresh, new world began."[13] While again overstated, this observation is nothing new. It has been recognized by those who have already been cited above (Hauerwas and Willimon, Yoder, Scriven) and by others, such as Lesslie Newbigin and Jacques Ellul.

What is perhaps startling is that these who are calling attention to this shift and urging the church to be the church in the midst of a prevailing culture that is no longer Judeo-Christian are not evangelicals, as one might have expected. In fact, it is not entirely clear that most evangelicals really recognize the radical shift that has taken place.[14] Evangelicals tend to relate to the culture with an ahistorical moralism,[15] supported by a conversionist or transformationist model that now recognizes it cannot *entirely* support the dominant culture but must really transform it; so, evangelicals often turn to political protest or moral crusades. But what must be recognized is that the dominant culture can no longer be related to with the earlier conversionist or transformationist mentality, because between the public and those who are loyal to Christ there is a *fundamental* disagreement at the level of incompatible assumptions that make moralistic arguments ineffective at best and ridiculous-sounding at worst.[16]

Whether Hauerwas and Willimon were right in their conclusion that the Anabaptists did not withdraw from but were forced out of the culture, the situation today could be accurately described as just that. It is not that the church must take the exclusionist "Christ against culture" stance; it is that the culture has turned against Christ. And an appropriate response is demanded of the church.

This calls attention to one of the problems with Niebuhr's thesis. Though Anabaptists often *did* desire to set up alternative or countercultures, Niebuhr wrongly assumes that the church can always choose what relation it will have to the culture.[17] But the church does not always have a choice if it wants to remain the church in a dominant culture that is itself antithetical to the Christian worldview. (The circumstances surrounding the Barmen Declaration in Nazi Germany are testimony to that.) Again, perhaps Niebuhr could make this assumption given the Judeo-Christian milieu in which he wrote, but contemporary pluralism is not a factor in his analysis. The difference between the 1950s, when *Christ and Culture* was published, and the relativism of the 2000s can be seen within the history of American evangelicalism itself. Then it was important for evangelicals to distance themselves from their fundamentalist roots and enter into dialogue with the culture by insisting that "all truth is God's truth." But now, a few decades later, the same phrase takes on a different, ironic nuance in our pluralist culture: "*all* truth" means "*everybody's* truth is God's truth." The culture has shifted against Christ, and the church is *obliged* to respond accordingly. We cannot simply echo the same refrain about truth and expect it to be heard in the same way that it was thirty years ago.

Building on our discussion of pluralism and postmodernism in chapter 2, there are at least two characteristics of this "culture against Christ."

First, it is characterized by a "post-Constantinian" relativism or normative pluralism in which any kind of a "Christendom" is a thing of the past.[18] In other words, the consensus has broken down. This is dramatically borne out by the fact that 67 percent of the American population generally concur with the statement, "There is no such thing as absolute truth; different people can define truth in conflicting ways and still be correct."[19]

This becomes significant when one realizes that what underlies much of the debate over issues like abortion, homosexuality, and active euthanasia is the failure to arrive at a common definition of what it means to be *human* and what the purpose of human existence is.[20] Dealing with these issues in a moralistic manner or attempting to pass statewide legislation prohibiting such behaviors may have worked forty or fifty years ago. However, it will not work today. The dominant culture, characterized by relativism, is at odds with the church on a more fundamental level than evangelical leaders like John Willke, James Dobson, or Phyllis Schlafly seem to realize. George Hunsberger poignantly describes this failure to recognize the change in the church's "social location": "The Christendom experiment has run its course and is over, but our images and instincts are still formed by its memory. We play out the church's routine as though the concerns of the church and the quests of the culture go hand in glove."[21]

Second, the prevailing culture is characterized by the "post-Enlightenment" public atheism that Lesslie Newbigin elaborated.[22] As pointed out in chapter 2, we have divided the world into two realms. One realm is the public world of scientific fact that explains everything in terms of cause and effect relationships; we have agreed that in this realm some statements (such as "atoms exist") are true, and people would be fools to deny them. Pluralism is not allowed here. The other realm is the private world of religious beliefs and moral values, which are based on assumptions about the purpose of human existence, and where, as we have already mentioned, the culture is not in agreement. So, moral and religious statements are relegated to the realm of private opinion.

Those who are loyal to Christ cannot abide by a public atheism that dismisses the Christian claim that the risen Christ is Lord over all life—"public" and "private." To use Peter Berger's language, we inhabit a different

C. René Padilla (1932—)

Born in Ecuador, raised in Columbia, and now pastoring in Argentina, C. René Padilla is a leading evangelical theologian. With this unique Latin American perspective, he has become a prophetic voice. In his provocative *Mission Between the Times* (Eerdmans, 1985), Padilla demonstrates the deep impact a consumer mentality in North American culture has made upon the church. The Gospel has been reduced to just a spiritual and individualistic message that is confined to one's relationship with God. The result is a "God interested in the worship service but not in social problems, politics, business. . . ." Church growth strategies in North America even counsel a shallow Gospel that permits the materialist and racist to remain as such. Padilla indicts this message of conformism as a subversion of the Gospel. The North American church, "far from being a factor for the transformation of society, has become merely another reflection of society and . . . another instrument that society uses to condition people to its materialistic values."

By contrast, Padilla calls for a church that self-consciously manifests Christ's kingdom in history. The obedient church will bear the marks of Christ's mission: proclaiming the necessity of conversion to Jesus Christ, worshiping Jesus as Lord over all, instructing believers in a life of discipleship to their Lord, and demonstrating the Gospel through social service and confronting the powers of evil.

"plausibility structure" from our contemporaries.[23] The church claims that its moral stance and religious credo are statements about reality. But again, evangelicals are slow to recognize their own subtle conformity to the prevailing culture's ethos, for 53 percent of those who attend "evangelical" churches generally agree with the statement cited above regarding "absolute truth."[24] In fact, it would probably not be unusual to hear an evangelical say that Jesus Christ is Lord, and be quick to add, "At least that's my opinion."

Of course, one should not be surprised at the capitulation of much of the evangelical church to the dominant culture, *even in its moralistic reaction,* since pressures toward conformity to the ethos come through not only the schools and the media, but in the marketing philosophies and techniques that large segments of the church use to attempt to convert the culture.[25]

An Evangelical Response: Some Recommendations

What *should* be the evangelical response? The evangelical church must respond appropriately without adapting to the culture that has left it. What follows are three recommendations.

First, the evangelical church should welcome the disintegration of the consensus that no longer permits it to operate under old conversionist and transformationist paradigms, and see its own dislocation as an opportunity to be what Hauerwas and Willimon call "resident aliens." This is a call to a kind of Anabaptist vision that recognizes that culture cannot be escaped (one of Niebuhr's critiques of the caricatured antithesis position), but that the church's most effective witness is to be the church, faithful to the Gospel in a dominant culture whose fundamental assumptions are contrary to the Christian faith. It is unrealistic to yearn for the "good old days" (if they ever truly were) and to try to reestablish a kind of medieval *corpus christianum*.[26]

The evangelical church should see itself in exile, not unlike those in Babylon to whom Jeremiah addressed his letter of encouragement (Jer. 29:1–14). The exile motif allows the church to redefine itself theologically in distinction from and in proper relation to a culture with which it has been comfortable for too long and which it allowed to define the church when the church did not see itself in exilic terms.[27]

Second, though we might welcome the loss of the church's privileged status in the post-Constantinian, post-Enlightenment, postmodern culture, still the church must learn and teach the *Christian* metanarrative. We should not apologize for making universal claims about God as creator, about humans as fallen in sin, about Christ as the normative revelation of God, about redemption as solely available in Christ, and about the coming renewal of the creation when the kingdom of God is a completed reality. We are like the hero in a Walker Percy novel who is always a "bubble and a half off plumb"—we look strange to a world that has become comfortable with itself because we see the world in a different way, in the light of a defining story that embraces all time and all things (Eph. 1:3–23).

If the culture understands everything we do in worship, if the culture can make complete sense of our Christian practice, if the culture can understand our proclamation of a grace that cannot be earned, then we should probably be worried that we have not insisted on our metanarrative enough. The church lives its life and professes its faith in a way incomprehensible apart from the God revealed in Jesus Christ. Our morality does *not* make sense outside of the church and Jesus' vision of life. To the watching and listening world, severed from our master narrative, our actions and words look and sound like a foreign culture and foreign language.

By the way, learning a foreign language and the culture that goes with it is much easier when we are children. The church *must* teach the Christian metanarrative to its children. The question is: Whose master story *are* our children learning best and fashioning their lives after? What single event is their interpretive key to understanding history—the Holocaust, the American Revolution, the death and resurrection of Jesus Christ, or Kurt Cobain's suicide? By teaching the story, language, and practice of the master narrative centered in Christ we can help those in the church make sense of life; we can give them a sense of coherence in a fragmented, decentered world.

> "Christian ethics arise, in great part, out of something Christians claim to have seen that the world has not seen, namely, the creation of a people, a family, a colony that is a living witness that Jesus Christ is Lord." (Stanley Hauerwas and William H. Willimon, *Resident Aliens*, 72)

Third, if the church is to witness to the Christian metanarrative by *being* the church, and if the prevailing culture holds Christianity hostage to proofs for its truth in terms of the axioms of our society, then the church should move away from a defensive posture that employs a rationalist, evidentialist apologetic to an offensive stance that uses what Newbigin calls "the language of testimony"[28] which challenges the world to be accountable to the truth claims of the Gospel—to God's ongoing "story" of salvation as revealed in Christ and in which the church plays a central role.

This also calls into question the current fascination with church-growth movements that cater to the culture, beginning with the assumption that the church must answer questions posed by the culture, rather than the other way around. That is to say, over against a Tillichian move, the task is not so much "the interpretive matter of translating Jesus into modern categories but rather to translate the world to him . . . not to make the Gospel credible to the modern world, but to *make the world credible to the Gospel.*"[29]

Fourth, following from this last assertion, the church must seek to transform the culture not through the culture's means (Niebuhr's original conversionist and transformationist schemes), but through the church's faithful existence as it lives according to its eschatological vision. The evangelical church is in danger of failing to realize that the techniques of the culture are not neutral; they are laden with the ideological baggage of the culture. The medium through which the Gospel is communicated is also the message. Marketing philosophies that get the Gospel a "hearing" cannot keep means separated from ends.

The church-growth movement and market-driven churches (and even evangelical academics?) are successful in large part because they are aware that the Gospel must be told in terms appropriate to the secular culture. But as Logos Christology and Jesuit syncretism taught us, one cannot simply and uncritically adopt the culture's language and methods without risking the danger of losing the meaning and value of the message in the end.[30] With language and technique come cultural assumptions.

The one who understands this best is Jacques Ellul. And his insightful remarks about communism and fascism in *The Presence of the Kingdom* are easily applied to contemporary church-growth movements, Christian therapeutic emphases, cultural moralism, and political protests:

They are incapable of making a genuine revolution in our civilization because they accept the essential basis of this civilization, and confine themselves to moving along the line of its internal development. Thus, utilizing what this world offers them, they become its slaves, although they think that they are transforming it. All the revolutions, advocated both by communism and by fascism, are superficial modifications, which change nothing in the real problem of our day.[31]

Paying heed to Ellul's warning entails the church's careful attention, not to marketing and therapeutic techniques, not to moral persuasion and political protest, but to theological categories, such as: *Christology* and *theological anthropology*, so that we know what the consensus *should* be regarding the identity of the God "in whom we trust" and human nature; *soteriology*, so that we do not continue to lay a Pelagian foundation to our evangelistic efforts; *ecclesiology*, so that we have a post-Constantinian definition of the church that is a more authentic response to Christ's call and not a response to the world's call, and so that we can show a culture that functions on the basis of individualism and consumerism what it means to live in a covenant community that is based on a shared faith and love in a transcendent reality; and an *eschatology* that avoids both alarmism and triumphalism, while reminding the church that it is engaged in battle with "principalities and powers" that incarnate themselves into the dominant culture. That is to say, the church will transform culture, not by using the means of the *prevailing* culture, but simply by existing faithfully as the church in the world, theologically literate, informed by a vision of where God is taking history (not where the world wants to take it), and supported by a community of like-minded disciples. Grounded in a healthy ecclesiology and eschatology, the church can succeed in exposing the prevailing culture to the light of a transcultural Gospel that provides a radical alternative to the "plausibility structure" of our society. The world is to be judged and called to conversion by a reality that does not yet fully exist but that is being modeled by the church now. In this way the church lives in the culture as, what Newbigin calls, a "hermeneutic of the gospel"—living out a contrary form of life for the sake of the world. Again, recalling a point made in chapter 8, Ellul said it best:

> This, then, is the revolutionary situation: to be revolutionary is to judge the world by its present state, by actual facts, in the name of a truth which does not yet exist (but which is coming)—and it is to do so because we believe this truth to be more genuine and more real than the reality which surrounds us. Consequently it means bringing the future into the present as an explosive force. . . . Henceforth the revolutionary act forms part of history: it is going to create history, by inflecting it toward this future.[32]

The church is to be *both* transformationist *and* countercultural, but it is to be the former *by being* the latter with an apocalyptic consciousness and with the confidence that Christ's values and purposes *will* prevail in the world because they *are* reality.[33]

If the evangelical church does not respond appropriately to the prevailing culture in a manner suggested by the *non*-evangelicals that have been cited in this chapter, then it is liable to continue drifting in the direction of the "Christ-*of*-culture" nineteenth-century Protestant liberalism in its attempt to answer its "cultured despisers" on the culture's own terms. In the end, what may be transformed, to our detriment, is not culture, but Christ.

For Further Reflection

1. Do you agree with the authors that there is not a consensus in the United States on fundamental issues such as what it means to be human? What evidence can you give for your answer?
2. In practice, what will it mean for "the church to be the church" in a culture that does not share the church's Christian view of the world? Be specific.

For Further Reading

Dawn, Marva. *Is It a Lost Cause? Having the Heart of God for the Church's Children.* Grand Rapids: Eerdmans, 1997.

Hauerwas, Stanley. *After Christendom?* Nashville: Abingdon, 1991.

Hauerwas, Stanley, and William H. Willimon. *Resident Aliens.* Nashville: Abingdon, 1990.

Hunsinger, George. "Where the Battle Rages: Confessing Christ in America Today." *Dialog* 26/4 (Fall 1987): 264–73.

Newbigin, Lesslie. *Foolishness to the Greeks: The Gospel and Western Culture.* Grand Rapids: Eerdmans, 1986.

———. *The Gospel in a Pluralist Society.* Grand Rapids: Eerdmans, 1989.

Phillips, Timothy R., and Dennis L. Okholm. *Christian Apologetics in the Postmodern World.* Downers Grove, Ill.: InterVarsity, 1995.

Epilogue: The Legacy

The paternal side of the Zoblinskis originated from Poland. Tommy's great grandfather came over to the U.S. on a boat, and Tommy's father tells him stories that Mr. Zoblinski's father told him. When the families get together, Mr. Zoblinski and his brother (Tommy's uncle) trade notes about their latest attempts to make contact with what remains of the family in Poland. They have received some letters and photos. Hopefully, they will one day take a family trip to visit their ancestors' homeland.

One of the most exciting things that keeps Tommy and his father speculating is the discovery of a "legacy." In 1915, Tommy's great-great grandfather set aside some money for safe-keeping. Though none of the U.S. Zoblinskis can read the Polish document, from what little they can decipher and from what relatives in Poland have mentioned in letters, they speculate that the original investment, with 100 years of compounded interest, is to be divided evenly among all existing Zoblinski family members in the year 2015.

This is much like the situation in the evangelical Christian family. As we have seen, we have been left a legacy—a deposit—from our ancestors in the faith. And as it has been invested in those who follow, it has accrued interest: more people have joined the family, and our understanding of the faith, "once for all delivered to the saints" (Jude 3, RSV), is more richly understood and expressed (unlike the Polish document in the hands of the U.S. Zoblinskis).

The only way that Tommy and his relatives will claim the legacy (if indeed there is anything left to claim) is if they are very intentional about finding out what the legacy involves and how they can go about participating in it.

The only way that evangelical Christians can claim the legacy left to us by the folks we have met in these pages, is if we are intentional about discovering what it is that has been faithfully handed down to us and how we can be participants in it now.

Tommy would never have known about the legacy unless his father, uncle, and grandfather had passed it on. Neither will those who come after Tommy know the Zoblinski heritage unless he passes on the stories that have been told to him.

As Carl Henry reminds us (see appendix F), the torch is being passed to a new generation of evangelicals. Mistakes have been made; fruitful endeavors have been numerous. What a new generation does with the legacy it has been given will in large part determine the configuration of evangelical Christianity in the future. As one person put it: The church is always one generation away from extinction.

You have been welcomed to the family. You have been called by its name. You have been reminded to act in a manner reflecting the family's name. Living faithfully now is your responsibility. The next chapter is yours to write.

Appendices

Appendix A

Models of Church-World Relationships

H. Richard Niebuhr (*Christ and Culture*): 5 categories
  (1) "Christ against Culture" (ref. Tertullian; monasticism; Anabaptism)
  (2) "Christ the Transformer of Culture" (ref. Augustine; Calvin)
  (3) "Christ and Culture in Paradox" (ref. Luther)
  (4) "Christ above Culture" (ref. Aquinas and medieval synthesis)
  (5) "Christ of Culture" (ref. nineteenth-century liberal Protestants: Schleiermacher, Ritschl)

Ernst Troeltsch (*The Social Teachings of the Christian Churches*): 2 categories
  (1) "Sect-type Christianity": Church is a voluntary association, usually a small group of believers whose values differ from that of the culture; hostile toward and suspicious of the world; don't expect to see their views adopted by society in general nor to attract many followers; don't like to see church as an institution and seek to break down distinction of laity and clergy; often appeal to life and values of early church; often a rigorous lifestyle, stressing radical obedience to Christian ethics; emphasize individual religious experience.
  (2) "Church-type Christianity": Church is a large institution whose values contribute to society as a whole; expect to be socially acceptable with many followers and to exert a positive influence on society; expect their views to be sanctioned by the society in which they live.

Mary Jo Weaver (*Introduction to Christianity*): 4 categories
$$\longleftarrow \text{CHURCH} \quad \text{CULTURE} \longrightarrow$$
withdrawal | nonconformity /adaptation |domination
  (1) "*Withdrawal*" (GET OUT): motivated by desire for purity or perfection.

Physical withdrawal from a distracting world (e.g., monasticism).

Psychological withdrawal from an evil world (e.g., apocalyptic—Adventists, Jehovah's Witnesses, some fundamentalists and Pentecostals).

Cultural withdrawal from a threatening world (e.g., Anabaptists, such as Amish).

(2) *"Domination"* (STAY IN & CONVERT): motivated by desire to impose a Christian viewpoint on all members of society. Can include either a negative view of world (e.g., Religious Right) or a highly optimistic evaluation of human potential within the world (e.g., nineteenth-century Protestants). Calvin and the Reformed tradition fit in here, and so does Liberation theology. Do antiabortion groups (e.g., Operation Rescue)?

(3) *"Nonconformity"* (STAY IN OF NECESSITY): motivated by desire to distinguish the values of the Gospel from the culture to which and against which the church is seeking to witness. Refuses to conform to the established order; willing to criticize the policies and pursuits of the Establishment. Doesn't assume Christian religious values and beliefs are compatible with those of society or with the policies of government. But they don't write off the culture as irrelevant or as entirely evil (cf. "withdrawal"). Some aspects of the culture are accepted and adopted, but in other cases the church offers an alternative to the established order by its "corporate otherness" in its communal lifestyle. Puts little confidence in social structures; uses protest to confront culture. Groups that fit here include Sojourner's Fellowship, the Catholic Workers Movement (Dorothy Day), and the Mennonite Central Committee. Usually these folks are pacifists and lead "simple lifestyles."

(4) *"Adaptation"* (STAY IN & BE A PART OF IT): motivated by desire to achieve aims through cooperation with government whose aims are more often than not coextensive with the church's. Sees God still working in a world that is God's. Works by conforming, modifying, compromising, accommodating selves to the values of society, not in order to identify with society in such a way as to impose Christian values on everyone, but in order to influence. Usually see no reason in principle to oppose the policies and goals of the state, and when they do, often lobby through more culturally acceptable means than those of dissenters. They place confidence in social structures (e.g., voting, running candidates for office). Tolerant of pluralism. This includes most of the mainline Protestant denominations (e.g., Presbyterian Church U.S.A., Evangelical Lutheran Church of America, United Methodists).

Appendix B

In this article, the founder of *Sojourners* magazine, Jim Wallis, articulates a contemporary call for an antithesis. This is excerpted from "Advocate: The Vehicle for the Vision," in *Seeds of the Kingdom* (Washington, D.C.: *Sojourners* Magazine, 1977), 3–4. Reprinted with permission from *Sojourners*, 2401 15th St. NW, Washington, D.C. 20009; (202) 328–8842, fax (202) 328–8757.

Advocate: The Vehicle for the Vision

> From that time Jesus began to preach and say, "Repent; for the kingdom of heaven is at hand." (Matt. 4:16–17)

At the outset of his ministry, just following his temptation in the wilderness, Jesus here proclaims the coming of the kingdom and calls men and women to a complete change of heart and mind. . . . Jesus' first sermon calls us not to straight doctrine, nor to personal salvation, nor to social action, nor to charismatic experience, nor to contemplation, nor to class struggle, nor to liturgical renewal, he calls us to the kingdom of God. He says that entering the kingdom comes through repentance—*metanoia* in the Greek, meaning to have the whole form, character, and orientation of our lives undergo a radical transformation so that we might be equipped and prepared to participate in the new order that has come to change the world and us with it.

Matthew then reports that Jesus called a band of disciples to follow him and "they immediately left their nets, and followed him." From the calling of the disciples to the inauguration of the church at Pentecost, the life of the kingdom drives the believers to community and is meant to take

279

place in the context of a common shared life (Acts 2:42–47; 4:32–35). The life of the early Christian fellowships, as seen in the book of Acts and elsewhere in scripture, presents the Christian life as a common life, the life of a people more than the life of individuals.

The common life was not merely a futile experiment nor did this practice end at Jerusalem. Rather the common life and sharing is shown throughout the New Testament and became the distinguishing mark of the early church.

Most often we pass over the meaning of Pentecost and the Spirit's creation of a common life among the believers. In the New Testament there exists the most fundamental connection between the vision of the kingdom as a new order and the common life of the body of Christ as the vehicle of that new order. As the New Testament affirms a basic tension between the values and character of the kingdom of God and the assumptions and structure of the world, so the church is visioned as a new social reality that bears witness to the new order of the kingdom in the midst of the old. Always flowing from the call to repentance and to the kingdom is the invitation to join the new community, the voluntary society, the new peoplehood of those who have begun to experience the salvation of Christ and, together, bear witness to the new life and freedom which he brings.

Clearly, we are not left to determine the shape of our discipleship alone. God has given his people the gift of community.

A community of faith and struggle becomes imperative as a center of resistance to the old order and celebration of the new, an environment in which we find the healing of our own brokenness and a sign to the world of the new possibilities of life in Jesus Christ. This is the kind of faith community the New Testament calls the church. It can take different forms in different times and places but to be the church there must be community present among the believers. The gospel calls us not only to a new style of life but also to a new environment created by the Spirit to bring about our healing and the healing of the nations.

Thus the church's greatest failures in confronting sin and death in the world are not in merely failing to denounce the world's ills and problems, nor even in failing to effectively make social change, but rather stem from its failure to be what the church has been called to be, from failing to structure its life and action as that new community created by the work of Christ and empowered by the Holy Spirit to be a new social reality, a living testimony to the presence of the kingdom of God in the world. . . . The renewal of the church in our times will come about through the work of the Spirit in restoring and reconstituting the church as a local community whose common life bears the marks of radical obedience to the kingdom of God.

Therefore the making of community is essentially a revolutionary act. It is a revolutionary act because it purposes to detach men and women from their dependence upon the dominant institutions, powers, and idolatries of the world system and creates an alternative corporate reality based upon deviant social values, which challenges the hold of the world system over the lives of people. The most politically responsible undertaking for men and women of faith is to rebuild the church which, when biblically understood, is a spiritual task that creates a revolutionary situation. Repentance and redirection are possible for people only when they are presented with an alternative.

Our time is one of large-scale concentrated power, of giant corporate institutions whose influence is nearly all pervasive. We have grown to depend upon large corporations and state bureaucracies for our basic needs and, to a frightening extent, allowed these institutions to decide for us how we will live. In many ways, their values have become our own. Large institutions of concentrated power and influence consciously seek to bring people's lives into conformity with their will and purposes. Large-scale technology, huge amounts of private capital, and a growing economic and political centralization place tremendous power in the hands of a few people.

Most of our decisions are made for us by the institutions whose presence and authority we have all become so accustomed to. Power elites, whether they be the directors of corporate capitalism or of central state bureaucracies, act to control and dominate, removing the decision making process from the people who are affected by their decisions. Their predominance is unprecedented and is supreme in production, distribution and control of the economic process, in the political arena of public policy both domestic and foreign, in information, advertising, and the mass media, in education and cultural activities, in labor and the various professions, in the legal and judicial process. The population has forfeited decision making to such all powerful institutions in exchange for a "prepackaged" life of comfort, security, convenience. The public has become consumed with "needs" created by the controlling institutions and then fulfilled in ways to make the population into a dependent, servile, and docile mass society feverishly participating in its own dehumanization.

These dominant institutions control not only socio-economic and political systems but also shape cultural patterns and engineer the very personal values of populations. This is because the vast majority of the people depends upon them for their livelihood and security and cannot afford to fall out of favor with them. These institutions have developed sophisticated and intimidating methods of reward, punishment, and threat that can easily be enforced. In such a situation, the values and priorities of the institutions become the values and priorities of the people.

The greatest source of power these institutions have is not merely political or economic but is in the spiritual hold they have over people's lives. The very people who are, in a real sense, controlled by an institution become the chief source of support for the institution's perpetuation. People are turned into loyal employees, frenzied consumers, and obedient citizens— willing participants in their own dehumanization. In the biblical scheme of things, this is exactly how sin and death exercise their spiritual author- ity over people's lives.

For we are not contending against human foes, but against the principalities, against the powers, against the world rulers of this present darkness, against the spiritual hosts of wickedness in the heavenly places (Eph. 6:12).

The spiritual hold of the dominant institutions of the world system over people's lives must be broken. It is the refusal to give the demanded alle- giance, the withdrawal of loyalty and support, the ending of conformity to their purposes which is the greatest threat to the power of the principali- ties and powers. Without people's subservience and passive obedience, the powers of the world find their spiritual hold over people's lives rendered impotent. The treatment of Jesus at the hands of the authorities and the official paranoia over every radical dissenter in history demonstrates the deep fear of the principalities and powers when the legitimacy of their authority is challenged and a confrontation with the truth exposes the idol- atrous character of their power.

The gospel of salvation in Christ must be addressed to people's need to be freed from the idolatrous power and domination of the most powerful institutions of the world system. The action of God in changing people's lives and enabling them to live in a different way is at the heart of the gospel message. Throughout the Bible, the path of obedience to God is a com- munal pilgrimage, not merely an individual trek. Corporate strength and power cannot be countered through individual effort alone, but must be resisted with another form of corporate power with a different set of val- ues and assumptions. The dominance and control of the large institutions of the present system must and can be resisted with the new corporate strength that comes from a body of believers who share their lives together, support each other, take liability and responsibility for one another, hold each other accountable to a common commitment, reinforce a set of val- ues that is deviant from the larger society, and are empowered by the Holy Spirit.

The greatest influence on a person's life will be that institution or set of institutions on which the person feels most dependent for survival and sup- port. As long as most Christians are more dependent upon the powers and principalities of the world for their survival and security than they are upon the Christian community, the church cannot do anything other than con- form to the world. We must see through biblical eyes that our lives and our very spiritual survival personally, economically, and politically, must be centered in the Christian community. The community of the local church must become the most important and central corporate reality of our lives, the daily environment out of which our lives are lived, the fellowship of people that sustains and supports us. The church must represent a body of people who have committed their lives to one another in Christ, a communion of faith and trust in which everything is shared, a place where our lives and society are seen through the eyes of biblical faith, and a corporate sign of the transforming power of the gospel of the kingdom in this world.

Appendix C

In this address, Charles Colson, founder and chairman of Prison Fellowship Ministries, articulates a modern form of the conversionist stance. This is excerpted from a transcription of the undergraduate commencement speech given at Wheaton College on May 15, 1988. Used with permission.

The Crisis of Character

A crisis of character grips Western culture. The source of the crisis is not primarily political or economic, although it is certainly evidenced in those areas. . . . The most important thing about a culture takes place in the hearts of citizens, the people. Arnold Toynbee, unarguably the greatest historian of the twentieth century, said, "I think history is all really spiritual. When you strip the rind off the kernel, it is the history of peoples' relation with God, and through God with one another."

What then is the spirit of the age in which we live? What are the assumptions about God and the moral truth that define our culture? The answer, I believe, is that the West's historic transcendent vision has given way to a soulless and morally impoverished relativism.

The pervasive assumption of life today is that there is no transcendent morally binding source of authority or truth above the individual. . . . This did not happen through some humanist conspiracy hatched in the basement of CBS in New York. This has happened simply because we as a society have chosen for it to happen. It's everywhere justified in the name of pluralism and toleration. "Remember the old days, when people had these absolute ideas. They burned [individuals] . . . at the stake!" We modern

284

enlightened individuals avoid all that by recognizing no absolutes at all. Except, perhaps, the absolute of toleration.

This all sounds fine in theory. The problem is that you can't run a society on that. Because when a person is left to make moral decisions without some binding transcendent standard above himself, he will always make those choices on the basis of self-interest. Relativism inevitably leads to radical individualism, what in the old days we called just plain old-fashioned selfishness. It is hard to avoid the conclusion that relativism and radical individualism have eroded the vital element of character in American life. There is nothing left without a belief in a higher standard to restrain a person's passions.

What do we expect from a radical individual as a soldier? A Marine who sells secrets for sexual favors. What do we expect from a radical individualist businessman? You can expect insider traders who will betray public trust for private gain. What do we expect from radical individualism as politicians? People who vote immoral bloated deficits, and people who plagiarize, and people who can't restrain their glandular urges long enough to run a campaign for president. What do we expect from a radical individualist as a parent? Broken homes. . . . Only one out of five American families today fit the definition of a traditional American family. And what do we expect of a radical individualist as a minister? Prosperity preachers who defraud their supporters. Our society is in tatters for want of the cementing bonds of men and women of character.

How do we go about restoring the ethic to our society that gives us a standard, a transcendent value standard?

The first place to begin is not—as so many of our friends in the Religious Right believed earlier in this decade—by infiltrating politics. Politics depends on individuals of character, but it can't create character.

How do we effectively instill those moral habits which form character and cause people to rise above themselves? To morally educate, the first thing we have to do is to strengthen the family. The family is God's ordained instrument not only for propagating the human race, but for taking young children . . . and civilizing them, making them understand that they are part of a community. It is God's first school of moral instruction and there probably is no greater responsibility than [to] . . . be godly parents who model what a Christian family really is to a society in which the family is in disarray.

Second, the church has got to play a crucial role. Now philosophers [and] theologians will argue whether religion is necessary for morality. The fact of the matter is that religion has been the primary source of private morality and public virtue in our culture from the very beginning. The church, the body of Christ, has to be a community of character where we model those virtues of the common good, the transcendent values, the transcendent standards to a world that is so desperate to see relationships that have meaning.

And third, education. Alan Bloom says in his book, *The Closing of the American Mind,* no other area of our culture has been so touched by relativism. Tragically, higher education is often seen today as an instrument to train minds, rather than fill them. I suppose that is to be expected in a relativist society. If one point of view is as good as another point of view, how can anyone teach you that there is absolute truth? The point of your education is not just to train minds in academic skills, but to inculcate men and women with a passion for truth, informed by history and revelation. As Chesterton wrote so succinctly once, the object of opening the mind, as of opening the mouth, is to shut it on something solid. Russell Kirk once wrote that colleges and universities can't make . . . vicious students virtuous or stupid students wise. But they can endeavor to prove to their students that intellectual power is not hostile to moral worth. And from a Christian perspective, this process begins with a firm grounding in biblical truth and a knowledge of 2,300 years of moral tradition in the West. That hunger and passion for truth marks the educated Christian.

Your ability to cope with the present crisis of character will depend largely upon the strength of your convictions about the world and the philosophy of life which you have developed. Only such a view of life . . . [with] a transcendent standard will take you out of what Malcolm Muggeridge calls that dark little dungeon of your ego.

How to fight [this crisis of character]? Let me leave you today with two challenges.

First, you've got to learn to think Christianly about every aspect of life. Being Christian is not just going to church. Being Christian is to think about every issue of the day in the light of what we know to be biblical revelation and God's truth as it has been interpreted down through the centuries. Think of every issue in that context and then go out and be advocates for them.

I'm often asked because of my work in the prisons to address political groups, and recently I was invited to address the legislature in Texas on criminal justice reforms. Maybe this will give you an illustration of what I'm talking about. . . . During the course of my talk I told them not only about my own Christian experience, . . . but also about the fact that law must be in conformance with the law beyond the law or it can't possibly be a meaningful law. And finally, I ended up talking about the fact that they have to get prisoners out of prison and put them out on the street working and paying off their victims. Half of the prisoners in Texas are there for nonviolent offenses, where they are sitting at a cost of $20,000 a year to the taxpayers.

Afterwards . . . a number of the members of the legislature came over and . . . said, "Wow, that is a wonderful idea you gave us about restitution. Where did that come from?" I said, "Do you have a Bible at home? You go and dust it off, and turn to Exodus 20–22 and you will see that was God's law to Moses at Sinai, and look at what Jesus did with Zaccheus."

Restitution is a biblical truth. Now you can't stand up in front of that legislature and say, "Do this because the Bible says so," because they don't believe the Bible is true. But you can argue wisdom that you get from revelation. If you are thinking Christianly you can apply it—not proof-text it, not taking verses out of context, . . . taking Christian truth and applying it to today's problem and arguing and contending for the values of our culture. There is no other way that the mind of this culture can be captured other than Christian people who go from educated institutions like this and think Christianly and act Christianly.

Secondly, you have to be a people of character. And you'll be surprised how tough that's going to be. People will want you to compromise. . . . It's harder and harder to be a people of character. But you've got to do it. God's calling you to be a witness, a model to the world of what it means to stand for truth and righteousness and justice and honor and duty and all of those elements that make up character, which this society so desperately needs.

It can be costly. A few years ago, I was on an airplane flying to Boston. An Oriental man got up out of his seat as I was walking down the aisle. And he got all excited. "You're Chuck Colson, you're Chuck Colson." The people were trying to get in the plane behind me, so I sat him down quietly. But I couldn't stop him, he was so excited. He said, "I was seven years, seven months in prison, and my mother brought your book to me. I accepted Christ, turned my life around, I never thought I would meet you." Then he told me his name, Benigno Aquino. We became very good friends. I saw him many times in the United States.

He called me one day, and said, "I'm going back to the Philippines." I said, "Benigno, is that safe?" He said, "Yes, I've got to go back. My place is among my people. It's my duty, duty." I said, "You might get hurt." He said, "I don't have a thing to worry about. If I go back and there is a free election, I'll be elected president of the Philippines; if I go back and Marcos throws me into prison, I'll start Prison Fellowship. If I'm killed, I'll be with Jesus."

And with that he went back, and of course you know the story; he never got off the plane. He was shot dead going down the steps. His body lay on that tarmac. He was stopped, but what he stood for could not be stopped. That began a great spiritual movement through the Philippines in which two million people were on their knees at night praying because of that man's death. And two and one-half years later a peaceful bloodless revolution toppled the tyrant and brought freedom and democracy to his people.

That's character, that's honor, that's duty, that's a love for God's righteousness and justice; and that's the kind of passion we Christians have to have with reckless abandon—to walk into the world as instruments of God's holiness and righteousness, to bring character back into a society from which relativism and radical individualism has stripped it bare.

The answer is so clear, without a restoration of character this age cannot and indeed deserves not to be saved. What that means is that you must prize above all virtue, duty, honor, and your commitment to Christ over convenience, affluence, comfort and, yes, even life itself.

Appendix D

Mary Stewart Van Leeuwen, Professor of Psychology and Philosophy and Resident Scholar in the Center for Women in Leadership, Eastern College (Pa.), articulates a contemporary transformationist stance toward culture in this article which is excerpted from her commencement address to graduate students at Wheaton College on May 8, 1993. It is reprinted from the *Wheaton Alumni* 60 (autumn 1993), 10–11, and is used with permission.

Principalities, Powers, and Professionalism

The concept of worldviews is very close to the intellectual and theological heart of the Reformed, Christian tradition. It is also a topic that increasingly attracts the attention of thoughtful evangelicals who are striving to serve God in the pluralistic, interconnected world of the late twentieth century. James Sire, the former editor of InterVarsity Press, rightly notes that everyone has a worldview—that is, a set of rock-bottom, faith-based assumptions about the nature of reality. Furthermore, our worldviews are not confirmed or disconfirmed by scholarship or science. They are the base upon which we build our scholarship, our science, our professional life, and even our smallest everyday decisions and actions.

There was a time, in the heyday of logical positivism, when it was assumed that one could neatly separate neutral, scientific "facts" from the subjective "values" held by what was presumed to be a decreasing number of religious believers. But the insights of the postmodern philosophy of science have helped to put an end to that tidy dichotomy. We now know that even in the so-called hard sciences "facts are theory-laden and theories are underdetermined by facts." That is to say, the assumptions we make about reality interact with the doing of science in all its stages. Sometimes they help to advance scientific knowledge, and sometimes they hinder it. But in either case, they are unavoidable. As one of my Catholic colleagues in psychology once put it, "There is no such thing as immaculate perception."

When refracted through a Reformed lens, the concept of a specifically Christian worldview receives another important twist—an insistence upon the simultaneous working out of the themes of creation, sin, and redemption in all areas of life. According to Reformed creation theology, we are wrong to carve the world into separate spheres labeled "sacred" and "secular." We are not, for example, to label worship, Sunday School teaching, preaching, and church fellowship "sacred" while viewing television production, elementary school teaching, psychological counseling, business, politics, art, and scholarship as "secular." On the contrary, we are to proclaim that (in the words of Abraham Kuyper) "there is not one square inch of creation about which Jesus Christ does not say, 'That is mine.'"

As a Christian academic, I believe that this strong creation theology, with its negation of sacred/secular dualisms, is one of the most helpful contributions of Reformed folk to the cultural conversation. However, there is another side to the story. Our world, in all its creational diversity, does indeed belong to God. But it is also as C. S. Lewis said, "enemy-occupied territory." Because of the fallen mess of human existence, the very same creational structures which make for orderly life and God-celebrating diversity—gender, ethnicity, family, law, government, the arts, the academy, or the marketplace—are . . . powers which have not yet completely bowed the knee to Jesus Christ.

Lesslie Newbigin is a prolific Christian commentator who spent nearly forty years as a missionary to India before returning to his native Britain. His 1989 book, *The Gospel in a Pluralist Society*, contains a chapter titled "Principalities, Powers, and People" in which he gives a specifically New Testament twist to the topics of creation and sin as these are intertwined in contemporary life.

He begins by noting that on almost every page of the New Testament we come across words which speak, more or less interchangeably, of *power, authority, rule, elements, angelic forces*, and *dominion*. While these words obviously refer very frequently to God and God's kingdom, even more often they are used to refer to human rulers and authorities—or, more accurately, to the roles, the offices, or the structures which successive human beings have inhabited throughout history.

Thus, individual kings come and go; but kingship, as a structure, an element, or a power, remains. Individual students can come and go from a school; but the spirit, or ethos, or peculiar authority of the institution, remains. Members of a family come and go, but as any well-trained family therapist can affirm, families as a whole can remain in the grip of certain powers, or structures, or role-configurations which keep being played out, for better or for worse, from generation to generation.

These structures, elements, powers, or authorities are indeed spiritual; they are not reducible to "flesh and blood," as Paul reminds us in Ephesians 6, even though they require flesh-and-blood persons in order to be activated. They are also needful for orderly human life, and as such are "good creations of God." But, writes Newbigin:

> They can come to usurp the place to which they have no right, the place which belongs to Christ and to him alone. They can, as we say, become absolutized, and then they become demonic. The [state] power ordained by God in Romans 13 becomes the Beast of Revelation. The Torah, that loving instruction which God gives his people and the beauty of which is celebrated in Psalm 119, becomes a tyrant from which Christ has to deliver us. Tradition, the handing on of good practice from parent to child as it is so beautifully described in Deuteronomy [and in Proverbs] becomes an evil power which comes between human beings and the living God.

These are examples from the New Testament of the ways in which the powers created in and for Christ can become agents of tyranny. To put it a little differently, and here I am quoting Reformed theologian Lewis Smedes, "It is simple to make an idol: just slice one piece of created reality off from the whole and expect miracles from it."

As Christians working in human institutions, we are called to the admittedly difficult task of both affirming and negating much of what we see and partake of. For example, therapists are called to affirm the creational goodness of marriage as an institution, while refusing to condone the abuses of power between the sexes. Missionaries are to say "yes" to the rich diversity of cultures which God has permitted to arise as containers for human life, while saying "no" to runaway tribalism, nationalism, racism, and ethnocentrism.

Because all of these structures are both created and fallen, and because their positive and negative elements are at root spiritual realities which cannot be analyzed with merely human tools, it is often agonizingly difficult to know just when to say "yes" and when to say "no." Creational goodness and sinful distortion are often two sides of the same coin. The pursuit of a Christian professional life is fraught with difficulty. But "difficult" is not the same as "impossible." For, as Lesslie Newbigin reminds us:

> In the cross, Christ has disarmed the powers. He has unmasked them. . . . Cross and resurrection seen together mean both judgment and grace, both wrath and endless patience. God still upholds the structures; [for] without

them the world would collapse and human life would be unthinkable. But the structures lose their pretended absoluteness. . . . That is the bottom line for Christian thinking, and the starting point for Christian action in the affairs of the world.

How, then, asks Newbigin, are the thrones to be shaken? Through corporate prayer, proclamation, worship, and mutual accountability it is possible, by the grace of God, for us to discern when to exercise the "judgment that is inevitable in the light of the cross, and also the patience which is required of us as witnesses to the resurrection."

We will not see the structures of society as unalterable, sacred givens; but neither will we be anarchists who see it as our duty to destroy these structures before they destroy us. "We are rather [to be] patient revolutionaries," writes Newbigin, "who know that the whole creation, with all its given structures, is groaning in the travail of a new birth, and that we share this groaning and travail, this struggling and wrestling—but do so in hope, because we have already received, in the Spirit, the firstfruit of the new world."

Appendix E

This sermon, delivered on May 21, 1922, by Harry Emerson Fosdick, longtime pastor of Riverside Church in New York City, was one of the opening shots in the fundamentalist-modernist controversy. This clear and classic liberal statement is excerpted from *The Christian Century* (8 June 1922), 713–17.

Shall the Fundamentalists Win?

This morning we are to think of the Fundamentalist controversy which threatens to divide the American churches, as though already they were not sufficiently split and riven. . . .

The Fundamentalists see, and they see truly, that in this last generation there have been strange new movements in Christian thought. A great mass of new knowledge has come into man's possession: new knowledge about the physical universe, its origin, its forces, its laws; new knowledge about human history and in particular about the ways in which the ancient peoples used to think in matters of religion and the methods by which they phrased and explained their spiritual experiences; and new knowledge, also, about other religions and the strangely similar ways in which men's faiths and religious practices have developed everywhere.

Now, there are multitudes of reverent Christians who have been unable to keep this new knowledge in one compartment of their minds and the Christian faith in another. They have been sure that all truth comes from the one God and is his revelation. Not, therefore, from irreverence or caprice or destructive zeal, but for the sake of intellectual and spiritual integrity, that they might really love the Lord their God not only with all their heart and soul and strength, but with all their mind, they have been trying to see this new knowledge in terms of the Christian faith and to see the Christian faith in terms of this new knowledge. Doubtless they have made many mistakes. Doubtless there have been among them reckless radicals gifted with intellectual ingenuity but lacking spiritual depth. Yet the enterprise itself seems to them indispensable to the Christian Church. The new knowledge and the old faith cannot be left antagonistic or even disparate, as though a man on Saturday could use one set of regulative ideas for his life and on Sunday could change gear to another altogether. We must be able to think our modern life clear through in Christian terms and to do that we also must be able to think our Christian life clear through in modern terms.

There is nothing new about the situation. It has happened again and again in history, as, for example, when the stationary earth suddenly began to move and the universe that had been centered in this planet was centered in the sun around which the planets whirled. Whenever such a situation has arisen, there has been only one way out: the new knowledge and the old faith had to be blended in a new combination. Now, the people in this generation who are trying to do this are the liberals, and the Fundamentalists are out on a campaign to shut against them the doors of the Christian fellowship. Shall they be allowed to succeed?

It is interesting to note where the Fundamentalists are driving in their stakes to mark out the deadline of doctrine around the church, across which no one is to pass except on terms of agreement. They insist that we must all believe in the historicity of certain special miracles, preeminently the virgin birth of our Lord; that we must believe in a special theory of inspiration—that the original documents of the scripture, which of course we no longer possess, were inerrantly dictated to men a good deal as a man might dictate to a stenographer; that we must believe in a special theory of the atonement—that the blood of our Lord, shed in a substitutionary death, placates an alienated deity and makes possible welcome for the returning sinner; and that we must believe in the second coming of our Lord upon the clouds of heaven to set up a millennium here, as the only way in which God may bring history to a worthy denouement. Such are some of the stakes which are being driven, to mark a deadline of doctrine around the church. . . .

Let us face this morning some of the differences of opinion with which somehow we must deal.

We may as well begin with the vexed and mooted question of the virgin birth of our Lord. I know people in the Christian churches, ministers, missionaries, laymen, devoted lovers of the Lord and servants of the gospel, who, alike as they are in their personal devotion to the Master, hold quite different points of view about a matter like the virgin birth. Here, for exam-

ple, is one point of view: that the virgin birth is to be accepted as historical fact; it actually happened; there was no other way for a personality like
the Master to come into this world except by a special biological miracle.
That is one point of view, and many are the gracious and beautiful souls
who hold it. But, side by side with them in the evangelical churches is a
group of equally loyal and reverent people who would say that the virgin
birth is not to be accepted as an historic fact.

To believe in virgin birth as an explanation of great personality is one
of the familiar ways in which the ancient world was accustomed to account
for unusual superiority. Many people suppose that only once in history do
we run across a record of supernatural birth. Upon the contrary, stories of
miraculous generation are among the commonest traditions of antiquity.
Especially is this true about the founders of great religions. According to
the records of their faiths, Buddha and Zoroaster and Lao-Tse and Mahavira
were all supernaturally born. Moses, Confucius and Mohammed are the
only great founders of religion in history to whom miraculous birth is not
attributed. That is to say, when a personality arose so high that men adored
him, the ancient world attributed his superiority to some special divine
influence in his generation, and they commonly phrased their faith in terms
of miraculous birth. So Pythagoras was called virgin born, and Plato, and
Augustus Caesar, and many more. Knowing this, there are within the evangelical churches large groups of people whose opinion about our Lord's
coming would run as follows: those first disciples adored Jesus—as we do;
when they thought about his coming they were sure that he came specially from God—as we are; this adoration and conviction they associated
with God's special influence and intention in his birth—as we do; but they
phrased it in terms of a biological miracle that our modern minds cannot
use. So far from thinking that they have given up anything vital in the New
Testament's attitude towards Jesus, these Christians remember that the
two men who contributed most to the church's thought of the divine meaning of the Christ were Paul and John, who never even distantly allude to
the virgin birth. . . .

Consider another matter on which there is a sincere difference of opinion between evangelical Christians: the inspiration of the Bible. One point
of view is that the original documents of the scripture were inerrantly dictated by God to men. Whether we deal with the story of creation or the list
of dukes of Edom or the narratives of Solomon's reign or the sermon on
the mount or the thirteenth chapter of first Corinthians, they all came in
the same way and they all came as no other book ever came. They were
inerrantly dictated; everything there—scientific opinions, medical theories, historical judgments, as well as spiritual insights—is infallible. That is
one idea of the Bible's inspiration. But side by side with those who hold it,
lovers of the book as much as they, are multitudes of people who never

think about the Bible so. Indeed, that static and mechanical theory of inspiration seems to them a positive peril to the spiritual life. The Koran similarly has been regarded by Mohammedans as having been infallibly written in heaven before it came to earth. But the Koran enshrines the theological and ethical ideas of Arabia at the time when it was written. God an oriental monarch, fatalistic submission to his will as man's chief duty, the use of force on unbelievers, polygamy, slavery—they are all in the Koran. The Koran was ahead of the day when it was written, but, petrified by an artificial idea of inspiration, it has become a millstone about the neck of Mohammedanism.

When one turns from the Koran to the Bible, he finds this interesting situation. All of these ideas, which we dislike in the Koran, are somewhere in the Bible. Conceptions from which we now send missionaries to convert Mohammedans are to be found in the Book. There one can find God thought of as an oriental monarch; there, too, are patriarchal polygamy, and slave systems, and the use of force on unbelievers. Only in the Bible these elements are not final; they are always being superseded; revelation is progressive. The thought of God moves out from oriental kingship to compassionate fatherhood; treatment of unbelievers moves out from the use of force to the appeals of love; polygamy gives way to monogamy; slavery, never explicitly condemned before the New Testament closes, is nevertheless being undermined by ideas that in the end, like dynamite, will blast its foundations to pieces. Repeatedly one runs on verses like this: "It was said to them of old time. . . . but I say unto you"; "God, having of old time spoken unto the fathers in the prophets by divers portions and in divers manners, hath at the end of these days spoken unto us in his Son"; "The times of ignorance therefore God overlooked; but now he commandeth men that they should all everywhere repent"; and over the doorway of the New Testament into the Christian world stand the words of Jesus: "When he, the spirit of truth is come, he shall guide you into all the truth." That is to say, finality in the Koran is behind; finality in the Bible is ahead. We have not reached it. We cannot yet compass all of it. God is leading us out toward it. There are multitudes of Christians, then, who think, and rejoice as they think, of the Bible as the record of the progressive unfolding of the character of God to his people from early primitive days until the great unveiling in Christ; to them the Book is more inspired and more inspiring than ever it was before; and to go back to a mechanical and static theory of inspiration would mean to them the loss of some of the most vital elements in their spiritual experience and in their appreciation of the Book. . . .

Consider another matter upon which there is a serious and sincere difference of opinion between evangelical Christians: the second coming of our Lord. The second coming was the early Christian phrasing of hope. No one in the ancient world had ever thought, as we do, of development, progress, gradual change, as God's way of working out his will in human life and institutions. They thought of human history as a series of ages succeeding one another with abrupt suddenness. The Graeco-Roman world gave the names of metals to the ages—gold, silver, bronze, iron. The Hebrews had their ages too—the original paradise in which man began, the cursed world in which man now lives, the blessed messianic kingdom some day suddenly to appear on the clouds of heaven. It was the Hebrew way of expressing hope for the victory of God and righteousness. When the Christians came they took over that phrasing of expectancy and the New Testament is aglow with it. The preaching of the apostles thrills with the glad announcement, "Christ is coming!"

In the evangelical churches today there are differing views of this matter. One view is that Christ is literally coming, externally on the clouds of heaven, to set up his kingdom here. I never heard that teaching in my youth at all. It has always had a new resurrection when desperate circumstances came and man's only hope seemed to lie in divine intervention. It is not strange, then, that during these chaotic, catastrophic years there has been a fresh rebirth of this old phrasing of expectancy. "Christ is coming!" seems to many Christians the central message of the gospel. In the strength of it some of them are doing great service for the world. But unhappily, many so over-emphasize it that they outdo anything the ancient Hebrews or the ancient Christians ever did. They sit still and do nothing and expect the world to grow worse and worse until he comes.

Side by side with these to whom the second coming is a literal expectation, another group exists in the evangelical churches. They, too, say, "Christ is coming!" They say it with all their hearts; but they are not thinking of all external arrival on the clouds. They have assimilated as part of the divine revelation the exhilarating insight which these recent generations have given to us, that development is God's way of working out his will. They see that the most desirable elements in human life have come through the method of development. Man's music has developed from the rhythmic noise of beaten sticks until we have in melody and harmony possibilities once undreamed. Man's painting has developed from the crude outlines of the cavemen until in line and color we have achieved unforeseen results and possess latent beauties yet unfolded. Man's architecture has developed from the crude huts of primitive men until our cathedrals and business buildings reveal alike an incalculable advance and an unimaginable future. Development does seem to be the way in which God works. And these Christians, when they say that Christ is coming, mean that, slowly it may be, but surely, his will and principles will be worked out by God's grace in human life and institutions, until "he shall see of the travail of his soul and shall be satisfied."

. . . Multitudes of young men and women at this season of the year are graduating from our schools of learning, thousands of them Christians who may make us older ones ashamed by the sincerity of their devotion to God's will on earth. They are not thinking in ancient terms that leave ideas of progress out. They cannot think in those terms. There could be no greater tragedy than that the Fundamentalists should shut the door of the Christian fellowship against such.

I do not believe for one moment that the Fundamentalists should shut the door of the Christian fellowship against such.

I do not believe for one moment that the Fundamentalists are going to succeed. Nobody's intolerance can contribute anything to the solution of the situation which we have described. If, then, the Fundamentalists have no solution of the problem, where may we expect to find it?

The first element that is necessary is a spirit of tolerance and Christian liberty. When will the world learn that intolerance solves no problems? This is not a lesson which the Fundamentalists alone need to learn; the liberals also need to learn it. . . .

Nevertheless, it is true that just now the Fundamentalists are giving us one of the worst exhibitions of bitter intolerance that the churches of this country have ever seen. . . .

The second element which is needed if we are to reach a happy solution of this problem is a clear insight into the main issues of modern Christianity and a sense of penitent shame that the Christian church should be quarreling over little matters when the world is dying of great needs.

. . . The present world situation smells to heaven! And now, in the presence of colossal problems, which must be solved in Christ's name and for Christ's sake, the Fundamentalists propose to drive out from the Christian churches all the consecrated souls who do not agree with their theory of inspiration. What immeasurable folly!

Well, they are not going to do it; certainly not in this vicinity. . . . Never in this church have I caught one accent of intolerance. God keep us always so and ever increasing areas of the Christian fellowship: intellectually hospitable, open-minded, liberty-loving, fair, tolerant, not with the tolerance of indifference as though we did not care about the faith, but because always our major emphasis is upon the weightier matters of the law.

Appendix F

Carl F. H. Henry is recognized as the foremost evangelical theologian and statesperson. He has been a leading participant in evangelical institutions and causes from their beginning. Dr. Henry returned to Wheaton College, his alma mater, on April 30, 1990, and gave this message in chapel. This transcript is taken from the *Wheaton Alumni* 57 (June–July 1990), 12–14 and is used with permission.

Coming Home to Say Good-bye

I have come home this morning to say good-bye.

Since leaving Wheaton and Chicago with college and seminary degrees, I've shared in the beginnings of Fuller Seminary, of *Christianity Today* magazine, of the Institute for Advanced Christian Studies, and of the first great World Congress on Evangelism held in Berlin. Now it is time to come home and to say good-bye.

When Christ won my heart in 1933 I was already a Long Island editor and suburban reporter for New York dailies. My immediate superior deleted from all copy any mention of God. The world of religion lay snugly in the lap of modernism. It was not the Gospel of a crucified and risen Redeemer, but rather the social gospel of a coming Marxist millennium that prevailed in Protestant pulpits and publications. Modernism dominated the denominational colleges and seminaries, and it preempted public service radio time. So evangelical participation was excluded.

You must not, however, misjudge the modernists. They thought they were rescuing Christianity from fundamentalist and evangelical obscurantism. Modernists said many good things about Jesus and the Bible: Jesus towers higher than founders of the other world religions, they said, and the Bible surpasses other books in spiritual wisdom.

Yet the essence of modernism was its regard for the scientific method as the one reliable test of truth. Empirical verification requires that an event occur at least twice before one can be sure it has occurred once. In short, modernism presupposed the absolute uniformity of nature; it ruled out once-for-all miracles in advance.

Whatever tribute modernism paid to the Bible and to Jesus of Nazareth was hedged by a governing conviction that the miracles at the heart of evangelical theism and credal Christianity are mythical. Evangelical orthodoxy, or biblical theism, it therefore deplored as prescientific, unscientific, and antiscientific.

In this debate our Christian integrity was taken at stake, even the legitimacy of attending Wheaton College for liberal arts learning. We evangelicals were a lonely and beleaguered lot and much maligned. Some of that same hostility is emerging again today, despite the claim that 50 million Americans are born-again. The present adversarial context is not modernism, but humanism or raw naturalism.

Then as now we were involved in a collision of worldviews. We hungered for truth that exhibited the credibility of Christian belief and that unmasked the weaknesses and even pretensions of competing views. We hated the exams with an unholy disdain, but we wrestled them—Ken Taylor, who would give us *The Living Bible*; Sam and Howard Moffett who before its evangelistic explosion would return to Korea; Dayton Roberts who before the charismatic awakening would return with Grace Strachan to Latin America; Harold Lindsell who with Ken Taylor was on the Illinois state championship debate team; Eleanor Solteau who became a medical missionary among the Arabs in Palestine. There were others; the roster reads like an evangelical "Who's Who," and some are already with Christ in glory.

When in 1938 I graduated from Wheaton, the national radio networks apportioned free public service time only to the mainstream religions. The Federal Council of Churches reserved Protestant programming for ecumenists and opposed even the sale of network time to religious conservatives. That situation in part stimulated the formation in 1942 of the National Association of Evangelicals. It soon had a service constituency of over 10 million conservative Protestants. The evangelical resurgence was under way.

Five years later, in 1947, Dr. Wilbur Smith resigned from Moody Bible Institute, Dr. Everett Harrison from Dallas Seminary, and I from Northern Baptist Seminary, to share in founding Fuller Theological Seminary, the first interdenominational seminary west of the Mississippi. We dedicated it to biblical theology, biblical ethics, biblical apologetics, and biblical evangelism. Had Harold John Ockenga of Park Street Church followed through on his commitment to come as resident president, rather than functioning in absentia, the fortunes not only of Fuller but of all American evangelicalism would have been notably different. Dr. Charles Fuller had promised to sponsor Ockenga on television for a one-year trial run and that, I think, would have changed the course of American televangelism.

Also in 1947 Billy Graham, who had been a Wheaton sophomore during my senior year, became headline news when his Los Angeles crusade attracted Hollywood participants, and the Hearst papers front-paged him coast to coast. Almost from the beginning, Graham shocked the independent fundamentalists because he determined to win converts in modernist churches and included ecumenists on the platform.

That same year also appeared my *Uneasy Conscience of Modern Fundamentalism*. It lamented the withdrawal of fundamentalists from the sociocultural arena and urged them to sound the Christian claims in social affairs as well as in individual life. Soon it was followed by *Remaking the Modern Mind*, a declaration that the reigning philosophy had no legitimate claim to finality and judging it in the context of the Christian world-life view.

To summarize: in 1942, the National Association of Evangelicals; in 1947, Graham's evangelism, Fuller Seminary and *Uneasy Conscience*. . . .

In 1956 *Christianity Today* was launched. It quickly outstripped the pretentiously named *Christian Century* which for a half century had vocalized the ecumenical left in theology, politics, and economics.

By 1960 those of us specially interested in the scholarly side of evangelical witness were holding serious discussions about a Christian university in a major metropolitan area, notably New York City, where students could get hands-on training in virtually every career choice. Mainly for lack of consensus on the part of prospective major donors the effort was abandoned, and gave way to the more modest Institute of Advanced Christian Studies promotive of scholarly evangelical books. Others moved into the new evangelical opportunity.

In 1965 a fund-raising telethon by "Pat" Robertson launched the Christian Broadcasting Network, which gradually linked 190 stations in the U.S. and overseas by satellite. Oral Roberts, who had put healing evangelism on television a year earlier, opened Oral Roberts University in Tulsa in 1965.

In 1966, as a tenth anniversary project, *Christianity Today* sponsored our generation's first global evangelistic conclave, the World Congress on Evangelism in West Berlin; Graham was honorary chairman, and I was chairman. It was the father of Lausanne/74 and the grandfather of Manila/89, and it called for fidelity to the one God of justice and of justification.

Many of you in the last twenty years have shared in the excitement of and even participated in some of the events since then. In 1971 Jerry Falwell formed Liberty Baptist College in Lynchburg, where it has become Liberty University with 5,000 students. By the late 1970s "Pat" Robertson had established a full graduate university, now called Regent University, in Virginia Beach. Others of us meanwhile strove for a renewal of evangelical theology, which modernism, neo-orthodoxy, and humanism had sidelined, and to that end I wrote my own six-volume work on *God, Revelation and Authority,* to which *Time* magazine in 1976 devoted a full page.

Also in 1976 appeared the *Newsweek* cover story, "The Year of the Evangelical." It acknowledged that America's 50 million religious conservatives were the nation's fastest-growing spiritual force and noted that three presidential candidates professed to be born again. This astonishing evangelical initiative surprised Harvey Cox and other gurus of the secular city, who expected a religionless society, and it surprised also the ecumenists whose mainline churches were being sidelined. In that same year Chuck Colson emerged from Watergate notoriety to found Prison Fellowship Ministries, the most important evangelical humanitarian agency to appear since the founding of World Vision in the 1950s.

On almost every side, American fundamentalism by contrast was thought to be comatose and ready for early burial, despite its many day schools, and impressive Sunday Schools, and some notably large churches. It was assumed by the ecumenical movement, by the mainstream evangelicals, and by the charismatics, that fundamentalism was doomed for two reasons: first, its commitment to second degree separation—that is, separation both from the culture and from ecumenically-related churches; and second, its hostility to the Billy Graham Crusades because of Graham's inclusive sponsoring committees.

But Jerry Falwell rallied much of fundamentalist independency to the importance of political confrontation and in 1979 founded the Moral Majority for a national crusade that addressed ethical and social issues and involved a legislative lobby.

All wings of the conservative religious thrust were now aggressively in motion—fundamentalists, evangelical, charismatic—while ecumenical churches were losing prestige, numbers, and finances as their constituencies increasingly fell away.

Then, a decade later, occurred the charismatic televangelism calamities involving Oral Roberts, Jim Bakker, and Jimmy Swaggart, as well as a number of noncharismatic pastors and leaders. In a single decade the secular city refocused its perception of the evangelical movement and blunted its initiative. The secular media revived the specter of Elmer Gantry along with the old modernist prejudices and viewed evangelical orthodoxy in a context of psychological manipulation and financial exploitation.

You have much to forgive our generation for bequeathing to you this "bag of worms" with your evangelical heritage. But you also inherit a worldwide evangelistic initiative, an unprecedented theological and commentary literature, improved Bible translations, evangelical colleges and seminaries crowded with students, multitudes of churches where the Gospel is now preached, and an enlarging door to the political arena. I dare say also that the 1989 Evangelical Affirmations [held at Trinity Evangelical Divinity School] conference enabled evangelicals to regain some of their stride and that the recent pressures for financial integrity and accountability strengthened the movement overall.

In this somewhat murky firmament your own star is now rising. None of us who came before you from the halls of Wheaton was a C. S. Lewis, an Aleksandr Solzhenitsyn, a Nobel prizewinner. But among you this morning may well be a future Jonathan Salk, a Supreme Court Justice like Sandra O'Connor, a president of one of the Big Ten universities, a future Augustine to do battle with the intellectual Philistines of our time.

I must not mislead you, however, by an in-house perspective. The world-spirit outside these walls is deepening its hostility to a supernatural faith. When Protestant modernism dominated into the 1930s, religious humanists who rejected the supernatural were a meager minority. Neo-orthodoxy, paced by Karl Barth and Emil Brunner, put both modernism and humanism on the defensive by its summons to hear the transcendent Word of the self-revealing God. It left its mark even upon evangelical seminaries and religious colleges ready to compromise biblical authority. Yet in the great secular universities mediating scholars like Tillich and Barth and Brunner had little more impact than did consistent evangelicals. It was secular humanism that took the initiative in public education, in the mass media, and in the political realm: God was excluded from public significance, religion was assigned only an internal subjective importance, reality was reduced to impersonal processes and quantum events, all philosophical principles and moral imperatives were held to be culture-relative, and all life was declared to be temporal so that the cemetery becomes your final destiny and mine.

In today's cultural setting, therefore, the intellectual initiative is no less hostile to the faith than was that which greeted us students of an earlier generation. Secular humanism is in fact moving downward rather than upward; in short, humanism is losing its humanitarianism and channeling into raw naturalism. That is why my last book, *Twilight of a Great Civilization*, warns that midnight may soon overtake Western culture unless Judeo-Christian theism reverses the present convictional stance. That is also why Chuck Colson warns in *Against the Night, Living in the New Dark Ages* that, if Anglo-American culture collapses, many churches already compromised by its concessions may not survive its nightfall.

We know that the world lies in the lap of the evil one and that mere social bandaids will neither change it nor long preserve it. We know that our divine mandate is to preach the forgiveness of sins on the ground of Christ's atonement and to proclaim to the world the standards by which God will finally judge it. We know that the risen Jesus has life-transforming power to make obedient disciples of a motley company of young converts like ourselves. We know that in his sovereign providence God can enable us to penetrate the world with a living witness to the truth and power of evangelical theism. In that awesome task I wish you Godspeed. May you share as we did in the splendor of a spiritual sunrise and not only in the sad defection of a secular society. Our turning decade of the century needs a vanguard of future heroes with a special glow, the glow of royal purple. "For Christ and His Kingdom" is still a noble hallmark. Remember who your ruler is. Don't forget his daily briefing and, above all else, hold his commands in honor.

Almost all my teachers are gone, or I would pay them public tribute. They labored for little of this world's goods, but they knew us by name and they wanted us above all else to serve God well and to honor our Wheaton heritage. You do not know who most of them were, or know many of us who studied hard under them, even as the next generation will remember too few of your present mentors and—amid the onrush of modernity—might all too soon forget some of you. But you differ from us in one notable respect: this is your moment. The flaming light, the torch, is being passed to you. Don't let it slip or lose your stride.

And good-bye, until we meet again.

Notes

1. All in the Family

1. See Virgil Vogt, "Economic Koinonia," *Post-American* 4 (June/July 1975), 22–27.
2. For a defense of this position, see David Chilton, *Productive Christians in an Age of Guilt-Manipulators: A Biblical Response to Ronald J. Sider* (Tyler, Tex.: Institute for Christian Economics, 1982); John Jefferson Davis, *Your Wealth in God's World* (Phillipsburg, N.J.: Presbyterian and Reformed, 1984).
3. This term originates from Nicholas Wolterstorff, *Reason within the Bounds of Religion,* 2d ed. (Grand Rapids: Eerdmans, 1984).
4. Quoted in T. H. L. Parker, *Karl Barth* (Grand Rapids: Eerdmans, 1970), 17.
5. Arthur C. Cochrane, *The Church's Confession under Hitler* (Philadelphia: Westminster, 1962), 87, 120–21.
6. "The Guiding Principles of the Faith Movement of the 'German Christians,' June 6, 1932" in Cochrane, *Church's Confession,* 222–23. Here the term "evangelical" is used differently than above. In contemporary German, the term *evangelisch* is synonymous with Protestant or Lutheran. See also Robert P. Ericksen, *Theologians under Hitler: Gerhard Kittel, Paul Althaus and Emmanuel Hirsch* (New Haven, Conn.: Yale University Press, 1985).
7. John Leith, *Introduction to the Reformed Tradition: A Way of Being the Christian Community* (Philadelphia: Westminster, 1980), 17–31.

2. Browsing the Worldview Catalog

1. See Nicholas Wolterstorff, *Reason within the Bounds of Religion,* 2d ed. (Grand Rapids: Eerdmans, 1984).
2. See Robert C. Roberts, *The Strengths of a Christian* (Philadelphia: Westminster, 1984), 26–27.
3. Brian J. Walsh and J. Richard Middleton, *The Transforming Vision: Shaping a Christian World View* (Downers Grove, Ill.: InterVarsity, 1984), 35; James W. Sire, *The Universe Next Door: A Basic World View Catalog* (Downers Grove, Ill.: InterVarsity, 1988), 18.
4. Carl Sagan, *Cosmos* (New York: Random House, 1980), 4.
5. Paul Kurtz, ed., *Moral Problems in Contemporary Society: Essays in Humanistic Ethics* (Englewood Cliffs, N.J.: Prentice-Hall, 1969), 3.
6. Humanist Manifesto II; For more information, see the American Humanist Association Web page at *http://www.infidels.org/org/aha/documents/manifesto2.html.*

7. Mary Farrell Bednarowski, *New Religions and the Theological Imagination in America* (Bloomington, Ind.: Indiana University Press, 1989), 7.

8. Marilyn Ferguson, *The Aquarian Conspiracy: Personal and Social Transformation in the 1980s* (Los Angeles: J. P. Tarcher, 1980), 98, 382.

9. Barbara Marx Hubbard, *The Hunger of Eros* (Harrisburg, Pa.: Stackpole, 1976), 54–55.

10. C. S. Lewis, *Mere Christianity* (New York: Macmillan, 1952), 48–50.

11. Harold S. Kushner, *When Bad Things Happen to Good People* (New York: Avon, 1981), 134.

12. Ibid., 81.

13. Rosemary Radford Ruether, "Feminism and the Jewish Christ in Dialogue," in *The Myth of Christian Uniqueness: Toward Pluralistic Theologies of Religions,* ed. John Hick and Paul F. Knitter (Maryknoll, N.Y.: Orbis, 1987), 141.

14. John Hick, *An Interpretation of Religion: Human Responses to the Transcendent* (New Haven, Conn.: Yale University Press, 1989), 8.

15. Alan Ehrenhalt, *The Lost City: Discovering the Forgotten Virtues of Community in the Chicago of the 1950s* (New York: Basic Books, 1995), 272.

16. Roger Lundin, "The Pragmatics of Postmodernity," in Timothy R. Phillips and Dennis L. Okholm, eds., *Christian Apologetics in the Postmodern World* (Downers Grove, Ill.: Inter-Varsity, 1995), 38.

17. Ibid., 31.

3. Revelation: The Source of Our Christian Identity

1. We will be using the personal pronoun "he" to refer to God. This does not imply that God is male, since God has no gender. But it is the best we can do with human language, since we do not want to lose the personal nature of God with an impersonal pronoun or an awkwardly sounding and tediously repetitive use of the word "God."

2. *Institutes* 1.6.1.

3. "Scripture alone" did not mean that they simply ignored the writings of Christians during the previous fifteen centuries. The Reformers still believed that tradition gives us valuable insights. As Barth put it, they became fellow students of the Bible with those Christians who had come before. Think of it this way: we join people like Augustine, Aquinas, and Luther in one giant Bible study throughout history; that is why it is important to "listen" to brothers and sisters who are now part of the church triumphant—whose insights into scriptural truths are found in their writings.

4. Note that God's revelation of himself is always mediated through something human: through human flesh (Jesus of Nazareth), human language (Scripture), a human institution (the church). God discloses himself on our level—in earthy, human, worldly ways. He accommodates himself to our ability to understand, because we would not be able to understand him on his own level. As John Calvin put it, God speaks to us as parents speak to their baby—with a lisp.

5. The Greek style and vocabulary of the Apostle John is simple when compared with that of the Gospel writer Luke; the Book of Revelation is very rough Greek, and there are many misspellings and grammatical irregularities.

6. The heat of battles with liberals over the authority of Scripture (which we will look at later in this book) led fundamentalists and evangelicals to insist on the *inerrancy* of Scripture (with reference to the original documents). The argument is that since God is true and omniscient, and since each word in the Bible is inspired by him, then each word of the Bible is infallibly true. In recent years some evangelicals have found the word "inerrant" too strident—a negative word that has various meanings and does not tell us what the Bible is. So these evangelicals have opted for something like "completely reliable and absolutely authoritative" instead of "inerrant." This is essentially the point made in *The Chicago Statement on Biblical Inerrancy* when it states that "inerrant" signifies "the quality of

being free from all falsehood or mistake and so safeguards the truth that Holy Scripture is entirely true and trustworthy in all its assertions."

7. Calvin, *Institutes* 1.7.4.

8. Ibid., 1.7.2.

9. Ibid., 1.7.5.

10. This early document, also called *The Teaching of the Twelve Apostles*, can be found in Cyril C. Richardson, ed., *Early Christian Fathers*, Library of Christian Classics, vol. 1 (Philadelphia: Westminster, 1963), 161–82.

11. The word canon was first applied to Scripture by Athanasius in A.D. 373 to designate the "divinely inspired books of Scripture." Athanasius's list of the canonical books of the Bible in A.D. 367 is the same list we have today in our Bibles. The table of contents may have been the same as early as A.D. 200, but we cannot be absolutely certain until Athanasius's list.

12. In addition, Jesus promised them the Holy Spirit as their inspiration to guide them "into all truth," as well as "teach" and "remind" them of "everything" he had said to them (John 14:26; 15:26; 16:13–15). Paul recognized this when he stated that the church is God's people, built on the foundation of prophets and *apostles*, with Jesus himself as the chief cornerstone (Eph. 2:20).

13. The *Acts of Paul* is an example of the questionable literature. This work dating in the late 100s attempted to expand our knowledge of Paul. Included is one story, where Paul has been sentenced to fight the lions. "At dawn there was a cry from the citizens: 'Let us go to the spectacle! Come, let us see the man who possesses God fighting with the beasts!' . . . So when he had taken his place . . . ordered a very fierce lion, which had but recently been captured, to be set loose against him. . . . 'Away with the sorcerer! Away with the poisoner!' But the lion looked at Paul, and Paul at the lion. Then Paul recognized that this was the lion which had come and been baptized. And borne along by faith, Paul said: 'Lion, was it thou whom I baptized?' And the lion in answer said to Paul: 'Yes.' Paul spoke to it again and said: 'And how wast thou captured?' The lion said with one voice: 'Even as thou, Paul'" (Wilhelm Schneemelcher, ed., *New Testament Apocrypha* [Philadelphia: Westminster, 1963ff], 1:392–4).

The Gospel of Thomas is one example of the heretical literature circulating. This is a collection of sayings purportedly by Jesus. Included are the following: (25) "Jesus said: Love thy brother as thy soul; keep him as the apple of thine eye." (114) "Simon Peter said to them: Let Mary go forth from among us, for women are not worthy of the life. Jesus said: Behold, I shall lead her, that I may make her male, in order that she also may become a living spirit like you males. For every woman who makes herself male shall enter into the kingdom of heaven" (Schneemelcher, *New Testament Apocrypha*, 1:511–22).

14. Actually, McGrath was explaining what "theology" does. (See his *A Cloud of Witnesses* [Grand Rapids: Zondervan, 1990].) Doctrines spring from and become material for theology, because theology is literally the words or study of God, done according to rules. (It is not mere opinion, but a discipline that every believer does to one extent or another. Some even make a career out of it. That can be both good and bad!) A fuller definition of theology would be: "a human response to the revelation of God done within and for the Christian church that engages in critical reflection for responsible talk about God." This is what we will deal with below.

15. Ericksen, *Theologians Under Hitler*, 48.

16. Ibid., 87, 42.

17. Charles Malik, *The Two Tasks* (Westchester, Ill.: Cornerstone, 1980), 32.

4. Setting the Stage: The Creation of the World and Human Beings

1. See Proverbs 8:29, Jeremiah 5:22, and Psalm 104:7–9. Note the disciples' question in Luke 8:25, as well as the description of the "new heaven and new earth" that includes no more sea (Rev. 21:1).

2. See E. A. Burtt, *The Metaphysical Foundations of Modern Science* (Garden City, N.Y.: Doubleday Anchor, 1954); Diogenes Allen, *Christian Belief in a Postmodern World: The Full Wealth of Conviction* (Louisville: Westminster/John Knox, 1989), chap. 1.

3. "Think of a country where people were admired for running away in battle or where a man felt proud of double-crossing all the people who had been kindest to him. You might just as well try to imagine a country where two and two made five. Men have differed as regards what people you ought to be unselfish to—whether it was only your own family, or your fellow countrymen, or everyone. But they have always agreed that you ought not to put yourself first. Selfishness has never been admired" (Lewis, *Mere Christianity*, 19).

4. Sometimes people think of the created world as intrinsically evil because they do not realize that the Bible uses the word "world" in two different ways. It is used in Romans 8:18–25 in the sense of God's created world that he originally declared good, that subsequently fell into the bondage of sin, and which awaits the completion of its release and redemption from that bondage. However, it is used in Romans 12:2 and 1 John 2:15–17 to refer to a philosophy of life that is set against God's purposes—what we oftentimes mean when we say that some person or act is "worldly." For a helpful discussion, see Robert Webber, *The Church in the World* (Grand Rapids: Zondervan/Academie, 1986), appendix A.

A similar confusion occurs when people interchange "body" (*soma* in Greek, usually, though not always, referring to our whole personal life that can be used either for good or evil [see 1 Cor. 6:13, 15, 19–20]) and "flesh" (*sarx* in Greek, which usually refers to the principle of sin that is within us and is set against the Spirit of God [see Rom. 7:5–6, 17–20]). These confusions have often led people to assume that the physical body is bad.

5. For an interesting introduction to theology that looks at the world through such a community lens, see Stanley J. Grenz, *Created for Community: Connecting Christian Belief with Christian Living* (Wheaton, Ill.: Victor/BridgePoint, 1996).

6. As we will note later, this point is made profoundly in John 1:14 where the background to the word "dwelt" is the tabernacle of God in the wilderness. "The Word became flesh and tabernacled among us."

5. After the Fall: Sin and Its Consequences

1. Of course, there is a religious counterpart to all of this. Legalism is also a lie that religious folks often build their lives around. (See 1 Tim. 4:1–5.) And such a lie is as difficult to deal with as that which the secular culture tries to sell us, because in a legalistic religious community one is made to feel abnormal if he or she does not fall in line.

2. The image is not obliterated, but warped or distorted. See Genesis 9:6 and James 3:9 which indicate that the image was still there after the Fall.

3. Walter Brueggemann, *Genesis* (Atlanta: Westminster John Knox, 1982), 53.

4. This is a controversial and difficult issue. Many evangelicals interpret Genesis as ordaining a complementarian relationship between husband and wife. For example, the *Danvers Statement* (1987) of the Council of Biblical Manhood and Womanhood states that "Adam's headship in marriage was established by God before the Fall, and was not a result of sin." Typically, the order of creation is seen as mandating a hierarchy, which they support from Paul's statement as well, that woman was created for man (1 Cor. 11:8–9). A strong case, however, can be made that the creation narrative has a different emphasis. Adam's problem is that he is isolated and lonely in creation; there is nothing else he can relate to as a person. As Scripture describes his plight, "But for Adam no suitable helper

was found" (Gen. 2:20). "The Hebrew term 'helper' ought not be interpreted in the sense of serving as an assistant. The Hebrew word . . . which means 'other' or 'helper,' also refers to one who saves or delivers. Apart from this verse it is only used with reference to God in relationship to Israel (Deut. 33:7; Pss. 33:20; 115:9)" (Stanley Grenz, *Sexual Ethics: A Biblical Perspective* [Dallas: Word, 1990], 19). At the creation of Eve, Adam joyously declares: she is "bone of my bones and flesh of my flesh" (Gen. 2:23). Eve is not in a subservient position but elevated. For she rescues him from solitude and thus represents the "crown of creation" (Grenz, *Sexual Ethics*, 28). See also Willard M. Swartley, *Slavery, Sabbath, War, and Women: Case Issues in Biblical Interpretation* (Scottdale, Pa.: Herald, 1983).

5. John Francis Kavanaugh, *Following Christ in a Consumer Society* (Maryknoll, N.Y.: Orbis, 1981), 34.

6. Hallelujah, What a Savior: God's Salvific Work in Jesus Christ

1. See Bettie J. Eadie, *Embraced by the Light* (Placerville, Calif.: Gold Leaf, 1992).

2. They also saw that our salvation was at stake if this were not true, for "what has not been assumed cannot be healed." If God did not assume our full humanity—body and soul—then our full humanity could not be saved.

3. The term *testament*, as in the Old and New Testaments, means the same thing as a covenant. A *covenant* is a relational term that refers to an agreement between two parties. God's covenants originate solely through his initiative; it is God's free and thus gracious decision to deliver and redeem sinners. The unfolding drama of God's covenant in the two testaments is beautifully rendered in Walter Wangerin's "re-presentation" of the biblical story entitled *The Book of God* (Grand Rapids: Zondervan, 1996).

4. That is why the Ten Commandments consist of two tables, one dealing with humanity's responsibilities to God and the second with other humans.

5. We are borrowing an allusion to the church's halfhearted response to Jesus' radical call to discipleship from Thomas Kelly, *A Testament of Devotion* (1941; reprint, San Francisco: HarperSanFrancisco, 1992). In chiding the church for making religion a dull habit instead of a burning fever, he poignantly remarks: "Religion as a dull habit is not that for which Jesus lived and died," p. 53.

6. Perhaps Jesus learned this from his mother. Mary obeyed the call of God for her life by becoming pregnant while she was betrothed to Joseph. At the least she risked public disgrace through divorce (since betrothal was everything in marriage short of sexual intercourse and could only be terminated by divorce); at the worst she risked being executed by stoning.

7. Rollo May, *Love and Will* (New York: Norton, 1969).

8. There are various images of the atonement in the New Testament, all of which are necessary for a complete understanding of the work of Christ on the cross on our behalf: (1) the "classical" theory emphasizes Christ's payment of a ransom on our behalf by giving his life (Mark 10:45); (2) the "Christus Victor" theory emphasizes Christ's victory over his enemies (Col. 2:15); and (3) the "Latin" theory emphasizes Christ's substitutionary sacrifice as the lamb (John 1:36; Heb. 2:17) who satisfies the wrath of God. Also, St. Paul focuses on the legal penalty Christ took upon himself for us, the lawbreakers (Rom. 5:6–11; 2 Cor. 5:19–21).

7. Already but Not Yet: The Church and the Kingdom

1. See Flannery O'Connor, "The River," in *The Complete Stories* (New York: Farrar, Straus and Giroux, 1977), and *The Violent Bear It Away* (New York: Farrar, Straus and Giroux, 1960).

2. The image of baptism as jumping onto a moving train is taken from Stanley Hauerwas and William H. Willimon, *Resident Aliens* (Nashville: Abingdon, 1990).

3. For an excellent development of this point see Darrell L. Guder, *Be My Witnesses* (Grand Rapids: Eerdmans, 1985), 40–44, 91–96.

4. By "locus" we mean the place or, in this case, institution where something occurs—a center of activity or concentrated reality. As a beehive is the locus of honey production, so the church is the visible human institution in which the results of Christ's salvific kingdom work occur as in no other place or institution.

5. This twofold pattern is implicit within Jesus' imperative: "Those who would come after me must deny themselves and take up their cross and follow me" (Mark 8:34, NIV:ILE). The cross is an instrument of death; thus, our mission is not to elevate ourselves but to lay down our lives to follow him who died and rose again so that we might live.

6. Dietrich Bonhoeffer, *Life Together* (New York: Harper and Row, 1954), 17–39.

7. Jacques Ellul, *The Presence of the Kingdom* (Colorado Springs: Helmers and Howard, 1989), 38–39.

8. Hans Küng, *The Church* (New York: Doubleday, 1967), 90–94.

8. Back to the Future

1. While other biblical writers do not explicitly mention a millennium, implicit support comes from 1 Corinthians 15:22–24:

> For as in Adam all die, so also in Christ all will be made alive. But each in his own order: Christ the first fruits, [i.e., the life, death and resurrection of Jesus Christ], then at his coming, those who belong to Christ [i.e., the Second Coming, perhaps at the time of Armageddon]. Then comes the end, when he delivers the kingdom to God the Father after destroying every rule and every authority and power [i.e., the end, the Last Judgment and creation of a new heaven and new earth]. (RSV)

These verses appear to refer to three separate events. And they can be interpreted as implying that just as there is a temporal gap between Christ's first coming and his second, so also there is a period of time between the second coming and the final judgment. Between the second and third set of events is when the millennium perhaps occurs.

2. Richard Mouw, *When the Kings Come Marching In* (Grand Rapids: Eerdmans, 1983), 13.

3. See Norris Magnuson, *Salvation in the Slums: Evangelical Social Work 1865–1920* (Grand Rapids: Baker, 1990).

9. How the Family Got Its Start: The Early Church

1. These categories are derived from Stanley Hauerwas and William H. Willimon, *Resident Aliens* (Nashville: Abingdon, 1989), and H. Richard Niebuhr, *Christ and Culture* (New York: Harper and Row, 1951). Refer to appendix A for a summary of categories espoused by Ernst Troeltsch, Niebuhr, and Mary Jo Weaver.

2. For example, refer to the dispute that is recorded in Acts 6:1–6. Here the "Hebrew" Jewish-Christian widows were being treated differently than the "Greek" Jewish-Christian widows when it came to the distribution of aid. The former were people who had resisted the influence of Greek culture, while the latter were those who had melded aspects of the culture with their religious orientation. Since the latter were the ones being slighted, the early church responded magnanimously by appointing seven deacons who were from the "Greek" Jewish-Christian group to oversee the equitable distribution of funds to all the widows. (We know this from the list of deacons' names; they were all Greek names, which the "Hebrews" would not have given their children.) The early church set a notable precedent, based on the mind of Christ (see Phil. 2:1–11): when there is a conflict, the first step

is not to demand *our* rights, but, in humility, to count others better than ourselves and to look out for the interests of others, as well as our own.

3. The word "apology" in this context refers to a defense of the faith. Thus, when Christians speak of *apologetics*, they are referring to the techniques and arguments used to defend Christian beliefs and practices.

4. For instance, Celsus, one of the harshest critics of Christianity, asked why God had not made the world perfect in the first place and why he took so long to fix it after it had gone wrong. He argued that the New Testament writers were biased biographers of Jesus and that Jesus had been born an illegitimate child and had learned black magic in Egypt. He was answered at great length by a Christian intellectual named Origen.

5. This was about the time of Nero and the infamous fire of Rome in A.D. 64.

6. One can see this in a correspondence between Pliny the Younger and the Emperor Trajan, epitomized in Trajan's reply to Pliny's request for guidance on the persecution of Christians: ". . . indeed nothing can be laid down as a general ruling involving something like a set form of procedure." (See *A New Eusebius*, ed. T. Stevenson (London: SPCK, 1957), 13–16.

7. This suspicion was what motivated Augustine to write his famous book *City of God*. In it he traced the history of the human race to demonstrate that Rome's problems were due to human sin that began with the Fall of the human race in Adam. As Augustine tried to show, if anything, Christianity was a help to the Roman state, not a hindrance. Why, Christians even prayed for the emperor. How could that be a threat to the empire?

8. The word "martyr" is related to the Greek word for "witness"—*martys*.

9. "Letter to Diognetus" in *Early Christian Fathers*, Library of Christian Classics 1, trans. and ed. Cyril R. Richardson (Philadelphia: Westminster, 1953), 217.

10. Tertullian, "On Idolatry," chap. 19 in *Ante-Nicene Fathers*, eds. Alexander Roberts and James Donaldson (Grand Rapids: Eerdmans, 1973), 3:73.

11. Tertullian, "On the Apparel of Women," chap. 13 in *ANF*, 4:25.

12. *Epistle to Barnabas*, chap. 19 in *ANF*, 1:48.

13. Augustus Neander, *Memorials of Christian Life* (London: Henry G. Bohn, 1852), 80.

14. Though not responding to rejection by the culture, Rodney Clapp, *Families at the Crossroads* (Downers Grove, Ill.: InterVarsity, 1995), argues for a similar understanding of the church in a chapter descriptively entitled "Church as First Family."

15. Neander, *Memorials*, 81.

16. Ibid., 59.

10. A Mixed Marriage: The Medieval Church

1. Cited in Henry Bettenson, *Documents of the Christian Church*, 2nd ed. (New York: Oxford University Press, 1963), 22.

2. Constantine would eventually become the sole ruler of the eastern and western halves of the empire in 324.

3. During the persecutions of the early church it was "easier" to keep higher moral and spiritual standards. Martyrdom was viewed as the supreme example of devotion to God—a measure of spirituality and degree of perfection. When the persecution ceased, the monks took the place of the martyrs as heroes of the church; monastics were called the "white martyrs."

4. Eventually, Rome would become the leading church of Western Christendom, while Constantinople would become the leader for the Eastern church.

5. Pope Boniface VIII reflected this theory in 1303: "By the words of the Gospel we are taught that the two swords, namely the spiritual authority and the temporal are in the power of the church. For when the apostle said, 'Here are two swords' (Luke 22:38)—that is in the church, since it was the apostles who were speaking—the Lord did not answer 'It is too much,' but 'It is enough.' Whoever denies that the temporal sword is in the power of Peter does not properly understand the word of the Lord when he said: 'Put up thy sword

into the sheath' (John 18:11). Both swords, therefore, the spiritual and the temporal, are in the power of the church. The former is to be used by the church, the latter for the church; the one by the hand of the priest, the other by the hand of kings and knights, but at the command and permission of the priest."

11. From Protest to Revolution: The Protestant Reformation

1. *Luther's Works* (Philadelphia: Muhlenberg, 1958), 32:112–13.

2. John Calvin was educated with such a benefice, thanks to the influence of his father, a secretary to a bishop.

3. Ozment makes this point very bluntly. "The clergy of the later Middle Ages might as readily seduce one's wife or daughter, confiscate one's land, and imprison or kill one as pardon one's sins" (Steven Ozment, *Protestants: The Birth of a Revolution* [New York: Doubleday, 1992], 22).

4. Fellowship with God was dependent upon moral likeness to God.

5. Timothy George, *Theology of the Reformers* (Nashville: Broadman, 1988), 25–26.

6. Roland H. Bainton, *Here I Stand* (Nashville: Abingdon, 1950), 78.

7. Ozment, *Protestants: The Birth of a Revolution,* 33.

8. Alister McGrath, *Reformation Thought: An Introduction* (New York: Blackwell, 1988), 72.

9. John Dillenberger, ed., *Martin Luther: Selections from His Writings* (Garden City, N.Y.: Doubleday Anchor, 1961), 340–41.

10. Ibid., 341.

11. Ibid.

12. *Luther's Works,* 24:174, 177.

13. Dillenberger, *Martin Luther,* 60.

14. Ibid., 75.

15. While promoting Luther's bold program, Zwingli claimed that he had learned his doctrine not from Luther but from God's Word.

16. Walter Klaassen, ed., *Anabaptism in Outline: Selected Primary Sources* (Scottdale, Pa.: Herald, 1981), 241.

17. The Anabaptists insisted that only adult believers should be baptized. Since everyone in Europe was baptized as an infant, many were "rebaptized." This scandalized many since it challenged the religious and political unity of European society.

18. Although they too affirm believer's baptism, Baptists are not usually Anabaptists; Baptists have tended to arise out of the Reformed, Lutheran, and Anglican traditions, or they have sprung up independently.

12. Anabaptists: The Church Living in Antithesis to the World

1. Peter Rideman, *Confession of Faith: Account of our Religion, Doctrine and Faith, Given by Peter Rideman of the Brothers Whom Men Call Hutterians* (Suffolk: Hodder and Stoughton, 1950), 50.

2. Ibid., 50–51.

3. Walter Klaassen, ed., *Anabaptism in Outline: Selected Primary Sources* (Scottdale, Pa.: Herald, 1981), 154.

4. Ibid., 156.

5. Ibid., 154.

6. Ibid., 156.

7. Ibid., 87.

8. Jesus acknowledged the pervasiveness of Satan's kingdom when he did not challenge Satan's offer of "all the kingdoms of the world" at his temptation (Luke 4:5–8).

9. For further elaboration of these two antithetical kingdoms, see Robert Friedmann, "The Doctrine of the Two Worlds," in *The Recovery of the Anabaptist Vision,* ed. Guy F. Hershberger (Scottdale, Pa.: Herald, 1957), 105–18.

10. John Leith, ed., *Creeds of the Church,* 3d ed. (Atlanta: John Knox, 1982), 285–86.

11. Klaassen, *Anabaptism in Outline,* 177.

12. *The Complete Writings of Menno Simons,* trans. Leonard Verduin, ed. John Christian Wenger (Scottdale, Pa.: Herald, 1956), 743. These criteria are an addition to the traditional Protestant signs of "pure doctrine" and a biblical use of "the sacramental signs." See also the important article by John Howard Yoder, "A People in the World," in John Howard Yoder, *The Royal Priesthood: Essays Ecclesiological and Ecumenical,* ed. Michael G. Cartwright (Grand Rapids: Eerdmans, 1994), 65–101. For another important exposition of these points see J. Lawrence Burkholder, "The Anabaptist Vision of Discipleship," in *The Recovery of the Anabaptist Vision,* ed. Guy F. Hershberger (Scottdale, Pa.: Herald, 1957), 135–51.

13. Klaassen, *Anabaptism in Outline,* 111.

14. *Complete Writings of Menno Simons,* 300; Klaassen, *Anabaptism in Outline,* 112. Ironically, during the Reformation period, one could be cleared of the crime of being an Anabaptist by cursing, dancing, getting drunk, quarreling, or coveting. Claus-Peter Clasen, *Anabaptism: A Social History, 1525–1618* (Ithaca, N.Y.: Cornell University Press, 1972), 143.

15. Klaassen, *Anabaptism in Outline,* 234. Some Anabaptist groups, such as the Hutterites, even repudiated the idea of private property for the sake of brotherly love.

16. Clasen, *Anabaptism: A Social History,* 187; Klaassen, *Anabaptism in Outline,* 241.

17. Klaassen, *Anabaptists in Outline,* 97.

18. Rideman, *Confession of Faith,* 38.

19. Ibid., 39–40.

20. Franklin H. Littell, "The Anabaptist Concept of the Church," in *The Recovery of the Anabaptist Vision,* ed. Guy F. Hershberger (Scottdale, Pa.: Herald, 1957), 127.

21. *Complete Writings of Menno Simons,* 334.

22. Leith, *Creeds of the Church,* 287.

23. Klaassen, *Anabaptism in Outline,* 252.

24. "Jesus People," *Christianity Today,* 14 September 1992, 20–25.

25. Klaassen, *Anabaptism in Outline,* 111.

26. Ibid., 112.

13. Martin Luther: The Conversionist Church

1. Note the New Testament evidence. Cornelius, the centurion, was converted through Peter's preaching; there is no indication that he deserted his military post. Paul's letters indicate that the early Christians were active in social and political positions. Among the more prominent are Erastus, the "director of public works" in Corinth (Rom. 16:23), and the saints in "Caesar's household" (Phil. 4:22) at Rome.

2. *Martin Luther: Selections from His Writings,* ed. John Dillenberger (Garden City, N.Y.: Anchor, 1961), 388.

3. *Martin Luther: Selections,* 370.

4. Carl E. Braaten, *No Other Gospel! Christianity among the World's Religions* (Minneapolis: Fortress, 1993), 128.

5. *Martin Luther: Selections,* 76.

6. Ibid., 383–85.

7. Braaten, *No Other Gospel,* 130.

8. Quoted in Eric W. Gritsch and Robert W. Jenson, *Lutheranism: The Theological Movement and Its Confessional Writings* (Philadelphia: Fortress, 1976), 139, from *Luther's Works,* 48:281–82.

9. *Luther's Works,* ed. Jaroslav Pelikan (St. Louis: Concordia, 1956), 21:106.

10. Ibid., 21:109.

11. *Luther: Selections,* 379.
12. Ibid.
13. *Luther's Works,* 21:117.
14. Ibid., 21:118.
15. Ibid., 21:13.
16. Webber, *Church in the World,* 101; Niebuhr, *Christ and Culture,* 149.
17. Quoted in William C. Placher, *A History of Christian Theology: An Introduction* (Philadelphia: Westminster, 1983), 187.
18. See Reinhold Niebuhr, "Proposal to Billy Graham," *The Christian Century,* 8 August 1956 (73/32): 921–22.

14. John Calvin: The Transformationist Church

1. *Institutes* 4.20.2.
2. Ibid., 2.8.38.
3. *Calvin: Commentaries,* Library of Christian Classics, vol. 23, ed. Joseph Haroutunian (Philadelphia: Westminster, 1958), 359.
4. *Institutes* 4.20.3.
5. "Geneva Catechism" in *Calvin: Theological Treatises,* Library of Christian Classics, vol. 22, ed. J. K. S. Reid (Philadelphia: Westminster, 1954), 91.
6. *Institutes* 1.15.3–4, 8.
7. Ibid., 4.20.3–6.
8. CR 43:208, quotation taken from John H. Leith, *John Calvin's Doctrine of the Christian Life* (Louisville: Westminster/John Knox, 1989), 44.
9. *Institutes* 1.15.4.
10. Leith, *Calvin's Doctrine of the Christian Life,* 190ff. See also *Institutes* 2.8.45ff., 4.20.24.
11. *Institutes* 2.12.2.
12. Ibid., 2.15.4.
13. John Calvin, *Commentaries on the Epistles to Timothy, Titus, and Philemon,* trans. William Pringle (Edinburgh: Calvin Translation Society; reprint, Grand Rapids: Baker, 1979), 90.
14. *Institutes* 4.12.1.
15. Ibid., 3.16.1. See also Wilhelm Niesel, *The Theology of Calvin,* trans. Harold Knight (Grand Rapids: Baker, 1980), 137.
16. *Institutes* 3.7.1, 3.20.42.
17. *Calvin: Theological Treatises,* 125. See also *Institutes* 2.15.5.
18. *Institutes* 3.20.42.; *Calvin: Theological Treatises,* 125.
19. *Institutes* 4.20.2.
20. Ibid., 2.8.38.
21. Ibid., 3.8.11.
22. Ibid., 2.8.54.
23. Ibid., 2.8.55.
24. John Calvin, *Commentaries on the New Testament,* ed. David Torrance and Thomas F. Torrance (Grand Rapids: Eerdmans, 1960), 1:193, 199.
25. *Calvin: Theological Treatises,* 125.
26. Quoted in Wilhelm Niesel, *Reformed Symbolics: A Comparison of Catholicism, Orthodoxy, and Protestantism,* trans. David Lewis (Edinburgh: Oliver and Boyd, 1962), 299, from John Calvin, *Opera,* 27: 467. See also *Institutes* 3.20.42.
27. Ronald S. Wallace, *Calvin's Doctrine of the Christian Life* (Grand Rapids: Eerdmans, 1959), 176–77, 185–86.
28. Quoted in Leith, *Calvin's Doctrine of the Christian Life,* 200, from OS 3:11.
29. *Institutes* 4.20.23.
30. Ibid., preface.

31. Ibid., 4.20.31.

32. Quoted in *Calvin: Institutes of the Christian Religion*, ed. John T. McNeill, trans. Ford Lewis Battles (Philadelphia: Westminster, 1960), 2:1519. The source is CR 41:25.

33. Richard L. Greaves, *Theology and Revolution in the Scottish Reformation* (Grand Rapids: Christian University Press, 1980), 138.

15. Slouching toward Secularism: Modernity and Accommodation

1. Paul Hazard, *The European Mind (1680–1715)* (New York: World, 1952).

2. Voltaire, *Dictionnaire Philosophique*, s.v., "Fanatisme, Fanaticism."

3. The difficulty is not that the earth cannot be considered the center. It could be. But the mathematical calculations and the number of orbits involved in thinking about the universe would become cumbersome. It was mathematic calculations that led people to question what our eyes tell us—namely, that the sun goes around the earth. The motionlessness of the earth, as well as the perfectly smooth orb that the moon was thought to be, were considered characteristics of creation's perfection.

4. For a good example of this, see Benjamin Franklin, *Autobiography and Other Writings*, ed. Russel B. Nye (Boston: Houghton Mifflin, 1958).

5. The traditional empirical arguments for God's existence assume the principle of causality in some form. They begin with a feature of this world—contingency, design—and seek its cause. It is precisely this move that Kant precludes. Our knowledge only concerns things as we experience them, not reality in itself. In addition, God has traditionally been defined so that he cannot be confined to experience and its causal, temporal, and spatial framework.

6. Perhaps you've heard of the story of scientists who were searching for the source of maggots in garbage. Unable to find their origin, they proposed that these worms were just spontaneously generated. It seems ridiculous to us now, because the principle of the interconnectedness of all events is so well ingrained in our view of things: every event has a horizontal cause. Everything in this world is conditioned or caused by something else so that there are no completely independent or original events.

7. William E. Hordern, *A Layman's Guide to Protestant Theology*, 2d ed. (New York: Macmillan, 1968), 33.

8. The same criticism may be made of the late twentieth-century search for the historical Jesus which has been popularized by the writings of members of the Jesus Seminar. Evangelical scholarship has been quick to point this out. Three of the best recent works are Gregory A. Boyd, *Cynic Sage or Son of God?* (Wheaton, Ill.: Victor/BridgePoint, 1995); Michael J. Wilkins and J. P. Moreland, eds., *Jesus Under Fire: Modern Scholarship Reinvents the Historical Jesus* (Grand Rapids: Zondervan, 1995); and Ben Witherington III, *The Jesus Quest: The Third Search for the Jew of Nazareth* (Downers Grove, Ill.: InterVarsity, 1995).

9. William Placher, *A History of Christian Theology: An Introduction* (Philadelphia: Westminster, 1983), 237–38.

10. Ibid.

11. Quoted in Gerhard Spiegler, *The Eternal Covenant: Schleiermacher's Experiment in Cultural Theology* (New York: Harper and Row, 1967), 17.

12. Adolf von Harnack, *The Essence of Christianity* (New York: Harper and Brothers, 1957), 13–14.

13. Russel H. Conwell, "Acres of Diamonds," in *Issues in American Protestantism: A Documentary History from the Puritans to the Present*, ed. Robert L. Ferm (Gloucester, Mass.: Peter Smith, 1976), 237.

16. We Are Family: American Evangelicalism and Its Roots

1. Charles Chauncey was the founder of the American Unitarian Association (which, in 1961, merged with the Universalists to form the "Unitarian Universalist Association").

2. George C. Bedell, Leo Sandon, Jr., and Charles T. Wellborn, *Religion in America* (New York: Macmillan, 1975), 143.

3. Ibid., 166.

4. George Marsden, *Fundamentalism and American Culture* (New York: Oxford University Press, 1980), 33.

5. Ibid., 34.

6. Ibid., 38.

7. Ibid.

8. For information about these, consult Donald Dayton, *Discovering an Evangelical Heritage*, 2d ed. (Peabody, Mass.: Hendrickson, 1988).

9. See Marsden, *Fundamentalism and American Culture*, 90–93, for what follows.

10. Ibid., 92.

11. Fundamentalists were dispensationalists who maintained that the supernatural gifts ended (e.g., speaking in tongues) with the New Testament. As a result, an occurrence of those supernatural gifts must be "demonic." Pentecostals, on the other hand, viewed tongues as a primary evidence that a believer had received the baptism in the Spirit.

12. For helpful discussions of recent modifications in dispensationalism, see Craig A. Blaising and Darrell L. Bock, *Progressive Dispensationalism* (Wheaton, Ill.: Victor/BridgePoint, 1993), and Robert L. Saucy, *The Case for Progressive Dispensationalism* (Grand Rapids: Zondervan, 1993).

13. For various descriptions of this cultural shift see Timothy R. Phillips and Dennis L. Okholm, eds., *Christian Apologetics in a Postmodern World* (Downers Grove, Ill.: InterVarsity, 1995).

14. See the indictments by Carl F. H. Henry, *Gods of This Age or—God of the Ages?* (Nashville: Broadman and Holman, 1994); Os Guinness and John Seel, eds., *No God but God: Breaking with the Idols of Our Age* (Chicago: Moody, 1992); Michael Scott Horton, ed., *Power Religion: The Selling Out of the Evangelical Church?* (Chicago: Moody, 1992); David F. Wells, *No Place for Truth: or, Whatever Happened to Evangelical Theology?* (Grand Rapids: Eerdmans, 1993), *God in the Wasteland: The Reality of Truth in a World of Fading Dreams* (Grand Rapids: Eerdmans, 1994); Cornelius Plantinga, Jr. and David F. Wells, "Evangelical Theology Today," *Theology Today* 51 (1995): 495–507.

15. James Davison Hunter, *Evangelicalism: The Coming Generation* (Chicago: University of Chicago Press, 1987), 34–40, 150–54, 180–86, *American Evangelicalism: Conservative Religion and the Quandary of Modernity* (New Brunswick, N.J.: Rutgers University Press, 1983), 84–91; David F. Wells, *No Place for Truth, God in the Wasteland;* Robert Brow, "Evangelical Megashift," *Christianity Today,* 19 February 1990, 12–14; Clark H. Pinnock and Robert C. Brow, *Unbounded Love: A Good News Theology for the 21st Century* (Downers Grove, Ill.: InterVarsity, 1994); Roger E. Olson, "Postconversative Evangelicals Greet the Postmodern Age," *Christian Century,* 3 May 1995, 480–83.

16. For two contrasting stances see, Phillip E. Johnson, *Reason in the Balance* (Downers Grove, Ill.: InterVarsity, 1995) and Stanley J. Grenz, *Theology for the Community of God* (Nashville: Broadman and Holman, 1994), 333.

17. Clark H. Pinnock, *A Wideness in God's Mercy: The Finality of Jesus Christ in a World of Religions* (Grand Rapids: Zondervan, 1992); John Sanders, *No Other Name: An Investigation into the Destiny of the Unevangelized* (Grand Rapids: Eerdmans, 1992); Timothy R. Phillips and Dennis L. Okholm, eds., *More Than One Way? Four Views on Salvation in a Pluralistic World* (Grand Rapids: Zondervan, 1995).

18. Timothy R. Phillips and Dennis L. Okholm, eds., *The Nature of Confession* (Downers Grove, Ill.: InterVarsity, 1996).

17. Recommendations for the Family in a Culture against Christ

1. See H. Richard Niebuhr, *Christ and Culture* (New York: Harper Torchbooks, 1951), 56. In fact, the word "Anabaptist" appears *nowhere* in the entire book, and Anabaptists are really not discussed. Niebuhr's primary models in the "Christ against Culture" paradigm are the early church, Tertullian, and Tolstoy.

2. See Hauerwas and Willimon, *Resident Aliens*, 40–42.

3. Ibid., 42.

4. Charles Scriven, *The Transformation of Culture: Christian Social Ethics after H. Richard Niebuhr* (Ann Arbor, Mich.: Books on Demand, n.d.).

5. Niebuhr, *Christ and Culture*, 45.

6. Ibid.

7. Scriven, *The Transformation of Culture*, 60ff. This gets independent confirmation in John Howard Yoder, *The Priestly Kingdom* (Notre Dame, Ind.: University of Notre Dame Press, 1988). In the chapter entitled "The Kingdom as Social Ethic," Yoder suggests that readers of *Christ and Culture* would be surprised by Niebuhr's earlier (1935) work *The Church against the World*, where he speaks of the church as being in bondage to idolatry, capitalism, nationalism, classism, optimistic humanism, and worthwhile social causes. Yoder notes the following about Niebuhr's early pronouncements, along with Wilhelm Pauck and Francis Miller: "This call to the church to rediscover an identity of her own, independent of the support of the world, as the prerequisite of a renewed validity in contributing to the world, did not mean a call to reach back to some phase of Protestant integrity. These writers . . . wrote from within the mainstream of institutionally cooperative, intellectually and socially liberal Protestants. It is perhaps partly for that reason that their witness has been forgotten.

"Richard Niebuhr never wrote his next book about the church against the world. One can even argue that his pluralistic typology later in *Christ and Culture* was his apology for backing away from so decisive a judgmental stance, or for not having found a church to fit that vision" (p. 90).

8. This is recognized by our contemporaries, such as Stanley Hauerwas and Alasdair MacIntyre. See the latter's *After Virtue*, 2d ed. (Notre Dame, Ind.: University of Notre Dame Press, 1984), esp. chap. 5.

9. This is Luther's question, too. The difference between the Lutheran and the Anabaptist who ask this question is in the conception of *loyalist* and in the answer each gives.

10. See Robert Wuthnow, *The Restructuring of American Religion* (Princeton: Princeton University Press, 1988), 244–50. His description of post-World War II conservative American Christianity fits the dualist Lutheran paradigm. Wuthnow argues that this holds true even for conservatives like Jerry Falwell who distinguished the kingdom of God from the U.S. as "God's chosen nation."

11. Niebuhr offers no critique of the conversionist model, which lends some credence to Hauerwas's and Willimon's suspicions that he *was* setting us up for approval of that option over against the other four.

12. Yoder, *The Priestly Kingdom*, 41–42. Cf. Ozment: "To reformers in any age, the experience [of reforms becoming law] is both exhilarating and demoralizing—exhilarating because their ideals at last gain the force of mandate, but demoralizing because those ideals are now at the mercy of the common man. Success brings both triumph and a new vulnerability" (Ozment, *Protestants: The Birth of a Revolution*, 89).

13. Hauerwas and Willimon, *Resident Aliens*, 15.

14. Of course, one might ask, "Who speaks for the 'evangelicals' here?" Since the denotation of the term is undergoing some rethinking, the answer to that might be difficult. One way of coming at this has been suggested by David F. Wells in a paper delivered at the Institute for the Study of American Evangelicals conference (Wheaton College, Spring

1992) entitled "On Being Evangelical: Some Differences and Similarities." He argues that in the last two decades evangelicals have moved from a confessionally centered unity to a *transconfessional* movement that has a minimal theological center; this is due to a growing diversity within evangelicalism and a growing influence from without, all centered around marketing techniques, managerial skills, personal experience, and (we would add) therapeutic models of pastoral ministry.

15. We owe this insight to Kenneth Myers in a lecture he gave at Wheaton College.

16. See Kenneth Myers, "A Better Way: Proclamation Instead of Protest" in *Power Religion,* ed. Michael Scott Horton (Chicago: Moody, 1992), 39–57.

17. This criticism was suggested by a Wheaton College colleague, Alan Jacobs.

18. The phrase "normative pluralism" comes from Keith Yandell of the University of Wisconsin in Madison. In a helpful distinction he argues that "descriptive pluralism" cannot be denied by the Christian and is even to be welcomed; there *are* many different religious and moral views "out there." But "normative pluralism" argues that all of these views have equal truth value, a claim that the Christian cannot accept.

19. George Barna, *What Americans Believe* (Ventura, Calif.: Regal, 1991), 83. Perhaps even more indicative is that the figure rises to 72 percent among the "Baby Busters." But perhaps most disheartening is that 73 percent of those associated with mainline Protestant churches concur with this statement.

One editorial in *Christianity Today* (9 March 1992) cited this statistic and then called for *more* sermonic arguments to show that the exclusive claims of Christ are "rationally superior"—to build a "reasonable case" for Christian doctrines. No doubt this can be done, but given Barna's statistics, one would have to conclude that that is precisely the wrong response to *this* culture.

20. If there *is* a consensus in our pluralistic culture it is perhaps that which Robert Bellah, et al., have suggested—namely, the agreement *not* to have a public morality except at a minimal level, backed by a Lockean freedom of the lone self-interested individual and by the establishment of government by social contract, defining humans as "relentless market maximizers." The "common good" is merely the sum of individual goods. The response of many churches is to appeal to "consumer Christians" to meet their needs, with little or no call for commitment or loyalty to the church community. See Robert N. Bellah, "Cultural Barriers to the Understanding of the Church and Its Public Role," *Missiology* 19 (4): 461–73. Also, see Robert Bellah, et al., *Habits of the Heart: Individualism and Commitment in American Life* (San Francisco: Harper and Row, 1985).

21. George R. Hunsberger, "The Newbigin Gauntlet: Developing a Domestic Missiology for North America," *Missiology* 19 (4): 391–408. Regarding our misperception of the culture, Kenneth Myers comments: "People do not want easy access to abortion clinics because laws are liberal; the laws are liberal because people want easy access to abortion clinics" (Myers, "A Better Way," 53).

It will be asserted later that the culture's definition of personhood is not the church's because the former does not share the latter's conviction that human nature is defined by Jesus Christ's full humanity and that the purpose of human existence is defined by Christian eschatology. The failure to recognize this and the persistence in relating to the culture at the level of moral and political appeals may not be far from the nineteenth-century Protestant liberal reduction of theology to ethics. See Adolf von Harnack's *What Is Christianity?*

22. Lesslie Newbigin, *Foolishness to the Greeks* (Grand Rapids: Eerdmans, 1986). For an excellent overview of Newbigin's agenda, see Hunsberger, "The Newbigin Gauntlet."

23. See Newbigin, *Foolishness to the Greeks,* 10ff., 62–63. A "plausibility structure" is "a social structure of ideas and practices that create the conditions determining what beliefs are plausible within the society in question," p. 10, n.1.

24. Barna, *What Americans Believe,* 85.

25. This can be seen in the responses Barna records in his survey. Though 66 percent of all people agree that "America is a Christian nation" and 81 percent agree that the Chris-

tian faith is relevant to the way they live today, what *Christian* means is questionable when 84 percent of those attending evangelical churches agree with the statement, "God helps those who help themselves"; 49 percent agree that "when it comes right down to it, one's first responsibility is to one's self"; 74 percent of the same group agree that "people are basically good"; and 56 percent say that "the purpose of life is enjoyment and personal fulfillment." See Barna, *What Americans Believe*, 80ff., 184ff. Significantly, the use of the media among evangelicals parallels the national average.

26. See Craig Van Gelder, "A Great New Fact of Our Day: America as Mission Field," *Missiology* 19 (4): 409–18. He writes: "We have lost the grand narrative, the storyline which gave direction and meaning to our lives as a society. . . . The overarching storyline has been lost and cannot be re-invented" (pp. 412–13).

27. See Hunsberger, "The Newbigin Gauntlet," 397, 401.

28. See Newbigin: "The conflict between the two views will not be settled on the basis of logical argument. The view will prevail that is seen to offer—both in theory and in practice—the widest rationality, the greatest capacity to give meaning to the whole of experience. This is as much a matter of faithful endeavor and costly obedience as of clarity and coherence of argument. It is at the heart of the biblical vision of the human situation that the believer is a witness who gives his testimony in a trial where it is contested. The verdict as to what stands and what falls will only be given at the end. To suppose that some kind of rationally conclusive 'proof' of one position or the other might be available now is to misunderstand the human situation" (Newbigin, *Foolishness to the Greeks*, 64).

Watson prefers to use "journalism" as the root metaphor of evangelism, though he finds Newbigin's "courtroom testimony" metaphor helpful as well. Watson is rightly trying to avoid the "salesperson" image of evangelism; we are communicating a message of good *news*, not hawking a commodity. But Newbigin's metaphor seems to have the added advantage of recognizing that persuasion is commanded of us—albeit the persuasion of courtroom testimony and not of sales techniques. Presumably, a good journalist only reports the news (though the presumption may be naive). See David Lowes Watson, "Christ All in All: The Recovery of the Gospel for North American Evangelism," *Missiology* 19 (4): 443–59; also see David Lowes Watson, "The Church as Journalist: Evangelism in the Context of the Local Church in the United States," *International Review of Mission* 72 (285): 57–74.

29. Hauerwas and Willimon, *Resident Aliens*, 24.

30. This point is made by the media-ecologist Neil Postman in his book *Amusing Ourselves to Death: Public Discourse in an Age of Television* (New York: Penguin, 1985), chap. 5. He writes, "Most Americans, including preachers, have difficulty accepting the truth . . . that not all forms of discourse can be converted from one medium to another. It is naive to suppose that something that has been expressed in one form can be expressed in another without significantly changing its meaning, texture, or value" (p. 117).

31. Jacques Ellul, *The Presence of the Kingdom*, 2d ed. (Colorado Springs: Helmers and Howard, 1989), 25.

32. Ibid., 38.

33. See Scriven, *The Transformation of Culture*, 181ff.

Glossary

adoptionism. The heresy that teaches Christ was a human creature gifted with divine powers and elevated to divine status as the adoptive, rather than the true and natural, Son of God.

Apollinarianism. The heresy named after a fourth-century bishop who taught that at the incarnation the divine Logos replaced the human spirit of Jesus, essentially taking on only a human body and soul; thus, Christ had a perfect divine nature but an incomplete human nature.

apologetics. The defense of the Christian faith, usually (but not necessarily) on intellectual grounds, which rebuts the attacks of detractors and recommends the faith to outsiders.

Arianism. The heresy named after a fourth-century churchman who taught that the Son was the first creature the Father made out of nothing. Through him all else was created, and as a consequence of his foreseen perfect obedience the Father bestowed on him the dignity of divine sonship.

canon. The authoritative collection of books of the Bible by which Christians are to measure their beliefs and practices. The earliest complete list that matches today's Bible is that of Athanasius in 367.

common grace. A term (in some ways unfortunate since grace is never "common") most often found in Reformed theology. It refers to the gifts God bestows on his fallen creation to sustain it in relative order, including his provision for human endeavors in government, the sciences, and the arts.

control beliefs. The most basic assumptions that guide our thinking about the world and our behavior.

deism. A natural and rational religion espoused by various people, especially in England during the eighteenth-century Enlightenment period. God is not seen as a personal deity, but as a creator who remains distant from his creation. At best, he involves himself with the world only to keep it on track. Some deists also held that we are to emulate God's moral attributes, for which we will be rewarded with a pleasant afterlife.

dispensationalism. An understanding of God's dealings with people throughout history as it is classically divided into seven ages or dispensations. The present church age is viewed as a parenthetical era in which the world is getting worse while awaiting Christ's imminent return. Old Testament promises made to Israel are sharply distinguished from God's dealings with the church. The view was spread in the nineteenth century by John Nelson Darby and C. I. Scofield and is often associated with premillennial pretribulational eschatology.

Docetism. A heresy often associated with Gnosticism that teaches the Son of God only appeared to be human in Jesus Christ.

dualism. Though there are different types of dualism, this volume generally uses the word to refer to the teaching that there are two fundamental eternal principles that are equal, independent, and opposed to each other.

eschatology. The study of last things or end times.

finite theism. Understandings of God that teach he is limited by, determined by, and partially dependent on another reality, such as the world. Process theology is one example.

general revelation. The disclosure of God through creation.

Gnosticism. A group of religions in New Testament times that sharply distinguished the good spiritual realm from the evil material realm. Gnostics typically held a docetic Christology and believed that the spiritual and material realms cannot be in immediate contact with each other.

illumination. Empowerment from the Holy Spirit by which believers are able to understand and apply God's Word (see 1 Cor. 2:14–16).

inspiration. From the Greek word *theopneustos,* which literally means "God breathed" (2 Tim. 3:16), inspiration refers to the supernatural work of God that enabled the biblical authors to write what he wanted.

justification. God's forgiveness and complete acceptance of the sinner, based upon the righteousness of Christ imputed to the one who receives it by faith.

Logos Christology. An understanding of Christ put forward especially by Apologists in the second and third centuries. They used the Greek word *logos* ("word"), found in John's gospel, to relate Christ to the Logos of Greek philosophy as the principle that orders the universe and to the Logos of certain Jewish circles as the agent of God's creative and revelatory acts.

Marcionism. The heresy named after a second-century churchman who taught that the God of Law in the Old Testament is not the God of Love revealed through Jesus Christ in the New Testament; accordingly, he rejected all of the Old Testament and accepted only Luke's gospel and ten of Paul's letters as canonical.

metanarrative. A term used to designate a "master story" that one uses as a grid or interpretive key for understanding everything.

millennium. Literally, a thousand years. Evangelical eschatologies largely revolve around different understandings of the thousand years mentioned in Revelation 20:1–6.

modernism. In theological circles it is most often associated with the tendency to accommodate religious teachings to contemporary thought. More generally it refers to the rational approach to reality that grew out of Western Europe during the Enlightenment.

monism. The belief that everything is ultimately one reality.

naturalism. The belief that matter is all that exists; the supernatural is denied. Atheism and humanism are naturalistic in their assumptions.

pantheism. The belief that all things are God.

pluralism. Religious and moral pluralism, used in a descriptive manner, is the acknowledgement that there are a variety of religious and moral beliefs and practices in the world. Used normatively, it implies that all religious and moral beliefs and practices are equally valid and true.

postmodernism. An overused term having several meanings. It often refers to a school of thought largely associated with several twentieth-century French philosophers. It also refers to the rejection of modernism's claim that there is an objective viewpoint from which all rational persons can reach common agreement about reality; as such it acknowledges the diverse perspectives of knowers who have been shaped by factors including community, gender, and race.

revelation. Literally, the "unveiling" of God. It refers to God's self-disclosure in creation, in Scripture, and preeminently in Jesus Christ.

sanctification. The lifelong process by which the justified sinner is made holy. Sanctification is accomplished in the believer's life through the work of the Holy Spirit and by the means of "putting on the new man" as evidenced in Bible study, prayer, worship, and acts of service.

sola Scriptura. A teaching associated with the Protestant Reformation that insists all that is necessary for salvation is clearly taught in the Bible (referred to as the "perspicuity of Scripture") and that the Bible is the ultimate authority in all things.

special revelation. God's saving self-disclosure through Jesus Christ, Scripture, and the church's proclamation of the gospel.

theism. The belief that God exists as a being who transcends the creation yet is involved in it.

theology. Literally, the "study of God." More specifically, it is a human response to God's prior revelation that proceeds according to certain rules and is done within and for the Christian church.

total depravity. A doctrine usually, though not exclusively, associated with Reformed theology. It teaches that sin infects every aspect of the creation and that human beings cannot deliver themselves out of this predicament.

Trinity. The unique Christian understanding of God as three persons (Father, Son, and Holy Spirit) in one divine being or substance (*homoousios*).

worldview. A loose English translation of the German *Weltanschauung*, which refers to an all-inclusive understanding of the world. It is a conceptual framework by which we interpret our experience and guide our actions.

Index

Alexander VI 167
Allen, Ethan 243
amillennial 126, 129–30, 131, 158
Amish 139
Anabaptists/Anabaptism 179–81, 182–95,
    196, 199, 201, 205, 209, 219,
    262–64, 268–69
Anglican tradition 178–79
Anselm of Canterbury 157, 161
Apocrypha 57–58
Apollinarius/Apollinarianism 94, 154
apologetics 70, 269, 311 n. 3
Apologists 143, 311 n. 3
Apostles' Creed 155–56
Aquinas, Thomas 157
Arius 93, 152
Arminianism 178, 242, 244
asceticism 156
Athanasius 93, 152–53
Auburn Affirmation 253
Augustine 118, 157–58, 265, 311 n. 7
authority 48, 61, 162–63, 168, 171–73,
    201, 212–14, 223, 233–34

baptism 109, 159, 163, 179–80
    believers' 186–87
    infant 179–80
    in the Spirit 316 n. 11
Baptists 177, 244
Barth, Karl 42
Benedictines 156
Berger, Peter 267–68
Bible. See Scripture, Holy

biblical criticism 229–30, 254
biblical literalism 249
biblical theology 62
Blackstone, W. E. 132
Blanchard, Charles 256
Blanchard, Jonathan 247
Blaurock, Georg 179
Book of Common Prayer 178
Brown, William Adams 235–36
Bryan, William Jennings 253

Calvin, John 52, 55, 77, 177–78, 209–21,
    265
canon 56–59, 173, 307 n. 11
Carnegie, Andrew 248
Carnell, Edward John 257
Charles the Great (Charlemagne) 160
Charles I 178
Charles V 166, 168
Chauncey, Charles 243
Christian college movement 258
Christian theism 35–36
Christianity Today 258–59
Church 64–65, 108–23, 211–12, 216–17,
    271–72
    accommodationist 140, 232–37
    Anabaptist 186–89
    antithesis 138–39, 156–57, 190–95, 196,
        199, 271
    conversionist 139–40, 196–208, 263,
        265, 269
    and culture 138–41, 180–81, 200–208,
        212–20, 233–38, 246–48, 253–60,
        262–72

early 141–49
medieval 156–64, 167–69
mission of 15–16, 64–65, 118–22,
    190–92, 202–5, 212, 215–18, 235
Reformation 166–81
and salvation history 109–10
transformationist 140, 158, 209–20,
    262–64, 268–72
Church of England. *See* Anglican tradition
Clement of Rome 159
community 73–74, 115–16, 173–74,
    186–87, 271
Congregationalists 243
Constantine 129, 150–52, 218
control beliefs 18–19, 23, 260
Conwell, Russell 237
Copernicus 224
Council of Nicaea 152
Council of Trent 222–23
covenant 95–96, 309 n. 3
covenantal theology 241
creation, doctrine of 67–77, 79–89, 183,
    197–99, 209–10, 308 n. 4
creation (cultural) mandate 75
Cromwell, Oliver 178
Cyprian (bishop of Carthage) 148, 159

Darby, John Nelson 248–49, 259
Decalogue. *See* Law
Darrow, Clarence 253
Darwin, Charles 228
Davenport, John 242–43
Decius 145
Definition of Chalcedon 154–55
Dei Filius 232
deism/deists 34–35, 77, 226, 243
Democritus 29
Descartes, Renè 225
Diakonia 115–16, 173–74, 191–92
Didache 56, 107
Diet of Worms 166, 175
Diocletian 145, 150
dispensational premillennialists 240
dispensationalism 127–28, 130–32, 248–49
Dixon, A. C. 252, 256
Dobson, James 267
Docetism 94
    and Jesus Christ 154
Dominicans 157
"Donation of Constantine" 161
Donatists 159

Dort, Synod of 178
double predestination 176
dualistic worldview (dualism) 27, 33–34, 68
Dwight, Timothy 243

Edict of Milan 151
Edward VI 178
Edwards, Jonathan 241–43
Elizabeth I 178
Ellul, Jacques 119, 270–71
Emerson, Ralph Waldo 244
English Civil War 178
Enlightenment 222–32
    in America 243
environment (nature) 75, 85, 96–100,
    117–18
eschatology 124–33, 271
ethics (moral values) 29–30, 32, 37–38,
    71–73, 202–4, 213–14, 265, 267–68
Eusebius 150–51
Evangelicalism 240–41, 246–48, 257–60,
    268–71
    distinctive elements of 15–16, 19–20,
    36–42, 166–67
Evangelicals for Social Action 259
evolution (Darwinism) 250–51, 257
excommunication 159, 162
ex nihilo 68

faith 59–60, 169–72
Fall. *See* sin
"False Decretals" 161
"feeling of absolute dependence" 235
Feuerbach, Ludwig 29
Finite theism 33–34
Finney, Charles Grandison 132, 247, 249,
    256
    and American Revivalism 244–45
Fish, Stanley 38
"Five Fundamentals" 252–53
Formula of Concord 175–76
Fosdick, Harry Emerson 236, 252, 254
Francis of Assisi 157
Franciscans 157
Franklin, Benjamin 34–35, 243
Freud, Sigmund 29, 228–29
Fuller Theological Seminary 257–58, 259
Fundamentalism/Fundamentalists 139,
    240–41, 244–46, 248–59, 266, 316
    n. 11
Fundamentals, The 251–52

Galerius 150
Galileo 224
General revelation 49–52
Geneva 177, 179, 219
German Christian Movement 18–19, 61
German higher criticism 251
Gilson, Etienne 262
Gnosticism/Gnostics 72–73, 93–94
God:
    the Creator 67–77
    Enlightenment view of 226–27
    as Love and Judge 104–5
    as revealed in Christ 91–93
    and revelation 49–52
    sovereignty and rule of 215–16
    as Trinity 152–55
Graham, Billy 258–59
Gray, James M. 256
Great Awakening 241–43
Great Commission 16, 58, 188
"Great Reversal" 255, 256–57
Grebel, Conrad 179
Gregory the Great 160

Harnack, Adolf von 234
Harvard University 241–43
Hauerwas, Stanley 262–63, 265–66, 268
Hegel, Georg Wilhelm Friedrich 227
Henry VIII 168, 178
Henry, Carl F. H. 258–59, 274
Hick, John 36–37
higher criticism. See German higher criticism
historical theology 64–65
Hobbes, Thomas 29
Hodge, Charles 249
holiness teaching 250–51
Holy Roman Empire 160
Holy Spirit 51, 54–55, 113, 172, 200, 255–56
homoiousion 152
homoousion 153
homosexuality 85, 267
Huguenots 177
"Humanist Manifesto II" 29–30
humanity 28–29, 32–33, 35–36, 49–52, 73–77, 79–89, 210–11, 223, 225–27, 271
Hume, David 226
Hunsberger, George 267

Hutter, Jacob 180
Hutterites 180

Ignatius of Antioch 159
illumination 54–55, 172
image of God 73–75, 80–81, 88
incarnation 103–4, 108
individualism 111
indulgences 168
inerrancy, biblical 250, 306 n. 6
Innocent III 162
inspiration 54–55, 250
interdict 162
International Prophetic Conference 249
InterVarsity Christian Fellowship 258
Irenaeus 159
Islam 35

Jefferson, Thomas 34–35, 243
Jesus Christ 15–16, 19, 25–26, 35–36, 50–51, 56, 271
    lordship of 16, 106, 109, 110–11, 118, 120–21, 132, 139, 190, 237–38
    and non-retaliatory love 191–92, 202–3, 214–15
    person of 91–93, 105–6, 152–55, 230, 234
    work of 16, 91–106, 108, 113–18, 125–31, 141, 169–70, 173–74, 184–85, 200, 202, 211–12, 215, 234–35, 309 n. 8
    See also incarnation
Jesus People USA 193, 194
John XXIII 232
Johnson, James Weldon 131
Judaism 35, 141–42, 148
Julius II 167
justification 113, 163, 168
    by faith alone 169–70, 174, 177, 202, 206

Kant, Immanuel 226–27, 233–34
Kato, Byang 63
kerygma 113
Keswick 250–51
Kierkegaard, Søren 115
Kingdom of God (Christ) 95–102, 109–21, 164, 183–84, 211–12
    See also spiritual kingdom
Knox, John 177, 218
koinonia. See community

Kushner, Harold 34
Kuyper, Abraham 25

Ladd, George Eldon 258
Law 88, 177, 183–85, 213, 255
Leo III 160–62
Locke, John 225–26
Logos (word) 142–43
    Christology 143, 270
    as reason and creation 71
Lord's Supper 115, 159, 176–78
Luther, Martin 55, 166–76, 196–208, 209,
    211–12, 213
Lutheranism 174–76, 263
Lyell, Charles 228

Machen, J. Gresham 249, 253
Malik, Charles 64
Manichaeism 33
Marburg 175
Marcion 58–59
marriage 76, 84–85, 219
martyrs/martyrdom 146, 311 n. 8, 311 n. 3
Marx, Karl 29
Mary (Queen of England) 178
Mathews, Shailer 235
May, Rollo 104
means of grace 115
Mears, Henrietta 258
medieval theological system 168
mendicant orders 157
Mennonites 180, 262
Methodists 244, 250
millennium 126–29
modernist controversy 252–53
modernists 240–41, 251
modernity (modernism) 222–23, 232–33,
    251–53, 259
monasticism 156–57, 159, 311 n. 3
monistic worldview 27, 28–33
Moody, D. L. 245–46
moral values. See ethics
Mosaic Covenant 96–97

National Association of Evangelicals 250–60
natural evil 85, 98, 115–16, 117
natural science 223–30, 232
naturalism 28–30
    and creation 70
nature. See environment
Nestorius 154

New Age 31–33, 93
New Covenant 98–99, 113, 180
"New Measures" 244–45
New Testament Canon 58–59
    See also Scripture, Holy
Newbigin, Lesslie 37, 266–67, 271
Newton, Isaac 224–25
Niagara Conference 249
Nicene Creed 93, 152–55
Niebuhr, H. Richard 262–67, 270
"Ninety-five Theses" 168
Novatians 159

Oberlin College 244, 247
Old Testament Canon 57–58
    See also Scripture, Holy
Origen 311 n. 4
original sin 86, 163
Orthodox Presbyterian Church 253

Padilla, C. René 268
paganism 146–48
Paine, Thomas 243
pantheism 30–33
    and creation 68
Pascal, Blaise 73
pax Romana 143–46
Peace of Augsburg 175
Pentecostals 257–58
Percy, Walker 80, 269
Perkins, John 117
persecution (early church) 144–46
Philip of Hesse 206–7
Philo 143
Pietist tradition 240, 246, 255–56
Pius V 178
Pius IX 232
pluralism/pluralist 36–38, 41, 92, 266–67,
    318 n. 18
Polycarp 147
"post-Enlightenment" 267
postmillennial 126, 128–29, 245, 254–55
postmodern philosophy of science 228
postmodernism 38–41, 267
predestination 175–76, 178
premillennialism 126, 130–32, 249, 255
    posttribulational 126–27
    pretribulational 127–28, 130
Presbyterians 241, 243
priesthood of all believers 173–74
Princeton Theological Seminary 240, 249

Princeton Theology 249–50
Princeton University 241
printers 172
Protestant liberalism 235–37, 272
Protestant Reformation 166–81
Protestant theology 169–74
purgatory 163, 168
Puritans/Puritanism 177, 178, 230–31, 241, 244

"Radical Reformation" 179
Ramm, Bernard 69
Rauschenbush, Walter 236, 254–55
reason 223
reconciliation 96, 106, 108, 116, 170
redemption 95, 98
Reformed Tradition (Calvinist) 176–78, 240–41, 241–44, 246, 249, 255
relativism 267
Religious Right 140
"Resident aliens" 268
revelation 49–55, 224, 226
Revivalism:
    American 241–46
    frontier 243–44
    urban 244–46, 250–51
Rinkart, Martin 204
Ritschl, Albrecht 234
Rorty, Richard 38, 39
Russell, Bertrand 29

sacerdotalism 159, 164
sacramental conception of salvation 163, 168–70
Sagan, Carl 28–29
salvation, 95–96, 104, 170, 174
    See also Jesus Christ, work of; justification; sacramental conception of salvation; sanctification
Salvation Army 247
sanctification 113–15, 211–12
Sankey, Ira D. 245
Satan 35, 86, 95–96, 99–102, 120–21, 126–29, 141, 158, 183–85, 200–201
Schlafly, Phyllis 267
Schleiermacher, Fredrich 233–35
Schleitheim Confession 186, 192
Schweitzer, Albert 230
scientific method 224–27
Scofield, C. I. 248, 250
Scofield Reference Bible 248

Scopes Trial 252–53
Scripture, Holy 16, 53–59, 233–37
    authority of 16, 55–56, 60–62, 171–73, 175, 306 n. 3, 306 n. 6
    Christocentricity of 47
    See also biblical criticism; theology
Scriven, Charles 263–64
search for the historical Jesus 230
Second Adam 94–95, 106
Second Great Awakening 243–44
secular humanism 28–30
secularization 230–32
Septuagint 57
service. See diakonia
sex 77
Simons, Menno 180, 189
simul justus et peccator 175
sin (the Fall) 35, 79–89, 94, 98, 112–13, 174, 183, 191, 198–99, 205, 210–11
Skinner, B. F. 29
Social Gospel Movement 236, 248, 255–56
Sojourners 259
sola Scriptura 53, 171–73, 174–76
special revelation 49–55
    See also Jesus Christ, person of; Scripture, Holy
spiritual kingdom 200–201, 212–14
Stowe, Harriet Beecher 216
Stylites 156
Syllabus of Errors 232
systematic theology 63–64

temporal kingdom 99, 200–208, 209, 212–14
ten Boom, Corrie 84
Ten Commandments. See Law
Tertullian 144, 146
Tetzel, Johann 168
theology 60–65
Thirty Years War 223
Toland, John 226
Torrey, Reuben 248, 252
total depravity 81
transcendentalism 244
"treasury of merit" 168
Trinity 153–55
Troeltsch, Ernst 262
"two swords theory" 151, 312 n. 5

Unitarian/Universalist 243, 316 n. 1

Valla, Lorenzo 161
Vatican Council I 232
Vatican Council II 232
Venerabilem (papal decree) 162
Visigoths 157

Warfield, Benjamin B. 249
Westminster Confession of Faith 250
Westminster Theological Seminary 253
Whitefield, George 242–43, 255
Whittemore, Emma 247
Willimon, William H. 262–63, 265–66, 268
Willke, John 267
worldview 22–42, 48

Christian 35–36, 59, 68–77, 79–89,
    91–95, 138, 266
types of 27–36
See also control beliefs
Worship 114–15
Wycliffe, John 178

Yale University 243
YMCA 247
Yoder, John Howard 265, 317 n. 7

Zoroastrianism 33
Zwingli, Ulrich 55, 167, 176–78